REPRODUCTION OF THE FIRST EDITION
COMMEMORATING
THE REBUILDING AND DEDICATION OF THE
NAUVOO TEMPLE
JUNE 2002

THE
RISE AND FALL OF NAUVOO
1900

BY ELDER B. H. ROBERTS

FOREWORD BY DAVID L. PAULSEN

A NOTE ON THE TEXT

Except for the front matter and foreword, this Commemorative edition of *The Rise and Fall of Nauvoo* by B. H. Roberts is an exact reprint of the 1900 first edition published in Salt Lake City.

First printed in the United States of America by *The Deseret News, Publishers* in 1900.

Reprint edition with a foreword by David L. Paulsen published by David L. Paulsen 2002.

Originally published: Salt Lake City : Deseret News, 1900.
Includes bibliographical references.

ISBN 0-934893-67-5

Front cover photograph courtesy of LDS Church Historical Department.

FOREWORD

David L. Paulsen

The rebuilding and rededication of the Nauvoo Temple has turned the hearts of Latter-day Saints toward Nauvoo and the triumphal and tragic events that unfolded there between 1838 and 1846. In 1900, these events were passionately chronicled by B. H. Roberts (1857–1933)—Mormon General Authority, historian and intellectual—in his classic work, *The Rise and Fall of Nauvoo.* This book has now been reissued to commemorate both the rededication of the temple and the courageous, faithful Saints who, under the strain of violent persecution, sacrificed all that they had, sometimes their very lives, to complete the sacred edifice. Their story needs to be not only read and remembered but also reprinted on the hearts of every succeeding generation of Latter-day Saints. No one tells their story with greater feeling or with deeper reverence and gratitude than B. H. Roberts. His retelling of the story is, itself, an important part of the legacy that needs to be preserved. The reissue of his classic work in an archival-quality binding will help to make this possible.

B. H. Roberts

Roberts's life story is one of high drama; space here permits a sketch of but a few scenes and settings: his quasi-abandonment as a child of four in England;[1] his immigration to the United States four years later[2] and his barefoot trek across the plains to the Salt Lake Valley;[3] his labor in his youth in the Ophir mines,[4] as a ranch and farm hand,[5] and as a blacksmith's apprentice, all the while thirsting for an education;[6] his quest to quench that thirst as he walked eleven miles daily from his home in Centerville to Salt Lake City to attend classes at the University of Deseret,[7] graduating in just one year as valedictorian;[8] his meteoric development from an illiterate English emigrant to a place of preeminence among LDS scholars; his church service as missionary,[9] mission president,[10] and member of the First Council of the Seventy;[11] his risking his life (while a mission president) by disguising himself as a rough mountaineer to retrieve the bodies of two Mormon missionaries slain in Tennessee by anti-Mormons;[12] his public lectures in many major U.S. cities on the restored gospel; his polygamous marriages[13] and consequent struggles with federal authorities—arrests, exile, prosecution, conviction and imprisonment;[14] his important role in the Utah State Constitutional Convention;[15] his election to the U. S. House of Representatives and his impassioned but unsuccessful bid (due to his polygamy) to be seated;[16] his conflicts—political, theological, and otherwise—with the Brethren, and his subsequent reconciliations;[17] his recruitment of Utah volunteers to serve in the armed forces during World War I and, although now over sixty, his service with them (both in the U.S. and overseas) as their chaplain. High drama, indeed! And much more could be added.

Of Roberts's early background and of his bootstrap rise to greatness, one experience is particularly significant:

> When Roberts was a lonely little waif in England, walking along a city street, he stopped to pick up a sheet of paper. It had fluttered down from an open window above him and landed near his path. He stared intently at the strange symbols. There was an intense longing to know what message the writing contained, but all his efforts failed to unlock the mystery of the written words. In almost hopeless desperation he asked himself:
>
> "Will the time ever come when I shall read books?"
>
> "Yea, and write them, too!" The quiet, piercing voice of inspiration burned this message upon his soul.[18]

By the end of his life, Roberts had published well over thirty books, more than three hundred articles, and more than a thousand sermons and discourses.[19] In weighing Roberts's accomplishments while considering that he was essentially self-taught, former LDS Church historian Leonard Arrington said: "This should give the modern generation of Mormon scholars ample cause for humility. Considering our enormous advantages, we ought to be making far greater contributions than we are."[20]

Arrington was among the first in our era to call attention to the significance of Roberts's work. In 1968, he distributed a questionnaire to fifty prominent LDS scholars, asking them to identify the five most outstanding intellectuals in Mormon history. Of thirty-eight respondents, thirty-five listed B. H. Roberts, nearly all of them ranking him first.[21] Nearly a quarter of a century later, Stan Larsen replicated Arrington's survey with remarkably similar results, except that Robert's preeminence was even more pronounced. Larsen sent out 152 questionnaires and received 94 responses. Roberts was listed most often, with 72 votes; Orson Pratt was second with 52. On the basis of his study, Larsen concluded, "What the present survey demonstrates is that sixty years after his death, B. H. Roberts remains the foremost intellectual in Mormonism, and if anything his position is even stronger now: in 1969 Roberts was 17 percent ahead of the second position; today he is 42 percent ahead."[22]

His recognized importance among Mormon thinkers no doubt serves as both causal explanation for and effect of the extensive publication or republication of works by or about Roberts over the past thirty years. Eight of his major works have already been reprinted or republished, some more than once.[23] Two biographies have been published—a short one by Robert Malan in 1966, and the more definitive biography by Truman Madsen in 1980. Finally, the last decade has seen the appearance of three of Roberts's never-before-published books: *Studies on the Book of Mormon,*[24] *The Autobiography of B. H. Roberts,* and, finally, what Roberts saw as his most important work—*The Truth, The Way, The Life: An Elementary Treatise in Theology.* After lying virtually forgotten for nearly sixty years, the manuscript was published twice in 1994[25] by two separate presses: Smith Research Associates,[26] and *BYU Studies.*[27] "The resurgence of interest in Roberts's work . . . , and the reissue of some of his writings are fortunate," said Sterling McMurrin, "for in him the Mormon people have a spokesman of uncommon stature and ability. His name should be kept very much alive by those who value the traditions of the Church, . . . or who have genuine appreciation for the ideas and institutions that have been the substance and strength of Mormonism."[28]

NOTES

1. Gary James Bergera, ed., *The Autobiography of B.H. Roberts* (Salt Lake City: Signature Books, 1990), 6.
2. Ibid., 4.
3. Ibid., 22–23.
4. Ibid., 48–51.
5. Ibid., 46.
6. Ibid., chap. 8.
7. Ibid., 68.
8. Ibid., 67.
9. Ibid., chaps. 11, 17.
10. Ibid., 136. He served as mission president two times.
11. Ibid., 174.
12. Ibid., chap. 17.
13. Ibid., 159.
14. Ibid., 175–80.
15. Ibid., chap. 21.
16. Ibid., chaps. 22–23.
17. Ibid., 254–57. These are not discussed by Roberts himself, but are addressed in the editor's afterword.
18. This statement was written and signed by B. H. Roberts in his own hand in a compilation of Seventies' Yearbooks, which Roberts presented to John Emmett, M.D., staff of Mayo Clinic, Rochester, Minnesota, and is quoted in Robert H. Malan, *B. H. Roberts: A Biography* (Salt Lake City: Deseret Book Co., 1966), 85. A slightly different account of the experience is contained in Roberts's biographical notes quoted in Truman G. Madsen, *Defender of the Faith: The B. H. Roberts Story* (Salt Lake City: Bookcraft, 1980), 21. See also Bergera, 16.

19. See the selected bibliography in Madsen, 441–43.
20. Leonard J. Arrington, "The Intellectual Tradition of the Latter-day Saints," *Dialogue: A Journal of Mormon Thought* 4 (Spring 1969): 24.
21. Ibid., 13, 22–24.
22. Stan Larson, "Intellectuals in Mormon History: An Update," *Dialogue: A Journal of Mormon Thought* 26 (Fall 1993): 187–89.
23. These include *Joseph Smith, the Prophet Teacher* (Princeton, NJ: Deseret Club, 1967); *The Mormon Doctrine of Deity* (Bountiful, UT: Horizon Publishers, 1976, 1982); *The Seventy's Course in Theology, Vols. I, II* (Dallas, TX: S.K. Taylor Publishing Co., 1976); also (Orem, UT: Grandin Book Co., 1994) as Vol. 5 of series entitled: Prominent Works in Mormon History; *Outlines of Ecclesiastical History* (Salt Lake City: Deseret Book Co., 1979); *A Comprehensive History of the Church* (Provo, UT: Brigham Young University Press, 1965, 1976), also (Salt Lake City: Deseret Book Co., 1982); *Defense of the Faith and the Saints,* Vol. I (West Jordan, UT: Early Church Reprints, 1981), *Defense of the Faith and the Saints,* Vol. I (West Jordan, UT: Early Church Reprints, 1983); *The Missouri Persecutions* (West Jordan, UT: Early Church Reprints, 1983); *The Rise and Fall of Nauvoo,* (West Jordan, UT: Early Church Reprints, 1981, 1983).
24. *Studies of the Book of Mormon,* 2d ed., with a new afterword (Salt Lake City: Signature Books, 1992); 1st ed. (Urbana: University of Illinois Press, 1895).
25. For fascinating essays telling the history of the manuscript from composition to publication, see James B. Allen, "The Story of *The Truth, The Way, The Life,*" and John W. Welch, "Introduction," in John W. Welch, ed., B.H. Roberts, *The Truth, The Way, The Life: An Elementary Treatise on Theology* (Provo, UT: BYU Studies, 1996).
26. *The Truth, The Way, The Life, An Elementary Treatise on Theology: The Masterwork of B. H. Roberts,* Stan Larson, ed., (San Francisco: Smith Research Associates, 1994).
27. *The Truth, The Way, The Life, An Elementary Treatise on Theology: The Masterwork of B. H. Roberts,* John W. Welch, ed., (Provo, UT: BYU Studies, 1994, 2d ed. 1996).
28. Sterling M. McMurrin, "Brigham H. Roberts, Notes on a Mormon Philosopher-Historian," written as an introduction to the reprint of *Joseph Smith, the Prophet-Teacher.*

THE

RISE AND FALL OF NAUVOO.

BY ELDER B. H. ROBERTS

AUTHOR OF "OUTLINES OF ECCLESIASTICAL HISTORY," "A NEW WITNESS FOR GOD," "THE MISSOURI PERSECUTIONS," "THE GOSPEL," SUCCESSION IN THE PRESIDENCY," ETC.

SALT LAKE CITY, UTAH:

THE DESERET NEWS, PUBLISHERS.

1900.

REPRODUCTION OF THE FIRST EDITION

COMMEMORATING

THE REBUILDING AND DEDICATION OF THE

NAUVOO TEMPLE

JUNE 2002

PREFACE.

THE RISE AND FALL OF NAUVOO is a companion volume and stands in historical sequence to "The Missouri Persecutions." It was written with the same object in view, *viz.*, "To place in the hands of the youth of the Latter-day Saints a full statement of the persecutions endured by the early members of The Church in this last dispensation; * * * that they may be made acquainted with the sacrifices which their fathers have made for the word of God and the testimony of Jesus Christ." And I indulge the same hope with reference to this book that I did with respect to "The Missouri Persecutions," *viz.*, that by "becoming acquainted with the story of the sufferings of the early Saints, the faith of the Gospel will become all the more dear to the hearts of their immediate posterity, and all the youth of Zion, for many generations to come."*

THE AUTHOR.

---

* See Preface to "The Missouri Persections."

CONTENTS.

INTRODUCTION.

Once in an ancient city, * * *
Raised aloft on a column, a brazen statue of Justice
Stood in the public square, upholding the scales in its left hand,
And in its right hand a sword, as an emblem that justice presided
Over the laws of the land, and the hearts and the homes of the people.
But in the course of time the laws of the land were corrupted;
Might took the place of right, and the weak were oppressed, and the mighty—
Ruled with an iron rod.—*Evangeline.*

QUEEN ANNE'S war was brought to a close by the treaty of Utrecht, in 1713. By this treaty the French province, Nova Scotia, was ceded by France to England; and, of course, the inhabitants, nearly exclusively French, and numbering some three thousand, became subjects of Great Britain. Less than half a century later, when the French and Indian war broke out, the French population had increased to eighteen thousand—outnumbering the English three to one. In fact the presence of the English amounted to nothing more than a military occupation of the peninsula. These French peasants, usually called Acadians, had brought under cultivation large tracts of land; owned about sixty thousand head of cattle; had built neat cottage homes, established peaceful hamlets, and lived in a state of plenty, but great simplicity. They were reputed to be a peaceable, industrious, and amiable race; governed mostly by their pastors, who exercised a paternal authority over them.

Thus dwelt together in love these simple Acadian farmers—
Dwelt in the love of God and of man. Alike were they free from
Fear, that reigns with the tyrant, and envy, the vice of republics.
Neither locks had they to their doors, nor bars to their windows;
But their dwellings were open as day, and the hearts of their owners;
There the richest were poor, and the poorest lived in abundance.

When the French and Indian war broke out, these people were quietly cultivating their farms, and manifested no warlike disposition. Still, the deputy governor of the province, Lawrence by name, pretended to fear an insurrection, should the French in Canada attempt an invasion of Acadia. Therefore when General Braddock met in council with the colonial governors at Alexandria, Lawrence urged the assembly to do something to overawe the French, and strengthen the English authority. A plan to humiliate the Acadians was decided upon, and placed in the hands of the infamous deputy governor, Lawrence, and Colonel Monckton to execute.

A fleet of forty vessels with three thousand regular troops on board, left Boston in May, 1755, and after a successful voyage anchored in Chignecto Bay. Landing their troops, they besieged Fort Beau-Sejour, which had been erected by the French, on the isthmus connecting Nova Scotia with New Brunswick. After a feeble resistance the fort capitulated, and in less than a month, with the loss of only twenty men, the English had made themselves masters of the whole country. The inglorious campaign was ended, but the fact still existed that the obnoxious Acadians outnumbered the English; and the question remained as it was before the invasion. The deputy governor convened a council "to consider what disposal of the Acadians the security of the country required." The result of the deliberations was this: The security of the country required the banishment of the entire French population!

Lawrence and his associates soon invented a scheme which furnished an excuse for carrying into effect this infamous order. An oath of allegiance was formulated to which the Acadians as consistent Catholics could not subscribe, without doing violence to their consciences. They refused to take the oath, but declared their loyalty to the English government. This they were told was insufficient. At one fell stroke they were adjudged guilty of treason, and the surrender of their boats and firearms demanded. To these acts of tyranny the Acadians submitted. They even offered to take the oath first required of them, but the deputy governor said the day of grace was past; that once having refused to take it, they must now endure the consequences.

Their lands, houses and cattle were declared forfeited; their peaceful hamlets were laid waste; their houses given to the flames; the fruits of years of honest industry and strict economy were wantonly destroyed, and the people driven to the larger coast towns. In one district two hundred and thirty-six houses were burned to the ground at once. Part of the inhabitants who had escaped to the woods beheld all they possessed wickedly destroyed by bands of marauders, without making any resistance until their place of worship was wantonly set on fire. Exasperated by this unhallowed deed, they rushed from their hiding places, killed about thirty of the incendiaries, and retreated to the woods.

To render this scheme of tyrannical banishment completely effective, further treachery was necessary. In each district the people were commanded to meet at a certain place and day on important business, the nature of which was carefully concealed from them, until they were assembled and surrounded by English troops; then the inhuman edict of banishment was announced to the heart-broken peasants. Very little time was allowed them for preparation. In mournful crowds they were driven to the beach. Women with white faces pressed their babes to their hearts; children dumb with terror clung to their parents; the aged and the infirm as well as the young and strong shared the common fate.

At the large village of Grand Pre, when the moment for embarkation arrived, the young men, who were placed in the front, refused to move; but files of troops with fixed bayonets forced obedience. As soon as they were on board the British shipping, heavy columns of black smoke ascending from Grand Pre announced to the wretched Acadians the destruction of their lovely village.

The embarkation of these peasants, and the burning of Grand Pre is thus described by Longfellow:

Thus to the Gaspereau's mouth moved on that mournful procession.
There disorder prevailed, and the tumult and stir of embarking.
Busily plied the freighted boats; and in the confusion
Wives were torn from their husbands, and mothers, too late, saw
their children

Left on the land, extending their arms with wildest entreaties.

* * * * * * * * * * *

Suddenly rose from the South a light, as in Autumn the blood red
Moon climbs the crystal walls of heaven, and o'er the horizon
Titan-like, stretches its hundred hands upon mountain and meadow,
Seizing the rocks and the rivers, and piling huge shadows together;
Broader and ever broader it gleamed on the roofs of the village,
Gleamed on the sky and the sea, and the ships that lie in the road-stead.
Columns of shining smoke uprose and flashes of flame were
Thrust through their folds and withdrawn, like the quivering hands of a martyr.
Then as the winds seized the gleeds and the burning thatch, and, uplifting,
Whirled them aloft through the air, at once from a hundred house-tops
Started the sheeted smoke with flashes of flame intermingled.
These things beheld in dismay the crowd on the shore and on ship-board.
Speechless at first they stood, then cried aloud in their anguish,
"*We shall behold no more our homes in the village of Grand Pre.*'

The property which had before escaped the hands of the spoilers was now laid waste on the plea of discouraging the return of the exiles, who, through their blinding tears, saw the land of their homes and their hopes fade from view.

No preparations had been made for their settlement elsewhere; nor did they receive any compensation for their property from which they were forced, or that had been wickedly destroyed. In a starving and penniless state, they were put ashore in small groups at different points along the coast of

New England, where many of them perished through the hardships they endured. A pathetic representation of their wrongs was addressed to the English government, and by reference to solemn treaties made between them and the provincial government, they proved their banishment to be "as faithless as it was cruel." "No attention, however," says Marcus Wilson, "was paid to this document, and so guarded a silence was preserved by the government of Nova Scotia upon the subject of the removal of the Acadians, that the records of the province make no allusion whatever to the event."

After the close of the French and Indian war, France ceded all her possessions in Canada to victorious England. The case of the Acadians was again brought before the English government, but no compensation was ever allowed them for the outrages committed against them. The property of which they were ruthlessly plundered was never restored. They were allowed to return to the province, and, on taking the customary oaths, could receive lands; but of the eighteen thousand that were banished, less than two thousand returned:

Still stands the forest primeval; but under the shade of its branches
Dwells another race, with other customs and language.
Only along the shore of the mournful and misty Atlantic
Linger a few Acadian peasants, whose fathers from exile
Wandered back to their native land to die in its bosom.

For such atrocious acts as these, we find no apologist among our historians. On every hand they meet with execration. Such wanton cruelty—such palpable violations of human rights are stains upon the escutcheon of the nation that permits them to be perpetrated within her borders.

It is quite generally supposed that such atrocious crimes as this against the French peasants of Acadia are only to be met with in former ages or among non-Christian countries. But in writing the history of the Rise and Fall of Nauvoo—strange as it may appear, and almost past believing—it is my task to relate events which have taken place in the nineteenth century, in this age of boasted enlightenment and toleration, that shall make the expulsion of the French peasants from Acadia pale in comparison with them; events which have occurred in the United States, the boasted asylum for the oppressed of all nations; events which would be more in keeping with the intolerance of the dark ages and the cruelty of Spain, during the reign of the inquisition, than in this age and in this nation. What events are these that so thunder in the index? Such deeds as outrage humanity, and well-nigh destroy one's confidence in human governments; mock justice; deride the claims of mercy; and pull down the wrath of an offended God upon the people who perform them, and upon the government which allows them to go unwhipped of justice. Listen to the history of the Rise and Fall of Nauvoo.

THE
RISE AND FALL OF NAUVOO.

CHAPTER I.

NAUVOO.

THE history of the Rise and Fall of Nauvoo is worthy the attention of the readers of this book because its story is connected with one of the most important religious movements of this or any other age; and with the life and death of one of the world's greatest and most unique characters, the Prophet Joseph Smith. It is worthy of the reader's attention because the religious institution founded under God by this man—the Church of Jesus Christ of Latter-day Saints—survives him, and presents to the world the greatest religious wonder of the age, a right conception of which cannot be formed without a knowledge of this Nauvoo period of the history of The Church; a period which is essentially a formative one, especially in regard to what may be considered the higher and more complex doctrines of Mormonism. It was in Nauvoo that Joseph Smith reached the summit of his remarkable career. It was in Nauvoo he grew bolder in the proclamation of those doctrines which stamp Mormonism as the great religion of the age. It was in Nauvoo that Joseph Smith's life expanded into that eloquent fullness which gives so much promise of what that man will be in eternity. It was in Nauvoo he contended against a world of opposition; against the power of falsehood and misrepresentation; against priestcraft;

against corruption in high places; from here he corresponded with statesmen, and rebuked demagogues; from here he went to martyrdom—to seal his testimony with his blood. And after his death, it was from here his people fled to the wilderness in the most remarkable exodus of modern times. The Church fled into the wilderness—not, however to be hidden from the world, but to be lifted up on high as an ensign to the nations, to be as a city sitting upon a hill that cannot be hid, but on the contrary, from its lofty eminence challenges the attention of the world. In Illinois, as in Missouri, the religious toleration guaranteed in the Constitutions of both the State of Illinois and of the United States—religious toleration, at once the boast and pride of Americans, and also the test of true enlightenment and the highest civilization—this vaunted toleration was in Nauvoo put to the test and found wanting. That is, before the exodus of The Church from Nauvoo, it became evident that a people accepting what to their neighbors was a singular faith, and one that was unpopular withal, could not live in peace among their fellow-citizens of other faiths, and hence the exodus, not only from Nauvoo but from the entire State of Illinois and also from the United States. The Latter-day Saints, in a word, were expatriated from the United States,* and sought an asylum in the wilderness, and among tribes of savages. From whence, after half a century, that same Church emerges, enlarged, prosperous, more firmly rooted in safety and in strength of faith than ever before—a greater enigma to the religious world than when it made its exodus from Illinois.

All these things have a relation to Nauvoo, for The Church had a sort of second birth there, which makes the Rise and Fall of Nauvoo a theme of peculiar interest to those interested

---

* When the Mormon Pioneers arrived in the Salt Lake valley, that whole intermountain region still belonged to the republic of Mexico.

in what the world calls Mormonism. And who is not or should not be interested in a religious movement of such proportions, of such pretensions and of such achievements in the face of such opposition as it has met? * * * * * *

Nauvoo, then, its rise and its fall, is to be the subject of my discourse. The word Nauvoo comes from the Hebrew, and signifies beautiful situation; "carrying with it also," says the Prophet Joseph Smith, "the idea of rest." And, indeed, the location of the city is beautiful. No sooner does one come in view of it than he exclaims, "It is rightly named!" The city, or at least the marred remains of it, stands on a bold point around which sweeps the placid yet majestic "Father of Waters"—the Mississippi. The city is at least half encircled by that noble stream. From its banks the ground rises gradually for at least a mile where it reaches the common level of the prairie that stretches out to the eastward, farther than the eye can reach, in a beautifully undulating surface, once covered by a luxuriant growth of natural grasses and wild flowers, with here and there patches of timber; but now chequered with meadows, and, at the time of my visit, in 1885, with fields of waving corn.

Opposite Nauvoo, on the west bank of the river, the bluffs rise rather abruptly, almost from the water's edge, and are covered, for the most part, with a fine growth of timber. Nestling at the foot of one of the highest of these bluffs, and immediately on the bank of the river, is the little village of Montrose, to which I shall have occasion to refer in these pages. Back of these bluffs before mentioned, roll off the alternate prairie and woodlands of Iowa. Between Montrose and Nauvoo, and perhaps two thirds of the distance across the river from the Illinois side, is an island, from three-fourths of a mile to a mile in length, and from fifty to one or two hundred yards in width, having its greatest extent north and south.

Nauvoo is situated just at the head of what are usually called the Des Moines Rapids, about one hundred and ninety miles above St. Louis. These rapids were a serious obstacle to the navigation of the Mississippi at this point, in an early day, as in the season of low water they could not be passed by the steamboats plying the river. This difficulty of late, however, has been obviated by the general government building a fine canal, running parallel with the west bank of the river, from Keokuk to Montrose, a distance of twelve or fifteen miles. I was unable to learn the cost of the construction, but judge it must have required at least several millions of dollars.

Such is the location of Nauvoo; such its immediate surroundings. It now remains for me to relate the events which led to the establishment of a thriving city on the site we have briefly described; how it was converted from a sickly wilderness to the most desirable section of the great State of Illinois; and then how, through acts of injustice and treachery, some of its principal founders were murdered and the rest of its inhabitants cruelly driven from the city by mob violence into the wilderness; and how the city sank from its prosperous condition, to become the semi-desolate place it is today; and, what is of more importance, to trace the development of that faith taught by Joseph Smith, which is destined to become, and indeed now is, one of the world's great religions.

CHAPTER II.

THE RECEPTION OF THE EXILES IN ILLINOIS.

IN what is properly a companion volume to this—"The Missouri Persecutions"—I have told how the Latter-day Saints were driven from Missouri under a threat of extermination from the executive of that State, Lilburn W. Boggs. When fleeing from Missouri, where they had suffered so much from mob violence, and from the State government officials, the Mormon exiles crossed the Mississippi into the State of Illinois, at the point near where the city of Quincy is located—in fact, at the Quincy Ferry. Their destitute condition, together with the injustice they had suffered in Missouri—the spectacle of a people in free America being driven from their homes and exiled from one of the States of the American Union because of religious beliefs—aroused the indignation and excited the sympathy of the people of Quincy and vicinity. A kind reception was given to the exiles by the people of this section of Illinois, one very similar to that given to many of the same people by the inhabitants of Clay County, when a cruel persecution had driven some twelve hundred of them from their homes in Jackson County, Missouri, five years before.* The Democratic Association of Quincy was especially active in the interests of the exiles. In the month of February a meeting was called by this association to inquire into the situation of the Mormon exiles. At this first meeting all that

---

* Missouri Persecutions, Chapter xiv.

was done was to pass a resolution, to the effect that the people called Latter-day Saints were in a situation requiring the aid of the people of Quincy. A committee of eight was appointed to call a general meeting of both citizens and Mormons, and to receive a statement from the latter of their condition, with a view to relieving their necessities. The committee was instructed to get the Congregational church in which to hold the next meeting, but the directors having in charge that building would not allow it to be used for that purpose. I speak of this to show the kind of charity existing in the breasts of some pretended followers of Him who taught that charity was the crowning virtue. Failing to secure the church, the second meeting was held in the courthouse.

At this meeting the special committee appointed at the first meeting reported its labors. The committee had received statements from Sidney Rigdon and others in relation to the expulsion of the Mormons from Missouri, and suggested a series of resolutions setting forth that the exiled strangers were entitled to the sympathy and aid of the people of Quincy;

That a numerous committee, composed of individuals from every part of the town, be appointed to allay the prejudices of the misguided citizens of Quincy, and explain that it was not the design of the exiled Saints to lower the wages of the laboring classes, but to secure something to save them from starvation;

That a standing committee be appointed to relieve, so far as in their power, the wants of the destitute and homeless; and to use their utmost endeavors to procure employment for those who were able and willing to labor.

The report closed by saying:—

We recommend to all the citizens of Quincy that in all their intercourse with the strangers, they use and observe a becoming decorum and delicacy, and be particularly careful not to indulge in any conversation or expression calculated to wound their feelings, or in any way to reflect upon those who, by every law of humanity, are entitled to our sympathy and commiseration.

This good work begun by the Democratic Association was continued by them, and substantial assistance was given to the suffering Saints through their exertions. At a subsequent meeting of the association the following resolutions were adopted:

That we regard the right of conscience as natural and inalienable, and the most sacredly guaranteed by the Constitution of our free government;

That we regard the acts of all mobs in violation of law; and those who compose them individually responsible, both to the laws of God and man, for every depredation committed upon the property, rights, or life of any citizen;

That the inhabitants upon the western frontier of the State of Missouri, in their late persecution of the people denominated Mormons, have violated the sacred rights of conscience and every law of justice and humanity;

That the governor of Missouri, in refusing protection to this class of people, when pressed upon by a heartless mob, and turning upon them a band of unprincipled militia, with orders encouraging their extermination, has brought a lasting disgrace upon the State over which he presides.

Thus with expressions of sympathy and material aid did the people of Quincy assist the exiles and bid them hope for better days. Nor was this kindly feeling confined to the people of Quincy and vicinity; it extended throughout the State; and especially was it exhibited by some of the leading men thereof, including Governor Carlin, Stephen A. Douglas, Dr. Isaac Galland and many others.

CHAPTER III.

COMMERCE—LAND PURCHASES.

IN the fall of 1838 a brother by the name of Israel Barlow left the State of Missouri under the exterminating order of Governor Boggs. By missing his way, or, what is more likely, directed by the hand of a kind Providence, he did not leave the State by the same route as the great body of his people, but taking a northeasterly course, struck the Des Moines River a short distance above its mouth, in the Territory of Iowa. He was without food and destitute of clothing. Making his wants known to the people living in that locality, they kindly supplied him with food and raiment. To them he related the story of the persecution of the Latter-day Saints in Missouri, and how his people, poor and destitute as himself, were fleeing from the State *en masse*. His relation of the sufferings of the Saints, and the cruelties heaped upon them by their heartless persecutors, enlisted the sympathies of his hearers, and they gave him letters of introduction to several gentlemen, among which was one to Dr. Isaac Galland, a gentleman of some influence living at Commerce, a small settlement on the banks of the Mississippi, in Illinois, and which afterward became the site of Nauvoo.

Dr. Galland owned considerable land in Commerce, and he wrote the Saints located in Quincy that several farms could doubtless be rented in his locality, and that perhaps some fifty families could be accommodated at Commerce. In addition to this offer of lands made to The Church, another and a previous one had been made of twenty thousand acres, between the Des

Moines and the Mississippi rivers. This tract could have been purchased at two dollars per acre, to be paid in twenty annual payments without interest. A conference was convened at Quincy in February, and the advisability of making the purchase and settling the Saints in a body came up for consideration. It was decided by the conference that it was not advisable to locate lands at that time.

Subsequently, however, on the ninth day of March, the Saints having received further offers of land in Illinois and Iowa, called another public meeting and appointed a committee to go and examine the lands offered. In Iowa, the people and officers of the Territory expressed a kindly feeling toward the exiled Saints. The governor of Iowa—Robert Lucas—had known the Saints in Ohio, and testified to Dr. Galland that the Mormon people, when they were in Ohio, were good citizens, and he respected them as such now, and would treat them accordingly, should they, or any part of them, decide to settle in his Territory. The statement is made in answer to a letter of inquiry on the subject of the Mormons settling in Iowa. He wrote to Dr. Isaac Galland as follows:

EXECUTIVE OFFICE, IOWA, BURLINGTON
March. 1839.

DEAR SIR —On my return to this city, after a few weeks' absence in the interior of the Territory, I received your letter of the 25th ultimo, in which you give a short account of the sufferings of the *people called Mormons*, and ask "whether they could be permitted to purchase lands, and settle upon them, in the Territory of Iowa, and there worship Almighty God according to the dictates of their own consciences, secure from oppression," etc.

In answer to your inquiry, I would say, that I know of no authority that can constitutionally deprive them of this right. They are citizens of the United States, and are entitled to all the rights and privileges of other citizens. The 2nd section of the 4th Article of the Constitution of the United States (which all are solemnly bound to support), declares that the "citizens of each State shall be entitled to all the privileges and immunities of citizens of the several States." This privilege extends in full force to the Territories of the United States. The first Amendment to the Constitution of the United States declares that "Congress shall make no law respecting an establishment of religion, or prohibiting the free exercise thereof."

The Ordinance of Congress of the 13th July, 1787, for the government of the Territory northwest of the river Ohio, secures to the citizens of said Territory, and the citizens of the States thereafter to be formed therein, certain privileges which were, by the late Act of Congress organizing the Territory of Iowa, extended to the citizens of this Territory.

The first fundamental Article in that Ordinance, which is declared to be forever unalterable, except by common consent, reads as follows, to-wit: "No person demeaning himself in a peaceable and orderly manner, shall ever be molested on account of his mode of worship, or religious sentiments in said Territory."

These principles, I trust, will ever be adhered to in the Territory of Iowa. They make no distinction between religious sects. They extend equal privileges and protection to all; each must rest upon its own merits, and will prosper in proportion to the purity of its principles, and the fruit of holiness and piety produced thereby.

With regard to the peculiar people mentioned in your letter, I know but little. They had a community in the northern part of Ohio for several years; and I have no recollection of ever having heard in that State of any complaints against them from violating the laws of the country. Their religious opinions, I consider, has nothing to do with our political transactions. They are citizens of the United States, and are entitled to the same political rights and legal protection that other citizens are entitled to.

The foregoing are briefly my views on the subject of your inquiries.

With sincere respect,

I am your obedient servant,

ROBERT LUCAS.

To ISAAC GALLAND, Esq., Commerce, Illinois.

This communication Dr. Galland sent to the Quincy *Argus*, accompanied by the following note:

COMMERCE, ILLINOIS,
April 12, 1839.

MESSRS. EDITORS:—Enclosed I send you a communication from Governor Lucas of Iowa Territory. If you think the publication thereof will in any way promote the cause of justice, by vindicating the slandered reputation of the people called Mormons, from the ridiculous falsehoods which the malice, cupidity and envy of their murderers in Missouri have endeavored to heap upon them, you are respectfully solicited to publish it in the *Argus*. The testimony of Governor Lucas as to the good moral character of these people, I think will have its deserved influence upon the people of Illinois, in encouraging our citizens in their humane and benevolent exertions to relieve this distressed people, who are now wandering in our neighborhoods without comfortable food, raiment, or a shelter from the pelting storm.

I am, gentlemen, very respectfully,
Your obedient servant,
ISAAC GALLAND.

In conversation with Dr. Galland, Isaac Van Allen, Esq., attorney-general for the same Territory (Iowa), gave him to understand that he would, so far as within his power, protect the Mormon people from insult and injury. It was these assurances of sympathy and protection which led to a reconsideration of the conclusion of the former conference, and the appointment of a committee to examine the lands offered. But little or nothing was ever done by this committee.

On the twenty-second of April, 1839, the Prophet Joseph joined the exiled Saints at Quincy. After a cruel imprisonment of over five months, he had escaped from his persecutors while en route from Liberty prison, Clay County, to Columbia, Boone County, to which he and his companions in prison had taken a change of venue for trial. The guards got drunk and were evidently willing for their prisoners to escape. At any rate, the Prophet, in stating the circumstance in his history, says: "We thought it a favorable opportunity to make our escape; knowing that the only object of our enemies was our destruction; and likewise knowing that a number of our brethren had been massacred by them on Shoal Creek, amongst whom were two children; and they had sought every opportunity to abuse others who were left in the State; and that they were never brought to an account for their barbarous proceedings, but were winked at and encouraged by those in authority. We thought that it was necessary for us, inasmuch as we loved our lives, and did not wish to die by the hand of murderers and assassins; and inasmuch as we loved our families and friends, to deliver ourselves from our enemies." And so the Prophet and his companions escaped and arrived in Quincy as already stated.

I need not stop to undertake a description of the scenes of this exiled people welcoming their youthful Prophet into their midst, after such trials as they had passed through, in which the strength of each man's soul and love for his brethren had been tested. The Saints had seen their Prophet and his fellow prisoners betrayed into the hands of a merciless enemy, and knew that a court-martial of the Missouri State militia had condemned him and his companions to be shot in the public square at Far West. They had seen him and his fellow-prisoners torn away from their parents and families, and their people, under circumstances the most distressing. They had been told by the haughty commander-in-chief of the mob militia forces which invested Far West—General Clark—that the doom of their leaders was sealed, and they need not expect, nor even let it enter into their hearts that they would be permitted to see them again. Many of them had seen him chained like a felon, standing before unjust judges, whose hearts were filled to overflowing with hatred towards him. Contrary to every principle of justice, he had been sent to languish in prison in the midst of his enemies; while they themselves, with bursting hearts and blinding tears, were compelled to sign away their lands and homes at the muzzle of the musket and flee from the Christian State of Missouri, under the exterminating order issued by Governor Boggs. Yet in all these trials, from the dangers of the murderous militia camps, from the malice of corrupt courts, and the injustice of drunken juries, and at last from the prison's gloom, a kind Providence had delivered him, and he was again in their midst, again with them to still their fears and direct their movements.

His presence was the signal for action. He arrived in Quincy on the 22nd of April. The day following he spent in greeting his friends, and receiving visits from the brethren; but on the twenty-fourth he called and presided over a conference, at which, in connection with Bishop Knight and Alanson Ripley, he was appointed to go to Iowa to select a place for the gathering of the exiled Saints. The conference also advised the brethren, who could do so, to go to Commerce and locate in Dr. Galland's neighborhood.

On the first of May the committee purchased a farm of one hundred and thirty-five acres, for which they agreed to pay five thousand dollars; also another and a larger farm of Dr. Galland for nine thousand dollars. The committee desired that these farms should be deeded to Alanson Ripley, but Sidney Rigdon, manifesting a rather sour disposition, said that no committee should control any property that he had anything to do with. So the purchase made of Dr. Galland was deeded to Sidney Rigdon's son-in-law, G. W. Robinson, with the understanding that he should deed it to The Church as soon as it was paid for according to the contract. This was the first purchase of lands made in Commerce. The place is thus described by Joseph: "When I made the purchase of White and Galland, there was one stone house, three frame houses, and two block-houses, which constituted the whole city of Commerce."

This small collection of houses was immediately on the banks of the river, and scattered between them and what afterwards became the south part of the city of Nauvoo, were one stone and three log houses. It was one of these humble dwellings that Joseph moved into on the tenth of May, 1839. Back some distance from the river, however, were other dwellings scattered over the country, one of which was the home of Daniel H. Wells, a justice of the peace for the district of Commerce, and who afterwards became a prominent Church leader, one of the counselors, in fact, in the First Presidency of The Church.

Later, when referring to the purchase of lands about Commerce, the Prophet Joseph said:

> The place was literally a wilderness. The land was mostly covered with trees and bushes, and much of it was so wet that it was with the utmost difficulty that a footman could get through, and totally impossible for teams. Commerce was unhealthy, very few could live there; but believing that it might become a healthy place by the blessing of heaven to the Saints, and no more eligible place presenting itself, I considered it wisdom to make an attempt to build up a city.

Having spoken of the first purchase of lands at Commerce, it may not be amiss here to say that subsequently more extensive purchases were made of Dr. Galland and Messrs. Hubbard, Wells, Hotchkiss and others. Considerable difficulty and embarrassment to Joseph personally and to The Church in general arose over misunderstandings about the Hotchkiss land purchase. Hotchkiss sold to Joseph for The Church upwards of five hundred acres of land in Commerce, for which he was to receive fifty-three thousand five hundred dollars, half to be paid in ten years, and the remainder in twenty years. This amount was secured to Hotchkiss & Company by two notes, one payable in ten years and the other in twenty, signed by Joseph Smith, Hyrum Smith and Sidney Rigdon. The difficulty connected with this extensive land purchase arose from some exchanges that were made of property in the east, by some of the Saints, for its equivalent in value in land out of the Hotchkiss purchase in Commerce; the matter, however, was finally amicably settled.

The terms on which Dr. Galland let The Church have lands were extremely advantageous to the Saints. He sold at a reasonable rate, and on long credit, that the people might not be distressed in paying for the inheritance they purchased. In addition to the first purchase, he exchanged lands with the Saints in the vicinity of Commerce for lands in Missouri, to the value of eighty thousand dollars. And he gave them a good title to the same. He is described as a man of literary attainments and extensive information and influence. All of which he used for the good of the exiled Saints in giving them a standing among his friends. Finally he joined The Church, thus casting his lot with the exiled people he had assisted, and from that time until his death, partook of their joys and their sorrows; shared their fortunes and reverses.

In addition to these land purchases, The Church made others; some of them even more extensive than those already mentioned. The village of Nashville, in Lee County, Iowa, and twenty thousand acres of land adjoining, was bought, though upon what terms the purchase was made cannot be learned. Another purchase also in Iowa was made by Bishop Knight, and a settlement was started there called Zarahemla, which was opposite Nauvoo. This place was organized into a stake* of

---

* A stake of Zion is a territorial division of The Church that embraces several wards or branches. The stake is presided over by a president, who must be a High Priest, assisted by two counselors, also High Priests. There must also be in each stake of Zion a high council, consisting of twelve High Priests, over which council the presi-

Zion, but in January, 1842, the stake organization was discontinued; though Zarahemla continued as an organized branch of The Church.

Stakes of Zion in the following year were organized at Lima, in Illinois; also at Quincy, in Adams County, for the benefit of the Saints who continued there. Another stake was organized at Columbus, in Adams County, Illinois, known as Mount Hope stake; besides these stakes, branches of the Church were organized in various parts of Lee County, Iowa, and Adams and Hancock counties, Illinois. But as Nauvoo rose from the swamps and underbrush of Commerce, and, under the industry and enterprise of the Saints, and the blessings of a kindly disposed Providence, developed into a healthy, beautiful and prosperous commercial and manufacturing city, these stake organizations in the surrounding country were discontinued, and Nauvoo became the one great gathering place of the Saints.

---

dency of the stake preside. This high council constitutes the judicial power (ecclesiastical) of the stake, to which appeals lie from the bishops' courts.

CHAPTER IV.

"AS FLIES IN THE OINTMENT."

HAVING described the site of Nauvoo, and related the circumstances connected with its establishment as a gathering place of the Saints, it is necessary to return to the consideration of some events which occurred at Quincy during the sojourn of the Saints at that place.

Paul, in his day, told the Hebrews that all were not Israel that were of Israel: so all were not Saints that flocked into Quincy with the exiles from Missouri; many of them were altogether unworthy of the association of the people of God. These preyed upon the hospitality of the people of Quincy to such an extent, that The Church by action of a conference authorized Elder John Taylor, then one of the Twelve Apostles, and who afterwards became President of the Church, to write the following letter, which was printed in the Quincy *Argus:*

In consequence of so great an influx of strangers, arriving in this place daily, owing to their late expulsion from the State of Missouri, there must of necessity be, and we wish to state to the citizens of Quincy and the vicinity, through the medium of your columns, that there are many individuals among the numbers who have already arrived, as well as among those who are now on their way here, who never did belong to our Church, and others who once did, but who, for various reasons, have been expelled from our fellowship. Among these are some who have contracted habits which are at variance with principles of moral rectitude (such as swearing, dram-drinking, etc.,) which immoralities the Church of Latter-day Saints is liable to be charged with, owing to our amalgamation under our late existing circumstances. And as we as a people do not wish to lay under any such imputation, we would also state, that such individuals do not hold a name or a place amongst us; that we altogether discountenance everything of the kind, that every person once belonging to our community, contracting or persisting in such immoral habits, have hitherto been expelled from our society; and that such as we may hereafter be informed of, we will hold no communion with, but will withdraw our fellowship from them.

We wish further to state, that we feel laid under peculiar obligations to the citizens of this place for the patriotic feelings which have been manifested, and for the hand of liberality and friendship which was extended to us, in our late difficulties; and should feel sorry to see that philanthropy and benevolence abused by the wicked and designing people, who under pretense of poverty and distress, should try to work up the feelings of the charitable and humane, get into their debt without any prospect or intention of paying, and finally, perhaps, we as a people be charged with dishonesty.

We say that we altogether disapprove of such practices, and we warn the citizens of Quincy against such individuals who may pretend to belong to our community.

I have given this letter *in extenso*, because it bears upon its face the evidence of the honesty of The Church, and its disposition to treat the people of Illinois, who had so nobly and kindly received its members in the days of their distress, with candor. It also tells us of a class even then in The Church, who by the vileness of their lives gave some coloring to the charges subsequently so unjustly made against the whole Church; a class who brought upon The Church reproach; an unrighteous, apostate element, which lingered with The Church for the sake of advantage—the bane of the body religious.

CHAPTER V.

POLITICAL AGITATION.

ABOUT this time, too, the good feeling entertained toward the Saints by the people of Quincy and vicinity was not a little endangered through the unwise course of Lyman Wight. He began the publication of a series of letters in the Quincy *Whig*, in which he laid the responsibility of the outrages perpetrated against the Saints in Missouri upon the Democratic party, implicating not only the Democrats of Missouri, but indirectly the National Democratic party. This gave much dissatisfaction to members of that party in the vicinity of Quincy, a number of whom had been very active in assisting the Saints; and some of the leading men approached prominent brethren, who still remained in Quincy, and desired to know if The Church sustained the assertions of Lyman Wight. Elder R. B. Thompson wrote a letter to President Joseph Smith on the subject, in which he protested against the course taken by Lyman Wight, because of the influence it was having on many of those who had so nobly befriended the Saints in the day of their distress. Besides, it was altogether unjust, for no particular political party in Missouri was responsible for the cruelty practiced towards the Saints. Those who were in the mobs which robbed them of their homes, burned their houses, ran off their stock, and who whipped, murdered and finally drove the people from the State of Missouri, were made up of individuals of every shade of political faith, and of every religion, and many of no religion whatever. It was unfair, then, under these circumstances, that the responsibility should be laid at the charge of any one party or sect of religion. So that Wight's course was not only doing much mischief, but was also unjust.

To counteract the evil effect of Lyman Wight's communication to the *Whig*, Joseph Smith, Sidney Rigdon and Hyrum Smith, then the presiding quorum of the Church, published a letter in the *Whig*, from which I make the following quotation:

> We have not at any time thought there was any political party, as such, chargeable with the Missouri barbarities, neither any religious society, as such. They were committed by a mob, composed of all parties, regardless of difference of opinion, either political or religious.
>
> The determined stand in this State, and by the people of Quincy in particular, made against the lawless outrages of the Missouri mobbers by all parties in politics and religion, have entitled them equally to our thanks and our profoundest regards, and such, gentlemen, we hope they will always receive from us. * * * We wish to say to the public, through your paper, that we disclaim any intention of making a political question of our difficulties with Missouri, believing that we are not justified in so doing.

Lyman Wight was a bold, independent-spirited man; inclined to be self-willed and refractory. No one could control him; and even counsel or advice was usually disregarded—except it was from Joseph Smith. A few years subsequent to the time of which I am now writing, Lyman Wight himself said: "Joseph Smith is the only man who ever did control me; he is the only man who ever shall." But to Joseph's words Lyman Wight gave respectful attention, and bent his own strong will to comply with the wishes of the Prophet. He himself was a master spirit, and could apparently bring himself to acknowledge but one to whom he was willing to yield his own judgment and his own will, and that one was Joseph Smith. It is said by those acquainted with him, that in the Prophet's hands his spirit was as pliable as that of a child.

It was one of Joseph's peculiar characteristics to be able to control men—men, too, who were themselves master spirits; who were themselves naturally leaders; and it is seldom, indeed, that such characters are willing to take a second place. But in the presence of Joseph they seemed naturally to accord him the leadership. He was a leader even among master spirits; a leader of leaders; and it may not be amiss here to briefly inquire into the apparently mysterious influence which the Prophet exerted over the minds of others, by reason of which he controlled them, since this particular instance in which Lyman Wight figures, illustrates it.

In reply to the letter of R. B. Thompson, Joseph admitted that the course of Wight was unfair, and said: The Church was not willing to make of their troubles a political question; but he also said that he considered it to be "the indefeasible right of every free man to hold his own opinion in politics and religion;" and therefore would have it understood that, as an individual, Lyman Wight had the right to entertain and express whatever opinion he pleased in regard to their troubles in Missouri; only intimating that care should be taken not to set forth individual views as the views of The Church. In writing to Lyman Wight on the subject, Joseph did not upbraid him, nor peremptorily order him to discontinue the publication of his letters, or retract them, but he informed him that the matter had been considered in a council of The Church, and that the result was that his course was disapproved. But Joseph took occasion to express his confidence in Wight's good intentions, and said:

Knowing your integrity of principle, and steadfastness in the cause of Christ, I feel not to exercise even the privilege of counsel on the subject, save only to request that you will endeavor to bear in mind the importance of the subject, and how easy it might be to get a misunderstanding with the brethren concerning it; and though last, but not least, that whilst you continue to go upon your own credit, you will steer clear of making The Church appearas either supporting or opposing you in your politics, lest such a course may have a tendency to bring about persecution on The Church, where a little wisdom and caution may avoid it. I do not know that there is any occasion for my thus cautioning you in this thing, but having done so, I hope it will be well taken, and that all things shall eventually be found to work together for the good of the Saints. * * * With every possible feeling of love and friendship for an old fellow-prisoner and brother in the Lord, I remain, sir, your sincere friend.

Throughout this whole affair it will be observed that Joseph starts out with the idea that every individual is absolutely free and independent as to entertaining views and in giving expression to them, both in politics and religion, so long as he makes no one else responsible for them; that in correcting Lyman Wight, he does it by appealing to the man's reason, and by pointing out the possible result of his course, which may be avoided by a little discretion; while the whole communication breathes such a spirit of confidence in the man he is correcting, and love for him as an "old fellow-prisoner," that it was altogether irresistible. And this is the secret of Joseph's power to control his brethren. There was no petty tyranny in his government. He was above that. Every right he claimed for himself, he accorded to others; while his mildness in correcting errors and his unbounded love for his brethren knit them to him in bands stronger than steel. It was ever his method to teach correct principles and allow men to govern themselves.

CHAPTER VI.

A DAY OF GOD'S POWER.

DURING the summer of 1839 the Saints who had been driven from Missouri continued to gather at Nauvoo and settle on the lands which had been purchased by The Church authorities. The violent persecution they had passed through in Missouri had well nigh wrecked the people. They had been stripped of their earthly possessions, until they were reduced to the most abject poverty. And the exposure and hardships endured made them an easy prey to the malaria that infected Nauvoo and vicinity. Another thing which doubtless contributed to make them unable to resist the ravages of disease, was the fact that a period of relaxation was following the intense excitement under which they had lived for more than two years.

The spirit has such power when it is once thoroughly aroused, that for a time it so braces up the body as to make it almost impregnable to disease and unconscious of fatigue. But this cannot continue long. It wears out the body; and as soon as the excitement is removed, then comes the period of relaxation and the body sinks down from sheer exhaustion.

Such was the condition of the exiled Saints who came flocking into Nauvoo, in the summer of 1839. They had reached a haven of rest. The fearful strain on the nervous system under which they had labored during the mobbings in Missouri and their flight from that State was removed; and they fell down in Nauvoo exhausted, to be a prey to the deadly malaria prevalent in that locality. Such was their condition on the morning of the 22nd of July. Joseph's house was crowded with the sick whom he was trying to nurse back to health. In his door-yard were a number of people camped in tents, who had but newly arrived, but upon whom the fever had seized. Joseph himself was prostrate with sickness, and the general distress of the Saints weighed down his spirit with sadness. While still thinking of the trials of his people in the past, and the gloom that then overshadowed them, the purifying influence of God's Spirit rested upon him and he was immediately healed. He arose and began to administer to the sick in his house, all of whom immediately recovered. He then healed those encamped in his door-yard, and from thence went from house to house calling on the sick to arise from their beds of affliction, and they obeyed and were healed.

In company with P. P. Pratt, Orson Pratt, John Taylor, Heber C. Kimball, and John E. Page, he crossed the river to Montrose, and healed the sick there. One case is mentioned by all who have written on the subject as being very remarkable. This was the case of Elijah Fordham. He was almost unconscious and nearly dead. Bending over him, the Prophet asked the dying man if he knew him, and believed him to be a servant of God. In a whisper he replied that he did. Joseph then took him by the hand, and with an energy that would have awoke the dead, he commanded him in the name of Jesus Christ to arise from his bed and walk. Brother Fordham leaped from his bed, removed the bandages and mustard plasters from his feet, dressed himself, ate a bowl of bread and milk, and accompanied the Prophet to other houses on his mission of love.

All day the work continued; and to the Saints who witnessed the remarkable manifestation of God's power in behalf of the sick, the twenty-second day of July, 1839, is remembered with gratitude to Almighty God, who through the demonstration of His power that day, gave an indisputable witness to the world that He was with Joseph Smith, and had authorized him to speak in the name of Jesus Christ. To the Saints it was a testimony that God was with them; for they witnessed a fulfillment of God's ancient promise to His people, viz.—

Is any sick among you? Let him call for the Elders of the Church; and let them pray over him, anointing him with oil, in the name of the Lord: and the prayer of faith shall save the sick, and the Lord shall raise him up.*

And again:

These signs shall follow them that believe: In My name shall they cast out devils; they shall speak with new tongues; * * * they shall lay hands on the sick and they shall recover.†

These ancient promises to God's people had also been renewed to the Latter-day Saints in modern revelations to the Church through the Prophet Joseph himself:

As I said unto mine apostles I say unto you again, that every soul who believeth on your words, and is baptized by water for the remission of sins, shall receive the Holy Ghost; and these signs shall follow them that believe. In my name they shall do many wonderful works:

In my name they shall cast out devils;

In my name they shall heal the sick;

In my name they shall open the eyes of the blind, and unstop the ears of the deaf; and the tongue of the dumb shall speak; and if any man shall administer poison unto them it shall not hurt them. * * * But a commandment I give unto them, that they shall not boast themselves of these things, neither speak them before the world.‡

Again, I say, to the Saints who witnessed the demonstration of God's power on the 22nd of July, 1839, in the healing of the

---

*James v: 14, 15.

†Mark xvi: 17.

‡Doc. & Cov., Sec. lxxxiv. The revelation was given in September, 1832.

sick in fulfillment of these promises ancient and modern, it was a witness to them that God was with them and with their Prophet.

CHAPTER VII.

DEPARTURE OF THE TWELVE FOR ENGLAND.

A REVELATION had been received by the Prophet Joseph on the eighth of July, 1838, in which a commandment was given to fill up the quorum of the Twelve Apostles by ordaining John Taylor, John E. Page, Wilford Woodruff, and Willard Richards to take the places of those who had fallen through apostasy. The following spring "let them depart," said the revelation, "to go over the great waters, and there promulgate my Gospel, the fullness thereof, and bear record of my mame. Let them take leave of my Saints in the city of Far West, on the twenty-sixth day of April next, on the building spot of my house." By the twenty-sixth of April, the day set for them to take leave of the Saints to start on their mission, nearly all the members of The Church had been driven from Far West. I have already related, however, in "The Missouri Persecutions" how five of the Apostles and several who were to be ordained returned by different routes to Far West, met with a few of the Saints there and fulfilled the mandates of this revelation, notwithstanding the boasts of the mob that it should fail.* For some time the Apostles who started from the public square at Far West for England were detained to aid in settling the Saints at Nauvoo, but the latter part of the summer of 1839 found them making every exertion to continue their journey.

Wilford Woodruff and John Taylor were the first of the quorum to leave Nauvoo for England. Elder Woodruff at this

---

* Missouri Persecutions, Chapter XLVIII.

time was living at Montrose, and was rowed across the river in a canoe by Brigham Young. On landing, he lay down to rest on a side of sole leather, near the post office. While there Joseph came along and said: "Well, Brother Woodruff, you have started on your mission?"

"Yes, but I feel and look more like a subject for the dissecting room than a missionary," was the reply.

"What did you say that for?" asked Joseph. "Get up and go along, all will be well with you."

Shortly afterwards Elder Woodruff was joined by Elder Taylor, and together they started on their mission. On their way they passed Parley P. Pratt, stripped, bareheaded and barefooted, hewing some logs for a house. He hailed the brethren as they passed and gave them a purse, though he had nothing to put in it. Elder Heber C. Kimball, who was but a short distance away, stripped as Elder Pratt was, came up and said: "As Brother Parley has given you a purse, I have a dollar I will give you to put in it." And mutually blessing each other, they separated to meet again in foreign lands.

On the twenty-ninth of August, Parley P. Pratt and his brother Orson started for England, leaving Nauvoo in their own carriage.

On the fourteenth of the following month Brigham Young left his home at Montrose and started for England. He had been prostrated for some time by sickness, and at the time of starting on his mission was so feeble that he had to be assisted to the ferry, only some thirty rods from his house. All his children were sick, and he left his wife with a babe but ten days old, and in the poorest of circumstances, for the mobs of Missouri had robbed him of all he had. After crossing the river to the Nauvoo side, Israel Barlow took him on a horse behind him and carried him to the house of Elder Heber C. Kimball, where his strength altogether failed him, and he had to remain there for several days, nursed by his wife, who, hearing that he was unable to get farther than Brother Kimball's, had crossed the river from Montrose to care for him.

On the eighteenth of the month, however, Brigham, in company with Heber C. Kimball, made another start. A brother by the name of Charles Hubbard sent a boy with a team to take them a day's journey on their way. Elder Kimball left his wife in bed shaking with ague, and all his children sick. It was only by the assistance of some of the brethren that Heber himself could climb into the wagon. "It seemed to me," he remarked afterwards in relating the circumstance, "as though my very inmost parts would melt within me at the thought of leaving my family in such a condition, as it were, almost in the arms of death. I felt as though I could scarcely endure it."

"Hold up!" said he to the teamster, who had just started. "Brother Brigham, this is pretty tough, but let us rise and give them a cheer." Brigham, with much difficulty, rose to his feet, and joined Elder Kimball in swinging his hat and shouting, "Hurrah, hurrah, hurrah for Israel!" The two sisters hearing the cheer came to the door—Sister Kimball with great difficulty—and waved a farewell; and the two Apostles continued on their journey without purse, without scrip, for England.

The departure of Elders George A. Smith, Reuben Hedlock, and Theodore Turley was but little less remarkable. They were feeble in health, in fact, down with the ague. Before they were out of sight of Nauvoo their wagon upset, and spilled them down the bank of the river. Elders Smith and Turley were unable to get up, not because of any injuries they had received, but because of their illness. Elder Hedlock helped them into their wagon and they resumed their journey. They had not proceeded far when they met some gentlemen who stopped their team and said to the driver: "Mr., what graveyard have you been robbing?" The remark being elicited by the ghostly appearance of the Elders *en route* for England.

Thus in sickness and poverty, without purse and without

scrip, leaving their families destitute of the comforts of life, with nothing but the assurances of the people, who were as poor as themselves, that they should be provided for, the Twelve turned their faces toward Europe, to preach the Gospel to the highly civilized peoples of the world. Shaking with the ague, and then burning up with the fever; now in the homes of the wealthy, then in the hovels of the poor; now derided by the learned and self-styled refined, and now welcomed by the poor of this world who rejoiced in the message they bore—they journeyed on, never looking back, nor complaining of the hardships through which they were called to pass for the Master's sake. They had ringing in their ears the words of Jesus:

"He that loveth father or mother, houses or lands, wives or children more than he loveth me is not worthy of me." And again they had the promise: "There is no man that hath left houses, or parents, or brethren, or wife, or children for the kingdom of God's sake, who shall not receive manifold more in this present time, and in the world to come life everlasting."

With this warning and this promise before them, they made their way by different routes, but at last met in England, where an effectual door was opened for the preaching of the Gospel, and thousands with joy embraced the truth.

These men went out weeping, bearing precious seed; they returned in time bringing their sheaves with them, and had joy in their harvest. And what shall separate these men who endured so much for the Gospel's sake, from the love of God? "Shall tribulation, or distress, or persecution, or famine, or nakedness, or peril, or sword?" "Nay, in all these things they shall be more than conquerors through Him that loved them."

CHAPTER VIII.

THE "TIMES AND SEASONS."

THE power of the press in sustaining the work he had begun, was early recognized by Joseph Smith and his associates; and it was this recognition of its powers which led him to establish, as early as possible, a paper that would be under the control of The Church, voice its sentiments and defend its principles. The Church had been organized but eighteen months, and its membership was very small when a conference held in Ohio authorized the purchase of a press, and instructed W. W. Phelps to begin the publication of a paper in Independence, Missouri. In June, 1832, the first number of that paper, the *Evening and Morning Star*, was published.

The following year the *Evening and Morning Star* press was broken and the type scattered by the mob, which collected at Independence to drive the Saints from Jackson County. The press and the book-binding property were never again restored to The Church, though the *Star* afterwards reappeared in Kirtland, edited by Oliver Cowdery.

Another periodical was also published in Kirtland called *The Saints' Messenger and Advocate*, the first number of which appeared in December, 1833. This periodical was superceded in a few years—1837—by the *Elders' Journal*. But when Joseph Smith and Sidney Rigdon had to flee from Kirtland for their lives, in the spring of 1838, the press and type on which the *Journal* was printed were removed to Far West. Here an effort was made to re-issue the *Journal*, Sidney Rigdon being appointed editor. But again the assembling of angry mobs hindered the work. And the night that General Lucas' mob-militia force surrounded Far West, this press and type were buried in the dooryard of a brother by the name of Dawson. The form for a number of the *Elders' Journal* was buried, with the ink on it, in the hurry to get it safely hidden from the enemy. It remained in its grave until taken up by Elias Smith, Hyrum Clark and some others, and taken to Commerce, where, in the fall of 1839, it was set up in a cellar, through which a spring of water was running, and on it was published the *Times and Seasons.*

This periodical was issued first as a sixteen page monthly, but afterwards became semi-monthly. Its first editor and manager was Don Carlos Smith, the youngest brother of Joseph Smith, who learned the printer's art in the office of Oliver Cowdery, and at the time he took charge of the *Times and Seasons* was but twenty-four years of age. His associate was Ebenezer Robinson. The paper was first issued in November, 1839.

Don Carlos Smith continued to act as editor of this paper until his death, which occurred on the seventh of August, 1841. Ebenezer Robinson then became the editor and Elder Robert B. Thompson was appointed to assist him. The manner in which the paper was conducted was very unsatisfactory to The Church authorities, and the Twelve Apostles took charge of it with Elders John Taylor and Wilford Woodruff as its managers, and President Joseph Smith as editor-in-chief. It was conducted by these parties for about a year, when the Prophet Joseph resigned the editorial chair, and Elder John Taylor was assigned to the position of chief editor, and kept that place until the discontinuance of the publication, in consequence of the Saints being driven from Nauvoo. It was a valuable means of communication for The Church authorities, as they were enabled to reach the Saints through its columns notwithstanding their scattered condition; and in its pages are collected the principal historical events which occurred in the early days of The Church; which, in connection with the principles and doctrine expounded by its editors, and the communications from the Prophet, make it of inestimable value to the student of Church history or the development of Church doctrine.

CHAPTER IX.

AN APPEAL TO THE GENERAL GOVERNMENT FOR REDRESS OF GRIEVANCES.

IT will be remembered by those who have read "The Missouri Persecutions," that Sidney Rigdon was released from prison in Liberty, Missouri, before Joseph and the other brethren escaped. On his arrival in Quincy, his position as one of the presidents of The Church, his education and eloquence, gave him the attention of the leading citizens of Quincy, and particularly enlisted the sympathy of Governor Carlin, of Illinois. By coming in contact with him, and relating the cruelties practiced against the Saints in Missouri, he conceived the altogether fanciful and utterly impracticable idea of impeaching the charter of Missouri on an item in the Constitution, viz: "that the general government shall give to each State a republican form of government." And it was his point to prove that such a government did not exist in Missouri. His plan was to present the story of the Saints' wrongs to the governors of the respective States, before the assembly of the several legislatures, and induce as many of them as possible to bring the case before the legislatures in their messages. Another part of the plan was to have a man at each State capital armed with affidavits that would give the necessary information to the legislatures. After the action of the State legislatures the case was to be presented to the national Congress for its consideration and action.

To carry out his plans George W. Robinson was appointed to take affidavits and collect general information bearing on the subject, and Sidney Rigdon himself secured letters of introduction to the governors of several States and to the President of the United States from Governor Carlin, of Illinois, and Governor Robert Lucas, of Iowa. On the fifth of May, 1839, however, at a conference of The Church held near Quincy, Joseph Smith presiding, the gigantic and fanciful scheme conceived by Sidney Rigdon was considered and somewhat reduced of its unwieldy proportions by the conference simply resolving:

> That this conference send a delegate to the city of Washington to lay our case before the general government; and that President Rigdon be the delegate: and that Colonel Lyman Wight be appointed to receive the affidavits which are to be sent to the city of Washington.

Here the matter rested for a time through the inactivity of President Rigdon, whose ardor in the work of God about this time began to wane.

In consequence of the inactivity and lack of interest manifested by Sidney Rigdon in going to Washington to present the case of the Latter-day Saints *vs.* the State of Missouri to the President and Congress of the United States, at a High Council meeting, held at Commerce on the twentieth of October, 1839, the Prophet Joseph was appointed to be the delegate to Washington, and a few days later Sidney Rigdon and Elias Higbee were appointed by the same council to assist him in this mission.

As a contrast between the two men, Sidney Rigdon and Joseph Smith, I call attention to the fact that after his appointment to go to Washington to petition the general government for a redress of grievances, in behalf of the Saints, Sidney Rigdon had allowed nearly six months to pass away without doing anything; but the ninth day after Joseph was appointed to this mission he was found leaving Commerce with a two-horse carriage, accompanied by Rigdon, Higbee and Orin P. Rockwell, *en-route* for Washington. The Prophet was always prompt in action. There were no tedious delays in anythinghe under took;

no letting "I dare not wait upon I would, like the old cat 'i the adage." His motto for the commencement of his career had been, "When the Lord commands, do it." And it was pretty much the same thing when a council of the Priesthood, or himself individually, had determined upon any particular course of action, he at once set himself about performing it.

The mission for the city of Washington passed through Springfield, the capital of the State of Illinois, on their journey, and here met with Dr. Robert D. Foster, who afterwards, as we shall see, became prominently connected with events at Nauvoo. Elder Rigdon being ill, Dr. Foster administered medicines to him, journeying with Joseph's party for several days for that purpose. At last, however, Elder Rigdon became so weak that it became necessary to leave him near Columbus, Ohio; and Orin P. Rockwell and Dr. Foster remained with him, while Joseph and Judge Higbee continued their journey to Washington.

It was during this journey, too, that Joseph met another man destined to perform a prominent part in the drama enacted at Nauvoo. This was William Law, whom Joseph's party met at Springfield, Illinois. He was then leading a small company of Saints from Canada to Nauvoo. Joseph's company remained several days at Springfield, and he preached there several times, staying at the home of James Adams, the probate judge of that county. Judge Adams treated the Prophet with the kindness of a father.

An incident occurred as the party approached Washington which borders on the domain of the romantic, or perhaps may be considered to enter directly into it. The coachman stopped his horses in front of one of the many public houses they passed *en route*, to get his grog, when the horses took fright, and dashed down the road at break-neck speed. The passengers, as might be expected, became terror-stricken, and one woman in her excitement tried to throw her babe out of the window; she was prevented, however, by Joseph, who calmed her fears, and persuaded the rest of the passengers to keep their seats. He then opened the door of the coach and succeeded in climbing up the side of the vehicle, and reaching the driver's seat. Gathering up the reins, he stopped the horses before any accident occurred either to coach or passengers.

It is needless to say that Joseph's heroism drew from his fellow-passengers their warmest expressions of admiration and gratitude. No terms were sufficiently strong to convey their admiration of his daring. Among the passengers were several members of Congress who proposed mentioning the incident to Congress, for they believed that body would reward Joseph's conduct by some public act. With this object in view they asked for his name, and were doubtless dumfounded to learn that they had been saved from their imminent peril by the courage of the Mormon Prophet. At any rate the profusion of thanks and admiration was stayed, "and," says Joseph, "I heard no more of their praise, gratitude or reward." Need one stop to moralize on the littleness of man when he allows prejudice to dictate his action instead of reason?

It was on the twenty-eighth of November, 1839, that Joseph and Judge Elias Higbee arrived in Washington, and took up their abode at an unpretentious boarding house, on the corner of Missouri and Third Streets. They were very much cramped on account of means, as the people they represented were poor in this world's goods, and unable to supply the means necessary to enable their delegates to indulge in the luxurious style of living usually adopted by those who go to the seat of government on special missions.

The day following his arrival, Joseph obtained an interview with President Martin Van Buren, who had been elected to the presidency by the Democratic party. I give Joseph's own account of this visit to President Van Buren, that our readers may judge of the impression he made upon the Prophet, and what the Prophet thought of Congress generally:

On Friday, the twenty-ninth, we proceeded to the house of the President. We found a very large and splendid palace, surrounded with a splendid enclosure, decorated with all the fineries and elegancies of the world. We went to the door and requested to see the President, when we were immediately introduced into an upper apartment, where we met the President, and were introduced into his parlor, where we presented him with our letters of introduction. As soon as he had read one of them, he looked upon us with a kind of half frown and said: "What can I do? I can do nothing for you! If I do anything, I shall come in contact with the whole State of Missouri."*

I cannot determine whether it was on the occasion of this visit that President Van Buren made use of the expression, "Your cause is just, but I can do nothing for you," or whether he so expressed himself at some subsequent meeting. But under date of February 6th, 1840, Joseph remarks, in speaking of his mission to Washington:

During my stay I had an interview with Martin Van Buren, the President, who treated me very insolently, and it was with great reluctance he listened to our message, which, when he heard, he said: "Gentlemen, your cause is just, but I can do nothing for you. If I take up for you, I shall lose the vote of Missouri." His whole course went to show that he was an office-seeker, that self-aggrandizement was his ruling passion, and that justice and righteousness were no part of his composition.

As this language is somewhat different to that reported by Joseph on the occasion of his first visit to the President, I am inclined to the opinion that the language attributed to him in the latter quotation was used at some subsequent meeting to the first. I again quote from Joseph's letter to Hyrum:

Now we shall endeavor to express our feelings and views con-

---

*Letter to Hyrum Smith, Dec. 5, 1839.

cerning the President, as we have been eye-witness to his majesty. He is a small man, sandy complexion, and ordinary features, with frowning brow, and considerable body, but not well proportioned as to his arms and legs, * * * and in fine, to come directly to the point, he is so much of a fop or a fool (for he judged our cause before he knew it), we could find no place to put truth into him. We do not say the Saints shall not vote for him, but we do say boldly, that we do not intend he shall have our votes.

Joseph speaks very highly of the senators and representatives from Illinois, who rendered him some considerable assistance in getting a hearing before a congressional committee, but he was not favorably impressed with congressmen or their conduct on the whole. He says:

For a general thing there is but little solidity and honorable deportment among those who are sent here to represent the people, but a great deal of pomposity and show. * * * There is such an itching disposition to display their oratory on the most trivial occasions, and so much etiquette, bowing and scraping, twisting and turning, to make a display of their witticism, that it seems to us rather a display of folly and show, more than substance and gravity, such as becomes a great nation like ours. However, there are some exceptions.

After the meeting with the President, a meeting with the Illinois delegation in Congress was arranged, to take into consideration the best means of getting the wrongs of the Saints before Congress. This meeting took place on the sixth of December. A Mr. Robinson of that delegation, whether a member of the House or Senate I do not know, took a stand against the Saints presenting any claims to be liquidated by the United States; but Joseph contended against him, and presented the constitutional rights of the people, and Mr. Robinson promised to reconsider the subject, and at the meeting the next day it was decided that a memorial and petition be drawn in concise form and presented by Judge Young, who had taken a lively interest in the cause of the Saints. At this stage of the proceedings, Joseph and Judge Higbee learned that it was necessary to have more positive testimony on the subject in hand, so that they sent to Nauvoo and a very large number of affidavits were taken and forwarded to Washington to sustain the statements to be presented to Congress.

The petition presented to Congress related the outrages committed against the Saints at considerable length, from the commencement of difficulties in Jackson County, in the autumn of 1833, until their final expulsion from the State in the winter of 1838-9; and made emphatic the infamy of Governor Boggs' exterminating orders, which gave the coloring of authority for the action of the State mob-militia. They said in their statement of wrongs that if given an opportunity they could prove every allegation they made against the State of Missouri. And that "neither the Mormons as a body, nor as individuals of that body, had been guilty of any offense against the laws of Missouri, or of the United States: but their only offense had been their religious opinions."

In conclusion the petition represents that for the wrongs endured—

> The Mormons ought to have some redress; yet how and where shall they seek and obtain it?
>
> Your Constitution guarantees to every citizen, even the humblest, the enjoyment of life, liberty and property. It promises to all their religious freedom, the right to worship God beneath their own vine and fig tree, according to their own conscience. It guarantees to all the citizens of the several States the right to become citizens of any one of the States, and to enjoy all the rights and immunities of the citizens of the State of his adoption. Yet of all these rights have the Mormons been deprived. They have, without a cause, without a trial, been deprived of life, liberty and property. They have been persecuted for their religious opinions. They have been driven from

the State of Missouri at the point of the bayonet, and prevented from enjoying and exercising the rights of citizens of the State of Missouri. It is the theory of our laws, that for the protection of every legal right, there is a legal remedy. What, then, we would ask, is the remedy for the Mormons? Shall they appeal to the legislature of the State of Missouri for redress? They have done so. They have petitioned, and these petitions have been treated with silence and contempt. Shall they apply to the federal courts? They were, at the time, citizens of the State of Missouri. Shall they apply to the courts of the State of Missouri? Whom shall they sue? The order for their destruction, their extermination, was granted by the executive of the State of Missouri. Is not this a plea of justification for the loss of individuals, done in pursuance of the order? If not, before whom shall the Mormons institute a trial? Shall they summon a jury of the individuals who composed the mob? An appeal to them were in vain. They dare not go to Missouri to institute a suit, their lives would be in danger.

For ourselves we see no redress, unless it be awarded by the Congress of the United States. And we here make our appeal as *American citizens*, as *Christians*, and as *men*—believing the high sense of justice which exists in your honorable bodies, will not allow such oppression to be practiced upon any portion of the citizens of this vast republic with impunity, but that some measure which your wisdom may dictate, may be taken, so that the great body of people who have been thus abused, may have redress for the wrongs which they have suffered.

The statement of wrongs and petition for their redress was introduced into the Senate by Judge Young, and referred to the committee on judiciary of which General Wall was chairman.

At this stage of the proceedings Joseph left Washington and went to Philadelphia, where he labored in the ministry among the Saints; but Judge Elias Higbee was left in Washington to look after the interest of the petitioners before the Senate committee. The subject was held under advisement and discussed occasionally,until the fourth of March, 1840, when the committee reported. That report was of a character to crush forever the hopes of obtaining, at the hands of the general government, any redress for the outrages perpetrated against them in Missouri. The report said that after full examination and consideration, the committee unanimously concurred in the opinion: "That the case presented for their investigation is not such a one as will justify or authorize any interposition of this government."

They stated that the wrongs complained of were not alleged to have been committed by officers of the United States; that the charges were all against the citizens and authorities of the State of Missouri; that the petitioners were citizens or inhabitants of Missouri; that the grievances complained of were committed within the territory of Missouri; and for these reasons the Senate judiciary committee did "not consider themselves justified in inquiring into the truth or falsehood of facts charged in the petition." The committee represented that if the charges were true, then the petitioners must seek redress in the courts of judicature, either of Missouri or of the United States, whichever might have jurisdiction in the case. "Or," said the report, "the petitioners may, if they see proper, apply to the justice and magnanimity of the State of Missouri—an appeal which the committee feel justified in believing will never be made in vain by the injured or oppressed." The report said that it could not be presumed that a State wanted either the power or lacked the disposition to redress the wrongs of its own citizens, committed within its own territory, "whether they proceed from the lawless acts of her officers or any other person."

The report closed by asking the passage of the following resolution:

Resolved, That the committee on the judiciary be discharged from the further consideration of the memorial in this case; and that the memorialists have leave to withdraw the papers which accompany their memorial.

The resolution was passed without dissent, and thus the appeal to Congress for redress of the outrages committed against the Saints by Missouri ended.

At a conference of The Church held in April following, a number of resolutions were adopted, regretting and condemning the action of the Senate judiciary committee, and approving the course pursued by their delegation to Congress, Joseph Smith, Sidney Rigdon and Elias Higbee, and requesting them to continue their exertions to obtain redress for a suffering people as opportunities became more favorable for such efforts, and if at last all hopes of obtaining satisfaction for the injuries done us be entirely blasted, that they then "appeal our case to the Court of Heaven, believing that the Great Jehovah, who rules over the destiny of nations, and who notices the falling sparrows, will undoubtedly redress our wrongs, and ere long avenge us of our adversaries."

CHAPTER X.

ORSON HYDE'S MISSION TO JERUSALEM.

THOSE who have read "The Missouri Persecutions," will remember the disaffection of Orson Hyde at Far West, and the statements he made in connection with Thomas B. Marsh against The Church, in the autumn of 1838—that time when men's hearts were failing them for fear, and death and destruction were rife; when even strong hearts grew faint and brave cheeks were blanched. Well, as stated in the account of his disaffection, like Peter of old, this modern Apostle wept bitterly for his error, returned to The Church, was forgiven; and during the conference held at Commerce in April, 1840, he was called to go on a mission to Jerusalem.

It appears that Elder Hyde in a heavenly vision saw himself on the Mount of Olives blessing the land for the return of the people of Judah, hence, that he might be obedient to the vision, he was appointed to go to that land for the purpose mentioned. In the letter of appointment, which the Prophet gave him, occurs the following passage:

> The Jewish nation have been scattered abroad among the Gentiles for a long period; and in our estimation the time of the commencement of their return to the Holy Land has already arrived. * * * It is highly important, in our opinion, that the present views and movements of the Jewish people be sought after, and laid before the American people for their consideration, their profit and their learning.

On the 15th of the same month that Elder Hyde was called, he left his family at Nauvoo and started for Jerusalem without purse or scrip. The next day he met with John E. Page, who subsequently to the conference at which Orson Hyde had been called, was appointed to go with him to the Holy Land.

They traveled through several States together, preaching as they went. In the city of Cincinnati they succeeded in raising up a large and prosperous branch of The Church; and while Elder Page remained in Cincinnati to strengthen the Saints, Elder Hyde made his way to New York.

These labors consumed the summer of 1840, and in January, 1841, the word of the Lord came to the Prophet Joseph saying that he was not well pleased with the long delays of his servants in starting on their mission to Jerusalem, and they were requested to hasten their departure. In the meantime, however, Elder Page had lost the spirit of his appointment and had no disposition to go, but Orson Hyde on the receipt of this reproof set sail at once from New York for England.

It is not our design to follow him through all his meanderings in Europe, or relate his trials or his perils in crossing the mighty seas, and passing through states in which war was raging. He succeeded in reaching the Holy City some time in October, and on the twenty-fourth of that month, 1841, early in the morning, was seated on the Mount of Olives, as he had seen himself in vision; and wrote the prayer he had to offer in behalf of the Jews and their city, which had been for so long a time trodden down of the Gentiles.

In that prayer he referred to the prophecies of God's servants in relation to the Jews and Jerusalem, and asked that all might be fulfilled. He called for the richest blessings of heaven upon the Jews; he blessed, by virtue of his Priesthood, the city, the land, and all the elements, to the end that Judah might be gathered, Jerusalem rebuilt, and become an holy city, that the Lord's name might be glorified in all the earth. At the conclusion of his prayer, he says:

On the top of the Mount of Olives, I erected a pile of stones, as a witness according to ancient custom. On what was anciently called Mount Zion, where the temple stood, I erected another, and used the rod according to the prediction upon my head.

Just what he meant by saying that he had used the rod "according to prediction on his head," I have been unable to learn, except that it was a rod with which he had measured the city.

I have called the attention of my readers to this mission of Elder Hyde's to Jerusalem, because it doubtless has a greater significance than most people would be inclined to give it. The rebuilding of Jerusalem is regarded by Mormonism as of as much importance as the establishment of Zion; the gathering of the dispersed of Judah is as much a part of the great latter-day work as the reassembling of the other tribes of Israel; and the commencement of that work was made by Elder Hyde, when by the authority of his apostleship, he consecrated that land to the return of the house of Judah, to inhabit it, and rebuild their city according to the predictions of their prophets. It may be somewhat beyond the scope of this chapter to call attention to it, but surely it will be of interest to the reader to know that this apostolic mission and blessing upon the Holy Land has not been fruitless, but blessings as a result are flowing unto it, and the Jews are beginning to return to it. At the time of Apostle Hyde's visit and ceremonies on the Mount of Olives, but very few Jews were in the city or in Judea. As late as twenty years ago the consular reports show that there were not more than fifteen or twenty thousand Jews in all Jerusalem. But in a popular magazine for August, 1896, under the editorial caption—"The Plan for a Hebrew Nation"—the magazine said:

A movement of which Americans hear very little, but which may have an important effect upon the history of the coming century, is going forward upon the shores of the Mediterranean. This is the return of the Jews to their ancient home in Palestine—the Zionite movement it is called. For hundreds of years there has been talk of the Jew returning to Jerusalem. Through all his years of oppression and wandering, this vision of his native land has been held before his eyes by certain of his teachers. But it is only in the last twelve years, since the renewal of persecution in Russia, that the idea has taken shape. There are now more than four thousand colonists in Palestine. At Jaffa the schools are Hebrew, the ancient language being spoken altogether, and a Hebrew literature is being developed. The works of the great English, French and German authors are being translated, and writers of their own race are being encouraged.

The Zionite movement is backed by the influence of the Rothschilds and other great Jewish families and societies, and as we see its stirring in every country, we can believe it only requires a great popular leader to make it one of the important movements in history. That it is not purely religious, but racial, is proven by the co-operation of Rabinowitz, the Christian Jew who became so well known here during the World's Fair Congress. There is already one Jewish Christian colony in Palestine. * * * As a Jewish state, Palestine might well become a country that would claim consideration among the family of nations. If the Zionite continues to grow, such a result is almost assured.

During the same month, namely, in its impression of August 11th, 1896, the St. Louis *Globe-Democrat* published the following:

Only two decades ago there were not more than fifteen or twenty thousand Jews in Jerusalem. At that [time] no houses were to be found outside the walls of the city. Since then many changes have taken place and the Hebrew population—mainly on account of the increase of the Jewish immigration from Russia—now stands at between sixty and seventy thousand. Whole streets of houses have been built outside the walls on the site of the ancient suburban districts, which for hundreds of years have remained deserted. It is not, however, only in Jerusalem itself that the Jews abound, but throughout Palestine they are buying farms and establishing themselves in a surprisingly rapid manner. In Jerusalem they form at present a larger community than either the Christian or the Mohammedan.

CHAPTER XI.

DEATH'S HARVEST IN NAUVOO—RETURN OF PRODIGALS.

DURING the summer of 1840, death reaped a rich harvest in Nauvoo. Before his ruthless stroke fell many worthy Saints who had been connected with The Church from the time it was founded. Among the first to fall was Bishop Edward Partridge. He died on the twenty-seventh of May, in the forty-sixth year of his age. He was the first Bishop in The Church, and in that capacity had presided over the Saints who gathered to Zion, in Jackson County, Missouri, during the years 1831-33. Joseph described him as a "pattern of piety," and the Lord himself declared that he was like Nathaniel of old—his heart was pure before him, and he was without guile. His life was indeed an eventful one. He was called from his merchandizing, and became a preacher of righteousness. Much, in fact all, of his riches fell into the hands of the mobs of Jackson County, in the autumn of 1833, and upon his meek and uncovered head fell a double portion of their fury. Five years later, he passed through those trying times experienced by the Saints in their exodus from the State of Missouri, under the exterminating order of the infamous Governor Boggs; and at that time, he again saw the fruits of his industry fall a prey to the rapacity of his relentless enemies. Stripped of his earthly possessions and broken in health, he reached Commerce, but the trials through which he passed had proven too much for his constitution, which was never robust, and he passed away, a victim to the intolerance and religious bigotry of this generation.

In September of the same year Father Joseph Smith,

Patriarch to The Church, and father of the Prophet Joseph, was "gathered to his final home," in the sixty-ninth year of his age. He was baptized on the sixth day of April, 1830, and was one of the six who organized The Church on that date. Indeed he was the one who first received the testimony of his son after the angel Moroni visited him on that memorable night of September 21, 1823; and it was he who first exhorted his prophet son to be faithful and diligent to the message he had received. He endured many persecutions on account of the claims made by his son Joseph to being a prophet of God; for Joseph's declarations that he had received heavenly visions and revelations together with a divine commission to preach the Gospel of Christ, not only brought upon himself the wrath of the ungodly, but involved his whole family in the persecutions which followed him throughout his life. Of these things, however, his father never complained, but endured all things patiently, and with true heroism, and ever supported his son in carrying out the counsels of Heaven. He was born on the twelfth of July, 1771, in Topsfield, Massachusetts; and was the second of the seven sons of Asahel and Mary Smith; his forefathers being among those who early came from England to Massachusetts. He was a large man, ordinarily weighing two hundred pounds, was six feet two inches tall, and well proportioned, strong and active; and he stood unbowed beneath the accumulated sorrows and hardships he had experienced during his nearly three score and ten years of sojourn in this life. The exposures, however, that he suffered in the exodus from Missouri brought on him consumption, of which he died. His was an unassuming nature—noted mostly, perhaps, for its sincerity and unwavering integrity. He was a child of nature, and one of nature's noblest; his life had been spent in parts remote from the busy marts, where "wealth accumulates and men decay;" and he had passed through his probation on earth without being corrupted by the evil influences of luxury or enervating civilization. He was a type of men, so well described by one of our poets, in the following lines:

Simple their lives—yet theirs the race
When liberty sent forth her cry,
Who crowded conflicts deadliest place,
To fight—to bleed—to die;
Who stood on Bunker's heights of red,
By hope through years were led—
And witnessed Yorktown's sun
Shine on a nation's banner spread,
A nation's freedom won!

Such was the character of the first Patriarch of The Church in this dispensation.

Another circumstance of interest in Nauvoo during this eventful summer of 1840 was the return of a number of prodigals to The Church. I have already stated the case of Orson Hyde. Frederick G. Williams was dropped from his position as counselor to the Prophet in November, 1837, and in March, 1839, was excommunicated at a conference in Quincy, Illinois. At the April conference in 1840, however, he came before the assembled Church and "humbly asked forgiveness, and expressed his determination to do the will of God for the future." He was forgiven by the Saints but was never restored to his former position in the First Presidency.

About the time Thomas B. Marsh and Orson Hyde fell during the trying scenes in Missouri, W. W. Phelps and Oliver Cowdery left The Church. Elder Phelps was a man who had been of great service to The Church and to the Prophet in a literary way, though some of his work in that line was marred by pedantic verbosity, and pretension to a knowledge of ancient languages which was not justified by any extended acquaintance he had of them. Still, he it was who in the early rise of The Church gave the cast to very much of The Church literature, and, as I remarked, he had been useful to The Church and the Prophet in the capacity of an editor and writer.

During the summer of 1840 he began to feel his way back from his apostasy into The Church. He had seen his folly and began to tremble at the gulf which opened at his very feet to devour him. He felt debased and humbled, and most piteously begged to be forgiven and taken back in the confidence of his brethren and the Saints. So interesting are the circumstances connected with his return that I give *in extenso* the letters which passed between himself and the Prophet.

W. W. PHELPS' LETTER TO JOSEPH SMITH.

DAYTON, OHIO, June 29, 1840.

BROTHER JOSEPH—I am alive, and with the help of God I mean to live still. I am as a prodigal son, though I never doubt or disbelieve the fullness of the Gospel. I have been greatly abused and humbled, and I blessed the God of Israel when I lately read your prophetic blessing on my head, as follows:

"The Lord will chasten him because he taketh honor to himself, and when his soul is greatly humbled he will forsake the evil. Then shall the light of the Lord break upon him as at noonday, and in him shall be no darkness," etc.

I have seen the folly of my way, and I tremble at the gulf I have passed. So it is, and why I know not. I prayed and God answered, but what could I do? Says I, "I will repent and live, and ask my old brethren to forgive me, and though they chasten me to death, yet *I will die* with them, for their God is my God. The *least place with them* is enough for me, yea it is bigger and better than all Babylon." Then I dreamed that I was in a large house with many mansions, with you and Hyrum and Sidney, and when it was said, "Supper must be made ready," by one of the cooks, I saw no meat, but you said there was plenty, and showed me much, and as good as I ever saw; and while cutting to cook, your heart and mine beat within us, and we took each other's hand and cried for joy, and I awoke and took courage.

I know my situation, you know it, and God knows it, and I want to be saved if my friends will help me. Like the captain that was cast away on a desert island; when he got off, he went to sea again, and made his fortune the next time—so let my lot be. I have done wrong, and am sorry. The beam is in my own eye. I have not walked with my friends according to my holy anointing. I ask forgiveness in the name of Jesus Christ of all the Saints, for I will do right, God helping me. I want your fellowship; if you cannot grant that, grant me your peace and friendship, for we are brethren, and our communion used to be sweet, and whenever the Lord brings us together again, *I will make all the satisfaction on every point that Saints or God can require.* Amen.

W. W. PHELPS.

Elders Hyde and Page, *en route* for the east on their mission to Jesusalem, met with Phelps at Dayton, and at his request these brethren added the following to his communication:

Brother Phelps requests us to write a few lines in his letter, and we cheerfully embrace the opportunity. Brother Phelps says he wants to live; but we do not feel ourselves authorized to act upon his case, but have recommended him to you; but he says his poverty will not allow him to visit you in person at this time, and we think he tells the truth. We therefore advise him to write, which he has done.

He tells us verbally, that he is willing to make any sacrifice to procure your fellowship, life not excepted, yet reposing that confidence in your magnanimity that you will take no advantage of this open letter and frank confession. If he can obtain your fellowship, he wants to come to Commerce as soon as he can. But if he cannot be received into the fellowship of The Church, he must do the best he can in banishment and exile.

Brethren, with you are the keys of the Kingdom; to you is power given to "exert your clemency, or display your vengeance." By the former you will save a soul from death, and hide a multitude of sins: by the latter you will forever discourage a returning prodigal, cause sorrow without benefit, pain without pleasure, ending in wretchedness and despair. But former experience teaches that you are workmen in the art of saving souls; therefore with the greater confidence do we recommend to your clemency and favorable consideration, the author and subject of this communication. "Whosoever will, let him take of the water of life freely." Brother Phelps says he will, and so far as we are concerned, we say he may.

In the bonds of the covenant,

ORSON HYDE,
JOHN E. PAGE.

To this piteous appeal from one who had wandered far from the fold, and who had been torn by the thorns, the Prophet wrote a most worthy reply—a reply which clearly indicates that the spirit of the Master burned brightly in the breast of the servant.

JOSEPH SMITH'S LETTER TO W. W. PHELPS.

NAUVOO, HANCOCK CO., ILLINOIS, July 22, 1840.

DEAR BROTHER PHELPS—I must say that it is with no ordinary feelings I endeavor to write a few lines to you in answer to yours of the 29th ultimo; at the same time I am rejoiced at the privilege granted me.

You may in some measure realize what my feelings, as well as Elder Rigdon's and Brother Hyrum's were, when we read your letter—truly our hearts were melted into tenderness and compassion when we ascertained your resolves, etc. I can assure you I feel a disposition to act on your case in a manner that will meet the approbation of Jehovah, (whose servant I am) and agreeably to the principles of truth and righteousness which have been revealed; and inasmuch as long-suffering, patience and mercy have ever characterized the dealings of our Heavenly Father towards the humble and penitent, I feel disposed to copy the example, cherish the same principles, and by so doing be a savior of my fellow men.

It is true, that we have suffered much in consequence of your behavior—*the cup of gall, already full enough* for mortals to drink, was indeed *filled to overflowing* when *you* turned against us. One with whom we had oft taken sweet counsel together, and enjoyed many refreshing seasons from the Lord—"had it been an enemy, we could have borne it." "In the day that thou stoodest on the other side, in the day when strangers carried away captive his forces, and foreigners entered into his gates, and cast lots upon Far West, even thou wast as one of them; but thou shouldest not have looked on the day of thy brother, in the day that he became a stranger, neither shouldest thou have spoken proudly in the day of distress."

However, the cup has been drunk, the will of our Father has been done, and we are yet alive, for which we thank the Lord. And having been delivered from the hands of wicked men by the mercy of our God, we say it is your privilege to be delivered from the powers of the adversary, be brought into the liberty of God's dear children, and again take your stand among the Saints of the Most High, and by diligence, humility, and love unfeigned, commend yourself to our God, and your God, and to The Church of Jesus Christ.

Believing your confession to be real, and your repentance genuine, I shall be happy once again to give you the right hand of fellowship, and rejoice over the returning prodigal.

Your letter was read to the Saints last Sunday, and an expression was taken, when it was unanimously—

Resolved, That W. W. Phelps should be received into fellowship.

"Come on, dear brother, since the war is past,
For friends at first are friends again at last."

Yours as ever,

JOSEPH SMITH, JR.

Some time after this, when laying out work for the brethren to do, in a sudden burst of kindness he said to his secretary:

Write Oliver Cowdery, and ask him if he has not eaten husks long enough. If he is not almost ready to return, be clothed with robes of righteousness, and go up to Jerusalem. Orson Hyde hath need of him.

A letter was written accordingly, but the Prophet's generous tender of forgiveness and fellowship called forth no response from Oliver Cowdery, once the second Elder of The Church, and the first to make public proclamation of the Gospel to the world. Subsequently, however, he did return, namely in 1848.

It may not be amiss here to call the attention of the reader to a peculiarity of Mormonism, which is illustrated, not only by this case of Phelps, but by a multitude of other cases of the same character; and that is: whenever the religion of the Latter-day Saints—the Gospel of Jesus Christ—takes hold of men, and conviction of its truth has struck deep into the human soul, they may through transgression lose the fellowship of the Saints and of The Church; they may wander out upon the hills and through the deserts, away from the fold, but they can never forget the sweet communion of the Spirit of God, which they enjoyed before their fall; nor can they forget the fact that they once knew that Mormonism was true. The recollection of those things operates upon the mind, and not unfrequently leads to a sincere repentance; and it has often happened, in the experience of The Church, that men who through transgression turned away from the truth, after thorns have torn their flesh, and the wild briar stripped them of their covering, they return and humbly beg to be re-admitted into their Father's house. Lucifer-like, they cannot forget the heights from which they fell, they cannot all forget the splendor of that glory and the happiness of that peace they enjoyed in God's Kingdom, and wicked indeed must that heart become, that these recollections will not lead to repentance. May not they have so far transgressed that they cannot repent, and are beyond even the desire for forgiveness? Are they not the sons of perdition? Thank God, their numbers are few!

Again, those who fall away from Mormonism carry with them the evidences of that fall. Unbelievers say to Mormons, "Come out of the darkness of your superstitions into God's sunlight of freedom"—but when one looks upon the fate, the condition and experience of those who have denied the faith, he receives small encouragement to obey the summons. Seldom indeed are they prospered even in the affairs of this world, and the canker-worm gnawing within, writes upon their faces the anguish of heart which their lying lips deny. They smile, but smiling suffer; the heart still beats, but brokenly lives on; and who so blind that he would exchange the peace, the joy, the holy aspirations and assurances which the Gospel brings, for the unrest, the gloom, darkness, uncertainty and fearfulness, which forever haunt the mind of the apostate? Only those who would exchange the glorious light of heaven for the murky blackness of hell.

CHAPTER XII.

JOHN C. BENNETT.

ABOUT this time, there were other characters which had become attracted to The Church, and who became prominent in the events which occurred at Nauvoo. Among them was Dr. John C. Bennett, described as "a man of enterprise, extensive acquirements, and of independent mind, one calculated to be of great benefit to The Church." His attention had been attracted to the Mormon people during their persecutions in Missouri. At that time he was brigadier-general of the "Invincible Dragoons" of Illinois, and wrote to the leaders of The Church in the hours of their deepest distress, proffering to go to their assistance with all the forces he could raise in Illinois, as his bosom swelled with indignation at the treatment the Saints received at the hands of the cruel but cowardly Missourians. That proffered service, however, was not accepted; doubtless because the Saints depended for vindication of their reputation, and redress of their wrongs, upon the officers of the State and Nation, rather than upon adventurers who offered their service to wage war upon their enemies. But after the Saints began gathering at Commerce, he again expressed a desire to connect his fortunes with theirs.

As this man may properly be regarded as the "Benedict Arnold" of The Church at Nauvoo, I shall take the liberty of now noting a few expressions in his first letters to Joseph the Prophet, which, if they fail to adorn a tale, they will at least point a moral.

When he contemplated joining his fortunes with The

Church at Commerce, he held the position of quartermaster-general in the militia of the State of Illinois, a position he did not wish to resign. Indeed he expressed a desire to hold the position for a number of years. He was also a physician with an extensive practice, and sent extracts from the Louisville *Courier-Journal* which gave evidence of high standing in his profession. Writing of these things to Joseph, he said:

I do not expect to resign my office of quartermaster-general of the State of Illinois, in the event of my removal to Commerce, unless you advise otherwise. I shall likewise expect to practice my profession, but at the same time your people shall have all the benefit of my speaking power, and my untiring energies in behalf of the good and holy faith.

In a communication following the one from which I make the above quotation he said:

You are aware that at the time of your most bitter persecution, I was with you in feeling, and proffered you my military knowledge and powers.

The egotism of the man plainly appears in these expressions, and manifests a spirit that is altogether at variance with the humility required by the Gospel, and doubtless that self-importance laid the foundation of his subsequent fall. While Joseph extended a hearty welcome to the doctor to come to Nauvoo, he by no means held out very flattering inducements to him, as may be seen by Joseph's letters to him in answer to those of Bennett's, expressing his determination to join the Saints at Commerce. He said:

I have no doubt that you would be of great service to this community in practicing your profession, as well as those other abilities of which you are in possession. Though to devote your time and abilities in the cause of truth and a suffering people, may not be the means of exalting you in the eyes of this generation, or securing you the riches of this world, yet by so doing you may rely on the approval of Jehovah, "that blessing which maketh rich and addeth no sorrow." * * * Therefore, my general invitation is, let all who will come, come and partake of the poverty of Nauvoo, freely.

I should be disposed to give you a special invitation to come as early as possible, believing you will be of great service to us. However, you must make your own arrangements according to your circumstances. Were it possible for you to come here this season to suffer affliction with the people of God, no one will be more pleased to give you a cordial welcome than myself.

Surely this was frank enough, and ought to have dispelled from the doctor's mind, if at that time such ideas lurked there, all thoughts of winning worldly fame, or gratifying vain ambition, by linking his fortunes with those of The Church of Jesus Christ.

CHAPTER XIII.

RENEWAL OF HOSTILITIES BY MISSOURI.

IT would appear that Hatred's hunger is never fed; it seems to possess an appetite which is insatiable, and can never feel at ease so long as the object of its detestation remains within its reach; and even when that object is removed beyond the immediate power of Hatred to do it harm, as the dragon of the apocalypse when he could not follow the woman he had persecuted into the wilderness, cast out of his mouth a flood of water after her to destroy her—even so Hatred, when baffled in his efforts to destroy his victims, sends out floods of falsehood to overwhelm them by infusing his own venom into the breasts of others; that that destruction which he could not bring to pass himself, might be brought about by another.

Such was the course of hate-blinded Missouri towards the Saints of God, whom she had driven beyond her borders. Seeing that she had not destroyed them, but that they were now upon the eve of enjoying an era of prosperity such as they had never enjoyed while within her borders, she employed all her cunning to incite the hatred of the citizens of Illinois against them. But this was not easy of accomplishment; and at first, the misrepresentations of a State that had been guilty of such outrages as those committed by Missouri against the Latter-day Saints, had but little weight in Illinois.

Finding that their accusations against the people whom they had so wronged had little or no effect, an effort was made to give coloring to their statements; and stolen goods were conveyed from Missouri to the vicinity of Commerce, so that when they were found, suspicion might rest upon the people in whose neighborhood the stolen articles were discovered.

Nor did their outrages stop at this. But doubtless being emboldened by reason of the general government's refusing to make any effort to redress the wrongs of the Saints, a company of men led by William Allensworth, H. M. Woodyard, Wm. Martin, J. H. Owsely, John Bain, Light T. Lait and Halsay White, crossed over the Mississippi to Illinois, at a point a few miles above Quincy, and kidnapped Alanson Brown, James Allred, Benjamin Boyce and Noah Rogers; and without any writ or warrant of any character whatever, they dragged them over to Missouri, to a neighborhood called Tully, in Lewis County. These unfortunate men were imprisoned for a day or two in an old log cabin, during which time their lives were repeatedly threatened. At one time Brown was taken out, a rope placed around his neck, and he was hung up to a tree until he was nearly strangled to death. Boyce at the same time was tied to a tree, stripped of his clothing and inhumanly beaten. Rogers was also beaten, and Allred was stripped of every particle of clothing, and tied up to a tree for the greater part of the night, and threatened frequently by a man named Monday, exclaiming: "G—d d—n you, I'll cut you to the hollow." He was finally, however, released without being whipped.

After they had received this inhuman treatment, their captors performed an act purely Missourian in its character, that is, they gave them the following note of acquittal:

TULLY, MISSOURI, July 12, 1840.

The people of Tully, having taken up Mr. Allred, with some others, and having examined into the offenses committed, find nothing to justify his detention any longer, and have released him.

By order of the committee.

H. M. WOODYARD.

As soon as the people of Commerce and vicinity were informed of this outrage, Gentiles as well as Mormons were loud in their condemnation of it, and at once a mass meeting was called, and resolutions were adopted, expressing their unqualified indignation, and calling upon the governor of Illinois to take the necessary steps to punish those who had committed this outrage, and by vindicating the law, give the Missourians to understand there was a limit beyond which their deeds of violence must not pass.

D. H. Wells, not then a member of The Church, and George Miller were appointed a committee to wait upon Governor Carlin, and lay the case before him. For this purpose they repaired to Quincy, and at the recital of the cruelties practiced upon the men who were the victims of the Missourians, the governor's wife, who was present at the interview, was moved to tears, and the governor himself was greatly agitated. He promised to counsel with the State attorney, who by law was made his adviser, and promised to take such steps as the case seemed to require, and the law to justify. Just what was done by Governor Carlin, however, I am unable to learn; but one thing is certain, and that is, the guilty parties were never brought to justice, nor even to a trial—indeed it may be that even then the love which Governor Carlin once had for the Saints, and which at last became dead, had begun to grow cold.

Scarcely had the excitement occasioned by the kidnapping of Allred and his associates subsided, when Governor Boggs of Missouri made a requisition on Governor Carlin, of Illinois, for the persons of Joseph Smith, Jr., Sidney Rigdon, Lyman Wight, P. P. Pratt, Caleb Baldwin and Alanson Brown, as fugitives from justice. Governor Carlin granted the requisition—was it another case of Herod and Pilate being made friends over the surrender of God's Prophet? But fortunately when the sheriff went to Commerce with his requisition, Joseph and his brethren were not at home, and could not be found; so that the officers returned without them. These men were not fugitives from justice, no process had ever been found against them, the governor himself had connived at their escape from the hands of the officers charged with the duty of conducting them from Liberty, Clay County, to Boone County;* and these men did not feel disposed to try again "the solemn realities of mob law in Missouri."

These circumstances gave the Saints to understand that their peace in their beautiful situation on the banks of the placid, grand, old Mississippi was not to be without alloy; the goal of their final triumph and rest had not been reached. These incidents were a premonition of danger; they were indeed the few drops of rain which sometimes precede the storm, but a kind Providence shut out from their vision how fierce that storm would be, or how would they have had the courage to meet it?

---

* Missouri Persecutions, Chapter XLVII.

CHAPTER XIV.

FOUNDING A CITY.

MEANTIME Commerce had become Nauvoo. The city of Nauvoo was incorporated by act of the legislature of Illinois, on the fourteenth of December, 1840. The charter granted on that date described the boundaries of the city, but gave to the citizens—whom it erected a body corporate and politic—the right to extend the area of the city whenever any tract of land adjoining should have been laid out into town lots and recorded according to law. The city council was to consist of a mayor, four aldermen and nine councilors to be elected by the qualified voters of the city. The first Monday in February was appointed for the first election of officers.

The charter granted to the citizens of Nauvoo the most plenary powers in the management of their local affairs. Indeed, about the only limit placed upon their powers was, that they do nothing inconsistent with the constitution of the United States, and the State constitution of Illinois. But inside of those lines they were all powerful to make and execute such ordinances as in the wisdom of the city council were necessary for the peace, good order, and general welfare of the city. It afterwards became a question in the State as to whether or not powers too great had not been granted the city government—but of that I shall have occasion to speak further on.

The leading men of the State appeared not only willing but anxious to grant the privileges of this city government to the Saints. S. H. Little, of the upper house of the State legislature, especially stood by the Saints, and pleaded for their rights;

together with Messrs. Snyder, Ralston, Moore, Ross and Stapp; while Mr. John F. Charles, the representative to the lower house from the district in which Nauvoo was located, manfully discharged his duties to the Nauvoo portion of his constituents, by using all his energy to secure them their city government.

An incident connecting Abraham Lincoln with the passage of this charter may not be without interest. The State of Illinois was at that time divided into two political parties, Whigs and Democrats. Both parties were friendly to the Saints, who considered themselves equally bound to both parties for acts of kindness. Lincoln was a Whig, and in the November election his name was on the State electoral ticket as a Whig candidate for the State legislature. But many of the people of Nauvoo, wishing to divide their vote, and to show a kindness to the Democrats, erased the name of Lincoln, and substituted that of Ralston, a Democrat. It was with no ill feeling, however, towards Mr. Lincoln that this was done, and when the vote was called on the final passage of the Nauvoo charter, he had the magnanimity to vote for it; and congratulated John C. Bennett on his success in securing its enactment.

The Saints rejoiced in the prospects of liberty secured to them by their city government, and of it Joseph said:

> I concocted it for the salvation of The Church, and on principles so broad, that every honest man might dwell secure under its protecting influences, without distinction of sect or party.

An inspection of the charter will bear out this opinion of it, for while it was "concocted for the salvation of The Church," it by no means secured that salvation by trespassing upon the rights of others, but by recognizing the rights of the Saints to be equal to the rights of other citizens. Nor was it intended that Nauvoo should be an exclusive city for people of the Mormon faith; on the contrary, all worthy people were invited to come and assist to build it up and partake of its liberty and anticipated prosperity. An official proclamation, issued over the signatures of Joseph Smith, Sidney Rigdon and Hyrum Smith, who then constituted the First Presidency of The Church, contains the following passage:

We wish it likewise to be distinctly understood, that we claim no privileges but what we feel cheerfully disposed to share with our fellow-citizens of every denomination, and every sentiment of religion; and therefore say, that so far from being restricted to our own faith, let all those who desire to locate in this place (Nauvoo) or the vicinity, come, and we will hail them as citizens and friends, and shall feel it not only a duty, but a privilege to reciprocate the kindness we have received from the benevolent and kind-hearted citizens of the State of Illinois.

And as an earnest of the intention, so far as the Saints were concerned, of carrying out in practice these liberal sentiments and extending equal rights to people of all religious persuasions, among the first acts of the city council was the passage of the following ordinance, introduced by Joseph Smith:

SECTION I. Be it ordained by the city council of the city of Nauvoo that the Catholics, Presbyterians, Methodists, Baptists, Latter-day Saints, Quakers, Episcopalians, Universalists, Unitarians, Mohammedans, and all other religious sects and denominations, whatever, shall have free toleration and equal privileges in this city; and should any person be guilty of ridiculing and abusing, or otherwise deprecating another, in consequence of his religion, or of disturbing or interrupting any religious meeting within the limits of this city, he shall, on conviction before the mayor or municipal court, be considered a disturber of the public peace, and fined in any sum not exceeding five hundred dollars, or imprisoned not exceeding six months, or both, at the discretion of said mayor and court.

The second section made it the duty of all municipal officers to notice and report any violation of the law—and in fact, of any other law of the city—to the mayor; and the municipal officers were authorized to arrest all violators of this law, either with or without process; so that the fullest religious liberty was secured to all sects, and all religions, and to people of no religion at all if any such there should be. Under such an ordinance, people could worship Almighty God according to the dictates of their consciences, without fear of molestation from any one; but they were restrained from interfering with the religion or mode of worship of their fellows—they were told, in a manner, that their liberties ended where those of other people commenced.

On the first of February, 1841, the first election for members of the city council took place, as provided by the city charter. John C. Bennett was chosen mayor; William Marks, Samuel H. Smith, D. H. Wells, and N. K. Whitney, aldermen; Joseph Smith, Hyrum Smith, Sidney Rigdon, Chas. C. Rich, John T. Barnett, Wilson Law, Don C. Smith, J. P. Greene and Vinson Knight, councilors. On the third of the month the city council was organized, by appointing the following officers: marshal, H. G. Sherwood; recorder, James Sloan; treasurer, R. B. Thompson; assessor, James Robinson; supervisor of streets, Austin Cowles.

Mayor Bennett, the same day, delivered his inaugural address. After making several recommendations to the council relative to the establishment of an educational institution, a militia, the enactment of a temperance ordinance, and other measures affecting the manufacturing and commercial interests of the city; and further recommending that the protecting ægis of the corporation be thrown around every moral and religious institution of the day, which was in any way calculated to ennoble or ameliorate the condition of the citizens, he concluded his speech in these words:

As the chief magistrate of your city, I am determined to execute all State laws, and city ordinances passed in pursuance of law, to the very letter, should it require the strong arm of military power to enable me to do so. As an officer, I know no man; the peaceful, unoffending citizen shall be protected in the full exercise of all his civil, political and religious rights, and the guilty violator of the law shall be punished without respect to persons.

The first act of the city council, after its organization, was to express its gratitude for its privileges and powers conferred upon the city by its charter. For this purpose the following resolution was introduced by Joseph Smith, and adopted:

Resolved, by the city council of the city of Nauvoo, that the unfeigned thanks of this community be respectfully tendered to the governor, council of revision, and legislature of the State of Illinois, as a feeble testimonial of their respect and esteem of noble, high-minded, and patriotic statesmen; and as an evidence of gratitude for the signal powers recently conferred—and that the citizens of Quincy be held in everlasting remembrance for their unparalleled liberality and marked kindness to our people, when in their greatest state of suffering and want.

The next move was to pass a temperance ordinance, which practically made Nauvoo a prohibition city—that is, so far as prohibitory ordinances prohibit.

CHAPTER XV.

THE NAUVOO LEGION.

THE Nauvoo charter proper really contained two other charters, viz: One for the establishment of a university within the limits of the city "for the teaching of the arts and sciences, and learned professions," and another for the organization of an independent military body to be called the "Nauvoo Legion."

An ordinance was passed on the third of February, in relation to the university, appointing a chancellor and board of regents. A site for a building was selected, and plans of the structure were drawn, but that was as far as the matter went, as the city had no funds with which to proceed with the work of construction.

An ordinance was also passed on the above date authorizing the organization of the Nauvoo Legion. The original provision in the Nauvoo charter establishing this military body provided that the city council might organize the inhabitants of the city, subject to military duty under the laws of the State, into an independent body of militia; and a subsequent amendment to the charter extended the privilege of joining the Legion to any citizen of Hancock County, who might by voluntary enrollment desire to do so; and in that event he was to have all the privileges to be enjoyed by members of that organization. The charter provided that the officers of the Legion should be commissioned by the governor; and that the members thereof be required to perform the same amount of military duty as the regular militia of the State; they were to be at the disposal of the mayor inexecuting the laws and ordinances of the city, and the laws of the State; and also at the disposal of the governor for the public defense, and the execution of the laws of the State and of the United States; and were entitled to their proportion of the public arms; but were exempt from all military duty not specified in these provisions.

The commissioned officers of the Legion were constituted its court-martial, which was its law-making department; but no law inconsistent with either the Constitution of the United States or the State of Illinois was to be enacted by this court. The privilege of organizing the citizens of Nauvoo, and as many of the citizens of Hancock County as might desire to unite with them, into an independent military body, was highly gratifying to the people of Nauvoo, but more especially so to Joseph Smith, who, in speaking of it, in a proclamation to the Saints scattered abroad, said:

> The Nauvoo Legion embraces all our military power, and will enable us to perform our military duty by ourselves, and thus afford us the power and privileges of avoiding one of the most fruitful sources of strife, oppression and collision with the world. It will enable us to show our attachment to the State and Nation, as a people, whenever the public service requires our aid, thus proving ourselves obedient to the paramount laws of the land, and ready at all times to sustain and execute them.

The city ordinance provided that the Legion should be divided into two cohorts, the horse troops to constitute the first cohort, and the infantry the second. The commander-in-chief of the Legion was to be known as the lieutenant-general, who was also made the reviewing officer and president of the court-martial and Legion. His staff was to consist of two principal aides-de-camp with the rank of colonel of cavalry; and a guard of twelve aides-de-camp with the rank of captain of infantry; and a drill officer, with the rank of colonel of dragoons, to be the chief officer of the guard.

The second officer was a major-general, to act as the secretary of the court-martial and Legion. His staff consisted of an adjutant; surgeon-in-chief, a cornet, quartermaster, paymaster, commissary, and chaplain; all to hold the rank of colonel of cavalry; besides these, there were to be in his staff, a surgeon for each cohort, quartermaster sergeant, sergeant-major, and a chief musician—with the rank of captain of light infantry; and two musicians with the rank of captain of infantry. Besides these officers there were created by the ordinance an adjutant and inspector-general; and a brigadier-general to command each cohort. The staff of each brigadier-general consisted of an aide-de-camp with the rank of lieutenant-colonel of infantry, and when not otherwise in service, these brigadiers had access to the staff of the major-general.

The ordinance organizing this body of militia provided that the court-martial should adopt for the Legion, so far as practicable, the discipline, drill, uniform, rules and regulations of the United States army. And a law passed by the court-martial shortly after its organization, required all male citizens within the limits of Nauvoo, between the ages of eighteen and forty-five, excepting such as were exempted from service under the laws of the United States, to perform military duty under the penalty of being fined for absence from general parades, as follows: generals, twenty-five dollars; colonels, twenty dollars; captains, fifteen dollars; lieutenants, ten dollars; and musicians and privates, five dollars. For absence from company parades—of course without good reason for the absence—the fines were fixed at these rates: commissioned officers, five dollars; non-commissioned officers, three dollars; and musicians and privates, two dollars.

The first election of officers of the Legion took place on the fourth of February, 1841; and resulted in Joseph Smith being unanimously chosen lieutenant-general; John C. Bennett, major-general; Wilson Law, brigadier-general of the first cohort;

and Don Carlos Smith, brigadier-general of the second cohort. The staffs of the respective generals were chosen from the leading citizens of Nauvoo, some of whom were not members of the Mormon Church. There were but six companies at the time the Legion was organized, in February, 1841, but in September following, the number of men had increased to one thousand four hundred and ninety; and at the time of the Prophet Joseph's death, some three years later, the Legion numbered about five thousand.

With such strict regulations, accompanied by a natural enthusiasm for military display, and drilled by competent military officers, it is not to be wondered at if the Legion became the best body of militia in the State of Illinois. It excited the jealousy and envy of the rest of the militia in the surrounding counties, and all the laudable efforts of the Legion to become an efficient body of militia, with a view of assisting in the execution of the State and National laws, if occasion should require, were construed by their enemies to mean a preparation for rebellion, and the establishment and spread of the Mormon religion by conquests of the sword, as, it is alleged, Mohammed established his religion. Thus the forming of an independent body of militia, enabling the Saints to perform their military duty by themselves, which the Prophet fondly hoped would remove "one of the most fruitful sources of strife, oppression and collision with the world," and which he further hoped would give the Saints, as a people, an opportunity of showing their attachment to the State and Nation, whenever the public service required their aid —by the misrepresentation of their enemies, was made one of the principal rocks of offense, and was used to excite the apprehensions and prejudices of the good people of Illinois.

The people of the United States have always been jealous of military power, and hence have been careful in forming their political institutions to subordinate the military to the civil authority, except in times of actual war; and, therefore, notwithstanding the very good intentions of the Saints at Nauvoo, it was a very easy matter for their enemies to excite the prejudice and awaken the fears of the people of Illinois by pointing to the existence of this elaborate and efficient military organization with its frequent musters and parades, and captained by a great religious leader, whom, notwithstanding his virtues and the uprightness of his intentions—they had come to regard as a wild, religious fanatic, prepared to go to what lengths they knew not in the promulgation of his religion. Hence that which was to be a bulwark to the city, and a protection to the Saints, was transformed by their enemies into an occasion of offense, and an excuse for assailing them.

CHAPTER XVI.

RECONSTRUCTION OF QUORUMS—THE NAUVOO HOUSE AND THE TEMPLE.

IN the meantime important changes in The Church organization were pending. An important revelation was received on the nineteenth of January, 1841,* which provided for filling the vacancies in the several quorums and a reconfirmation of all the authorities of the Church. Hyrum Smith, who had stood in the position of counselor to his brother Joseph, since the apostasy of F. G. Williams and his expulsion from The Church, on the seventh of November, 1837—was appointed to succeed his father as Patriarch to The Church; to hold the sealing blessings of The Church, even the Holy Spirit of promise, whereby the Saints are sealed up unto the day of redemption, that they may not fall, notwithstanding the day of temptation that might come upon them. He was also appointed a prophet, seer, and revelator, as well as Joseph with whom he was to act in concert, and from whom he was to receive counsel. The Prophet was to show unto him the keys whereby he might ask and receive, "and be crowned with the same blessing and glory and honor and priesthood, and gifts of the priesthood that once were put upon him that was my servant Oliver Cowdery."

Joseph Smith was given, as the presiding Elder of The Church, to be a translator, a revelator, a seer and prophet. Sidney Rigdon was admonished of his neglect of duty, and of his lack of faith; he was told, however, if he would repent of his

---

* Doctrine and Covenants, Section 124.

sins, and stand in his place and calling, he might continue to act as counselor to Joseph, and the Lord promised to heal him, and make him powerful in testimony. The reason for this admonition, as one may judge from the spirit of it, was that he to whom it was given had become sour in his feelings toward the work of God. His ardor was cooling, and his zeal, which at times had been inordinate, seemed now to be oozing out of his disposition.

William Law, whom, it will be remembered, Joseph first met when *en route* for Washington—Law then leading a small company of Saints to Nauvoo from Canada—was appointed to fill the vacancy in the First Presidency made by the appointment of Hyrum Smith to the office of Patriarch. And such blessings and spiritual powers were pronounced upon him by the Lord, as seldom falls to the lot of man. On condition of his faithfulness he was to have power to heal the sick, cast out devils, be delivered from those who administered unto him poison, and the serpent that might lay hold upon his heel; "And what if I will," said the Lord, "that he should raise the dead, let him not hold his voice."

Brigham Young was appointed the president of the Twelve Apostles, and liberty was given to appoint another man to fill the vacancy made in the quorum through the death of David W. Patton, who was killed by the mob, at the battle of Crooked River, in Missouri. The High Council for Nauvoo was named, and a presidency given to the High Priests; the seven presidents of the Seventies were appointed; and all the quorums of the Priesthood both in the Melchisedek and Aaronic divisions were set in order, so far as the appointment of presidents was concerned.

Besides setting the Priesthood in order, the Lord in this revelation required that a house should be built to His name; "a house worthy of all acceptation; that the weary traveler may find health and safety while he contemplates the word of the

Lord;" and the Prophet Joseph and his family were to have a right of permanent residence in it. It was to be known as the "Nauvoo House," and built unto the name of the Lord. The possession of individual stock was to range from fifty dollars to fifteen thousand dollars; no person being allowed to put in less than fifty, nor more than fifteen thousand. And it was specially provided that none but those who believed in the Book of Mormon and the revelations of God were to be permitted to hold stock in the house.

In addition to this commandment to build the Nauvoo House, the Lord told the Saints that there was not a place found on the earth to which He might come and restore that which was lost, or which he had taken away, even the fullness of the Priesthood; nor was there a baptismal font upon the earth where the Saints might be baptized for the dead.

The doctrine of baptism for the dead had been made known to the Saints some time previous to this, and the ordinance had been performed in the Mississippi and other convenient places; but this is an ordinance of God's house, and cannot be acceptable to Him when performed elsewhere, only in the days of the poverty of His people. And as more prosperous times had dawned upon The Church, the Saints were required to build a temple to the name of the Most High; and they were further told that they were granted sufficient time to build a temple, and if they failed to build it at the expiration of that appointed time, they should be rejected as a Church together with their dead. To show to The Church the importance of erecting this temple, the Lord reminded them how He had commanded Moses to build a tabernacle, that the children of Israel could bear with them into the wilderness, that those ordinances might be revealed which had been hidden from before the foundation of the world. Therefore said the Lord—

Let this house be built unto my name that I may reveal mine

ordinances therein, unto my people. For I design to reveal unto my Church things which have been kept hid from before the foundation of the world, things that pertain to the dispensation of the fullness of times; and I will show unto my servant Joseph all things pertaining to this house, and the Priesthood thereof. * * * And ye shall build it on the place where you have contemplated building it, for that is the spot which I have chosen for you to build it.

The location which the Saints had contemplated as the site for the temple was on a bold eminence overlooking the river, the landscape on the Iowa side, and all the surrounding country for miles around. It was not only by far the noblest site in Nauvoo for a temple, but ideal in its fitness.

CHAPTER XVII.

THE CONFERENCE OF APRIL 6TH, 1841.

THE sixth of April, 1841, was a memorable day in the history of Nauvoo. That day the corner stones of the great temple which God by revelation had commanded His people to build were to be laid. To the Prophet Joseph the day must have been a veritable gleam of sunshine amid the constantly renewing storms of his eventful career. It was a beautiful day, clear and balmy—propitious for the exercises to take place.

Early in the morning there was a hurrying to and fro in the streets of militiamen, for the presence of sixteen uniformed companies of the Nauvoo Legion was to add brightness and interest to the imposing ceremonies. A great procession was formed and marched to the temple site. Here the Legion was formed in a hollow square surrounding the excavations made for the foundation of the temple and enclosing the officers of the Legion, choir, citizens and prominent Elders of The Church who were to lay the corner stones of that structure. Sidney Rigdon was the orator of the occasion; and, doubtless owing to the recent admonition he had received in the revelation from the Lord—to which reference has been made—he was aroused from his lethargy for the time. At any rate, on this occasion he spoke with his old fervor and eloquence. He reviewed the trials of the past, the blessings they then enjoyed, the brightening prospects of the future, and dwelt at some length upon the importance of building temples, and the labor to be performed in them.

At the conclusion of the oration, at the direction of the

First Presidency, the architects lowered the southeast corner-stone to its place, and Joseph Smith said:

This principal corner-stone in representation of the First Presidency, is now duly laid in honor of the great God; and may it there remain until the whole fabric is completed; and may the same be accomplished speedily; that the Saints may have a place in which to worship God, and the Son of Man have where to lay His head.

To wbich Sidney Rigdon added:

May the persons employed in the erection of this house be preserved from all harm while engaged in its construction, till the whole is completed, in the name of the Father, and of the Son, and of the Holy Ghost. Even so, amen.

Thus were laid the corner-stones of the Nauvoo Temple, amid the rejoicing of the Saints; and even strangers forgot their prejudices and joined with hearty good will, as interested spectators of the proceedings. "Such an almost countless multitude of people," says one enthusiastic account of the scenes of the day, written at the time, "moving in harmony, in friendship, in dignity, told with a voice not easily misunderstood, that they were a people of intelligence, and virtue, and order; in short, that they were Saints; and that the God of love, purity and light, was their God, their exemplar and director; and that they were blessed and happy."

While on this subject, I quote the instructions on temple building from the history of the Prophet:

If the strict order of the Priesthood were carried out in the building of temples, the first stone will be laid at the southeast corner, by the First Presidency of The Church. The southwest corner should be laid next. The third, or northwest corner next; and the fourth or northeast corner the last.

The First Presidency should lay the southeast corner-stone, and dictate who are the proper persons to lay the other corner-stones.

If a temple is built at a distance, and the First Presidency are not present, then the quorum of the Twelve Apostles are the proper persons to dictate the order for that temple; and in the absence of the Twelve Apostles, then the presidency of the stake will lay the southeast corner-stone. The Melchisedek Priesthood laying the corner-stones on the east side of the temple, and the Lesser Priesthood those on the west side.

During the remaining days of the conference, opened with such splendid ceremonies, the Saints were instructed in principle and doctrine, the quorums of the Priesthood were arranged in their proper order and the important questions of business put to each quorum separately and voted upon; especially the names of those whom God had appointed and reappointed to fill the respective positions alluded to in the revelation above quoted.

Besides this, the several charters of Nauvoo, the Legion, University, Agricultural and Manufacturing Association, Nauvoo House Association, etc., were read and accepted by the people. Lyman Wight was sustained to fill the vacancy in the quorum of the Twelve. John C. Bennett was presented in connection with the First Presidency as assistant President until Sidney Rigdon's health should be restored. Everything necessary for the welfare, happiness and prosperity of the Saints was considered, and preparations made to push the work of God forward in all its departments. The conference lasted from Wednesday morning until Sunday night; and is one of the most important ever held by The Church.

Indeed the circumstances surrounding the Saints at the time were of a character to bid them hope that Nauvoo would be to them "a safe retreat." The friendship of nearly all of the leading men of the State; the universal sympathy felt by the people of Illinois for the victims of Missouri's fury; the action of the State legislature in granting the several charters noted in chapter fifteen—all supported the hopes entertained.

CHAPTER XVIII.

PROPHET'S TRIAL AT MONMOUTH.

EARLY in the summer of 1841, an event happened which threatened the peace of the inhabitants of Nauvoo. When busily intent in the performance of some labor, or duty, or even when in pursuit of pleasure, how often it happens that we work on, or enjoy our pleasure in the bright sunshine, without ever thinking of storms, until a sudden clap of thunder startles us, and looking up we see that dark clouds have arisen above the horizon; the bright skies are rapidly becoming overcast—a storm is impending! So it was with the Saints at Nauvoo concerning the matter of which we speak. It fell upon them as unexpectedly as falls a thunderbolt from a cloudless sky.

It occurred in this manner: When Hyrum Smith and William Law started on the mission to the Eastern States, to which they were appointed by the revelation of January 19, 1841, Joseph accompanied them as far as Quincy; and when returning to Nauvoo he stopped at Heberlin's hotel, on Bear Creek, some twenty-eight miles south of that city. While here a sheriff's posse under the direction of Thomas King, sheriff of Adams County, accompanied by an officer from Missouri, arrested him on a requisition from the governor of the State of Missouri. The warrant upon which the arrest was made was the one issued by the authorities of Missouri early in September, 1840; an effort to serve which was made on the fifteenth of that month, but the officers failed in their errand, as the brethren wanted, viz: Joseph Smith, Jr., Sidney Rigdon, Lyman Wight, P. P. Pratt, Caleb

Baldwin and A. Brown were not in Nauvoo, that is, they evaded arrest, as already related in a former chapter.

The complaint on which the requisition of the governor of Illinois was based charged that these men were fugitives from justice; and they were wanted in Missouri to answer to the old charges of "theft, arson and murder," supposed to have been committed in Caldwell and Daviess counties in the summer and fall of 1838.

What made Joseph's arrest more a matter of surprise to him was, that only a few hours previous to its being made, he had been in company with Governor Carlin at the latter's residence, and was treated with the greatest respect and kindness; yet not one word was said by the governor about the requisition made by Missouri for his arrest.

Joseph returned to Quincy in company with the sheriff's posse and secured a writ of *habeas corpus* from Charles A. Warren, master in chancery. The same evening, Saturday, June 5th, Judge Stephen A. Douglass arrived in Quincy, and appointed the hearing on the writ to take place the following Tuesday, at Monmouth, Warren County.

In the meantime the news of Joseph's arrest reached Nauvoo and created no little excitement. A party of seven men, under the leadership of Hosea Stout, left Nauvoo for Quincy, Sunday morning, in a skiff, to render the Prophet any assistance in their power, and prevent if possible his enemies taking him to Missouri. They struggled against a head-wind all day, but reached Quincy at dusk, only to learn that Joseph had gone to Nauvoo in charge of Sheriff King and another officer; there was nothing for them to do but to return.

Sheriff King was taken sick at Nauvoo, but Joseph nursed him with all the tenderness of a brother, and the day following Monday, started for Monmouth, accompanied by a large number of the leading men of Nauvoo, and the sheriff, whom Joseph cared for personally during the journey of seventy-five miles. The party arrived at Monmouth on Tuesday, but at the request of the State attorney, who claimed he was not prepared on the case, the hearing was postponed until the next day.

The appearance of Joseph in Monmouth caused considerable excitement. He was invited to preach, but thought it best, as he was a prisoner, not to do so; but he appointed Amasa Lyman to preach in the court room on Wednesday evening.

The prejudice of the people of Monmouth was as excessive as it was blind. They employed at their own expense several attorneys to assist the prosecution, and declared that if there were any lawyers in the district who would even undertake the defense of the Prophet, they never need look to the people of that county again for political favors. But there were strong men in attendance at the court, men not to be frightened by such threats, and whose souls despised the petty minds that could frame them; Joseph, therefore, was ably defended by Messrs. Charles A. Warren, Sidney H. Little, O. H. Browning, James H. Ralston, Cyrus Walker, and Archibald Williams.

The pleadings of the lawyers for the defense were peculiarly affecting, since all of them were more or less acquainted with the condition of the Saints when they fled from the violence of Missourians to Illinois. O. H. Browning had seen several of these companies of Saints in their flight and could trace them by the blood left in their footprints on the snow; his recital of their sufferings moved Judge Douglass, most of the officers of the court and the spectators to tears. One of the brethren present who wrote an account of the trial for the Nauvoo papers says:

He [Mr. Browning] concluded his remarks by saying, To tell the prisoner to go to Missouri for a trial was adding insult to injury, and then said: "Great God! Have I not seen it? Yes, my eyes have beheld the blood-stained traces of innocent women and children, in the dreary winter, who had traveled hundreds of miles barefoot, through frost and snow, to seek a refuge from their savage pursuers. 'Twas a scene of horror, sufficient to have enlisted the sympathy of an adamantine heart. And shall this unfortunate man, whom their fury has seen proper to select for sacrifice, be driven into such a savage land, where none dare to enlist in the cause of justice? If there was no other voice under heaven ever to be heard in this cause, gladly would I stand alone, and proudly spend my latest breath in defense of an American citizen."

The lawyers for the prosecution, according to Joseph's own account, acted honorably and confined themselves to the merits of the case, excepting two—Messrs. Knowlton and Jennings. They made an appeal both to the passions and prejudices of the people, and sought to create an excitement over the matter. Judge Douglass, however, was impartial in his rulings, and doubtless one officer of the court - the sheriff of Warren County—thought him severe in his efforts to protect the prisoner. The court room was densely packed and the judge ordered the sheriff to keep the spectators back; but this he neglected and the judge fined him ten dollars. In a few minutes the order to keep the spectators from crowding the prisoner and witnesses was repeated, and the sheriff told the court that he had ordered a constable to do it. "Clerk," said Judge Douglass, "add ten dollars more to that fine." This was effectual, the sheriff after that did his duty.

Joseph claimed in this case that he was unlawfully held a prisoner, and he could prove that the indictment upon which he was arrested had been obtained by fraud, bribery and duress. This line of defense, however, raised the question as to whether the court had the right to inquire into the merits of the case. A long debate between opposing counsel followed. But it will be remembered that an attempt to arrest Joseph on the requisition from the governor of Missouri had been made in September previous; and it appears that after the fruitless effort to make the arrest, the sheriff of Hancock County returned the writ; and the defense claimed that after the return of the writ to the executive, the defendant could not be again legally arrested upon it. It was upon this point that the court set Joseph at liberty. Following is Judge Douglass' decision on this point:

> The writ being once returned to the executive by the sheriff of Hancock County was dead, and stood in the same relationship as any other writ which might issue from the circuit court, and consequently the defendant cannot be held in custody on that writ.

On the other point in the case—as to whether evidence in the case was admissible—the judge withheld his opinion for further consideration, as the question was a grave one, involving the future conduct of the States in their relationship with each other; but on the ground that the writ was void, dead by reason of a former return being made on it by the sheriff of Hancock County, he ordered the discharge of the prisoner. And Missouri was again foiled in her designs upon the life of the Prophet.

At the conclusion of the trial Joseph ordered dinner for his company, which numbered by that time some sixty men. "And when I called for the tavern bill," says Joseph, "the unconscientious fellow replied, 'only one hundred and sixty dollars.'" Some time after this, in September following, Joseph sent the costs of this trial to the sheriff of Adams County, of which the following is a copy:

NAUVOO, September 30, 1841.

To the Deputy Sheriff of Adams County:

The following is a statement of my expenses, costs and liabilities, consequent upon my arrest and trial while in your custody, to-wit:

To amount of fees to Esquires Ralston, Warren & Co.	$250 00
To Esquires Little, Williams, Walker and Browning	100 00
To seven days for self, horse and carriage, @ $5.00 per day	35 00

To money spent during that time consequent upon arrest	60 00
To twelve witnesses	240 00
	$685 00

To which was added this note:

DEAR SIR —You will please take such measures as to put me in possession of the above amount, which is justly due me as above stated; to say nothing of false imprisonment and other expenses. * * *

Receive my respects, etc.

JOSEPH SMITH.

With the exception of the difficulty just considered, the summer of 1841 glided pleasantly by, bringing to the busy inhabitants of Nauvoo many occasions of social and spiritual enjoyment.

CHAPTER XIX.

EVENTS OF THE SUMMER OF 1841.

NAUVOO was the most promising and thrifty city in Illinois, and the fame thereof extended throughout the nation, due, in part, of course, to the peculiar religion of its inhabitants. Strangers from far and near made it a point to visit Nauvoo, and the peace, sobriety, industry and public spirit of the citizens challenged their admiration, whatever views they might entertain respecting their religion. A large bowery was constructed just west of the temple site where the people assembled for worship. Here the Prophet Joseph preached some of his most powerful discourses, and taught his people in the doctrine of the heavenly kingdom; and not unfrequently it happened that

> Fools who came to mock, remained to pray.

The Saints never intended to make either their city or the Nauvoo Legion exclusively Mormon.* On the contrary, the peo-

---

* The Legion is not, as has been falsely represented by its enemies, exclusively a Mormon military association, but a body of citizen soldiers organized (without regard to political preferences or religious sentiments) for the public defense, the general good, and the preservation of law and order—to save the innocent, unoffending citizens from the iron grasp of the oppressor, and perpetuate and sustain our free institutions against misrule, anarchy and mob violence; no other views are entertained or tolerated.—*Joseph Smith.* From an official letter published May 4, 1841.

ple at Nauvoo expressed a willingness to unite with their fellow-citizens in every good work and enterprise, and tolerate religious differences. Indeed, repeated invitations were sent out to the honorable men, not only of the State of Illinois, but of the United States, to men of capital and of influence and of integrity, asking them to come to Nauvoo, and assist in building up a glorious city.

In July, Sidney H. Little, of the State senate, was killed by leaping from his carriage, while his horse was unmanageable; and that the "Saints might mourn with those who are called to mourn," the eighteenth day of July was set apart as a day of fasting among the people of Nauvoo. By thus manifesting a feeling of sympathy and interest, they sought to cultivate peace and good-will among their fellow-citizens, and a number of honorable, and some of them influential men, while not accepting the faith of the Saints, became friendly disposed towards them, and associated with them in various business transactions.

But the good-will of the Saints was not very generally reciprocated by the people of Illinois; and there were, even at that early date, envyings and bitterness manifested by those who were jealous of the prosperity and increasing power of the Mormons in Nauvoo and vicinity. The same spirit existed to some extent in Iowa as will be seen by the following occurrence: General Swazey, in command of the militia of Iowa, Territory, invited Joseph and Hyrum Smith and General Bennett to attend the parade of the militia of that Territory at Montrose. The invitation was accepted, and General Swazey received his visitors courteously, and so did the militia. But during a recess in the exercises taken at noon, a Mr. D. W. Kilburn tried to create a disturbance by circulating the following note among the troops:

Citizens of Iowa—The laws of Iowa do not require you to muster or be reviewed by Joe Smith or General Bennett; and should they have the impudence to attempt it, it is hoped that every person having a proper respect for himself, will at once leave the ranks.

The facts are that these militia companies were not mustered by Joseph's order, nor did he expect to review them. He had simply accepted General Swazey's invitation to witness the movements of the troops as other spectators were doing, and neither Joseph nor Hyrum was in uniform. General Swazey had been several times invited to attend the drills and reviews of the Legion at Nauvoo, and he had simply returned the courtesy to the officers of the Legion. Kilburn's effort, however, to create a disturbance was not successful, though the papers of the State commented upon it, and some of them began to whisper that it was Joseph's ambition to build up a military church and extend his faith, "Mohammed-like," by the sword.

Early in the summer of 1841, in fact in the month of May, Joseph called upon the Saints everywhere to come into Hancock County, that there might be a concentration of effort to build up Nauvoo. The proclamation closed with these words:

> Let it therefore be understood that all the stakes excepting those in this county (Hancock) and in Lee County, Iowa, are discontinued; and the Saints instructed to settle in this county as soon as circumstances will permit.

The Twelve Apostles, whose departure from Nauvoo on their missions to England under very tryingcir cumstances, was related in a former chapter, returned during the summer, after accomplishing one of the most successful and remarkable missions in modern times. They were a tower of strength to Joseph, and he was not long in availing himself of their valuable support. At a special conference convened in Nauvoo on the sixteenth of August, 1841, Joseph said:

> The time had come when the Twelve should be called upon to

stand in their place next to the First Presidency; and attend to the settling of emigrants and the business of The Church at the stakes, and assist to bear off the kingdom victoriously to the nations.*

And he at once turned over to their management many of the temporal affairs, with which he had been perplexed, and devoted himself more exclusively to spiritual labors.

One of the most pleasing events that happened, during the summer of which I write, was the visit of the Indian chief Keokuk to Nauvoo. He was accompanied by Kiskukosh, Appenoose and about one hundred chiefs and braves of the Sac and Fox tribes, together with their families. They were brought over from the Iowa side on the ferry and two large flat boats. The band and a detachment of the Legion met them at the landing, but as soon as Keokuk failed to recognize Joseph among those who had come to bid him welcome, he refused to land or allow any of his party to go ashore until Joseph made his appearance. The arrangement had been made for the band and the detachment of the Legion to lead the dusky visitors to the grove where the Saints held their meetings; and there Joseph would have joined them. But Keokuk seemed to have his own ideas in relation to the etiquette to be observed at his reception, and waited until the Prophet met him at the landing and bade him welcome to Nauvoo.

At the grove Joseph addressed the Indians at some length, upon what the Lord had revealed to him concerning their forefathers, and recited to them the glorious promises contained in the Book of Mormon respecting themselves, the despised remnants of a once splendid race. How their hearts must have glowed and their eyes brightened as they listened to the young Prophet relate the story of their forefathers' rise and fall, and the bright promises held out to them of redemption from their

---

*Minutes of special conference, Aug. 16, 1841. Millennial Star, Vol. xviii, page 630.

fallen state! In conclusion Joseph counseled them to cease killing each other, and warring with other tribes or with the whites. To Joseph's speech Keokuk replied:

I have a Book of Mormon at my wigwam that you gave me a number of moons ago. I believe you are a great and good man. Keokuk looks rough, but I am a son of the Great Spirit. I have heard your advice. We intend to quit fighting, and follow the good talk you have given us.

After the "talk," they were feasted by the Saints with good food and dainties and melons. At the conclusion of the feast, they gave a specimen of their war dance to entertain the spectators, and then returned to the Iowa side of the river to their encampment.

Thus passed away the summer of 1841; and by the first of October—the date fixed for the semi-annual conference—the early autumn frosts had tinged the forest leaves with purple and gold, giving to the splendid scenery about Nauvoo an additional charm. President Joseph Smith was not present at the opening of the conference. He had that morning gone to assist in laying the corner-stone of the Nauvoo House which the Saints by revelation had been commanded to build;* and the conference was opened by President Brigham Young.

The principal subject brought before the people at this conference was the redemption of the dead, and building the temple. This matter appeared to impress itself upon the mind of Joseph with great force, and nothing, apparently, gave him more delight than to explain its importance to his people. Up to this time many baptisms for the dead had been performed in the river, but it was now announced that no more baptisms for the dead should be attended to, until it could be done in the

* Doctrine and Covenants, Section 124.

font of the Lord's house, for thus had the Lord commanded. The Saints, however, were not long denied the privilege of performing this work of baptism for their dead, as on the eighth of November, following the conference, a temporary baptismal font had been completed and dedicated in the basement of the temple.*

On the occasion of the angel Moroni's first appearance to Joseph Smith, in 1823, he repeated to the young Prophet the words of Malachi, recorded in the fourth chapter of the Book of Malachi, the fifth and sixth verses, though quoting somewhat differently from the language of King James' translation, as follows:

Behold, I will reveal unto you the Priesthood, by the hand of Elijah the prophet, before the coming of the great and dreadful day of

---

* The font was constructed of pine timber, and put together of staves tongued and grooved, oval shaped, sixteen feet long east and west, and twelve feet wide, seven feet high from the foundation, the basin four feet deep; the moulding of the cap or base was formed of beautiful carved wood in antique style, and the sides were finished with panel work. There were steps leading up and down into the basin in the north and south sides, guarded by side railings. The font stood upon twelve oxen, four on each side and two at each end, their heads, shoulders and forelegs projecting out from under the font. They were carved out of pine plank, glued together, and copied after the most beautiful five-year-old steer that could be found in the country. * * * The oxen and ornamental mouldings of the font were carved by Elder Elijah Fordham, from New York. * * * The font was inclosed by a temporary frame building sided up with split oak clap-boards, with a roof of the same material, but was so low that the timbers of the first story o the temple were laid above it. The water was supplied from a well thirty feet deep in the east end of the basement. This font was built for the baptism for the dead until the temple could be completed, when a more durable one was to take its place.—*Millennial Star*, Volume XVIII, 744.

the Lord; and he will plant in the hearts of the children the promises made to the fathers, and the hearts of the children shall turn to their fathers; if it were not so, the whole earth would be utterly wasted at his coming.

In fulfillment of this promised visitation, in April, 1836, Elijah the prophet appeared to Joseph Smith and Oliver Cowdery and said:

Behold, the time has fully come, which was spoken by the mouth of Malachi, testifying that he (Elijah) should be sent before the great and dreadful day of the Lord come, to turn the hearts of the fathers to the children, and the children to the fathers, lest the whole earth be smitten with a curse. Therefore the keys of this dispensation are committed into your hands, and by this ye may know that the great and dreadful day of the Lord is near, even at the doors.

And now when something like peace had come to The Church, and settled conditions obtained, the Prophet of God began to unfold the doctrine of salvation for the dead—the application of those principles of salvation to past generations who had lived upon the earth when neither the Gospel nor divine authority to administer its ordinances were among men.

In addition to the main idea of this doctrine which he taught with such great power, the following gems are gathered from his teachings at this conference, chiefly relating to the same subject:

The proclamation of the first principles of the Gospel, was a means of salvation to men individually, and it was the truth and not men that saved them; but men by actively engaging in rites of salvation substantially became instruments in bringing multitudes of their kindred into the Kingdom of God. [And hence] he presented baptism for the dead as the only way by which men can appear as saviors on Mount Zion.

* * *

The difference between an angel and a ministering spirit: the one [the first] is a resurrected or translated body with its spirit ministering to embodied spirits; the other a disembodied spirit visiting and ministering to disembodied spirits.

* * *

Jesus Christ became a ministering spirit (while his body was laying in the sepulchre) to the spirits in prison, to fulfill an important part of his mission, without which he could not have perfected his work or entered into his rest. After his resurrection he appeared as an angel to his disciples.

* * *

Translated bodies cannot enter into rest until they have undergone a change equivalent to death.

* * *

Translated bodies are designed for future missions.

* * *

The angel which appeared to John on the Isle of Patmos was a translated or resurrected body.

* * *

Jesus Christ went in body after his resurrection to minister to translated and resurrected bodies.

* * *

It is no more incredible that God should *save* the dead than that he should raise the dead.

* * *

There is never a time when the spirit is too old to approach God.

* * *

All are within the reach of pardoning mercy, who have not committed the unpardonable sin, which hath no forgiveness, neither in this world, nor in the world to come. There is a way to release the spirit of the dead; that is by the power and authority of the Priesthood—by binding and loosing on earth. This doctrine appears glorious, inasmuch as it exhibits the greatness of divine compassion and benevolence in the extent of the plan of human salvation.

This glorious truth is well calculated to enlarge the understanding, and to sustain the soul under troubles, difficulties, and distresses.

For illustration, suppose the case of two men, brothers, equally intelligent, learned, virtuous and lovely, walking in uprightness and in all good conscience, so far as they had been able to discern duty from the muddy stream of tradition, or from the blotted page of the book of nature. One dies and is buried, having never heard the Gospel of reconciliation; to the other the message of salvation is sent, he hears and embraces it, and is made the heir of eternal life. Shall the one become a partaker of glory, and the other consigned to hopeless perdition? Is there no chance for his escape? Sectarianism answers, none! none!! none!!! Such an idea is worse than atheism. The truth shall break down and dash in pieces all such bigoted Pharisaism; the sects shall be sifted, the honest in heart brought out, and their priests left in the midst of their corruption.

* * *

This doctrine presents in a clear light the wisdom and mercy of God in preparing an ordinance for the salvation of the dead, being baptized by proxy, their names recorded in heaven, and they judged according to the deeds done in the body. This doctrine was the burden of the Scriptures. Those Saints who neglect it, in behalf of their deceased relatives, do it at the peril of their own salvation. The dispensation of the fullness of times will bring to light the things that have been revealed in all former dispensations; also other things that have not been before revealed.

* * *

Another interesting feature of the conference was the report made by the Prophet of The Church property in his charge as trustee-in-trust for The Church. He also took occasion to report the amount of his own earthly possessions, of which the following is a copy:

Old Charley, a horse given to him several years before in Kirtland; two pet deers; two old turkeys and four young ones; an old cow given to him by a brother in Missouri; old Major, a dog; his wife, children, and a little household furniture!

Surely his earthly possessions did not far exceed those of Him who had not where to lay His head!

CHAPTER XX.

INTRODUCTION OF THE NEW MARRIAGE SYSTEM.

ANOTHER matter of very great importance, and one which has exercised a great influence upon the course of events in the history of The Church—and especially upon the events of this Nauvoo period—belongs to the spring and summer of 1841; and many things of our history will be all the plainer if the matter referred to be considered now. I refer to the introduction, in practice, of the marriage system which afterwards obtained in The Church. The chief and greatest feature of this marriage system—celestial marriage it is called by The Church, because it is the marriage system that obtains in celestial worlds—is the eternity of the marriage covenant. "Until death us do part" is usually the mutual covenant of man and woman in the orthodox "Christian" marriage ceremony.* That is, the marriage covenant is understood among "Christians" generally as being a matter that pertains to time only, the contract obligations ending with death. But this celestial marriage system of The Church regards the incident of death not at all, but makes the covenant of marriage for time and for all eternity; a covenant which is sealed and ratified by that power of the Priesthood in the administrator which binds on earth and it is bound in heaven.† That is, the covenant of

---

* See The Book of Common Prayer, Church of England, article, Solemnization of Matrimony.

†Jesus said unto Peter: I will give unto thee the keys of the kingdom of heaven: and whatsoever thou shalt bind on earth shall be bound in heaven: and whatsoever thou shalt loose on earth shall be loosed in heaven.—Matt. xvi: 19.

marriage holds good through time and will be in effect and of binding force in and after the resurrection. In other words this marriage system regards man as enduring eternally, and formulates his marriage covenants in harmony with that view of him. Of course this contemplates the continuation of the marriage state in eternity. Not only the spiritual and intellectual companionship, but all the relations of the wedded state, with the joys of parentage—the power of endless lives being among the means of man's exaltation and glory. That this is a view of marriage quite distinct from the usual "Christian" view, goes without saying. It throws a new light upon man's future existence. It destroys the vagueness which through nearly all ages like a mystic pall has hidden the glory and exaltation destined for man in the future eternities of God. It should be said, in this connection, that the revelations of God to Joseph Smith even before this marriage system was made known, held out to man the hope of a tangible future existence in a resurrected, immortal body of flesh and bones quickened by the spirit, and clothed with the glory of immortal youth. The future life was to be a reality, not a land of shadows; his heavenly home was to be upon the earth, after it had become sanctified and made a celestial sphere. His relations with his kindred and friends were to be of a nature to satisfy the longings of the human heart for society, for fellowship; and needed only the revelation of this marriage system to complete the circle of his promised future felicity. For grant to man in his resurrected state a real, tangible existence; an immortal youth that knows no pain or sickness or disease; the power to "hive" knowledge and wisdom as the centuries, the millenniums and eternities roll by; grant him the power to build and inhabit; to love and be loved; and add to that the power of endless lives—the power and privilege to perpetuate his race under an eternal marriage covenant—grant this, and the future happiness, exaltation and glory of man stands revealed as being absolutely without limitations, and far greater and beyond in majesty anything within our power to conceive in our present state of semi-dullness.

I say that the primary principle of the marriage system of The Church is the eternity of the marriage covenant; but owing to the fact that the system also includes the doctrine of a plurality of wives, the importance and grandeur of the doctrine of the eternity of the marriage covenant to a very great extent has been lost sight of in the discussion of and the popular clamor concerning the plurality feature of this new marriage system. The revelation making known this marriage doctrine came about in this way: First it should be stated—and it is evident from the written revelation itself, which bears the date of July 12th, 1843,*—that the doctrine was revealed and the practice of it began before the partial† revelation now in the Doctrine and Covenants was written. As early as 1831 the rightfulness of a plurality of wives under certain conditions was made known to Joseph Smith. In the latter part of that year, especially from November 1831, and through the early months of 1832, the Prophet with Sidney Rigdon as his assistant was earnestly engaged at Hiram, a village in Portage County, near Kirtland, Ohio, in translating the Jewish scripture.‡ It must have been while engaged in that work that the evident approval of God to the plural marriage system of the ancient patriarchs attracted the Prophet's attention and led him to make those inquiries of the Lord to which the opening paragraphs of the written revelation refer, viz:—

Verily, thus saith the Lord unto you, my servant Joseph, that in-

---

* See Doc. and Cov. Sec. 132: 52.

† *Ibid*, verse 66.

‡ See Millennial Star, Vol. XIV. (Supplement) pp 80,83; also pp. 114 and 116 same volume. Doc. and Cov. Sec. 76: 11-16.

asmuch as you have inquired of my hand, to know and understand wherein I, the Lord, justified my servants Abraham, Isaac and Jacob; as also Moses, David and Solomon, my servants, as touching the principle and doctrine of their having many wives and concubines: behold! and lo, I am the Lord thy God, and will answer thee as touching this matter.

The doctrine revealed at that time to the Prophet, however, was not to be made known to the world; but Joseph did make known what had been revealed to him to a few trusted friends, among whom were Oliver Cowdery and Lyman E. Johnson, the latter confiding what the Prophet had taught him to Orson Pratt, his missionary companion. With these and a few other exceptions, perhaps, the knowledge of the truth and righteousness of this principle of the future marriage system of The Church was locked up in the bosom of the Prophet of God.

About 1840, however, the Prophet began to be moved upon to make known the doctrine to others. He taught the principle to Joseph Bates Noble for one, as early as the fall of 1840. According to the affidavit of Noble, given before James Jack, a notary public, in and for the county of Salt Lake, Utah, in June, 1869, Joseph Smith declared to Noble that "he had received a revelation from God on the subject, and that an angel of the Lord had commanded him (Joseph Smith) to move forward in the said order of marriage; and further, that the said Joseph Smith requested him (Joseph B. Noble) to step forward and assist him in carrying out the said principle." This same man Noble gives the following affidavit with reference to the introduction of the practice of this principle by Joseph Smith, the Prophet:

Territory of Utah, } ss
County of Salt Lake, }

Be it remembered that on this 26th day of June, A. D. 1869, personally appeared before me, James Jack, a Notary Public in and for said county, Joseph Bates Noble, who was by me sworn in due form of law, and upon his oath saith, that on the fifth day of April, A. D., 1841, at the City of Nauvoo, County of Hancock, State of Illinois, he married or sealed Louisa Beaman, to Joseph Smith, President of the Church of Jesus Christ of Latter-day Saints, according to the order of celestial marriage revealed to the said Joseph Smith.

(Signed) JOSEPH B. NOBLE.

Subscribed and sworn to by the said Joseph Bates Noble the day and year first above written.

JAMES JACK, Notary Public.

The introduction of the practice of plural marriage by the Prophet then began even before the return of the Twelve from England. On their return Joseph soon began to teach the principle to them, and urged upon them the importance of putting it into practice. The dread with which the doctrine was regarded, the prejudices against it in the hearts of those faithful men who accepted it as a revelation from God through the Prophet, are all illustrated in the reflections and testimony of Elder John Taylor, one of the Twelve at that time, and subsequently the President of the Church. And here let me repeat what I said in his biography some years ago: "The world never made a greater mistake than when it supposed that plural marriage was hailed with delight by the Elders who were commanded of the Lord to introduce its practice in this generation. They saw clearly that it would bring additional reproach upon them from the world; that it would run counter to the traditions and prejudices of society, as, indeed, it was contrary to their own traditions; that their motives would be misunderstood or misconstrued. All this they saw, and naturally shrunk from the undertaking required of them by the revelation of God." And now Elder Taylor:—

Joseph Smith told the Twelve that if this law was not practiced, if they would not enter into this covenant, then the Kingdom of God could not go one step further. Now, we did not feel like preventing the Kingdom of God from going forward. We professed to be the

Apostles of the Lord, and did not feel like putting ourselves in a position to retard the progress of the Kingdom of God. The revelation says that "All those who have this law revealed unto them must obey the same." Now, that is not my word. I did not make it. It was the Prophet of God who revealed that to us in Nauvoo, and I bear witness of this solemn fact before God, that he did reveal this sacred principle to me and others of the Twelve, and in this revelation it is stated that it is the will and law of God that "all those who have this law revealed unto them must obey the same."

I had always entertained strict ideas of virtue, and I felt as a married man that this was to me, outside of this principle, an appalling thing to do. The idea of going and asking a young lady to be married to me when I had already a wife! It was a thing calculated to stir up feelings from the innermost depths of the human soul. I had always entertained the strictest regard of chastity. I had never in my life seen the time when I have known of a man deceiving a woman—and it is often done in the world, where, notwithstanding the crime, the man is received into society and the poor woman is looked upon as a pariah and an outcast—I have always looked upon such a thing as infamous, and upon such a man as a villain. * * * Hence, with the feelings I had entertained, nothing but a knowledge of God, and the revelations of God, and the truth of them, could have induced me to embrace such a principle as this.

We [the Twelve] seemed to put off, as far as we could, what might be termed the evil day.

Some time after these things were made known unto us, I was riding out of Nauvoo on horseback, and met Joseph Smith coming in, he, too, being on horseback. * * * I bowed to Joseph, and having done the same to me, he said: "Stop;" and he looked at me very intently. "Look here," said he, "those things that have been spoken of must be fulfilled, and if they are not entered into right away the keys will be turned."

Well, what did I do? Did I feel to stand in the way of this great, eternal principle, and treat lightly the things of God? No. I replied: "Brother Joseph, I will try and carry these things out."

So indeed he did, for within two years, in Nauvoo, he

married Elizabeth Haigham, Jane Ballantyne and Mary A. Oakley.

After this the testimony is abundant that plural marriage as well as marriage for eternity was abundantly practiced in Nauvoo,* though the revelation which made its rightfulness known was not written until July 12th, 1843.

I have remarked in the opening of this chapter that the consideration of this subject at this period of Nauvoo's history would aid the reader to understand more clearly many things in the subsequent events we have to relate. It is to be observed first of all that this principle of plural marriage had to be introduced secretly; first, because of the traditions and prejudices of the Saints themselves; and, secondly, because of the advantage that their enemies surrounding them would have when once the doctrine was publicly proclaimed. This enforced secrecy, then, which a reasonable prudence demanded, gave rise to apparent contradictions between the public utterances of leading brethren in The Church and their practice. Wicked men took advantage of the situation and brought sorrow to the hearts of the innocent and reproach upon The Church. Some, possessed of a zeal without wisdom, knowing of this doctrine, hastened without authority to make public proclamation of it and had to be silenced, as, for instance, a number of Elders who were reproved by Hyrum Smith for preaching this doctrine at a branch of The Church at China Creek, near Nauvoo;† and later one Hiram Brown who did the same thing in Lapeer County, Michigan; for which he was disfellowshiped from The Church and notified by Joseph and Hyrum to attend the con-

---

* See a collection of affidavits on this subject in the Historical Record, Andrew Jenson, compiler; and also affidavits in Succession in Presidency, 2nd edition.

† See Times and Seasons for March, 1844.

ference in April of that year to give a further account of his proceedings.*

Then again there were others who falsely taught that the Prophet approved of promiscuous intercourse between the sexes, and that there was no sin in such relations so long as they were kept secret and brought no scandal upon the community. This afforded villains their opportunity, and such men as John C. Bennett; the Laws, Wilson and William; Dr. Foster; the young Higbees, Chancy L., and Francis M.; and others, to reap their harvest of wickedness. There was necessarily enough of mystery in the movements of the Prophet and his faithful brethren connected with the matter of plural marriage to give something of color to the false statements of these wretches, and hence many otherwise good people were deceived. The duty of the Prophet and his associates, however, to denounce this wickedness that had crept into The Church was not shirked by the leading Elders of The Church. The Prophet was bold in his denunciation of the evil and snatched the masks from the faces of corrupt men, and did all in his power to protect the innocent from the deceptions of the vicious, though it pluck down upon his own head the vengeful wrath of the ungodly. With this situation in mind I am sure the reader will better appreciate the many complications which follow.

In ordor that the reader who is a stranger to Mormonism may see how far the principle of the eternity of the marriage covenant and the plural marriage system of The Church is removed from the sensuality that is often attributed to it, I quote *in extenso*, in concluding this chapter, the revelation which justifies and authorized it:

Verily, thus saith the Lord unto you, my servant Joseph, that inasmuch as you have inquired of my hand, to know and understand

---

* See Times and Seasons for February 1st, 1844.

wherein I, the Lord, justified my servants Abraham, Isaac and Jacob; as also Moses, David and Solomon, my servants, as touching the principle and doctrine of their having many wives and concubines:

Behold! and lo, I am the Lord thy God, and will answer thee as touching this matter:

Therefore, prepare thy heart to receive and obey the instructions which I am about to give unto you; for all those who have this law revealed unto them must obey the same;

For behold! I reveal unto you a new and everlasting covenant; and if ye abide not that covenant, then are ye damned; for no one can reject this covenant, and be permitted to enter into my glory;

For all who will have a blessing at my hands, shall abide the law which was appointed for that blessing, and the conditions thereof, as were instituted from before the foundation of the world;

And as pertaining to the new and everlasting covenant, it was instituted for the fullness of my glory; and he that receiveth a fullness thereof, must and shall abide the law, or he shall be damned, saith the Lord God.

And verily I say unto you, that the conditions of this law are these:—All covenants, contracts, bonds, obligations, oaths, vows, performances, connections, associations, or expectations, that are not made, and entered into, and sealed, by the Holy Spirit of promise, of him who is anointed, both as well for time and for all eternity, and that too most holy, by revelation and commandment through the medium of mine anointed, whom I have appointed on the earth to hold this power, (and I have appointed unto my servant Joseph to hold this power in the last days, and there is never but one on the earth at a time, on whom this power and the keys of this Priesthood are conferred,) are of no efficacy, virtue or force, in and after the resurrection from the dead; for all contracts that are not made unto this end, have an end when men are dead.

Behold! mine house is a house of order, saith the Lord God, and not a house of confusion.

Will I accept of an offering, saith the Lord, that is not made in my name!

Or, will I receive at your hands that which I have not appointed!

And will I appoint unto you, saith the Lord, except it be by law, even as I and my Father ordained unto you, before the world was!

I am the Lord thy God, and I give unto you this commandment, that no man shall come unto the Father but by me, or by my word, which is my law, saith the Lord;

And everything that is in the world, whether it be ordained of men, by thrones, or principalities, or powers, or things of name, whatsoever they may be, that are not by me, or by my word, saith the Lord, shall be thrown down, and shall not remain after men are dead, neither in nor after the resurrection, saith the Lord your God;

For whatsoever things remain, are by me; and whatsoever things are not by me, shall be shaken and destroyed.

Therefore, if a man marry him a wife in the world, and he marry her not by me, nor by my word; and he covenant with her so long as he is in the world, and she with him, their covenant and marriage are not of force when they are dead, and when they are out of the world; therefore, they are not bound by any law when they are out of the world;

Therefore, when they are out of the world, they neither marry nor are given in marriage; but are appointed angels in heaven, which angels are ministering servants, to minister for those who are worthy of a far more, and an exceeding, and an eternal weight of glory;

For these angels did not abide my law, therefore they cannot be enlarged, but remain separately and singly, without exaltation, in their saved condition, to all eternity, and from henceforth are not Gods, but are angels of God, for ever and ever.

And again, verily I say unto you, if a man marry a wife, and make a covenant with her for time and for all eternity, if that covenant is not by me, or by my word, which is my law, and is not sealed by the Holy Spirit of promise, through him whom I have anointed and appointed unto this power—then it is not valid, neither of force when they are out of the world, because they are not joined by me, saith the Lord, neither by my word; when they are out of the world, it cannot be received there, because the angels and the Gods are appointed there, by whom they cannot pass; they cannot, therefore, inherit my glory, for my house is a house of order, saith the Lord God.

And again, verily I say unto you, if a man marry a wife by my word, which is my law, and by the new and everlasting covenant, and it is sealed unto them by the Holy Spirit of promise, by him who is anointed, unto whom I have appointed this power, and the keys of this Priesthood; and it shall be said unto them, ye shall come forth in the first resurrection; and if it be after the first resurrection, in the next resurrection; and shall inherit thrones, kingdoms, principalities, and powers, dominions, all heights and depths—then shall it be written in the Lamb's Book of Life, that he shall commit no murder whereby to shed innocent blood, and if ye abide in my covenant, and commit no murder whereby to shed innocent blood, it shall be done unto them in all things whatsoever my servant hath put upon them, in time, and through all eternity, and shall be of full force when they are out of the world; and they shall pass by the angels, and the Gods, which are set there, to their exaltation and glory in all things, as hath been sealed upon their heads, which glory shall be a fullness and a continuation of the seeds for ever and ever.

Then shall they be Gods, because they have no end; therefore shall they be from everlasting to everlasting, because they continue; then shall they be above all, because all things are subject unto them. Then shall they be Gods, because they have all power, and the angels are subject unto them.

Verily, verily I say unto you, except ye abide my law, ye cannot attain to this glory;

For straight is the gate, and narrow the way that leadeth unto the exaltation and continuation of the lives, and few there be that find it, because ye receive me not in the world, neither do ye know me.

But if ye receive me in the world, then shall ye know me, and shall receive your exaltation, that where I am, ye shall be also.

This is eternal lives, to know the only wise and true God, and Jesus Christ, whom he hath sent. I am he. Receive ye, therefore, my law.

Broad is the gate, and wide the way that leadeth to the deaths, and many there are that go in thereat; because they receive me not, neither do they abide in my law.

Verily, verily I say unto you, if a man marry a wife according to my word, and they are sealed by the Holy Spirit of promise, according to mine appointment, and he or she shall commit any sin or transgression of the new and everlasting covenant whatever, and all manner of blasphemies, and if they commit no murder, wherein they shed innocent blood—yet they shall come forth in the first resurrection, and enter into their exaltation; but they shall be destroyed in the flesh, and shall be delivered unto the buffetings of Satan unto the day of redemption, saith the Lord God.

The blasphemy against the Holy Ghost, which shall not be forgiven in the world, nor out of the world, is in that ye commit murder, wherein ye shed innocent blood, and assent unto my death, after ye have received my new and everlasting covenant, saith the Lord God; and he that abideth not this law, can in no wise enter into my glory, but shall be damned, saith the Lord.

I am the Lord thy God, and will give unto thee the law of my Holy Priesthood, as was ordained by me, and my Father, before the world was.

Abraham received all things, whatsoever he received, by revelation and commandment, by my word, saith the Lord, and hath entered into his exaltation, and sitteth upon his throne.

Abraham received promises concerning his seed, and of the fruit of his loins,—from whose loins ye are, namely, my servant Joseph,—which were to continue so long as they were in the world; and as touching Abraham and his seed, out of the world they should continue; both in the world and out of the world should they continue as innumerable as the stars; or, if ye were to count the sand upon the sea shore, ye could not number them.

This promise is yours, also, because ye are of Abraham, and the promise was made unto Abraham; and by this law are the continuation of the works of my Father, wherein he glorifieth himself.

Go ye, therefore, and do the works of Abraham; enter ye into my law, and ye shall be saved.

But if ye enter not into my law ye cannot receive the promise of my Father, which he made unto Abraham.

God commanded Abraham, and Sarah gave Hagar to Abraham to wife. And why did she do it? Because this was the law, and from Hagar sprang many people. This, therefore, was fulfilling among other things, the promises.

Was Abraham, therefore, under condemnation? Verily, I say unto you, Nay; for I, the Lord, commanded it.

Abraham was commanded to offer his son Isaac; nevertheless, it was written, thou shalt not kill. Abraham, however, did not refuse, and it was accounted unto him for righteousness.

Abraham received concubines, and they bear him children, and it was accounted unto him for righteousness, because they were given unto him, and he abode in my law, as Isaac also, and Jacob did none other things than that which they were commanded; and because they did none other things than that which they were commanded, they have entered into their exaltation, according to the promises, and sit upon thrones, and are not angels, but are Gods.

David also received many wives and concubines, as also Solomon and Moses my servants; as also many others of my servants, from the beginning of creation until this time; and in nothing did they sin, save in those things which they received not of me.

David's wives and concubines were given unto him, of me, by the hand of Nathan, my servant, and others of the prophets who had the keys of this power; and in none of these things did he sin against me, save in the case of Uriah and his wife; and, therefore he hath fallen from his exaltation, and received his portion; and he shall not inherit them out of the world; for I gave them unto another, saith the Lord.

I am the Lord thy God, and I gave unto thee, my servant Joseph, an appointment, and restore all things; ask what ye will, and it shall be given unto you according to my word:

And as ye have asked concerning adultery—verily, verily I say unto you, if a man receiveth a wife in the new and everlasting covenant, and if she be with another man, and I have not appointed unto her by the holy anointing, she hath committed adultery, and shall be destroyed.

If she be not in the new and everlasting covenant, and she be with another man, she has committed adultery;

And if her husband be with another woman, and he was under a vow, he hath broken his vow, and hath committed adultery,

And if she hath not committed adultery, but is innocent, and hath not broken her vow, and she knoweth it, and I reveal it unto you, my servant Joseph, then shall you have power, by the power of my Holy Priesthood, to take her, and give her unto him that hath not committed adultery, but hath been faithful; for he shall be made ruler over many;

For I have conferred upon you the keys and power of the Priesthood, wherein I restore all things, and make known unto you all things in due time.

And verily, verily I say unto you, that whatsoever you seal on earth, shall be sealed in heaven; and whatsoever you bind on earth, in my name, and by my word, saith the Lord, it shall be eternally bound in the heavens; and whosesoever sins you remit on earth shall be remitted eternally in the heavens; and whosesoever sins you retain on earth, shall be retained in heaven.

And again, verily I say, whomsoever you bless, I will bless, and whomsoever you curse, I will curse, saith the Lord; for I, the Lord, am thy God.

And again, verily I say unto you, my servant Joseph, that whatsoever you give on earth, and to whomsoever you give anyone on earth, by my word, and according to my law, it shall be visited with blessings, and not cursings, and with my power, saith the Lord, and shall be without condemnation on earth, and in heaven;

For I am the Lord thy God, and will be with thee even unto the end of the world, and through all eternity; for verily, I seal upon you your exaltation, and prepare a throne for you in the kingdom of my Father, with Abraham your father.

Behold, I have seen your sacrifices, and will forgive all your sins; I have seen your sacrifices, in obedience to that which I have told you; go, therefore, and I make a way for your escape, as I accepted the offering of Abraham, of his son Isaac.

Verily, I say unto you, a commandment I give unto mine handmaid, Emma Smith, your wife, whom I have given unto you, that she stay herself, and partake not of that which I commanded you to offer unto her; for I did it, saith the Lord, to prove you all, as I did Abraham; and that I might require an offering at your hand, by covenant and sacrifice;

And let mine handmaid, Emma Smith, receive all those that have been given to my servant Joseph, and who are virtuous and pure before me; and those who are not pure, and have said they were pure, shall be destroyed, saith the Lord God;

For I am the Lord thy God, and ye shall obey my voice; and I give unto you my servant Joseph, that he shall be made ruler over many things, for he hath been faithful over a few things, and from henceforth I will strengthen him.

And I command mine handmaid, Emma Smith, to abide and cleave unto my servant Joseph, and to none else. But if she will not abide this commandment, she shall be destroyed, saith the Lord; for I am the Lord thy God, and will destroy her, if she abide not in my law;

But if she will not abide this commandment, then shall my servant Joseph do all things for her, even as he hath said; and I will bless him and multiply him and give unto him an hundred-fold in this world, of fathers and mothers, brothers and sisters, houses and lands, wives and children, and crowns of eternal lives in the eternal worlds.

And again, verily I say, let mine handmaid forgive my servant Joseph his trespasses; and then shall she be forgiven her trespasses, wherein she has trespassed against me; and I, the Lord thy God, will bless her, and multiply her, and make her heart to rejoice.

And agair, I say, let not my servant Joseph put his property out of his hands, lest an enemy come and destroy him; for Satan seeketh to destroy; for I am the Lord thy God, and he is my servant; and behold! and lo, I am with him, as I was with Abraham, thy father, even unto his exaltation and glory.

Now, as touching the law of the Priesthood, there are many things pertaining thereunto.

Verily, if a man be called of my Father, as was Aaron, by mine own voice, and by the voice of him that sent me: and I have endowed him with the keys of the power of this Priesthood, if he do anything in my name, and according to my law, and by my word, he will not commit sin, and I will justify him.

Let no one, therefore, set on my servant Joseph; for I will justify him; for he shall do the sacrifice which I require at his hands, for his transgressions, saith the Lord your God.

And again, as pertaining to the law of the Priesthood: If any man espouse a virgin, and desire to espouse another, and the first give her consent; and if he espouse the second, and they are virgins, and have vowed to no other man, then he is justified; he cannot commit adultery, for they are given unto him; for he cannot commit adultery with that that belongeth unto him and to no one else;

And if he have ten virgins given unto him by this law, he cannot commit adultery, for they belong to him, and they are given unto him, therefore is he justified.

But if one or either of the ten virgins, after she is espoused, shall be with another man; she has committed adultery, and shall be destroyed; for they are given unto him to multiply and replenish the earth, according to my commandment, and to fulfill the promise which was given by my Father before the foundation of the world; and for their exaltation in the eternal worlds, that they may bear the souls of men; for herein is the work of my Father continued, that he may be glorified.

And again, verily, verily I say unto you, if any man have a wife, who holds the keys of this power, and he teaches unto her the law of my Priesthood, as pertaining to these things, then shall she believe, and administer unto him, or she shall be destroyed, saith the Lord your God, for I will destroy her; for I will magnify my name upon all those who receive and abide in my law.

Therefore, it shall be lawful in me, if she receive not this law, for him to receive all things, whatsoever I, the Lord his God, will give unto him, because she did not administer unto him according to my word; and she then becomes the transgressor; and he is exempt from the law of Sarah, who administered unto Abraham according to the law, when I commanded Abraham to take Hagar to wife.

And now, as pertaining to this law, verily, verily I say unto you, I will reveal more unto you, hereafter; therefore, let this suffice for the present. Behold, I am Alpha and Omega. Amen.

CHAPTER XXI.

CAMP FOLLOWERS.—BANKRUPTCY.

AMONG the most despicable occupations that men engage in, that of camp follower holds a front rank. By plundering the dead, by the practice of extortion upon the living, by taking advantage of the license and reign of terror that follows in the wake of an army, the camp follower plunders the terrified people, not unfrequently claiming to be authorized by the commanders of the army, in order to be more successful in his rapine. Thus he seeks to enrich himself upon the misfortunes and terrors of others and at the expense of the reputation of armies and their commanders. More loathsome are such characters than the vultures that hover about the fields made red by human gore, to glut themselves upon the festering, swollen bodies of the dead. Yet more to be despised than the camp follower is that man who will attach himself to a religious association with a view of profiting in schemes of villainy; and when discovered in his crimes throws the responsibility of his evil doing upon the leaders of said association, claiming that his crimes have been taught to him as a part of his religion! Such men are wholesale character assassins, for by their deeds virtuous communities are brought into disrepute, and reproach is cast upon their religion.

Some such characters had attached themselves to the Saints in Nauvoo and vicinity, and gave a coloring to the charges that were made against The Church, to the effect that the leaders thereof sanctioned stealing, so long as it was practiced on the Gentiles—those not belonging to The Church. Such were the rumors given out by some members of The Church engaged in this infamous business. On the eighteenth of November a nest of such vipers was uncovered at Ramus, near Nauvoo; and they were promptly excommunicated from The Church by the Apostles, who were holding a conference at the place on the date above mentioned. Both Joseph and Hyrum took advantage of the occasion to make affidavits before proper officers of the law to the effect that they had never given their sanction to such infamous doctrine as that attributed to them;* and the Twelve Apostles in an epistle to the public disavowed ever sanctioning the crime of theft.

Hyrum in his affidavit says:

I hereby disavow any sanction, or approbation by me of the crime of theft, or any other evil practice in any person or persons whatever, whereby either the lives or property of our fellow-men may be unlawfully taken or molested; neither are such doings sanctioned or approbated by the First Presidency or any other persons in authority or good standing in The Church, but such acts are altogether in violation of the rules, order and regulations of The Church, contrary to the teachings given in said Church, and the laws of both God and man.

In a public declaration to which Joseph appended his affidavit, the Prophet said:

It has been proclaimed upon the housetops and in the secret chamber, in the public walks and private circles throughout the length and breadth of this vast continent, that stealing by the Latter-day Saints has received my approval; nay, that I have taught them the doctrine, encouraged them in plunder, and led on the van--than which nothing is more foreign from my heart. I disfellowship the perpetrators of all such abominations; they are devils and not Saints, totally unfit for the society of Christians or men. It is true that

---

*Times and Seasons for December, 1841.

some professing to be Latter-day Saints have taught such vile heresies, but all are not Israel that are of Israel; and I want it distinctly understood in all coming time, that The Church over which I have the honor of presiding, will ever set its brows like brass, and its face like steel, against all such abominable acts of villainy and crime.

Nor were the Twelve less forcible in denouncing this iniquity. In an epistle printed at the same time with the above they said:

We know not how to express our abhorrence of such an idea, and can only say it is engendered in hell, founded in falsehood, and is the offspring of the devil; that it is at variance with every principle of righteousness and truth, and will damn all that are connected with it. * * * We further call upon The Church to bring all such characters before the authorities, that they may be tried and dealt with according to the law of God and delivered up to the laws of the land.

About this time, too, there were gangs of robbers operating up and down the Mississippi river from which the Saints suffered, as many of their horses and cattle were stolen; but more serious injury arose from the fact that the acts of these robbers were attributed to the Saints themselves, and did much to prejudice the minds of the public against them.

In the month of December the attempt to build up the town of Warren, located one mile south of Warsaw, was abandoned. As early as the fall of 1839 Daniel S. Witter, a man owning a sawmill at Warsaw, held out inducements to the First Presidency of The Church to settle at or in the vicinity of Warsaw, but the location where the Saints built up Nauvoo was considered preferable. Still Witter, Aldrich, Warren, and others continued to solicit the authorities of The Church to make an attempt to build up a city near Warsaw; and finally, in the spring of 1841, an agreement was entered into between The Church authorities and Witter, Warren and Aldrich—owners of the school section located just south of Warsaw—by which any of the Saints settling on this school section, already surveyed into town lots and called Warren, were to have certain privileges granted them.

In September, Willard Richards was located at Warsaw and made what preparations he could to receive settlers. Some few families of Saints gathered there, and in November two hundred and four emigrants from England were counseled to locate in that vicinity. But no sooner had preparations to build up the place been made than the citizens of Warsaw attempted to form an anti-Mormon association, and manifested other symptoms of an unfriendly character. They raised the rents—Mr. Witter himself raised one dollar per barrel on flour, while Aldrich forbade the people using the old wood on the school section. These unfriendly demonstrations led to the abandonment of the enterprise of building up Warren, and the Church authorities promptly advised the Saints who had located there to remove to Nauvoo.

The winter of 1841-2 was a busy one for Joseph and those who labored with him as his scribes. He read the proof-sheets of the Book of Mormon previous to its being stereotyped; and prepared that concise yet admirable historical sketch of the Rise and Progress of the Church, together with a summary of the principles it teaches—now known as the Articles of Faith—for Mr. Wentworth of Chicago, who was writing a history of Illinois. He also prepared for publication his translation of the Book of Abraham from Egyptian papyrus, and which in its importance as a record of the ancient saints brought to light in this age, stands only second to the Book of Mormon.

The Egyptian papyrus came into the possession of the Prophet through one Michael H. Chandler, who was traveling through Ohio exhibiting several Egyptian mummies and rolls of papyrus that were found in the coffin containing the mummies. Chandler claimed to have obtained the Egyptian treasures as a bequest from an uncle who had traveled in Egypt. But it matters little how Chandler came into possession of the mummies; the Saints in Kirtland purchased them, and the two rolls of papyrus proved to be the writings of Abraham and of Joseph who was sold into Egypt; and the record of Abraham, at least in part, was translated and published by the Prophet. Its importance is of the character above stated.*

These labors, together with instructing the Saints, attending debating schools, laboring in the city council, and organizing and instructing women's Relief Societies, occupied the attention of the Prophet until the opening of spring.

Meantime Nauvoo had been rapidly building up. Work on the temple and Nauvoo House was being pushed with considerable vigor; and many neat cottages had taken the place of the rude temporary cabins that had been constructed to shelter the people until their industry could win better homes. The population in the spring of 1842 was between eight and ten thousand. The stream of emigration from the British mission by that time had commenced to flow in and the new citizens assisted in no small degree to increase the prosperity of this central gathering place of the Saints.

But The Church had passed through a long period of disaster. Time and again the early members of The Church had been driven away from their homes, and while their faith in their religion remained unshaken, these frequent drivings and mobbings stripped them of their property and of course ruined their financial schemes; and though their prospects at Nauvoo began to brighten, the people were constantly plagued by the presentation of old claims upon them, their creditors making

*Those who would know more of this ancient record are referred to the Pearl of Great Price where they will find the translation of it; and for a pretty full consideration of its claims to being a genuine ancient record, and an inspired book, the reader is referred to "The Divine Authenticity of the Book of Abraham," by Elder George Reynolds.

small or no allowance for the disasters which had overtaken them. This was a constant draft upon their resources and a great hindrance to the growth of Nauvoo. Finally, as a means of protection against unreasonable, importunate creditors, a number of the leading brethren, among them the Prophet Joseph, took advantage of the bankrupt law. Under this law any one owing a certain amount more than he was able to pay, made out a schedule of his property and likewise of his debts, and placed both in the hands of an assignee, who paid his creditors whatever percentage of his debts his property amounted to; and the assignor could start again without being compelled to pay any of the old claims held against him previous to his declared insolvency. In whatever light this action on the part of the brethren may appear at first sight, an examination into all the circumstances will reveal the fact that as a means of self-protection it became absolutely necessary. They were financially down, and before they could rise to their feet, inexorable creditors were upon them to take away their substance. If it is possible for an individual or a company to be justified in taking advantage of the bankrupt law, then the Mormon leaders were. There was no effort on the part of those who took advantage of the bankrupt law to defraud their creditors. To parties with whom Joseph had contracted for lands, he wrote that he still considered his contracts with them as good; and in the case of the Hotchkiss purchase he proposed to renew the contract. This step placed the brethren beyond the power of their unjust creditors, and necessity compelled the action

CHAPTER XXII.

SUSPICIONS OF TREACHERY.

AS early as January, 1842, Joseph, as lieutenant-general of the Legion, issued orders for a general military parade and review of the Legion to take place on the seventh of May following. A subsequent order, issued in April, marking out the programme for the day's exercises, contained the following clause:

> At three o'clock p. m. the cohorts will separate and form in line of battle, the brigadiers assume their respective commands, and General Law's command [cavalry] will make a descent upon that of General Rich's [cohort C, infantry] in order of sham battle.

The lieutenant-general had invited the consolidated staff of the Legion to partake of a *repast militaire* on the occasion, at his house.

On the morning of the day appointed for the drill and review two thousand troops were in the field; and an immense concourse of spectators, both of Saints and strangers. Such was the interests taken in the movement of the people of Nauvoo, that a number of the prominent men of the State within reach of the city attended the review. Judge Stephen A. Douglass adjourned the circuit court, then in session at the county seat, Carthage, in order to attend. As soon as the lieutenant-general heard of the presence of Judge Douglass, he sent him an invitation to attend the military dinner given at his house, which the judge accepted.

It was a glorious day, passing off without noise or disorder;

and even the strangers expressed themselves as highly satisfied with what they had witnessed. But even during the brightest days clouds will sometimes drift across the sun's disc: so in the moments of man's supreme happiness, it often occurs that shadows arise to alarm his fears, and remind him how fleeting are the joys of this life—

> Some drops of joy with draughts of ill between;
> Some gleams of sunshine 'mid renewing storms,

are all that he may hope for. So was it with the principal founder of Nauvoo on the day of the sham battle. When the respective cohorts were drawn up in line of battle, facing each other, Major-General John C. Bennett rode up to General Smith and asked him to lead the charge of the first cohort, but Joseph declined. He next asked him to take a position in the rear of the cavalry without his staff during the engagement, but against this Captain A. P. Rockwood, the commander of Joseph's life guard, objected, and Joseph with his staff chose his own position.

Of this incident—and it is for this reason that I have referred to this parade and sham battle—Joseph remarks:

> If General Bennett's true feelings towards me are not made manifest to the world in a very short time then it may be possible that the gentle breathings of that Spirit which whispered to me on parade that there was mischief in that sham battle, were false; a short time will determine the point. Let John C. Bennett answer at the day of judgment, Why did you request me to command one of the cohorts, and also to take my position without my staff, during the sham battle on the seventh of May, 1842, where my life might have been forfeited and no man have known who did the deed?

This is about the first intimation that we have in any of The Church records of John C. Bennett's disaffection towards Joseph or The Church. Two years before he had come to Nauvoo

—then Commerce—filled with that fiery zeal "for the holy faith" which is only known to the newly-made convert. He was a man of considerable learning and ability, and devoted himself assiduously to bring to pass the prosperity of Nauvoo. He was of great service to Joseph as a lieutenant, and the Prophet was wont to say of him that he was about the first man he had about him who could do exactly what he wanted done, the way it should be done, and who would do it at once. In training the Legion and assisting in the drafting of the Nauvoo and other charters, he had rendered invaluable service; and had he possessed qualities of heart equal to those of his mind, he was calculated to have been a valuable acquisition to the city of Nauvoo. Nor am I willing to believe that his motives in uniting himself with The Church were altogether evil, notwithstanding his life previous to his joining The Church was immoral. I am quite willing to believe that when he came to the Saints it was his determination to reform and win for himself an honorable standing among his fellow-men; but the evil habits he had contracted were too strong for his will, and he sought the gratification of his lusts which led to his fall.

Soon after he settled at Nauvoo, he paid his addresses to a respectable young lady of the city, and she, believing him to be an honorable man, accepted them, and he promised to marry her. In the meantime, however, Joseph had received information from the vicinity of Bennett's former residence to the effect that the doctor was a wicked man, and that he had a wife and several children in McConnellsville, Morgan County, Ohio—a thing the doctor had kept concealed. Learning this, Joseph persuaded him to discontinue his attentions to the young lady; but he soon renewed them; whereupon Joseph threatened to expose him if he did not desist, which, to all appearances, had the desired effect.

Being foiled in his advances toward this young lady, and finding that Joseph stood like a lion in his path to prevent the accomplishment of his evil designs and protect the unsuspecting, he drew around him a covering of hypocrisy, carefully concealed his movements from the Prophet, and proceeded to teach some women, who only knew him as an honorable man, that promiscuous intercourse of the sexes was a doctrine believed in by the Latter-day Saints, and that there was no harm in it. In his first efforts he was unsuccessful; but in his subsequent advice, in the same line, he told them that Joseph and others of The Church authorities both sanctioned and practiced this wickedness, saying that the Prophet only denounced such things so vehemently in public, because of the prejudice of the people and the trouble it might create in his own house. In this manner he succeeded in overcoming the scruples of some of his dupes, and seduced several females. Nor did the evil end here. Bennett induced other men to adopt his evil practices; among them Francis M. and Chauncy L. Higbee. These men repeated the assertions made by the doctor, and thus the evil spread, and the reputation of the Prophet was being undermined.

But evils of this character cannot long be practiced without coming to light, and Doctor Bennett, finding that his corruption was about to be uncovered, began to prepare for the shock. When confronted with positive evidence that it was known that he had a wife and family, and that his seductions were also known, he attempted suicide by taking poison, and resisted the administration of antidotes, but he was rescued from this fate in spite of himself.

Before his evil course was known, arrangements were made to run the doctor for representative from the district in which Nauvoo was included, to the State legislature. But one day Joseph met the doctor in the presence of Squire Wells, and addressed him in substance as follows: "Doctor, I can sustain you no longer. Hyrum is against you, the Twelve are against you, and if I do not come out against sin and iniquity I shall myself be trodden under foot as a Prophet of God." That sentence sounded the death knell to the standing of Dr. Bennett in Nauvoo. Joseph had clung to him in the hope of reforming him, but that could no longer be expected; and when the Prophet let go his hold upon him, there was nothing could avert his downfall.

On the nineteenth of May Bennett resigned his position as mayor and Joseph was elected to that office. On this occasion, and before the whole city council, Joseph asked Doctor Bennett if he had anything against him, to which the doctor replied:

> I know what I am about, and the heads of The Church know what they are about, I expect; I have no difficulty with the heads of The Church. I publicly avow that if any one has said that I have stated that General Joseph Smith has given me authority to hold illicit intercourse with women he is a liar in the face of God. Those who have said it are damned liars; they are infernal liars. He never either in public or private gave me any such authority or license, and any person who states it is a scoundrel and a liar. * * * I intend to continue with you, and hope the time may come when I may be restored to full confidence and fellowship, and my former standing in The Church, and that my conduct may be such as to warrant my restoration, and should the time ever come that I may have the opportunity to test my faith, it will then be known whether I am a traitor or a true man.
>
> *Joseph*—Will you please state definitely whether you know anything against my character, either in public or private.
>
> *Doctor Bennett*—I do not. In all my intercourse with General Smith in public and in private he has been strictly virtuous.

In addition to this statement before the city council, Doctor Bennett made affidavit before Squire Wells to the same effect as the above.

On the twenty-sixth of May, the case of Bennett came up in the Masonic lodge, of which the doctor was a member, as were also nearly all the principal men of Nauvoo. In the presence of one hundred of the fraternity, he confessed his licentious practices, and acknowledged that he was worthy of the severest chastisement, yet he pleaded for mercy, and especially that he might not be published in the papers. So deep, apparently, was his sorrow, that Joseph pleaded for mercy in his behalf, and he was forgiven as a Mason; but previous to this, the First Presidency of The Church, the Twelve and the Bishop had sent a formal notice to him that they could not fellowship him as a member of The Church, but they withheld the matter from publication, at his earnest solicitation, because of his mother.

John C. Bennett, however, had fallen too far to recover from the effects of his deep transgression. He suddenly left Nauvoo, and soon afterward was found plotting with the enemies of the Saints for the destruction of The Church. By this time the Masonic lodge found that he was an expelled Mason, and had palmed himself off on the Nauvoo lodge as a Mason in regular standing, consequently he was disfellowshiped from the Nauvoo lodge, and was also cashiered by the court-martial of the Nauvoo Legion; and thus plucked of all his glory, he was left to wander as a vagabond and an outcast among men.

After he so suddenly left Nauvoo, he again said that the Prophet Joseph had authorized and encouraged sexual wickedness, and when confronted with his own affidavit, which declared Joseph to be a virtuous man, and a teacher of righteousness, and upright both in his public and private character, he claimed that he was under duress when he made that affidavit. But Squire Wells, before whom he had qualified to make his sworn statement, went before a justice of the peace, and made affidavit that during the time that this development of his wickedness was going on, and he making statements favorable to Joseph and The Church, that—

During all this time, if he (Doctor Bennett) was under duress or fear, he must have had a good faculty of concealing it; for he was at liberty to go and come when and where he pleased, so far as I am capable of judging.

Squire Wells further testifies in the same statement:

I was always personally friendly with him, after I became acquainted with him. I never heard him say anything derogatory to the character of Joseph Smith, until after he had been exposed by said Smith on the public stand in Nauvoo.

So soon as it was learned that the doctor had left Nauvoo, and was operating for the destruction of The Church, the whole case was published in the Nauvoo papers, and his corruption made known to the world. Those whom he had involved in his vile snares, both men and women, were brought before the proper tribunals of The Church; some of them were disfellowshiped, and others who sincerely repented were forgiven.

The only description I have seen of Doctor Bennett is given in the Essex County *Washingtonian*, published in Salem, Massachusetts, and that is contained in the issue of the fifteenth of September, 1842. According to that description he was a man five feet nine inches high, well formed, black hair sprinkled with grey, dark complexion, a rather thin face, and black, restless eyes.

The fall of Doctor Bennett added another evidence to the fact that neither natural nor acquired attainments, however brilliant they may be, can secure one a safe standing in the Church of Jesus Christ of Latter-day Saints, when not accompanied with righteousness of life. Moreover, experience has proven that to brilliancy of intellect highly cultivated, may be added inspired dreams, visions, the revelations of God, and the visitation of angels—and yet, if the daily life and conversation runs not hand in hand with righteousness, these things furnish at best but an insecure foundation on which to stand.

CHAPTER XXIII.

ATTEMPTED ASSASSINATION OF GOVERNOR BOGGS.

IT was rumored in Nauvoo about the middle of the month of May, 1842, that ex-Governor Boggs, of Missouri, had been assassinated by an unknown hand, at his residence in Independence, Jackson County, Missouri. The ex-governor, however, did not die from the wounds he received, but recovered in the course of several days. The assault made upon him by his enemy, whoever he might be, occurred on the sixth of May, in the year above named. He was seated in a room by himself, when some person discharged a pistol loaded with buckshot, through the adjoining window. Three of the shot took effect in his head—one of which, it was said, penetrated his brain. His son, hearing the shot, burst into the room and found him in a helpless condition. The pistol from which the shot was fired was found under the window, and there, too, were the footprints of the would-be assassin.

No sooner was the news of the affair heard than speculation was rife as to the parties who had perpetrated the deed; and in consequence of the infamous part taken by Boggs in driving the Saints from the State of Missouri, during the period that he was governor, it was not long before "Joe Smith and the Mormons" were accused of the deed. The Quincy *Whig*, in its issue of May 21st, said:

There are several rumors in circulation in regard to the horrid affair; one of which throws the crime upon the Mormons, from the fact, we suppose, that Mr. Boggs was governor at the time, and in no small degree instrumental in driving them from the State. Smith, too, the Mormon Prophet, as we understand, prophesied a year or so ago, his death by violent means. Hence, there is plenty of foundation for rumor.

To this statement the Prophet Joseph wrote a reply and sent it to the editor of the *Whig*, Mr. Bartlett:

DEAR SIR—In your paper of the 21st inst.,[May] you have done me manifest injustice, in ascribing to me a prediction of the demise of Lilburn W. Boggs, Esq., ex-governor of Missouri, by violent hands. Boggs was a candidate for the State senate, and, I presume, fell by the hand of a political opponent, with his hands and face yet dripping with the blood of murder; but he died* not through my instrumentality. My hands are clean and my heart pure, from the blood of all men.

As soon as Boggs recovered sufficiently, he went before Samuel Weston, a justice of the peace at Independence, and one of the characters that some of my readers of "The Missouri Persecutions" will remember as taking part in driving the Saints from their homes in Jackson County—before him Boggs made affidavit that he had reason to believe, from evidence and information then in his possession, that "Joseph Smith, the Mormon Prophet, was accessory before the fact of the intended murder;" and therefore applied to Thomas Reynolds, governor of Missouri, to make a demand on the governor of Illinois, to deliver Joseph Smith up to some person authorized to receive him on behalf of the State of Missouri, to be dealt with according to law.

Governor Reynolds promptly granted the request and made the demand on the governor of Illinois for the surrender of Joseph to one E. R. Ford, who was appointed the agent of

---

* It was then supposed that Boggs was dead. It was not until several days later that the news of his recovery reached Nauvoo or Quincy.

Missouri to receive him. In making the demand, Governor Reynolds said:

> Whereas it appears * * * that one Joseph Smith is a fugitive from justice, charged with being accessory before the fact, to an assault with intent to kill, made by one O. P. Rockwell, on Lilburn W. Boggs, in this State [Missouri]; and is represented to the executive department of this State as having fled to the State of Illinois; Now, therefore, I, * * * do by these presents demand the surrender and delivering of the said Joseph Smith, etc., etc.

We have given this extract for the requisition *verbatim*, because, in the first place, the affidavit of Boggs, upon the strength of which Governor Reynolds made his demand for the surrender of Joseph Smith, does not claim that he was a fugitive from justice, or that he had fled from the State of Missouri to Illinois; but on the contrary, the affidavit says that he was a "citizen or resident of Illinois," hence the statement of fact in the affidavit was not sufficient to justify the demand for Joseph Smith to be surrendered to Missouri. A person resident in a State may not be delivered up to the authorities of another State for alleged offenses, unless it is represented that he has fled from the State making the demand for his surrender, to escape from justice. This charge was not made by Boggs in his affidavit, which was Governor Reynolds' only authority for making the demand. But in what Boggs failed, Governor Reynolds made up; and upon his own responsibility, charged in his demand on Illinois that Joseph Smith was "a fugitive from justice," and had "fled to Illinois;" a statement that was at once untrue, and wholly gratuitous on the part of the executive of Missouri, and proves him to be a willing persecutor of the innocent. Secondly, it was this assumption on the part of Reynolds that did much towards making the demand on Illinois void. But more of this anon.

Governor Carlin, of Illinois, respected the demand of Missouri, and issued a warrant for the arrest of O. P. Rockwell as principal and Joseph Smith as accessory before the fact, in an assault with intent to kill, upon ex-Governor Boggs. The papers were placed in the hands of the deputy sheriff of Adams County,who,with two assistants, at once repaired to Nauvoo, and on the eighth of August, 1842, arrested the above named parties. There was no evasion of the officers, but the municipal court of Nauvoo, at once, on the application of the parties arrested, issued a writ of *habeas corpus*, requiring the officers having the prisoners in charge, to bring them before that tribunal, in order that the legality of the warrant under which they were arrested might be tested. This the sheriff refused to do, as he claimed that the municipal court had no jurisdiction in the case, but he left the prisoners in the care of the city marshal,without, however, leaving the original writ upon which alone they could be held; and the deputy sheriff and his assistants returned to Quincy; the prisoners being turned loose to go about their business.

During the absence of the deputy sheriff, Joseph had secured a writ of *habeas corpus* from the master in chancery, as it was questionable if the municipal court of Nauvoo had the authority to issue such writs in cases arising under the laws of the State or the United States.* The officers returned from Quincy on the tenth, but in the interim it had been decided by Joseph and his friends, that the best thing for himself and Rockwell to do under the excitement of public sentiment then exist-

---

* I say "questionable" as representing the views of the Prophet's friends. As a matter of fact, in my judgment, there could be no question about the municipal court having no such power. And if the letter of the Nauvoo charter justified the idea that the municipal court possessed any such power to interrupt the process of the State and United States courts, it was a manifest defect in the wording of the charter, a solecism that would render that part of the charter void.

ing was to keep out of the way for a season; so that the officers were unable to find them on their return.

Joseph crossed the river and stayed at his uncle John's house for a few days, in the settlement called Zarahemla; but on the night of the eleventh of August, he met by appointment his brother Hyrum, Rockwell, his wife Emma and several other friends at the south point of the island that stands midway in the river between Nauvoo and Montrose.

It had been rumored that the governor of Iowa had also issued a warrant for the arrest of Joseph and Rockwell, whereupon it was decided that it would be better for them to remain on the Illinois side of the river. Subsequent events, however, proved that this rumor was a false one. Joseph was rowed up the river by a Brother Dunham to a point near the home of a Brother Derby. Rockwell had been set ashore and had proceeded to the same point on foot, where he built a fire on the bank of the river, that Dunham might know where to land. At Derby's, the Prophet remained in hiding for some time, and Rockwell went east, remaining for several months in Pennsylvania and New Jersey.

From his place of concealment, Joseph directed the movements of the people at Nauvoo, and managed his own business through faithful agents, who met with him occasionally. Emma spent considerable of her time with him, and beguiled the loneliness of those weary hours of inactivity that he, whose life is the synonym for activity, had to endure.

During those days of exile, one gets a glimpse of the Prophet's private life and character, that in part explains the mystery of his power and influence over his friends and his people: —it was his unbounded love for them. Speaking of the meeting with his friends in the night at the island, in the account he gives of it in the Book of the Law of the Lord, he says:

How glorious were my feelings when I met that faithful and friendly band, on the night of the eleventh [of August], on the island at the mouth of the slough between Zarahemla and Nauvoo. With what unspeakable delight, and what transports of joy swelled my bosom, when I took by the hand, on that night, my beloved Emma—she that was my wife, even the wife of my youth, and choice of my heart. Many were the vibrations of my mind when I contemplated for a moment the many scenes we had been called to pass through, the fatigues and the toils, the sorrows and sufferings, and the joys and the consolations, from time to time, which had strewed our paths and crowned our board. Oh, what a commingling of thoughts filled my mind for the moment!—and again she is here, even in the seventh trouble—undaunted, firm and unwavering—unchangeable, affectionate Emma!

Of his brother Hyrum on the same occasion he says:

There was Brother Hyrum, who next took me by the hand—a natural brother. Thought I to myself, Brother Hyrum, what a faithful heart you have got! Oh, may the Eternal Jehovah crown eternal blessings upon your head, as a reward for the care you have had for my soul! Oh, how many are the sorrows we have shared together! and again we find ourselves shackled by the unrelenting hand of oppression. Hyrum, thy name shall be written in the Book of the Law of the Lord, for those who come after to look upon, that they may pattern after thy works.*

So he goes on to call the faithful by their names and record their deeds of love manifested towards himself, and pronounces his blessings upon them; and if, as one of old said, "We know that we have passed from death unto life because we love the brethren"—surely Joseph Smith possessed that witness—he loved his brethren better than his life!

---

* Some years before this, in December, 1835, Joseph said of Hyrum: "I could pray in my heart that all men were like my brother Hyrum, who possesses the mildness of a lamb, and the integrity of a Job, and in short, the meekness and humility of Christ; and I love him with that love that is stronger than death, for I never had occasion to rebuke him, nor he me."—Mill. Star, vol. vx. p. 521.

Some of the brethren proposed that Joseph should go up to the pine woods of Wisconsin, where a number of the brethren were engaged in getting out timber for the Temple and Nauvoo House, until the excitement should subside in Illinois. Of this proposition, Joseph said in a letter to Emma:

> My mind will eternally revolt at every suggestion of that kind. * * * My safety is with you if you want to have it so. * * * If I go to the pine country, you shall go along with me, and the children; and if you and the children go not with me, I don't go. I do not wish to exile myself for the sake of my own life. I would rather fight it out. It is for your sakes therefore that I would do such a thing.

This plan, however, was abandoned.

CHAPTER XXIV.

THE PROPHET'S TRIAL AT SPRINGFIELD—MISSOURI AGAIN THWARTED.

IT appears that Joseph had resolved to submit no longer to the injustice he had suffered from the hands of the people of Missouri. It was rumored that the officers on leaving Nauvoo, breathed out threats of returning with sufficient force to search every house in the city and vicinity; and Sheriff Ford, the agent of Missouri, threatened to bring a mob against the Mormons, if necessary to arrest the Prophet. Hearing these rumors, Joseph exchanged several letters with William Law, who had been recently elected major-general of the Legion, *vice* John C. Bennett, cashiered; in which he admonished him to have all things in readiness to protect the people in their rights, and not for one moment to submit to the outrages that were threatened.

"You will see, therefore," said he, in a letter written on the fourteenth of August, to Law, "that the peace of the city of Nauvoo is kept, let who will, endeavor to disturb it. You will also see that whenever any mob force or violence is used, on any citizen thereof, or that belongeth thereunto, you will see that force or violence is immediately dispersed, and brought to punishment, or meet it, and contest it at the point of the sword, with firm, undaunted and unyielding valor; and let them know that the spirit of old Seventy-six, and of George Washington yet lives, and is contained in the bosoms and blood of the children of the fathers thereof. If there are any threats in the city, let legal steps be taken against them; and let no man, woman or child be intimidated, nor suffer it to be done. Nevertheless, as I said in the first place, we will take every measure that lays in our power, and make every sacrifice that God or man could require at our hands, to preserve the peace and safety of the people without collision."

To these sentiments there was a willing response of acquiescence on the part of the major-general, and he pledged himself to faithfully carry out Joseph's orders, provided the emergency for doing so should arise. After a little, however, the excitement began to subside; and as Joseph's hiding place at Derby's was discovered by a young man who suddenly came upon him and his kind host while they were walking out in the woods for exercise, the Prophet moved quietly into the city, staying first at the house of one friend a day or two, and then removing to that of another.

In the meantime the case was plainly placed before Governor Carlin; and the course that Joseph had taken fully vindicated by letters written to him by Emma his wife, who displayed no mean ability in the correspondence she opened up with the governor, which so nearly concerned the peace of her family. She directed the attention of the governor to the fact that Joseph had not been in the State of Missouri for some three or four years—that if her husband had been accessory before the fact, to the assault upon ex-Governor Boggs, the crime, if committed at all—which she stoutly averred was not the case—was done in Illinois, and there was no law to drag a man from a State where the crime was committed, into a State where it had not been committed, for trial; and as her husband had not been in the State of Missouri for several years previous to the assault on Boggs, he could not have fled from the justice of that State, and therefore ought not to be given up under the fugitive-from-justice law.

Letters from many prominent citizens of Nauvoo were also sent to the governor; and the Female Relief Society called his attention to the threat of mob violence and invasion from Missouri, and asked that sufficient military protection might be given to insure the peace and safety of Nauvoo. All these things the governor treated lightly, and claimed that the only excitement that existed was with the Mormon people at Nauvoo, and nowhere else; and there was no need, he insisted, of taking the precautions hinted at by the people; though when talking on another subject he unwittingly remarked that persons were offering their services every day either in person or by letter, and held themselves in readiness to go against the Saints whenever he should call upon them; but he never had the least idea of calling on the militia, neither had he thought it necessary. He maintained that the proper thing for Joseph to do was to give himself up to the authorities of Missouri for trial, and he had no doubt that he would be acquitted. Judge Ralston asked him how he thought Mr. Smith would go through the midst of his enemies without being subject to violence; and how after his acquittal, he would be able to return to Illinois. To that proposition the governor could give no satisfactory answer, but made light of the whole matter. And in spite of all the protests sent in by the people of Nauvoo, he made a proclamation that as Joseph Smith and O. P. Rockwell had resisted the laws, by refusing to go with the officers who had them in custody, and had made their escape, he offered a reward of two hundred dollars for each or either of those "fugitives from justice." Governor Reynolds also offered a reward for their arrest, three hundred dollars for each one or either of them.

Joseph continued to remain in the city and moved about cautiously, attending to his business. A tide of popular prejudice had set in of such proportions that it seemed that it would overwhelm the Saints. It had been created largely through the misrepresentations of John C. Bennett, and Joseph at once determined to counteract it if possible. He ordered that a special conference be called to meet on the 29th of August, to appoint Elders of The Church to go through the State of Illinois and the east to flood the country with the truth in relation to Bennett's character. The conference was called, and in the interim documents and affidavits were prepared that the brethren might be armed with proofs in relation to the facts respecting Bennett and his misrepresentations.

The conference convened on the day appointed and Hyrum Smith addressed them on the mission that many of them were expected to take. At the conclusion of his remarks, Joseph suddenly stepped into the stand to the great joy of his people, many of whom thought he had gone to Washington, and others to Europe. His appearance created great cheerfulness and animation among the people. Joseph, naturally impulsive, was overjoyed to again stand before the Saints. He addressed them in more than his usual spirited manner and called upon the brethren to go through the States taking documents with them, "to show to the world the corrupt and oppressive conduct of Boggs, Carlin and others, that the public might have the truth laid before them." In response to this call to sustain the Prophet's character, three hundred and eighty Elders volunteered their services, and announced their willingness to go immediately.

For several days after the conference the Prophet continued about home, but it being revealed to him that his enemies were again on the move to take him, he found it necessary to drop out of sight. It was during this time of hiding that he wrote those instructions respecting baptism for the dead, contained in the 127th and 128th sections of the Book of Doctrine and Covenants.

But notwithstanding his enemies were on the watch for him, he now and then visited his home; and on the occasion of paying one of these visits to his family he nearly fell into the hands of the officers. He was at dinner with his family at the "Mansion," when Deputy Sheriff Pitman, of Adams County, and an assistant suddenly presented themselves at the door. Fortunately John Boynton, who was present, saw them first and went to the door to meet them. They asked him if Joseph Smith was present, to which he gave an evasive answer, saying that he had seen Joseph that morning, but did not say he had seen him since. During this conversation the Prophet stepped out of the back door, ran through the corn in his garden and so to the house of Bishop N. K. Whitney. Emma now engaged the sheriff in conversation. He said he wanted to search the house. She asked if he had a search warrant, to which he answered in the negative; but insisted on searching the house nevertheless, and as she knew that Joseph had escaped, she did not refuse. Of course the search was fruitless.

It was reported that a party of fifteen left Quincy with the sheriff the day before, and that they rode all night expecting to reach Nauvoo before daylight, surround the "Mansion," and capture Joseph. But in the night they got scattered and did not meet again, nor did Sheriff Pitman reach Nauvoo until about noon, when he made the effort above detailed.

About the first of October, Elder Rigdon and Elias Higbee were in Carthage, and from a conversation with Judge Douglass, they learned that Governor Carlin had purposely issued an illegal writ for the arrest of Joseph, thinking he would go to Carthage to be acquitted on *habeas corpus* proceedings before Judge Douglass; when an officer of the State would be present with a legal writ and serve it upon him immediately, and thus drag him to Missouri. The plot, however, was discovered in time to thwart it, and Joseph, in company with Elder John Taylor, Wilson Law and John D. Parker, left Nauvoo for the home of Elder Taylor's father, about a day and a half's ride from Nauvoo, and there the Prophet remained for about a week.

Meantime, through Major Warren, master in chancery, Joseph's case was presented to Justice Butterfield, of Chicago, and United States attorney for the district of Illinois. He wrote out an elaborate review of the case in which he claimed that Joseph could be released on a writ of *habeas corpus;* that he would have the right to prove that he was not in Missouri at the time the alleged crime was committed—that of necessity, if he was guilty of the crime with which he was charged, he must have committed it in Illinois, and therefore was not a fugitive from justice—and the governor of Illinois had no right to surrender him to the authorities of Missouri as such. Mr. Butterfield contended that a warrant for the action of the governor of a State, in delivering up a person to the authorities of another State, was found in that clause of the Constitution which says:

> A person charged in any State with treason, felony or other crime, who shall flee from justice, and be found in another State, shall, on demand of the executive authority of the State from which he fled, be delivered up, to be removed to the State having jurisdiction of the crime. (Constitution, Article 4; Section 2.)

Mr. Butterfield insisted that it was unnecessary to inquire into the laws that had been enacted by Congress on the subject, since:

> Congress has just so much power and no more than is expressly given by the said clause in the Constitution.

"What persons, then," he inquires, "can be surrendered up by the governor of one State to the governor of another?"

> First: He must be a person charged with treason, felony or other crime. It is sufficient if he be charged with the commission of crime, either by indictment found or by affidavit. Second: He must be a person who shall flee from justice, and be found in another State. It is not sufficient to satisfy this branch of the Constitution, that he should be "charged" with having fled from justice. Unless he has actually fled from the State, where the offense was committed, into another State, the governor of this State has no jurisdiction over his person and cannot deliver him up.

Mr. Butterfield reviewed the subject of *habeas corpus* writs and their operations both in England and the United States, and quoted a number of cases from the courts of New York, and the action of the executives of the several States to support the principles he contended for, and concluded his communication in these words:

> I would advise that Mr. Smith procure respectable and sufficient affidavits to prove beyond all question that he was in this State [Illinois] and not in Missouri at the time the crime with which he was charged was committed, and upon these affidavits, apply to the governor to countermand the warrant he has issued for his arrest. If he should refuse so to do, I am already of the opinion that, upon that state of facts, the supreme court will discharge him upon *habeas corpus.*

Joseph acted upon this advice, and sent agents with all the necessary papers to Springfield and applied to Governor Ford—Carlin's term of office in the meantime having expired—to revoke the writ and proclamation of ex-Governor Carlin for his arrest. The supreme court being in session, Governor Ford submitted the petition and all the papers pertaining thereto for their opinion, and they were unanimous in their belief that the Missouri writ was illegal, but were divided as to whether it would be proper for the present executive to interfere with the official acts of his predecessor, and therefore Governor Ford refused to interfere; but said, in a personal letter addressed to the Prophet:

> I can only advise that you submit to the laws and have a judicial investigation of your rights. If it should become necessary, for this purpose to repair to Springfield, I do not believe that there will be any disposition to use illegal violence towards you; and I would feel it my duty in your case, as in the case of any other person, to protect you with any necessary amount of force, from mob violence whilst asserting your rights before the courts, going to and returning.

This reply was endorsed by Mr. Butterfield and James

Adams, in whom Joseph had great confidence; and in conformity with the advice, Joseph was arrested by Wilson Law, on Carlin's proclamation. Application was made at Carthage for a writ of *habeas corpus* to go before the court at Springfield. No writ could be obtained at the court in Carthage, as the clerk had been elected to the State senate; but an order for such writ was issued on the master in chancery, and with that document Joseph, in the company of his brother Hyrum, John Taylor and others, and in charge of Wilson Law, started for Springfield, where they arrived in the afternoon of the thirtieth of December, 1842.

Judge Pope had continued his court two or three days in order to give Joseph's case a hearing, and in the first interview the judge had with him, agreed to try the case on its merits, and not dismiss it on any technicality. The deputy sheriff of Adams County was present, but refused at first to say whether he had the original writ or not; but finally King, his associate, admitted he had it.

Fearing that it was the object of these men to hold the original writ until after proceedings had concluded on the arrest made by virtue of Governor Carlin's proclamation, and thus create more trouble, a petition was made to Governor Ford to issue a new writ, that the case might come up on its merits, which was granted, and Joseph was arrested by Mr. Maxey, and a writ of *habeas corpus* was issued by the court; but as several days must elapse before a hearing could be had, Joseph was placed under $4,000 bonds, Wilson Law and General James Adams being his bondsmen.

At last the day of trial came on and the attorney-general of the State made the following objection to the jurisdiction of the court:

1. The arrest and detention of Smith, was not under or by color of authority of the United States, or of any officer of the United

States, but under and by color of authority of the State of Illinois, by the officer of the State of Illinois.

2. When a fugitive from justice is arrested by authority of the governor of any State, upon the requisition of the governor of another State, the courts of justice, neither State nor Federal, have any authority or jurisdiction to inquire into facts behind the writ.

These points were ably argued *pro* and *con* by Mr. Butterfield for the defense, and the attorney-general for the State. After giving a patient hearing, the court gave its opinion, saying in relation to the first objection, that, "The warrant on its face purports to be issued in pursuance of the Constitution and laws of the United States, as well as of the State of Illinois;" and therefore the court had jurisdiction.

"The matter in hand," said Judge Pope, "presents a case arising under the second section of article IV of the Constitution of the United States, and an act of Congress of February 12th, 1793, to carry it into effect. The Constitution says: 'The judicial power shall extend to all cases in law or equity arising under this Constitution, the laws of the United States, and treaties made, and which shall be made under their authority.'"

Therefore, on that line of reasoning, the judge concluded the court had jurisdiction. As to the second objection—the right of the court to inquire into facts behind the writ—the judge held it unnecessary to decide that point, as Smith was entitled to his discharge, for defect in the affidavit on which the demand for his surrender to Missouri was made. To justify the demand for his arrest the affidavit should have shown, "First, that Smith committed a crime; second, that he committed it in Missouri. And it must also appear 'that Smith had fled from Missouri.'" None of these things the affidavit of Boggs did, and the judge held that it was defective for those reasons, and added:

The court can alone regard the facts set forth in the affidavit of

Boggs as having any legal existence. The mis-recitals and over-statements in the requisition and warrant are not supported by oath and cannot be received as evidence to deprive a citizen of his liberty, and transport him to a foreign State for trial. For these reasons, Smith must be discharged.

And Joseph had scored another victory over his old enemies in Missouri.

CHAPTER XXV.

INCIDENTS OF THE TRIAL AND ACQUITTAL.

DURING the trial, excitement at times ran high and threatened to break out into acts of violence. When Joseph first made his way through the throng about the courthouse, some one in the crowd recognized him, and exclaimed: "There goes Smith now!" "Yes," said another, "and a fine looking man he is, too." "And as damned a rascal as ever lived!" put in a third. Hyrum Smith, overhearing the last remark said: "And a good many ditto!" "Yes," said the person addressed, "ditto, ditto, G—d d—n you, and every one that takes his part is as d—d a rascal as he is." "I am that man;" shouted Wilson Law, "and I'll take his part!" Whereupon both parties prepared for a fight; but Mr. Prentice, the marshal, interfered and quelled the disturbance; and the excitement soon quieted down.

During the progress of the trial the Prophet had good opportunity of associating with some of the leading men of the State, among them the judges of the supreme court, and Governor Ford, who ventured to caution the Prophet to have nothing to do with electioneering in political contests; a thing, the Prophet said in reply, he had never done. Governor Ford also told him that he had a requisition from the governor of Missouri for the arrest of himself and others on the old charge of treason, arson, etc., but he happened to know that the charges were dead. The State legislature was also in session and consequently there was a general gathering of the principal men of Illinois, and the Prophet extended largely his circle of acquaintances among them.

The time occupied by the trial kept Joseph and his party over one Sunday in Springfield, and the use of the hall of representatives was tendered him in which to hold religious services. The use of the hall was accepted and Orson Hyde preached in the forenoon, and Elder John Taylor in the afternoon; the services being largely attended by members of the legislature.

It required several days to make the journey from Springfield to Nauvoo, and the Prophet's party suffered no little from the extreme coldness of the weather. The news of Joseph's triumph had preceded him, and as his party approached the city, of which he was the chief founder, the people turned out almost *en masse* to bid him welcome to his home; and though there was little or none of the pomp and circumstance and splendor that attend the welcome of a king by his subjects, yet never did king receive more hearty or sincere welcome from his people than did Joseph from the citizens of Nauvoo.

The day following his return home the Prophet issued invitations to the Twelve Apostles and their wives and other leading citizens to attend a feast at his house in honor of his release from his enemies. The Twelve at the same time issued a proclamation inviting the Saints in Nauvoo to unite with them in dedicating Tuesday, the seventeenth of January, 1843, as "a day of humiliation, fasting, praise, prayer and thanksgiving before the Great Eloheim," because of the deliverance He had wrought out for His servant. The Bishops were instructed to provide suitable places in their respective wards for the people to meet in, and one or more of the brethren who had been with Joseph at Springfield, would be present to relate what had happened.

Although to relate here the circumstances that befell the man who was accused as the chief actor in the assault upon ex-Governor Boggs—O. P. Rockwell—takes us beyond many events of which we desire to speak, we think it proper to record how, after spending several months in the eastern States, he returned to St. Louis where he was recognized by Elias Parker, who made affidavit that he was the O. P. Rockwell advertised for in the papers, and on the fourth of March, 1843, was arrested by Mr. Fox, and taken to Independence for trial. Rockwell wrote from his prison in Independence to Bishop N. K. Whitney, for bail, which was fixed at five thousand dollars; but as the court in Missouri would only take some responsible person resident in Missouri, bail could not be secured for him.

I have not the space to give a detailed account of all Rockwell's adventures and sufferings during his weary imprisonment of nearly eight months. He suffered much cruelty in prison life, and when his case came before the grand jury there wasn't sufficient evidence to justify an indictment against him. But in the meantime he had made an effort to escape, and was held on a charge of jail-breaking, for which, when he came to be tried, he was sentenced to five minutes' imprisonment, though they kept him for several hours while an effort was made to trump up new charges against him.

One incident occurred during Rockwell's imprisonment that we can not pass without notice. Sheriff Reynolds made an effort to induce him to go to Nauvoo, and as the Prophet Joseph had great confidence in him, Reynolds' proposition was that he should drive Joseph in a carriage outside of Nauvoo, where the Missourians could capture him; and then, as to himself, he could either remain in Illinois, return to Missouri or go where he pleased. "You only deliver Joe Smith into our hands," said Reynolds, "and name your pile." "I will see you all damned first, and then I won't," replied Rockwell.

After meeting with many adventures he arrived in Nauvoo on an evening when there was a social party in progress at the Prophet's house. In the midst of the festivities Joseph observed a rough-looking man with long hair falling down over his shoulders, staggering among his guests as if intoxicated, and the suspicion arose at once that he was a Missourian. Joseph quietly spoke to the captain of police who was present, and told him to put the stranger out. A struggle ensued, and during its progress the Prophet had a full view of the man's face, and at once recognized his devoted friend O. P. Rockwell. It is needless to say he was given a hearty welcome or that the story of his adventures among the Missourians contributed no little to the enjoyment of the evening, though some portions of his narrative were so burdened with accounts of his sufferings and the cruelties practiced towards him, that they were calculated to produce sorrow rather than joy. But these feelings were banished by the fact that he was now delivered out of them all, and honorably discharged in fulfillment of the prophecy uttered by Joseph shortly after he heard of Rockwell's arrest in St. Louis, nearly a year before. The party which had been so rudely yet so pleasantly interrupted, proceeded, no one enjoying it more than the "long-haired stranger."

A few days, only, after the departure from Springfield of the Prophet and his party, John C. Bennett arrived there. The measures he then set on foot, and which produced, ultimately, what very nearly became serious results, may be judged from the following letter addressed to Sidney Rigdon and Orson Pratt, under date of January 10, 1843:

DEAR FRIENDS—It is a long time since I have written to you, and I should now much desire to see you; but I leave tonight for Missouri, to meet the messenger charged with the arrest of Joseph Smith, Hyrum Smith, Lyman Wight and others, for murder, burglary, treason, etc., etc., and who will be demanded in a few days on new indictments found by a grand jury of a called court on the original evidence, and in relation to which a *nolle prosequi* was entered by the district attorney.

New proceedings have been gotten up on the old charges, and no *habeas corpus* can then save them. We shall try Smith on the Boggs case, when we get him into Missouri. The war goes bravely on; and although Smith thinks he is now safe, the enemy is near, even at the door. He has awoke the wrong passenger. The governor will relinquish Joe up at once on the new requisition. There is but one opinion on the case, and that is, nothing can save Joe on the new requisition and demand, predicated on the old charges on the institution of new writs. He must go to Missouri; but he will not be harmed if he is not guilty; but he is a murderer, and must suffer the penalty of the law. Enough on this subject.

I hope that both of your amiable families are well, and you will please to give to them all my best respects. I hope to see you soon. When the officer arrives I shall be near at hand. I shall see you all again. Please write me at Independence immediately.

This letter was handed by Orson Pratt to Joseph, and was read by him to Sidney Rigdon and the company which gathered at the Nauvoo Mansion to celebrate the Prophet's release by a feast, to the discomfiture of Sidney Rigdon, who of course was averse to having it known that he held any correspondence with Bennett. The action of Orson Pratt in this matter paved the way for his return to his position in The Church, for he had been suspended from his quorum in the Priesthood, having been led to oppose the counsels and falsely accuse the Prophet, in consequence of the misrepresentations and malicious schemes of John C. Bennett. But after the above incident, he was re-baptized by the Prophet and received back into the quorum of the Apostles in full confidence and fellowship.

Meantime Nauvoo was growing. At this period—the winter of 1843—her inhabitants are variously computed from twelve to sixteen thousand. Her public buildings, chiefly the Temple and the Nauvoo House, were progressing rapidly. More pretentious buildings were being erected, and new additions to the original town plat were made, and the city, early in December, 1842, had been divided, ecclesiastically, into ten wards, and Bishops were appointed by the High Council to preside over each. The city council was active in passing ordinances to meet the growing necessities of a rapidly increasing population, looking especially to the cleanliness, health and morality of the city. In February, 1843, Joseph was elected a second time to be mayor, and all things considered, Nauvoo was rapidly approaching the high water mark of her prosperity.

CHAPTER XXVI.

DOCTRINAL DEVELOPMENT AT NAUVOO—INTERPRETATION OF THE SCRIPTURES.

AFTER the effort of the Prophet's enemies to drag him into Missouri on the charge of being an accessory before the fact in an attempt upon the life of ex-Governor Boggs, Nauvoo was granted a blessed season of peace, lasting from January, 1843, to the month of June following. It is well to note the circumstance, for Nauvoo had few such periods. Peace is essential to the growth of cities. Commerce flees from strife; and trade sinks into decay where conflicts distract the people. Nauvoo was favorably located and no city in the inland-West gave better promise of becoming an important center of domestic commerce, manufactures, and inland and river trade. With peace it could easily have become the rival of St. Louis or Chicago; and Kansas City and Omaha as outfitting points for the great West might scarcely have been known. In addition to being a center of trade, manufactures and domestic commerce, the presence of the Church of Jesus Christ of Latter-day Saints would have made it a shrine, a gathering place for the faithful from all parts of the world, and an educational center also; for already the charters were secured and the faculty chosen for a great university; and the keen interest which the Prophet and his followers had ever manifested in education gave every promise that Nauvoo in time would be one of the prominent centers of higher education in the United States.

The peace essential to this material and educational growth, however, was not granted to Nauvoo. Sectarian bitterness against the religion of the Prophet and his followers was too deep-rooted; political jealousy was too strong; and hence strife, plots, threats of violence, actual violence, rumors of invasions from Missouri, hints of assistance from mobs in Illinois, the frequent arrest of the founder of the city, the false reports that went abroad concerning its inhabitants—all combined to blight the growth which otherwise might have been hoped for from Nauvoo's favorable position and early development. But this lull referred to in that all but incessant storm which beat upon the uncovered head of Joseph Smith from the time he announced to the world a revelation from God until this period of grace—from January, 1843, to the June following—was employed by him to good advantage in the matter of the doctrinal development of The Church. It was in this period that he unfolded the doctrines which most distinguish The Church, which under God he had founded, from the sectarian churches founded by men. Unfortunately we do not have *verbatim* reports of his discourses during this period. Most of them were reported in long-hand by Willard Richards, his confidential friend and secretary, and Wilford Woodruff, one of the Twelve Apostles and noted among other things for daily journalizing events passing under his observation. But these reports are not *verbatim*, and there doubtless exist many verbal inaccuracies, and often the impression of the idea left upon the mind of the reporter rather than the idea itself. But notwithstanding some verbal inaccuracies that may exist, and even the statement of the impression of ideas for the ideas themselves, still these long-hand reports of the discourses of the Prophet, stand among the most valued documents of our annals.

Without strict regard to the chronological order in which occur his discourses, conversations, letters, and revelations quoted in the following pages of the chapters devoted to doctrinal subjects, I wish to present the substance of his teachings within the period named.

THE FUNCTIONS OF THE PRIESTHOOD TO BLESS.

To Orson Hyde, one of the Twelve, somewhat given to prophesying calamities and speaking with severity to those slow to receive his words, the Prophet took occasion to say in a council meeting of the Twelve:

> I told Elder Hyde that when he spoke in the name of the Lord, it should prove true; but he must not curse the people—rather bless them.

A remark which at once recognizes the power of that Priesthood held by Orson Hyde—even though he curse the people—but he more especially points out the fact that the chief function of that Priesthood is to bless and not curse.

THE SCRIPTURES AND THEIR INTERPRETATION.

Occasionally the Prophet expounded the Scriptures, and in this he was most happy: not so much on account of his knowledge of ancient languages—though that knowledge, when his opportunities for acquiring it are taken into account, was surprisingly extensive—as from that divine inspiration which so mightily rested upon him at times. Of the Bible itself the Prophet said:

> I believe the Bible as it read when it came from the pen of the original writers. Ignorant translators, careless transcribers, or designing and corrupt priests have committed many errors.

As an example of the errors which had crept into the holy record he put in contrast the following:

> It repented the Lord that he had made man on the earth.—Genesis v: 6.

God is not a man, that he should lie; neither the son of man that he should repent.—Numbers xxiii: 19.

His exegesis, which at once harmonizes the conflicting passages, and satisfies the understanding, is as follows:

It ought to read: It repented *Noah* that God had made man. This I believe, and then the other quotation [meaning the second] stands fair. If any man will prove to me by one passage of holy writ one item I believe to be false, I will renounce and disclaim it as far as I have promulgated it.

In like manner he set the following passage right, Hebrews VI: 1-6.

The first principles of the Gospel, as I believe, are, *Faith, Repentance, Baptism* for the remission of sins, with the promise of the *Holy Ghost.* Look at Hebrews VI: 1, for contradictions! "Therefore *leaving* the principles of the doctrine of Christ, let us go on unto perfection." If a man *leaves* the principles of the doctrine of Christ, how can he be saved in the principles? This is a contradiction. * * * I will render it as it should be: "Therefore *not* leaving the principles of the doctrine of Christ, let us go on unto perfection, not laying again the foundation of repentance from dead works, and of faith towards God," etc.

In like manner he pointed out a solecism in the Lord's prayer. It reads in our common version:

Lead us not into temptation, but deliver us from evil, for thine is the kingdom, the power, etc.

In contrast with this may be placed the statement of James:

Let no man say when he is tempted, I am tempted of God: for God cannot be tempted with evil, *neither tempteth he any man.*—James I: 13.

Then why pray to God the Father—

And lead us not into temptation?

The Prophet's exegesis was:

The passage should read: And *leave* us not—or, suffer us not to be led, into temptation, for thine is the kingdom, etc.

Again, in a public discourse he dealt with the following passage:

Among those that are born of women, there hath not arisen a greater prophet than John the Baptist: nevertheless, he that is *least* in the kingdom of heaven is greater than he.

Taking up the first part of the question, viz: the greatness of John, he thus expounded it:

Firstly, he [John] was trusted with a divine mission of preparing the way before the face of the Lord. Whoever had such a trust committed to him before or since? No man. Secondly, he was intrusted with the important mission, and it was required at his hands to baptize the Son of Man. Whoever had the honor of doing that? Whoever had so great a privilege and glory? Whoever led the Son of God into the waters of baptism, and had the privilege of beholding the Holy Ghost descend in the form of a dove, or rather in the sign of a dove, in witness of that administration? * * * Thirdly, John at that time was the only legal administrator in the affairs of the kingdom there was then on earth and holding the keys of power. The Jews had to obey his instructions or be damned by their own laws, and Christ Himself fulfilled all righteousness in becoming obedient to the law which He had given to Moses on the mount, and thereby magnified it and made it honorable, instead of destroying it. The son of Zachariah wrested the keys, the kingdom, the power, the glory, from the Jews, by the holy anointing and decree of heaven; and these three reasons constitute him the greatest Prophet born of women.

Taking up the second part of the subject—"He that is least in the kingdom of heaven is greater than he," [i. e., greater than John]—it was made easy to understand in the following manner:

How was the least in the kingdom of heaven greater than he

[John]? In reply, I ask who did Jesus have reference to as being the least? Jesus was looked upon as having the *least* claim in all God's kingdom, and was *least* entitled to their credulity as a Prophet, as though he had said: "He that is *considered* the least among you, is greater than John—that is myself."

Explaining the matter of interpretation itself, he said:

> What is the rule of interpretation? Just no interpretation at all. Understand it precisely as it reads. I have a key by which I understand the Scriptures. I inquire, what was the question which drew out the answer or caused Jesus to utter the parable? * * * To ascertain its meaning, we must dig to the root and ascertain what it was that drew the saying out of Jesus.

While this was said especially in relation to the parable of the prodigal son, it may well be given a wider application; and it will be found a great aid in arriving at the truth of many supposedly hard sayings of the Scriptures. But while this key or rule of interpretation was doubtless of great service to the Prophet in his study of the scriptures, he was helped in another and a more important way to understand them; to understand them in a manner which I cannot explain better than by quoting a passage with which he dealt at an earlier date than the period with which I am now dealing, but which is of such moment and helps to illustrate the work we find him doing at Nauvoo during this interim of peace, that we can well afford to stop and consider it. As early as 1831 the Prophet with Sidney Rigdon set about the task of bringing forth a new and inspired translation of the Bible. Their work extended also into the year 1832. On the 16th day of February of that year, they came, in the course of their work, to the twenty-ninth verse of the fifth chapter of John's Gospel, speaking of the resurrection of the dead, concerning those who shall hear the voice of the Son of Man, and shall come forth, and which in our common version stands:

> And shall come forth; they that have done good, unto the resur-

rection of life; and they that have done evil, unto the resurrection of damnation.

But to the Prophet it was given:

* * * And shall come forth: they who have done good in the resurrection of the just, and they who have done evil, in the resurrection of the unjust.

Then follows upon this rendering of the passage by the Spirit, a revelation concerning the future state of man and the different degrees of glory which he will inherit, the like of which is not to be found elsewhere in all that is written among the children of men; and which, in part, I quote. Reverting to the passage as given by the Spirit, the Prophet says:

Now this caused us to marvel, for it was given unto us of the Spirit; and while we meditated upon these things, the Lord touched the eyes of our understandings and they were opened, and the glory of God shone round about;

THE VISION OF THE SON'S GLORY.

And we beheld the glory of the Son, on the right hand of the Father, and received of his fullness;

And saw the holy angels, and they who are sanctified before his throne, worshiping God, and the Lamb, who worship him for ever and ever.

And now, after the many testimonies which have been given of him, this is the testimony last of all, which we give of him, that he lives;

For we saw him, even on the right hand of God, and we heard the voice bearing record that he is the Only Begotten of the Father—

That by him and through him, and of him the worlds are and were created, and the inhabitants thereof are begotten sons and daughters unto God.

THE FALL OF LUCIFER.

And this we saw also, and bear record, that an angel of God who was in authority in the presence of God, who rebelled against the Only Begotten Son, whom the Father loved, and who was in the bosom of the Father—was thrust down from the presence of God and the Son,

And was called Perdition, for the heavens wept over him—he was Lucifer, a son of the morning.

And we beheld, and lo, he is fallen! is fallen! even a son of the morning.

And while we were yet in the Spirit, the Lord commanded us that we should write the vision, for we beheld Satan, that old serpent —even the devil—who rebelled against God, and sought to take the kingdom of our God, and his Christ,

Wherefore he maketh war with the saints of God, and encompasses them round about.

And we saw a vision of the sufferings of those with whom he made war and overcame, for thus came the voice of the Lord unto us.

Thus saith the Lord, concerning all those who know my power, and have been made partakers thereof, and suffered themselves, through the power of the devil, to be overcome, and to deny the truth and defy my power—

They are they who are the sons of perdition, of whom I say that it had been better for them never to have been born,

For they are vessels of wrath, doomed to suffer the wrath of God, with the devil and his angels in eternity;

Concerning whom I have said there is no forgiveness in this world nor in the world to come,

Having denied the Holy Spirit after having received it, and having denied the Only Begotten Son of the Father—having crucified him unto themselves, and put him to an open shame.

These are they who shall go away into the lake of fire and brimstone, with the devil and his angels,

And the only ones on whom the second death shall have any power;

Yea, verily, the only ones who shall not be redeemed in the due time of the Lord, after the sufferings of his wrath;

For all the rest shall be brought forth by the resurrection of the dead, through the triumph and the glory of the Lamb, who was slain, who was in the bosom of the Father before the worlds were made.

And this is the gospel, the glad tidings which the voice out of the heavens bore record unto us,

That he came into the world, even Jesus, to be crucified for the world, and to bear the sins of the world, and to sanctify the world, and to cleanse it from all unrighteousness;

That through him all might be saved whom the Father had put into his power and made by him,

Who glorifies the Father, and saves all the works of his hands, except those sons of perdition, who deny the Son after the Father has revealed him;

Wherefore, he saves all except them they shall go away into everlasting punishment, which is endless punishment, which is eternal punishment, to reign with the devil and his angels in eternity, where their worm dieth not, and the fire is not quenched, which is their torment;

And the end thereof, neither the place thereof, nor their torment, no man knows,

Neither was it revealed, neither is, neither will be revealed unto man, except to them who are made partakers thereof:

Nevertheless I, the Lord, show it by vision unto many, but straightway shut it up again;

Wherefore the end, the width, the height, the depth, and the misery thereof, they understand not, neither any man except them who are ordained unto this condemnation.

And we heard the voice, saying, Write the vision, for lo! this is the end of the vision of the sufferings of the ungodly!

OF THOSE WHO INHERIT THE CELESTIAL GLORY.

And again, we bear record, for we saw and heard, and this is the testimony of the gospel of Christ, concerning them who come forth in the resurrection of the just;

They are they who received the testimony of Jesus, and believed on his name and were baptized after the manner of his burial, being buried in the water in his name, and this according to the commandment which he has given,

That by keeping the commandments they might be washed and cleansed from all their sins, and receive the Holy Spirit by the laying on of the hands of him who is ordained and sealed unto this power,

And who overcome by faith, and are sealed by the Holy Spirit of promise, which the Father sheds forth upon all those who are just and true.

They are they who are the church of the first born.

They are they into whose hands the Father has given all things—

They are they who are Priests and Kings, who have received of his fullness, and of his glory,

And are Priests of the Most High, after the order of Melchisedek, which was after the order of Enoch, which was after the order of the Only Begotten Son;

Wherefore, as it is written, they are Gods, even the sons of God—

Wherefore all things are theirs, whether life or death, or things present, or things to come, all are theirs and they are Christ's and Christ is God's;

And they shall overcome all things;

Wherefore let no man glory in man, but rather let him glory in God, who shall subdue all enemies under his feet—

These shall dwell in the presence of God and his Christ for ever and ever.

These are they whom he shall bring with him, when he shall come in the clouds of heaven, to reign on the earth over his people.

These are they who shall have part in the first resurrection.

These are they who shall come forth in the resurrection of the just.

These are they who are come unto Mount Zion, and unto the city of the living God, the heavenly place, the holiest of all.

These are they who have come to an innumerable company of angels, to the general assembly and church of Enoch, and of the first born.

These are they whose names are written in heaven, where God and Christ are the judge of all.

These are they who are just men made perfect through Jesus the mediator of the new covenant, who wrought out this perfect atonement through the shedding of his own blood.

These are they whose bodies are celestial, whose glory is that of the sun, even the glory of God, the highest of all, whose glory the sun of the firmament is written of as being typical.

THOSE OF THE TERRESTRIAL GLORY.

And again, we saw the terrestrial world, and behold and lo, these are they who are of the terrestrial, whose glory differs from that of the church of the first born, who have received the fullness of the Father, even as that of the moon differs from the sun in the firmament.

Behold, these are they who died without law,

And also they who are the spirits of men kept in prison, whom the Son visited, and preached the gospel unto them, that they might be judged according to men in the flesh,

Who received not the testimony of Jesus in the flesh, but afterwards received it.

These are they who are honorable men of the earth, who were blinded by the craftiness of men.

These are they who receive of his glory, but not of his fullness.

These are they who receive of the presence of the Son, but not of the fullness of the Father;

Wherefore they are bodies terrestrial, and not bodies celestial, and differ in glory as the moon differs from the sun.

These are they who are not valiant in the testimony of Jesus; wherefore they obtain not the crown over the kingdom of our God.

And now this is the end of the vision which we saw of the terrestrial, that the Lord commanded us to write while we were yet in the Spirit.

THOSE WHO INHERIT THE TELESTIAL GLORY.

And again, we saw the glory of the telestial, which glory is that of the lesser, even as the glory of the stars differs from that of the glory of the moon in the firmament.

These are they who received not the gospel of Christ, neither the testimony of Jesus.

These are they who deny not the Holy Spirit.

These are they who are thrust down to hell.

These are they who shall not be redeemed from the devil, until the last resurrection, until the Lord, even Christ the Lamb shall have finished his work.

These are they who receive not of his fullness in the eternal world, but of the Holy Spirit through the ministration of the terrestrial;

And the terrestrial through the ministration of the celestial;

And also the telestial receive it of the administering of angels who are appointed to minister for them, or who are appointed to be ministering spirits for them, for they shall be heirs of salvation.

SUMMARY OF THE GREAT VISION.

And thus we saw in the heavenly vision, the glory of the telestial, which surpasses all understanding,

And no man knows it except him to whom God has revealed it.

And thus we saw the glory of the terrestrial, which excels in all things the glory of the telestial, even in glory, and in power, and in might, and in dominion.

And thus we saw the glory of the celestial, which excels in all things—where God, even the Father, reigns upon his throne for ever and ever;

Before whose throne all things bow in humble reverence and give him glory for ever and ever.

They who dwell in his presence are the church of the first born, and they see as they are seen, and know as they are known, having received of his fullness and of his grace;

And he makes them equal in power, and in might, and in dominion.

And the glory of the celestial is one, even as the glory of the sun is one.

And the glory of the terrestrial is one, even as the glory of the moon is one.

And the glory of the telestial is one, even as the glory of the stars is one, for as one star differs from another star in glory, even so differs one from another in glory in the telestial world;

For these are they who are of Paul, and of Apollos, and of Cephas.

These are they who say they are some of one and some of another—some of Christ and some of John, and some of Moses, and some of Elias, and some of Esaias, and some of Isaiah, and some of Enoch;

But receive not the gospel, neither the testimony of Jesus, neither the prophets, neither the everlasting covenant.

Last of all, these all are they who will not be gathered with the saints, to be caught up unto the church of the first born, and received into the cloud.

These are they who are liars, and sorcerers, and adulterers, and whoremongers, and whosoever loves and makes a lie.

These are they who suffer the wrath of God on the earth.

These are they who suffer the vengeance of eternal fire.

These are they who are cast down to hell and suffer the wrath of Almighty God, until the fullness of times when Christ shall have subdued all enemies under his feet, and shall have perfected his work,

When he shall deliver up the kingdom, and present it unto the Father spotless, saying—I have overcome and have trodden the wine-press alone, even the wine-press of the fierceness of the wrath of Almighty God.

Then shall he be crowned with the crown of his glory, to sit on the throne of his power to reign for ever and ever.

But behold, and lo, we saw the glory and the inhabitants of the telestial world, that they were as innumerable as the stars in the firmament of heaven, or as the sand upon the sea shore,

And heard the voice of the Lord, saying—these all shall bow the knee, and every tongue shall confess to him who sits upon the throne for ever and ever;

For they shall be judged according to their works, and every man shall receive according to his own works, his own dominion, in the mansions which are prepared,

And they shall be servants of the Most High, but where God and Christ dwell they cannot come, worlds without end.

This is the end of the vision which we saw, which we were commanded to write while we were yet in the Spirit.

But great and marvelous are the works of the Lord, and the mysteries of his kingdom which he showed unto us, which surpasses all understanding in glory, and in might, and in dominion,

Which he commanded us we should not write while we were yet in the Spirit, and are not lawful for man to utter;

Neither is man capable to make them known, for they are only to be seen and understood by the power of the Holy Spirit, which God bestows on those who love him, and purify themselves before him;

To whom he grants this privilege of seeing and knowing for themselves;

That through the power and manifestation of the Spirit, while in the flesh, they may be able to bear his presence in the world of glory.

And to God and the Lamb be glory, and honor, and dominion for ever and ever. Amen.

CHAPTER XXVII.

DOCTRINAL DEVELOPMENT AT NAUVOO—THE KINGDOM OF GOD AND THE RESURRECTION.

IT should be remembered that the preaching of Alexander Campbell, the founder of the "Church of the Disciples," or "Christians," had a widespread influence in the western States of the Union, including Illinois. Among other things taught by him in his public ministry was that the baptism of John was not identical with Christian baptism, and that the Kingdom of God was not set up in the earth until after the Son of God was glorified and the day of Pentecost was come. It was perhaps because of the very extended acceptance of these views throughout the West which led the Prophet to make the following comprehensive remarks about the baptism of John and the Kingdom of God.

OF JOHN'S BAPTISM.

Some say the Kingdom of God was not set up until the day of Pentecost, and that John did not preach the baptism of repentance for the remission of sins; but I say, in the name of the Lord, that the Kingdom of God was set up on the earth from the days of Adam to the present time. * * * As touching the Gospel and baptism that John preached, I would say that John came preaching the Gospel for the remission of sins; he had his authority from God, and the oracles of God were with him, and the Kingdom of God for a season seemed to rest with John alone. * * * John was a priest after the order of Aaron and had the keys of that Priesthood, and came forth preaching repentance and baptism for the remission of sins, but at the same time cries out, "There cometh one after me more mighty than I, the latchet of whose shoes I am not worthy to unloose;" and Christ came according to the words of John, and he was greater than John, because He held the keys of the Melchisedek Priesthood and Kingdom of God, and had before revealed the Priesthood to Moses; yet Christ was baptized by John to fulfill all righteousness. * * * [John] preached the same Gospel and baptism that Jesus and the Apostles preached after him. The endowment was to prepare the disciples for their mission unto the world.

OF THE KINGDOM OF GOD.

Whenever there has been a righteous man on earth unto whom God revealed His word and gave power and authority to administer in His name, and where there is a priest of God—a minister who has power and authority from God to administer in the ordinances of the Gospel and officiate in the Priesthood of God—there is the Kingdom of God; and in consequence of rejecting the Gospel of Jesus Christ and the Prophets whom God had sent, the judgments of God have rested upon peoples, cities and nations, in various ages of the world, which was the case with the cities of Sodom and Gomorrah, which were destroyed for rejecting the Prophets. * * * Whenever men can find out the will of God, and find an administrator legally authorized from God, there is the Kingdom of God; but where these are not, the Kingdom of God is not. All the ordinances, systems and administrations on the earth are of no use to the children of men, unless they are ordained and authorized of God; for nothing will save a man but a legal administration; for none other will be acknowledged either by God or angels. * * *

* * * Some say the Kingdom of God was not set up until the day of Pentecost, and that John did not preach the baptism of repentance for the remission of sins; but I say, in the name of the Lord, that the Kingdom of God was set up on the earth from the days of Adam to the present time. * * * Now I will give my testimony. I care not for man. I speak boldly and faithfully, and with authority. How is it with the Kingdom of God? Where did the Kingdom of God begin? Where there is no Kingdom

of God, there is no salvation. What constitutes the Kingdom of God? Where there is a Prophet, a Priest, or a righteous man unto whom God gives His oracles, there is the Kingdom of God; and where the oracles of God are not, there the Kingdom of God is not. In these remarks I have no allusion to the kingdoms of the earth. We will keep the laws of the land; we do not speak against them; we never have, and we can hardly make mention of the State of Missouri, of our persecutions there, etc., but what the cry goes forth that we are guilty of larceny, burglary, arson, treason, murder, etc., etc., which is false. We speak of the Kingdom of God on the earth, not the kingdoms of men. * * * But, says one, the Kingdom of God could not be set up in the days of John, for John said the Kingdom was at hand. But I would ask if it could be any nearer to them than to be in the hands of John? The people need not wait for the day of Pentecost to find the Kingdom of God, for John had it with him, and he came forth from the wilderness, crying out "Repent ye, for the Kingdom of Heaven is nigh at hand," as much as to say, "Out here I have got the Kingdom of God, and I am coming after you; and if you don't receive it, you will be damned," and the Scriptures represent that all Jerusalem went out unto John's baptism. There was a legal administrator, and those that were baptized were subjects for a king; and also the laws and oracles of God were there, therefore the Kingdom of God was there, for no man could have better authority to administer than John, and our Savior submitted to that authority Himself by being baptized by John, therefore the Kingdom of God was set up on the earth even in tho days of John.

* * * Again, he says, "Except ye are born of the water and of the Spirit, ye cannot enter into the Kingdom of God; and though the heavens and earth should pass away, my words should not pass away." If a man is born of water and of the Spirit, he can get into the Kingdom of God. It is evident the Kingdom of God was on earth, and John prepared subjects for the Kingdom, by preaching to them and baptizing them, and he prepared the way before the Savior, or came as a forerunner, and prepared subjects for the preaching of Christ, and Christ preached through Jerusalem on the same ground where John had preached, and when the Apostles were raised up, they worked in Jerusalem and Jesus commanded them to tarry

there until they were endowed with power from on high. Had they not work to do in Jerusalem? They did work and prepared a people for the Pentecost. The Kingdom of God was with them before the day of Pentecost, as well as afterwards.

It is evident from all this that, speaking broadly, with the Prophet the Kingdom of God was the government of God on earth and in heaven—whether that government was manifested through the authority of a single individual or a complete system of ecclesiastical or national government. This is, however, speaking broadly, not to say loosely; and in the same manner that the subject is spoken of in holy scripture where the phrases *Kingdom of God, Kingdom of Heaven, the Church of Christ, Church of God, the Church,* etc., are often used interchangeably and indiscriminately to represent in a general way that divine institution which God in whole or in part from time to time establishes to help man in the matter of his salvation. But it is proper for the reader to know that Joseph Smith when speaking strictly recognized a distinction between "The Church of Jesus Christ" and the "Kingdom of God." And not only a distinction but a separation of one from the other. The Kingdom of God according to his teaching is to be a political institution that shall hold sway over all the earth; to which all other governments will be subordinate and by which they will be dominated. Of this Kingdom Christ is the King; for He is to reign "King of Kings" as well as "Lord of Lords." While all governments are to be in subjection to the Kingdom of God, it does not follow that all its members will be of one religious faith. The Kingdom of God is not necessarily made up exclusively of members of the Church of Christ. In fact the Prophet taught that men not members of The Church could be, not only members of that Kingdom, but also officers within it. It is to grant the widest religious toleration, though exacting homage and loyalty to its great Head, to its institutions, and obedience to its laws.

On the other hand the Church of Christ is purely an ecclesiastical organization, comprising within its membership only those who have embraced the Gospel of Jesus Christ; who inwardly have accepted its principles in their faith, and outwardly have received the rites and ceremonies it prescribes. Of this Church Jesus Christ is the Head, since He is to be "Lord of Lords" as well as "King of Kings." The Church is peculiarly Christ's. It bears His name. It is composed of members who, while not behind others in doing Him homage, as the head of the Kingdom of God, accept Him as more than the King of Kings—they accept Him as Lord—as Lord of Lords, as Redeemer—Savior—God. But the Church of Christ, precious as it is; beloved by its great Head; in the harmony of its truth, perfect; in the beauty of its holiness, passing all praise; in its power of salvation, absolute—yet the Church of Christ will doubtless stand under the protecting ægis of the Kingdom of God in common with other systems of religion, enjoying only such rights as will be common to all. And while the Church of Christ will enjoy to the full her privileges, promulgate her faith without let or hindrance, make known the truth she holds and her saving grace and power, and manage her own affairs—yet she will not usurp the prerogative of the Kingdom of God, nor interfere with those outside the pale of her jurisdiction—outside of her membership. Such, in substance, was the teaching of the Prophet on this subject. Not publicly, or at least not very publicly; but he taught the foregoing in the counsels of the Priesthood as many testify, and effected an organization as a nucleus of the Kingdom above referred to of which some who were not in The Church were members.

It will be understood, then, that what I have quoted from the Prophet's discourses on the subject of the Kingdom of God is spoken broadly; in a sense which recognizes the Kingdom of God simply as the government of God on earth or in heaven; and whether represented by a single individual holding divine authority,or a regular system of government; and which, loosely, may be and is applied to the Church of Christ, or some part thereof.

THE GLORIOUS COMING OF THE SON OF GOD.

It was this year, 1843, that the speculations of William Miller fixed upon for the glorious coming of the Son of God, to reign with His Saints on the earth for a thousand years. Though Mr. Miller was but a religious enthusiast, yet his teachings and his deductions from the prophecies of Daniel and John the Revelator created no little stir throughout the United States, and many thousands of people were looking for the appearing of the Lord Jesus Christ, expecting the resurrection of the dead to begin, and the promised reign of righteousness to follow. The agitation concerning this great event naturally led to many inquiries being submitted to the Prophet concerning it, and he did not hesitate to boldly cross the statements of Mr. Miller on the subject, and contradict his deductions based upon the predictions of the prophets. Joseph Smith stood at the head of the Dispensation of the Fullness of Times, and he knew too well the then present status of the work of God to be deceived into believing that the time for the coming of the Son of God had arrived. The great preliminary work which is to precede that great event had not been accomplished, and until that work was done the Prophet knew that Jesus would not come in the clouds of heaven in power and great glory. It was reported in the Chicago *Express* that one Hyrum Redding had actually seen the promised sign of the coming of the Son of Man, concerning which Joseph in a communication to the *Times and Seasons* said:

Mr. Redding may have seen a wonderful appearance in the clouds one morning about sunrise, (which is nothing very uncommon in the winter season,) he has not seen the sign of the Son of Man, as foretold by Jesus; neither has any man, nor will any man, until after the sun has been darkened and the moon bathed in blood; for the Lord hath not shown me any such sign; and as the prophet saith, so it must be: "Surely the Lord God will do nothing, but He revealeth His secret unto His servants the prophets." (See Amos, III, 7.) Therefore hear this, O earth: The Lord will not come to reign over the righteous, in this world, in 1843, nor until everything for the Bridegroom is ready.

Referring again to the subject, some time later, he said, in a public discourse—

I was once praying very earnestly to know the time of the coming of the Son of Man, when I heard a voice repeat the following: "Joseph, my son, if thou livest until thou art eighty-five years old, thou shalt see the face of the Son of Man; therefore let this suffice, and trouble me no more on this matter." I was left thus without being able to decide whether this coming referred to the beginning of the millenium or to some previous appearing, or whether I should die and thus see His face. I believe that the coming of the Son of Man will not be any sooner than that time.

On still another occasion the Prophet said:

Were I going to prophesy I would say the end will not come in 1844, 5 or 6, or in forty years. There are those of the rising generation who shall not taste death until Christ comes. I was once praying earnestly upon this subject, and a voice said unto me, "My son, if thou livest until thou art eighty-five years of age, thou shalt see the face of the Son of Man." I was left to draw my own conclusion concerning this: and I took the liberty to conclude that if I did live to that time, He would make His appearance. But I do not say whether He will make His appearance or I shall go where He is. I prophesy in the name of the Lord God, and let it be written, The Son of Man will not come in the clouds of heaven till I am eighty-five years old. [He] then read the fourteenth chapter of Revelations, 6th and 7th verses: "And I saw another angel fly in the midst of heaven, having the everlasting gospel to preach unto them that dwell on the earth, and to every nation, and kindred, and tongue, and people, saying with a loud voice, Fear God and give glory to him for the hour of his judgment is come." And Hosea 6th chapter, after two days, etc.,—2,520 years; which brings it to 1890. The coming of the Son of Man never will be—never can be till the judgments spoken of for this hour are poured out; which judgments are commenced. Paul says: "Ye are children of the light and not of the darkness, that that day should overtake you as a thief in the night." It is not the design of the Almighty to come upon the earth and crush it, and grind it to powder, but He will reveal it to His servants the prophets. Judah must return, Jerusalem must be rebuilt, and the Temple, and water come out from under the Temple, and the waters of the Dead Sea be healed. It will take some time to build the walls of the city and the Temple, etc., and all this must be done before the Son of Man will make His appearance. There will be wars and rumors of wars, signs in the heaven above and on the earth beneath, the sun turned into darkness and the moon to blood, earthquakes in divers places, the seas heaving beyond their bounds; there will appear one grand sign of the Son of Man in heaven. But what will the world do? They will say it is a comet, a planet, etc. But the Son of Man will come as the sign of the coming of the Son of Man which will be as the light of the morning cometh [coming] out of the east.

I would again remind the reader that these reports of remarks and discourses of the Prophet's are imperfect, having been written in long-hand, and in part from memory and therefore really are only synopses of what was said. I call attention to this at this point because the imperfections in construction of the above are very apparent, so also the fact that the report in this case is very much abbreviated. Still the substance—the great facts concerning the work to precede the coming of the Son of Man, and the prediction that the Son of Man will not come until that work is performed, are all there, and that is the important thing.

Of the appearance of the Savior when He does come, the Prophet said;

When the Savior shall appear, we shall see Him as He is. We shall see that He is a man like ourselves, and the same sociality which exists among us here will exist among us there, only it will be coupled with eternal glory, which glory we do not now enjoy.

OF THE RESURRECTION.

No less interesting were the Prophet's teaching on the subject of the resurrection of the dead. To a remark of Elder Orson Pratt's to the effect that a man's body changes every seven years, the Prophet replied:

There is no fundamental principle belonging to a human system that ever goes into another in this world or in the world to come. I care not what the theories of men are. We have the testimony that God will raise us up, and He has the power to do it. If any one supposes that any part of our bodies, that is, the fundamental parts thereof, ever goes into another body he is mistaken.

Speaking of the desirability of an honorable burial, and of living and dying among friends in connection with the resurrection, the Prophet said at the funeral services held in honor of Lorenzo D. Barnes, who had died while on a mission to England:

I believe those who have buried their dead here, their condition is enviable. Look at Jacob and Joseph in Egypt, how they required their friends to bury them in the tomb of their fathers. See the expense which attended the embalming and the going up of the great company to the burial. It has always been considered a great calamity not to obtain an honorable burial; and one of the greatest curses the ancient prophets could put on any man was that he should go without a burial. * * * * * * * * * I would esteem it one of the greatest blessings if I am going to be afflicted in this world, to have my lot cast, where I can find brothers and friends all around me. But this is not the thing I referred to: it is to have the privilege of having our dead buried on the land where God has appointed to gather His Saints together, and where there will be none but Saints, where they may have the privilege of laying their bodies where the Son of Man will make His appearance, and where they may hear the sound of the trump that shall call them forth to behold Him, that in the morn of the resurrection they may come forth in a body, and come up out of their graves and strike hands immediately in eternal glory and felicity, rather than be scattered thousands of miles apart. There is something good and sacred to me in this thing. The place where a man is buried is sacred to me. This subject is made mention of in the Book of Mormon and the Scriptures. Even to the aborigines of this land, the burying places of their fathers are more sacred than anything else. When I heard of the death of our beloved Brother Barnes, it would not have affected me so much if I had the opportunity of burying him in the land of Zion. * * * I have said, Father, I desire to die here among the Saints. But if this is not Thy will, and I go hence and die, wilt Thou find some kind friend and bring my body back, and gather my friends who have fallen in foreign lands, and bring them up hither, that we may all lie together. * * * * * * * * * * If tomorrow I shall be called to lie in yonder tomb, in the morning of the resurrection let me strike hands with my father, and cry, "My father, father!" and he will say, "My son, my son!" as soon as the rocks rend and before we come out of our graves. And may we contemplate these things so? Yes, if we learn how to live and how to die. When we lie down we contemplate how we may rise up in the morning: and it is pleasing for friends to lie down together, locked in the arms of love, to sleep and wake in each others' embrace and renew their conversation. * * * * * * Would you think it strange if I relate what I have seen in vision in relation to this interesting theme? Those who have died in Jesus Christ may expect to enter into all that fruition of joy, when they come forth, which they possessed or anticipated here. So plain was the vision, that I actually saw men, before they had ascended from the tomb, as though they were getting up slowly. They took each other by the hand, and said to each other, "My father, my son, my mother, my daughter, my brother, my sister." And when the voice calls for the dead to rise, suppose I am laid by the side of my father, what would be the first joy of my heart? To meet my father, my mother, my brother, my sister and when they are by my side, I embrace them, and they me. It is my meditation all the day, and more than my meat and drink, to know how I shall make the Saints of God comprehend the visions that roll like an overflowing surge before my mind. * * * Lay hold of these things, and let not your knees or joints tremble, nor your heart faint; and then what can earthquakes, wars and tornadoes do? Nothing. All your losses will be made up to you in the resurrection, provided you continue faithful, by the vision of the Almighty I have seen it. * * * More painful to me are the thoughts of annihilation than death. If I had no expectation of seeing my father, mother, brothers, sisters and friends again, my heart would burst in a moment, and I should go down to my grave. The expectation of seeing my friends in the morning of the resurrection cheers my soul and makes me bear up against the evils of life. It is like their taking a long journey, and on their return we meet them with increased joy. God has revealed His Son from the heavens, and the doctrine of the resurrection also, and we have a knowledge that those we bring here God will bring up again clothed upon and quickened by the Spirit of the Great God, and what mattereth it, whether we lay them down, or we lay down with them, when we can keep them no longer? Then let them sink down like a ship in a storm—the mighty anchor holds her safe. So let these truths sink down in our hearts, that we may even here begin to enjoy that which shall be in full hereafter. Hosanna, hosanna, hosanna to Almighty God, that rays of light begin to burst forth upon us even now!

GOD'S AND ANGELS' TIME.

In answer to the question, "Is not the reckoning of God's time, angels' time, prophets' time and man's time according to the planet on which they reside?" I answer, yes. But there are no angels who minister to this earth but those who belong or have belonged to it. The angels do not reside on a planet like this earth; but they reside in the presence of God, on a globe like a sea of glass and fire, where all things for their glory are manifest—past, present and future,and are continually before the Lord.

THE EARTH IN ITS SANCTIFIED STATE.

The following is an entry in his journal:

Saturday, 18th of February [1843.] While at dinner I remarked to my family and friends present, that when the earth was sanctified and became like a sea of glass, it would be one great Urim and Thummim and the Saints could look in it and see as they are seen.

Later in public, on the same subject, he said:

The place where God resides is a great Urim and Thummim. This earth in its sanctified and immortal state, will be made like unto crystal and will be a Urim and Thummim to the inhabitants who dwell thereon, whereby all things pertaining to an inferior kingdom or all kingdoms of a lower order, will be manifest to those who dwell on it; and this earth will be Christ's. Then the white stone mentioned in Revelation II: 17, will become a Urim and Thummim to each individual who receives one, whereby things pertaining to a higher order of kingdoms, will be made known, and a white stone is given to each of those who come into the celestial kingdom, whereon is a new name written, which no man knoweth save he that receiveth it. The new name is the key word.

CHAPTER XXVIII.

DOCTRINAL DEVELOPMENT—PROPHECIES.

THIS period under consideration was rich in prophecies. The boldness of Joseph Smith's predictions was startling; but it is to be remarked that they have been fulfilled as fast as the wheels of time have brought them due.

A PREDICTION UPON THE PRESENT GENERATION.

I prophesy, in the name of the Lord God of Israel, anguish and wrath and tribulation and the withdrawing of the Spirit of God from the earth await this generation, until they are visited with utter desolation. This generation is as corrupt as the generation of the Jews that crucified Christ; and if He were here today and should preach the same doctrine He did then, they would put Him to death. I defy all the world to destroy the work of God, and I prophesy they never will have power to kill me till my work is accomplished, and I am ready to die.

PROPHECY ON WAR.

I prophesy in the name of the Lord God, that the commencement of the difficulties which will cause much bloodshed previous to the coming of the Son of Man will be in South Carolina. It may probably arise through the slave question. This a voice declared to me while I was praying very earnestly on the subject, December 25th, 1832.

These remarks were made in April, 1843, at a place called Raymus, near Nauvoo; and the incidental reference to what a voice had declared to him respecting the war to begin in South Carolina, is doubtless an allusion to the more formal prophecy on that great subject, and which I consider of so much importance that while it does not strictly belong to the period under consideration, I give it *in extenso*, as connected with the lesser prophecy quoted above.

PROPHECY ON THE WARS OF THE LAST DAYS.

Verily, thus saith the Lord, concerning the wars that will shortly come to pass, beginning at the rebellion of South Carolina, which will eventually terminate in the death and misery of many souls.

The days will come that war will be poured out upon all nations, beginning at that place;

For behold, the Southern States shall be divided against the Northern States, and the Southern States will call on other nations, even the nation of Great Britain, as it is called, and they shall also call upon other nations, in order to defend themselves against other nations; and thus war shall be poured out upon all nations.

And it shall come to pass, after many days, slaves shall rise up against their masters, who shall be marshalled and disciplined for war:

And it shall come to pass also, that the remnants who are left of the land will marshal themselves, and shall become exceeding angry, and shall vex the Gentiles with a sore vexation;

And thus with the sword, and by bloodshed, the inhabitants of the earth shall mourn; and with famine, and plague, and earthquakes, and the thunder of heaven, and the fierce and vivid lightning also, shall the inhabitants of the earth be made to feel the wrath, and indignation and chastening hand of an Almighty God, until the consumption decreed, hath made a full end of all nations;

That the cry of the saints, and of the blood of the saints, shall cease to come up into the ears of the Lord of Sabaoth, from the earth, to be avenged of their enemies.

Wherefore, stand ye in holy places, and be not moved, until the day of the Lord come; for behold it cometh quickly, saith the Lord. Amen.

I do not hesitate to refer to this prophecy as one of the

boldest, most forceful and remarkable ever uttered by a prophet of God in either ancient or modern times; and its exact and minute fulfillment to be read in the history of the United States and other countries is as astonishing as the prediction is bold.* This prophecy was given in December, 1832; and the Elders in those days, at least a number of them, carried manuscript copies of it with them on their missionary journeys, and frequently read it to their congregations in various parts of the United States. In Volume XIII of the *Millennial Star*, published in 1851, pages 216, 217, is an advertisement of a new publication to be called the *Pearl of Great Price.* In the announced contents is named this revelation of December, 1832, on war, with the statement that it had "never before appeared in print." Subsequently, but in the same year, 1851, the *Pearl of Great Price* with this prophecy in it, word for word as it is here quoted, was published by Franklin D. Richards, in Liverpool, England. There are copies of the first edition still extant.

PREDICTION THAT THE SAINTS WOULD REMOVE TO THE ROCKY MOUNTAINS AND BECOME A GREAT PEOPLE.

No less remarkable perhaps was the Prophet's great prediction of the sixth of August, 1842, given in his history under that date and published in the *Millennial Star*,† concerning the removal of the Latter-day Saints to the Rocky Mountains, then a thousand miles beyond the frontiers of the United States; but of which I shall not say more here as it is to receive consideration in a subsequent chapter.

PROPHECY UPON THE HEAD OF STEPHEN A. DOUGLASS.

In the daily journal of Wm. Clayton, who at the time the

---

* For the consideration of the fulfillment of this prophecy the reader is referred to the writer's "New Witness for God," ch. XXIII.

† Vol. xix, page 630.

following prophecy was made was private secretary of the Prophet, and almost his constant companion—under date of May 18th, 1843, occurs the following entry concerning a visit with the Prophet to Judge Douglass at Carthage:

Dined with Judge Stephen A. Douglass, who is presiding at court. After dinner Judge Douglass requested President Joseph to give him a history of the Missouri persecutions; which he did in a very minute manner for about three hours. He also gave a relation of his journey to Washington City, and his application in behalf of the Saints to Mr. Van Buren, the President of the United States, for redress, and Mr. Van Buren's pusillanimous reply: "Gentlemen, your cause is just, but I can do nothing for you," and the cold, unfeeling manner in which he was treated by most of the senators and representatives in relation to the subject, Clay saying, "You had better go to Oregon," and Calhoun shaking his head and solemnly saying, "It's a nice question; a critical question, but it will not do to agitate it." The judge listened with the greatest attention, and then spoke warmly in deprecation of the conduct of Governor Boggs and the authorities of Missouri, who had taken part in the extermination, and said that any people that would do as the mobs of Missouri had done ought to be brought to judgment; they ought to be punished. President Smith, in concluding his remarks, said that if the government which received into its coffers the money of citizens for its public lands, while its officials are rolling in luxury at the expense of its public treasury, cannot protect such citizens in their lives and property, it is an old granny anyhow, and I prophesy, in the name of the Lord God of Israel, unless the United States redress the wrongs committed upon the Saints in the State of Missouri and punish the crimes committed by her officers, that in a few years the government will be utterly overthrown and wasted and there will not be so much as a potsherd left, for their wickedness in permitting the murder of men, women and children and the wholesale plunder and extermination of thousands of her citizens to go unpunished, thereby perpetrating a foul and corroding blot upon the fair fame of this great republic, the very thought of which would have caused the high-minded and patriotic framers of the Constitution of the United States to hide their faces with shame. *Judge, you will aspire to the presidency of the United States; and if you ever turn your hand against me or the Latter-day Saints you will feel the weight of the hand of the Almighty upon you; and you will live to see and know that I have testified the truth to you, for the conversation of this day will stick to you through life. He appeared very friendly and acknowledged the truth and propriety of President Smith's remarks.*

This prophecy was published in Utah, in the *Deseret News* of September 24th, 1856; and afterwards in England in the *Millennial Star* of February, 1859. It is well known that Douglass did finally aspire to the Presidency of the United States, that he was nominated by a confident, aggressive party in 1860; and it is also known that in the elections of that year that party which had controlled the destinies almost uninterruptedly for forty years became demoralized; that Abraham Lincoln was triumphantly elected, receiving one hundred and eighty electoral votes, while Mr. Douglass received but 12; that Mr. Douglass some six weeks later died a disappointed not to say heart-broken man. All this is known, but it is not so generally known that on the twelfth of June, 1857, about one year after the prediction of his friend Joseph Smith was published in the *Deseret News*, in Utah, he most cowardly betrayed the people of that friend and united with their enemies in a most unjustifiable assault upon them, and in the fervor of his eloquence and to gain the favor of the populace, he cried out agaist them—

The knife must be applied to this pestiferous, disgusting cancer which is gnawing into the very vitals of the body politic. It must be cut out by the roots, and seared over by the red hot iron of stern and unflinching law. * * * Repeal the organic law of the Territory, on the ground that they are alien enemies and outlaws, unfit to be the citizens of a Territory, much less to ever become citizens of one of the free and independent States of this confederacy.*

---

*The speech is published in the *Missouri Republican* for June 18, 1857. For a more complete consideration of the prophecy, the reader is referred to the author's "New Witness for God," chapter xxii.

He little dreamed that in these utterances he was sealing his own political doom, and leaving on record an event that was to stand as a monument to the inspiration of Joseph Smith.

CHAPTER XXIX.

DOCTRINAL DEVELOPMENT AT NAUVOO—OF THE BEING AND NATURE OF GOD.

WHEN Joseph Smith in 1820 declared that he had in open vision seen God the Father and His Son Jesus Christ standing together above him in the air, surrounded by a glorious brilliancy of light which defied all description, and that God the Father pointed to Jesus and said:

"*Joseph, this is my beloved Son, hear Him*"—

it is quite evident that new ideas pertaining to God were about to be promulgated among men. The facts of this vision were quite at variance with the orthodox notions entertained about the Godhead. It is quite true that Christians talked about the Father and the Son, and as for the latter they had to concede that He was in the form of man, and remains so to this day, as they have no reason to believe that the all-glorious resurrected body of flesh and bones with which Jesus ascended to His Father has been dissolved and become incorporeal; but no orthodox Christian believed that the Father and the Son of the Scriptures were two distinct and separate individuals—a conclusion which this very first vision of the Prophet's forces upon the understanding if it is believed. The anthropomorphism of the vision is also too emphatic for the orthodox conception of God; for notwithstanding the Scriptures teach that man was created in the image of God;* and that Jesus Christ was the express image of His Father's person†—and certainly Jesus was in the form of man—yet the

* Genesis I, 26, 27.

† Heb., I, 3.

Christian orthodoxy gave such explanations of these facts of Scripture that they accepted not at all the idea that God the Father was a personage like unto man in form and as distinct as to His person from His Son Jesus Christ as is any father and son among men. The orthodox creed of the Godhead is as follows:

We believe in one God, the Father Almighty, the maker of all things visible and invisible; and in one Lord, Jesus Christ, the Son of God begotten of the Father, only begotten (that is) of the substance of the Father; God of God, Light of Light, very God of very God; begotten, not made; of the same substance with the Father, by whom all things are made, that are in heaven and that are in earth; who for us men, and for our salvation, descended and was incarnate, and became man; suffered and rose again the third day, ascended into the heavens and will come to judge the living and the dead; and in the Holy Spirit. But those who say there was a time when He [the Son] was not, and that He was not before He was begotten, and that He was made out of nothing or affirm that He is of any other substance or essence, or that the Son of God was created, and mutable, or changeable, the Catholic Church doth pronounce accursed.

This is the creed of St. Athanasius, formulated at the Council of Nice, A. D. 325, and is universally accepted by orthodox Christians. The explanation of the creed as given by Athanasius will also be of interest:

We worship one God in Trinity and Trinity in Unity; neither confounding the persons, nor dividing the substance. For there is one person of the Father, another of the Son, and another of the Holy Ghost. But the Godhead of the Father, Son and Holy Ghost is all one: The glory equal, the majesty co-eternal. Such as the Father is, such is the Son, and such is the Holy Ghost. The Father uncreate, the Son uncreate, and the Holy Ghost uncreate. The Father incomprehensible, the Son incomprehensible. The Father eternal, the Son eternal, and the Holy Ghost eternal. And yet these are not three eternals, but one eternal. As also there are not three incomprehensibles, nor three uncreated, but one uncreated and one incomprehensible. So likewise the Father is Almighty, the Son Almighty, and the Holy Ghost Almighty, and yet there are not three Almighties, but one Almighty. So the Father is God, the Son is God, and the Holy Ghost is God, and yet there are not three Gods, but one God.

It is of course apparent at a glance that the first great revelation to Joseph Smith declared facts in relation to the nature of God—His personality—the fact that the Father was distinct from the Son—the fact that there were two—or a plurality of Gods—which are at variance with the orthodox creed on the subject of Deity. This truth he continued to unfold from time to time, though the fullness and climax respecting this doctrine was reached at Nauvoo; and as it is the teachings of the Prophet and not a defense of them which I here wish to exhibit, I quote his own words:

GOD'S DISTINCT PERSONALITY.

The Father has a body of flesh and bones as tangible as a man's, the Son also, but the Holy Ghost has not a body of flesh and bones, but is a personage of spirit. Were it not so the Holy Ghost could not dwell in us. A man may receive the Holy Ghost, and it may descend upon him and not tarry in him.

THE HOLY GHOST A PERSONAGE.

The sign of the dove was instituted before the creation of the world, a witness of the Holy Ghost, and the devil cannot come in the sign of a dove. The Holy Ghost is a personage, and is in the form of a personage. It does not confine itself to the form of a dove, but in the sign of a dove. The Holy Ghost cannot be transformed into a dove; but the sign of a dove was given to John to signify the truth of the deed, as the dove is an emblem or token of truth and innocence.

IGNORANCE AS TO THE CHARACTER OF GOD.

It is necessary for us to have an understanding of God Himself in the beginning. There are but a very few beings in the world who understand rightly the character of God. The great majority of mankind do not comprehend anything, either that which is passed, or that which is to come, as it respects their relationship to God. They do not know neither do they understand the nature of that relationship, and consequently, they know but little above the brute beast, or more than to eat, drink and sleep. This is all man knows about God or His existence, unless it is given by the inspiration of the Almighty.

WHAT KIND OF A BEING GOD IS.

I want to ask this congregation, every man, woman and child, to answer the question in their own heart, what kind of a being God is. * * * God Himself was once as we are now, and is an exalted man, and sits enthroned in yonder heaven! That is the great secret. If the veil was rent today and the great God who holds this world in its orbit, and who upholds all worlds and all things by His power, was to make Himself visible, I say, if you were to see Him today, you would see Him like a man in form—like yourselves in all the person, image and very form as a man, for Adam was created in the very fashion, image and likeness of God, and received instruction from and walked, talked and conversed with Him, as one man talks and communes with another. * * * It is the first principle of the Gospel to know for a certainty the character of God and to know that we may converse with Him as one man converses with another, and that He was once a man like us; yea that God Himself, the Father of us all, dwelt on an earth, the same as Jesus Christ Himself did, and I will show it from the Bible.

PLURALITY OF GODS ESTABLISHED BY THE LANGUAGE OF GENESIS.

I shall comment on the very first Hebrew word in the Bible; I will make a comment on the very first sentence of the history of creation in the Bible—*Berosheit*. I want to analyze the word. *Baith*—in, by, through and everything else. *Rosh*—the head. *Sheit*—Grammatical termination. When the inspired man wrote it he did not put the *baith* there. An old Jew without any authority added the word: he thought it too bad to begin to talk about the head! It read first, "The head one of the Gods brought forth the Gods." That is the true meaning of the words. *Baurau* signifies to bring forth. If you do not believe it, you do not believe the learned man of God. Learned men can teach you no more than what I have told you. Thus the head God brought forth the Gods in the grand council. * * * The head God called together the Gods and sat in grand council to bring forth the world. The grand councilors sat at the head in yonder heavens and contemplated the creation of the worlds which were created at that time. * * * In the beginning, the head of the Gods called a council of the Gods, and they came together and concocted a plan to create the world and people it.

Later in dwelling on the same subject he said:

I will show from the Hebrew Bible that I am correct, and the first word shows a plurality of Gods, and I want the apostates and learned men to come here and prove to the contrary, if they can. An unlearned boy must give you a little Hebrew. *Berosheit baurau Eloheim ait aushamayeen uenhau auratis*, rendered by King James' translation: "In the beginning God created the heavens and the earth." I want to analyze the word *Berosheit*. *Rosh*, the head; *sheit*, a grammatical termination. The *Baith* was not originally put there when the inspired man wrote it, but it has been since added by an old Jew. *Baurau* signifies to bring forth; Eloheim is from the word *Elio*, God, in the singular number, and by adding the word *heim*, it renders it Gods. It read first, "In the beginning the head of the Gods brought forth Gods," or as others have translated it, "The head of the Gods called the Gods together."

SUSTAINED BY JOHN THE REVELATOR.

President Joseph Smith read the third chapter of Revelations, and took for his text first chapter, sixth verse: "And hath made us kings and priests unto God and his Father; to him be glory and dominion for ever and ever. Amen." It is altogether correct in the translation. Now you know that of late some malicious and corrupt men have sprung up and apostatized from the Church of Jesus Christ of Latter-day Saints, and they declare that the Prophet believes in a plurality of Gods, and lo and behold! we have discovered a very great secret, they cry: "The Prophet says there are many Gods, and this proves that he has fallen." * * * I will preach on the plurality of Gods. I have selected this text for that express purpose. I wish to declare I have always, and in all congregations when I have preached on the subject of the Deity, it has been the plurality of Gods. It has been preached by the Elders fifteen years. I have always declared God to be a distinct personage, Jesus Christ a separate and distinct personage from God the Father, and the Holy Ghost was a distinct personage and a Spirit; and these three constitute three distinct personages and three Gods. If this is in accordance with the New Testament, lo and behold, we have three Gods anyhow, and they are plural, and who can contradict it?

BY THE TESTIMONY OF PAUL.

Our text says: "And hath made us kings and priests unto God and *his Father*." The Apostles have discovered that there were Gods above, for Paul says God was the Father of our Lord Jesus Christ. * * * John was one of the men, and the Apostles declare they were made kings and priests unto God the Father of our Lord Jesus Christ. It reads just so in the Revelation. Hence the doctrine of a plurality of Gods is as prominent in the Bible as any other doctrine. It is all over the face of the Bible. It stands beyond the power of controversy. "A wayfaring man, though a fool, need not err therein." Paul says there are Gods many and Lords many. I want to set it forth in a plain and simple manner, but to us there is but one God—that is *pertaining* to us, and He is in all and through all. But if Joseph Smith says there are Gods many and Lords many, they cry, "Away with him, and crucify him, crucify him!" Mankind verily say that the Scriptures are with them. Search the Scriptures, for they testify of things that these apostates would gravely pronounce blasphemy. Paul, if Joseph Smith is a blasphemer, you are. I say there are Gods many, and Lords many, but to us only one; and we are to be in subjection to that one, and no man can limit the bounds or the eternal existence of eternal time. * * * Some say I do not interpret the Scriptures the same as they do. They say it means the heathen's gods. Paul says there are Gods many and

Lords many, and that makes a plurality of Gods, in spite of the whims of all men. Without a revelation I am not going to give them the knowledge of the God of heaven. You know and I testify that Paul had no allusion to the heathen gods. I have it from God, ard get over it if you can. I have a witness of the Holy Ghost, and a testimony that Paul had no allusion to the heathen gods in the text.

BY THE PHILOSOPHY OF ABRAHAM.

I want to reason a little on this subject. I learned it by translating the papyrus which is now in my house. I learned a testimony concerning Abraham, and he reasoned concerning the God of heaven. "In order to do that," said he, "suppose we have two facts; that supposes another fact may exist—two men on the earth, one wiser than the other, would logically show that another who is wiser than the wiser one may exist. Intelligences exist one above another, so that there is no end to them. If Abraham reasoned thus: If Jesus Christ was the Son of God, and John discovered that God, the Father of Jesus Christ, had a Father, you may suppose that He had a Father also. Where was there ever a son without a father? And where was there ever a father without first being a son? Whenever did a tree or anything spring into existence without a progenitor? And everything comes in this way. Paul says that which is earthly is in the likeness of that which is heavenly. Hence, if Jesus had a Father, can we not believe that He had a Father also? I despise the idea of being scared to death at such doctrine, for the Bible is full of it.

BY THE TESTIMONY OF JESUS.

I believe all that God ever revealed, and I never hear of a man being damned for believing too much; but they are damned for unbelief. They found fault with Jesus Christ because He said He was the Son of God, and made Himself equal with God. They say of me like they did of the Apostles of old, that I must be put down. What did Jesus say? "Is it not written in your law, I said, ye are Gods? If he called them Gods unto whom the word of God came, and the Scripture cannot be broken, say ye of him whom the Father has sanctified and sent into the world, Thou blasphemest, because I said I am the Son of God?" It was through Him that they drank of the spiritual rock.

Of course He would take the honor Himself. Jesus, if they were called Gods unto whom the word of God came, why should it be thought blasphemy that I should say I am the Son of God?*

HOW GOD CAME TO BE A GOD.

We have imagined and supposed that God was God from all eternity. I will refute that idea, and will take away the vail, so that you may see. * * * The Scriptures inform us that Jesus said, "As the Father hath power in Himself, even so hath the Son power"—to do what? Why, what the Father did. The answer is obvious—in a manner to lay down His body and take it up again. Jesus, what are you going to do? To lay down My life as My Father did and take it up again. Do you believe it? If you do not believe it you do not believe the Bible. Here then is eternal life, to know the only wise and true God, and you have got to learn to be Gods yourselves, and to be kings and priests to God, the same as all Gods have done before you, namely, by going from one small degree to another, and from a small capacity to a great one; from grace to grace, from exaltation to exaltation, until you attain to the resurrection of the dead and are able to dwell in everlasting burnings, and to sit in glory as do those who sit enthroned in everlasting power.

THE APPOINTMENT OF GODS.

The Scriptures are a mixture of very strange doctrines to the Christian world, who are blindly led by the blind. I will refer to another Scripture. "Now," says God, when He visited Moses in the bush, (Moses was a stammering sort of a boy like me,) God said, "Thou shalt be a God unto the children of Israel." God said, "Thou shalt be a God unto Aaron, and he shall be thy spokesman." I believe those Gods that God reveals as Gods to be sons of Gods, and all can cry, "Abba Father!" Sons of God who exalt themselves to be Gods, even

---

*I think in this last sentence the report is imperfect. The Prophet doubtless meant to represent Jesus as still talking, that is, as if the Prophet had said—*Jesus continues:* "If they were called, etc.

from before the foundation of the world and are the only Gods I have a reverence for.

THE APPOINTMENT OF OUR GOD.

The head of the Gods appointed one God for us; and when you take a view of the subject, it sets one free to see all the beauty, holiness and perfection of the Gods. All I want is to get the simple, naked truth, and the whole truth.

THE ONENESS OF GOD—IN WHAT IT CONSISTS.

Many men say there is one God; the Father, the Son and the Holy Ghost are only one God! I say that is a strange God anyhow —three in one, and one in three! It is a curious organization. "Father, I pray not for the world, but I pray for them which Thou hast given me." "Holy Father, keep through Thine own name those whom Thou hast given me, that they may be one, as we are." * * * I want to read the text to you myself: "I am agreed with the Father and the Father is agreed with Me, and we are agreed as one." The Greek shows that it should be "agreed." "Father, I pray for them which Thou hast given me out of the world, and not for these alone, but for them also which shall believe on me through their word, that they all may be agreed as Thou, Father, art agreed with me, and I with Thee, that they also may be agreed with us—" and all come to dwell in unity, and in all glory and everlasting burnings of the Gods; and then we shall see as we are seen, and be as our God, and He as His Father.

OF MAN AND HIS IMMORTALITY.

The doctrines which Joseph Smith taught respecting God were also calculated to have an effect on his teachings respecting man, and that it did so is evident from the following:

I have another subject to dwell upon which is calculated to exalt man. * * * It is associated with the subject of the resurrection of the dead, namely, the soul—the mind of man—the immortal spirit. Where did it come from? All learned men, and doctors of divinity say that God created it in the beginning; but it is not so: the very idea lessens man in my estimation. I do not believe the doctrine. I know better. Hear it, all ye ends of the world, for God has told me so, if you don't believe me, it will not make the truth without effect. * * * We say that God Himself is a self-existent being. Who told you so? It is correct enough, but how did it get into your heads? Who told you that man did not exist in like manner upon the same principles? God made a tabernacle and put a spirit into it, and it became a living soul. [Refers to the old Bible.] How does it read in the Hebrew? It does not say in Hebrew that God created the spirit of man. It says, "God made man out of earth and put into him Adam's spirit, and so became a living body." * * * I am dwelling on the immortality of the spirit of man. Is it logical to say that the intelligence of spirits is immortal, and yet that it had a beginning? The intelligence of spirits had no beginning, neither will it have an end. That is good logic. That which has a beginning may have an end. There never was a time when there were not spirits, for they are co-equal with our Father in heaven.

THE PROPHET'S VIEWS ON IMMATERIALITY AND ON CREATION.

There is no such thing as immaterial matter. All spirit is matter, but it is more fine or pure, and can only be discerned by purer eyes. We cannot see it; but when our bodies are purified, we shall see that it is all matter.

* * * You ask the wise doctors why they say the world was made out of nothing, and they will answer, "Don't the Bible say He created the world?" And they infer from that word *create* that it must be made out of nothing. Now the word create came from the word *baurau*, which does not mean to create out of nothing; it means to organize, the same as man would organize material and build a ship. Hence we infer that God had materials to organize the world out of—chaos—chaotic matter, which is element, and in which dwells all the glory. Elements had an existence from the time He [God] had. The pure principles of elements can never be destroyed, they may be organized and reorganized, but not destroyed. They had no beginning, and can have no end.

In order to present a more complete view of the importance

of man as connected with the work of his redemption, his future exaltation and glory, as taught by the Prophet, I quote two discourses of his preached in Nauvoo some time previous to the period under consideration. The first is an excerpt from remarks of the Prophet made in reply to certain questions about the Priesthood and other subjects; the second is from an article presented by him at the October conference of 1840:

I.

The Priesthood was first given to Adam; he obtained the First Presidency, and held the keys of it from generation to generation. He obtained it in the creation, before the world was formed, as in Gen. I, 20, 26, 28. He had dominion given him over every living creature. He is Michael, the Arch-Angel, spoken of in the Scriptures. Then to Noah, who is Gabriel; he stands next in authority to Adam in the Priesthood; he was called of God to this office, and was the Father of all living in his day, and to him was given the dominion. These men held keys first on earth, and then in heaven.

The Priesthood is an everlasting principle, and existed with God from eternity, and will to eternity, without beginning of days or end of years. The keys have to be brought from heaven whenever the Gospel is sent. When they are revealed from heaven it is by Adam's authority. Daniel VII, speaks of the Ancient of Days; he means the oldest man, our Father Adam, Michael; he will call his children together and hold a council with them to prepare them for the coming of the Son of Man. He (Adam) is the father of the human family, and presides over the spirits of all men, and all that have had the keys must stand before him in this grand council. This may take place before some of us leave this stage of action. The Son of Man stands before him, and there is given Him glory and dominion. Adam delivers up his stewardship to Christ, that which was delivered to him as holding the keys of the universe, but retains his standing as head of the human family.

The spirit of man is not a created being; it existed from eternity, and will exist to eternity. Anything created cannot be eternal; and earth, water, &c., had their existence in an elementary state, from eternity. Our Savior speaks of children and says, their angels always stand before my Father. The Father called all spirits before Him at the creation of man, and organized them. He (Adam) is the head and was told to multiply. The keys were first given to him, and by him to others. He will have to give an account of his stewardship and they to him.

The Priesthood is everlasting. The Savior, Moses, and Elias, gave the keys to Peter, James, and John, on the mount, when He was transfigured before them. The Priesthood is everlasting—without beginning of days or end of years; without father, mother, &c. If there is no change of ordinances, there is no change of Priesthood. Wherever the ordinances of the Gospel are administered, there is the Priesthood.

How have we come at the Priesthood in the last days? It came down, in regular succession. Peter, James, and John had it given to them, and they gave it to others. Christ is the great High Priest; Adam next. Paul speaks of The Church coming to an innumerable company of angels—to God, the Judge of all—the spirits of just men made perfect; to Jesus, the Mediator of the new covenant, &c., (Heb. III, 23.)

I saw Adam in the valley of Adam-ondi-Ahman. He called together his children and blessed them with a patriarchal blessing. The Lord appeared in their midst, and he (Adam) blessed them all, and foretold what should befall them to the latest generation. (See D. C., sec. III, pars. 28, 29.)

This is why Abraham blessed his posterity; he wanted to bring them into the presence of God. They looked for a city, &c. Moses sought to bring the children of Israel into the presence of God, through the power of the Priesthood, but he could not. In the first ages of the world they tried to establish the same thing; and there were Eliases raised up who tried to restore these very glories, but did not obtain them; but they prophesied of a day when this glory would be revealed. Paul spoke of the Dispensation of the Fullness of Times, when God would gather together all things in one, &c.; and those men to whom these keys have been given, will have to be there; and they without us cannot be made perfect.

These men are in heaven, but their children are on earth. Their bowels yearn over us. God sends down men for this reason. (Matt.

XIII, 41.) And the Son of Man shall send forth His angels, &c. All these authoritative characters will come down and join hand in hand in bringing about this work.

II.

In order to investigate the subject of the Priesthood, so important to this, as well as every succeeding generation, I shall proceed to trace the subject as far as I possibly can from the Old and New Testaments.

There are two Priesthoods spoken of in the Scriptures, viz., the Melchisedek and the Aaronic or Levitical. Although there are two Priesthoods, yet the Melchisedek Priesthood comprehends the Aaronic or Levitical Priesthood, and is the grand head, and holds the highest authority which pertains to the Priesthood, and the keys of the Kingdom of God in all ages of the world to the latest posterity on the earth, and is the channel through which all knowledge, doctrine, the plan of salvation, and every important matter is revealed from heaven.

Its institution was prior to "the foundation of this earth, or the morning stars sang together, or the Sons of God shouted for joy," and is the highest and holiest Priesthood, and is after the order of the Son of God, and all other Priesthoods are only parts, ramifications, powers, and blessings belonging to the same, and are held, controlled, and directed by it. It is the channel through which the Almighty commenced revealing His glory at the beginning of the creation of this earth, and through which He has continued to reveal Himself to the children of men to the present time, and through which He will make known His purposes to the end of time.

Commencing with Adam, who was the first man, who is spoken of in Daniel as being the "Ancient of Days," or in other words, the first and oldest of all, the great grand progenitor of whom it is said in another place he is Michael, because he was the first and Father of all, not only by progeny, but the first to hold the spiritual blessings, to whom was made known the plan of ordinances for the salvation of his posterity unto the end, and to whom Christ was first revealed, and through whom Christ has been revealed from heaven, and will continue to be revealed from henceforth. Adam holds the keys of the Dispensation of the Fullness of Times; i. e., the dispensation of all the times, have been and will be revealed through him from the beginning to Christ, and from Christ to the end of all the dispensations that are to be revealed: Ephesians, 1st chap., 9th and 10th verses, "Having made known unto us the mystery of his will, according to his good pleasure which he has purposed in himself: that in the dispensation of the fullness of times, he might gather together in one all things in Christ, both which are in heaven and which are on earth in him."

Now the purpose in Himself in the winding up scene of the last dispensation is that all things pertaining to that dispensation should be conducted precisely in accordance with the preceding dispensations.

And again: God purposed in Himself that there should not be eternal fullness until every dispensation should be fulfilled and gathered together in one, and that all things whatsoever, that should be gathered together in one in those dispensations unto the same fullness and eternal glory, should be in Christ Jesus; therefore He set the ordinances to be the same forever, and set Adam to watch over them, to reveal them from heaven to man, or to send angels to reveal them: Hebrews I, 14, "Are they not all ministering spirits, sent forth to minister to those who shall be heirs of salvation?"

These angels are under the direction of Michael or Adam, who acts under the direction of the Lord. From the above quotation we learn that Paul perfectly understood the purposes of God in relation to His connection with man, and that glorious and perfect order which He established in Himself, whereby He sent forth power, revelations, and glory.

God will not acknowledge that which He has not called, ordained and chosen. In the beginning God called Adam by His own voice. See Genesis 3rd chapter, 9th, 10th v., "And the Lord called unto Adam and said unto him, Where art thou? And he said, I heard thy voice in the garden, and I was afraid because I was naked, and hid myself." Adam received commandments and instruction from God; this was the order from the beginning.

That he received revelations, commandments and ordinances at the beginning is beyond the power of controversy; else how did they begin to offer sacrifices to God in an acceptable manner? And if they offered sacrifices they must be authorized by ordination. We read in Gen. 4th chap., 4th v., that Abel brought of the firstlings of the flock and the fat thereof, and the Lord had respect to Abel and to his offering. And, again, Hebrews XI, 4th, "By faith Abel offered unto God a more excellent sacrifice than Cain, by which he obtained witness that he was righteous, God testifying of his gifts; and by it he being dead, yet speaketh." How doth he yet speak? Why, he magnified the Priesthood which was conferred upon him, and died a righteous man, and therefore has become an angel of God by receiving his body from the dead, holding still the keys of his dispensation; and was sent down from heaven unto Paul to minister consoling words, and to commit unto him a knowledge of the mysteries of Godliness.

And if this was not the case, I would ask, how did Paul know so much about Abel, and why should he talk about his speaking after he was dead? Hence, that he spoke after he was dead must be by being sent down out of heaven to administer.

This, then, is the nature of the Priesthood; every man holding the presidency of his dispensation, and one man holding the presidency of them all, even Adam; and Adam receiving his presidency and authority from the Lord, but cannot receive a fullness until Christ shall present the Kingdom to the Father, which shall be at the end of the last dispensation.

CHAPTER XXX.

DOCTRINAL DEVELOPMENT AT NAUVOO—MISCELLANEOUS ITEMS.

IN this chapter I quote the sayings and instructions of the Prophet on a variety of topics, uttered principally within the period under consideration—from January to June 1843—though there are some exceptions.

THE VARIOUS KINDS OF BEINGS IN HEAVEN.

There are two kinds of beings in heaven, viz: Angels who are resurrected personages, having bodies of flesh and bones. For instance, Jesus said, "Handle me and see, for a spirit hath not flesh and bones as you see me have." Second, the spirits of just men made perfect, they who are not resurrected, but inherit the same glory.

HOW TO DETERMINE THE NATURE OF AN ADMINISTRATION.

When a messenger comes, saying he has a message from God, offer him your hand, and request him to shake hands with you. If he be an angel, he will do so, and you will feel his hand. If he be the spirit of a just man made perfect he will come in his glory, for that is the only way he can appear. Ask him to shake hands with you, but he will not move, because it is contrary to the order of heaven for a just man to deceive; but he will still deliver his message. If it be the Devil as an angel of light, when you ask him to shake hands, he will offer you his hand but you will not feel anything; you may therefore detect him. These are three grand keys whereby you may know whether or not any administration is from God.

THE PROPHET'S VIEW ON THE CREEDS OF MEN.

I cannot believe in any of the creeds of the different denominations, because they all have some things in them I cannot subscribe to, though all of them have some truth. I want to come up in the presence of God, and learn all things; but the creeds set up stakes and say, "Hitherto shalt thou come, and no further," which I cannot subscribe to.

THE PROPHET ON FRIENDSHIP.

Friendship is one of the grand fundamental principles of "Mormonism" to revolutionize and civilize the world, and cause wars and contentions to cease, and men to become friends and brothers. Even the wolf and the lamb shall dwell together; the leopard shall lie down with the kid; the calf and young lion, and the fatling; and a little child shall lead them; the bear and the cow shall lie down together, and the sucking child shall play on the hole of the asp and the weaned child shall play on the cockatrice's den, and they shall not hurt or destroy in all My holy mountain, saith the Lord of hosts. It is a time-honored adage that love begets love. Let us pour forth love—show forth all kindness unto all mankind and the Lord will reward us with everlasting increase; cast our bread upon the waters, and we shall receive it after many days, increased to a hundredfold.

ON THE POWER OF THE WORD OF GOD.

Every word that proceedeth from the mouth of Jehovah has such an influence over the human mind—the logical mind—that it is convincing, without other testimony. Faith cometh by hearing. If ten thousand men testify to a truth you know, would it add to your faith? No. Or will ten thousand testimonies destroy your knowledge of a fact? No. I don't want any one to tell me I am a prophet, or attempt to prove my word.

THE PROPHET ON THE LIBERTY OF CONSCIENCE AND THE CONSTITUTION OF THE UNITED STATES.

It is one of the first principles of my life and one that I have cultivated from my childhood, having been taught it by my father, to allow every one the liberty of conscience. I am the greatest advocate of the Constitution of the United States there is on the earth. In my feelings I am always ready to die in the protection of the weak and oppressed in their just rights. The only fault I find with the Constitution is, it is not broad enough to cover the whole ground.

Although it provides that all men shall enjoy religious freedom, yet it does not provide the manner in which that freedom can be preserved, nor for the punishment of government officers who refuse to protect the people in their religious rights, or punish those mobs, States or communities who interfere with the rights of people on account of their religion. Its sentiments are good, but it provides no means of enforcing them. It has but this one fault. Under its provision, a man or people who are able to protect themselves can get along well enough, but those who have the misfortune to be weak or unpopular are left to the merciless rage of popular fury. The Constitution should contain a provision that every officer of the government who should neglect or refuse to extend the protection guaranteed in the Constitution should be subject to capital punishment; and then the President of the United States would not say "Your cause is just but I can do nothing for you;" governors issue exterminating orders; or judges say, "The men ought to have the protection of law, but it won't please the mob; the men must die anyhow to satisfy the clamor of the rabble; they must be hung, or Missouri be damned to all eternity." Executive writs could be issued when they ought to be, and not be made instruments of cruelty to oppress the innocent, and persecute men whose religion is unpopular.

THE PROPHET'S COMMENT ON GOOD MEN.

I do not think there have been many good men on the earth since the days of Adam; but there was one good man and His name was Jesus. Many persons think a prophet must be a great deal better than anybody else. Suppose I would condescend—yes, I will call it condescend—to be a great deal better than any of you, I would be raised up to the highest heavens, and who should I have to accompany me? I love that man better who swears a stream as long as my arm, yet deals justice to his neighbors and mercifully deals his substance to the poor, than the long, smooth-faced hypocrite. I do not want you to think I am very righteous, for I am not. God judges men according to the use they make of the light which He gives them.

THE PROPHET'S ESTIMATE AND DESCRIPTION OF HIMSELF.

I am like a huge, rough stone rolling down from a high mountain, and the only polishing I get is when some corner gets rubbed off by coming in contact with something else, striking with accelerated force against religious bigotry, priest-craft, lawyer-craft, doctor-craft, lying editors, suborned judges and jurors, and the authority of perjured executives, backed by mobs, blasphemers, licentious and corrupt men and women, all hell knocking off a corner here and a corner there. Thus I will become a smooth and polished shaft in the quiver of the Almighty, who will give me dominion over all and every one of them, when their refuge of lies shall fail, and their hiding place shall be destroyed, while these smooth polished stones with which I come in contact become marred. * * * I am a rough stone. The sound of the hammer and chisel was never heard on me until the Lord took me in hand. I desire the learning and wisdom of heaven alone. I have not the least idea, if Christ should come to the earth and preach such rough things as He preached to the Jews, but that this generation would reject Him for being so rough.

OTHER WORLDS THAN OURS AND THEIR REDEMPTION.

Commenting on Revelation v: 13—"And every creature which is in heaven, and on the earth, and under the earth, and such as are in the sea, and all that are in them, heard I saying, Blessing, and honor, and glory, and power, be unto him that sitteth upon the throne, and unto the Lamb, for ever and ever"—the Prophet said:

I suppose John saw beings there of a thousand forms, that had been saved from ten thousand times ten thousand earths like this, strange beasts of which we have no conception; all might be seen in heaven. The grand secret was to show John what there was in heaven. John learned that God glorified Himself by saving all that His hands had made, whether beasts, fowls, fishes or men, and He will gratify Himself with them.

THE PROPHET'S DEFINITION OF THE WORD MORMON.

Before I give a definition, however, to the word Mormon, let me say that the Bible, in its widest sense, means good, for the Savior says, according to the Gospel of John, "I am the good shepherd," and it will not be beyond the common use of terms to say that good is among the most important in use, and though known by various names in different languages, still its meaning is the same, and is ever in opposition to bad. We say from the Saxon good; the Dane god; the Goth goda; the German gut; the Dutch goed; the Latin bonus; the Greek kalos; the Hebrew tob, and the Egyptian mon. Hence, with the addition of more, or the contraction mor, we have the word Mormon, which means, literally, more good.

MAKE YOUR CALLING AND ELECTION SURE.

Commenting on II Peter I, 5-10, and also verse 19, the Prophet said: Now there is some grand secret here, and keys to unlock the subject. Notwithstanding the Apostle exhorts them to add to their faith virtue, temperance, etc., yet he exhorts them to make their calling and election sure. And though they had heard an audible voice from heaven bearing testimony that Jesus was the Son of God, yet he says we have a more sure word of prophecy, whereunto ye do well that ye take heed as unto a light shining in a dark place. Now, wherein could they have a more sure word of prophecy than to hear the voice of God saying, "This is my beloved Son?" etc. Now for the secret and grand key. Though they might hear the voice of God and know that Jesus was the Son of God, this would be no evidence that their election and calling was made sure; that they had part with Christ, and were joint heirs with Him. They then would want that more sure word of prophecy, that they were sealed in the heavens and had the promise of eternal life in the kingdom of God. Then, having this promise sealed unto them, it was an anchor to the soul, sure and steadfast. Though the thunder might roll and the lightning flash and earthquakes bellow, and war gather thick around, yet this hope and knowledge would support the soul in every hour of trial, trouble and tribulation. Then knowledge through our Lord and Savior Jesus Christ is the grand key that unlocks the glories and mysteries of the Kingdom of heaven.

THE VALUE OF AGED MEN IN COUNCIL.

The way to get along in any important matter is to gather unto yourself wise men, experienced and aged men, to assist in council in all times of trouble. Handsome men are not apt to be wise and strong-minded; but the strength of a strong-minded man will generally create coarse features, like the rough, strong bough of the oak. You will always discover in the first glance of a man, in the outline of his features, something of his mind.

SALVATION—IN WHAT IT CONSISTS.

Salvation is nothing more nor less than to triumph over all our enemies and put them under our feet. And when we have power to put all enemies under our feet in this world, and a knowledge to triumph over all evil spirits in the world to come, then we are saved as in the case of Jesus, who was to reign until he had put all enemies under His feet, and the last enemy was death.

DESIRABILITY OF POSSESSING EARTHLY TABERNACLES.

Now, in this world mankind are naturally selfish, ambitious and striving to excel one above another, yet some are willing to build up others as well as themselves. So in the other world there are a variety of spirits. Some seek to excel. And this was the case with Lucifer when he fell. He sought for things which were unlawful. Hence he was cast down, and it is said he drew away many with him, and the greatness of his punishment is that he shall not have a tabernacle. This is his punishment. So the Devil, thinking to thwart the decree of God by going up and down in the earth seeking whom he may destroy any person that he can find that will yield to him, he will bind him, and take possession of the body and reign there, glorying in it mightily, not thinking that he had gotten a stolen tabernacle, and by and by some one having authority will come along and cast him out and restore the tabernacle to its rightful owner. But the devil steals a tabernacle because he has not one of his own, but if he steals one, he is always liable to be turned out of doors.

OF THE SPIRITS IN PRISON.

I will say something about the spirits in prison. There has been much said by modern divines about the words of Jesus (when on the cross] to the thief, saying, "This day shalt thou be with me in paradise." King James' translation makes it out to say paradise.

But what is paradise? It is a modern word, it does not answer at all to the original word that Jesus made use of Find the original of the word paradise. You may as easily find a needle in a haymow. Here is a chance for battle, ye learned men. There is nothing in the original word in Greek from which this was taken that signifies paradise, but it was, "This day thou shalt be with me in the world of spirits: then I will teach you all about it and answer your inquiries." And Peter says he went out and preached to the world of spirits (spirits in prison, 1st Peter, 3rd chapter, 19th verse), so that they who would receive it could have it answered by proxy by those who live on the earth. * * * Hades, the Greek, or Sheol, the Hebrew, these two significations means a world of spirits. Hades, Sheol, paradise, spirits in prison, are all one, it is a world of spirits. The righteous and the wicked will go to the same world of spirits until the resurrection. "I do not think so," says one. If you will go to my house any time, I will take my lexicon and prove it to you. The great misery of departed spirits in the world of spirits, where they go after death, is to know that they come short of the glory that others enjoy, and that they might have enjoyed themselves, and they are their own accusers.

THE PERSISTENCE OF OBTAINED INTELLIGENCE.

Whatever principle of intelligence we attain unto in this life, it will rise with us in the resurrection, and if a person gains more knowledge and intelligence in this life through his diligence and obedience than another, he will have so much the advantage in the world to come. There is a law, irrevocably decreed in heaven before the foundation of this world, upon which all blessings are predicated, and when we obtain any blessing from God, it is by obedience to that law upon which it is predicated.

THE DESIRABILITY AND POWER OF KNOWLEDGE.

If we get puffed up by thinking that we have much knowledge, we are apt to get a contentious spirit, and correct knowledge is necessary to cast out that spirit. The evil of being puffed up with correct [though useless] knowledge is not so great as the evil of contention. Knowledge does away with darkness, suspense and doubt, for these cannot exist where knowledge is. * * * In knowledge there is power. God has more power than all other beings, because He has greater knowledge, and hence He knows how to subject all other beings to Him. He has power over all. * * * It is not wisdom that we shall have all knowledge at once presented before us, but that we should have a little at a time; then we can comprehend it. * * * Add to your faith knowledge, etc. The principle of knowledge is the principle of salvation. This principle can be comprehended by the faithful and diligent; and every one that does not obtain knowledge sufficient to be saved will be condemned. The principle of salvation is given us through the knowledge of Jesus Christ.

CHAPTER XXXI.

THE PROPHET ARRESTED ON MISSOURI'S OLD CHARGES.

IF it should be asked what class of men can do the State the most harm, or the church most mischief, the universal answer would be—*traitors!* So patent is the correctness of the statement, that we deem it unnecessary to inquire into the reasons that lead to the conclusion. What state has perished but by traitor's hands? What patriot suffered, but by a traitor's perfidy? And so, as we proceed, we shall see that it was principally through the schemes of traitors that Nauvoo's budding prospects were blighted, and her virtuous people driven into the wilderness.

It will be remembered that in a former chapter a letter written by John C. Bennett to Sidney Rigdon and Orson Pratt is reproduced, in which he stated that he was then *en route* for Missouri for the purpose of getting out an indictment against Joseph for treason against that State, said to have been committed during the troubles at Far West, in the fall of 1838. Whether Bennett went to Missouri or not I cannot say, but through his influence the old charge of treason was revived, and an indictment found at a special term of the circuit court for Daviess County, Missouri, on the fifth of June, 1843; and on the thirteenth of the same month Governor Reynolds issued a requisition on the governor of Illinois for Joseph Smith, and appointed Joseph H. Reynolds the agent of Missouri to receive the Prophet from the authorities of Illinois. Accordingly the warrant for the arrest was placed in the hands of Harmon T. Wilson by Governor Ford, of Illinois, and Wilson and Reynolds started to find the Prophet.

In the meantime Joseph's friends were not inactive. The day before Governor Ford issued the warrant for the apprehension of the Prophet, he incidentally mentioned to Judge James Adams that a requisition had been made by Missouri for the arrest of Joseph, and that he should issue it the next day; whereupon Judge Adams dispatched an express from Springfield to Nauvoo with this information. The express arrived in Nauvoo on the sixteenth of June; but three days before, Joseph with Emma had left Nauvoo to visit Emma's sister, a Mrs. Wasson, living near Dixon in Lee County, a little more than two hundred miles north of Nauvoo. On the arrival of the messenger from Judge Adams, Hyrum Smith at once dispatched Stephen Markham and William Clayton to Joseph with the information. They left Nauvoo about midnight of the eighteenth, and sixty-six hours later arrived at Wasson's, having ridden two hundred and twelve miles in that time, changing horses only once and that near the end of the journey. Shortly after the arrival of Clayton, a Mr. Southwick of Dixon rode out to Inlet Grove, where Mr. Wasson lived, to inform Joseph that a writ was out for him, and for his pains and interest the Prophet paid him twenty-five dollars, though he had already been informed by Clayton and Markham.

After the receipt of this information, however, Joseph concluded to remain where he was, for, if he started for home, he might meet the officers where he had no friends, and be run over into Missouri among his enemies.

Just how the officers Wilson and Reynolds came to know of the whereabouts of Joseph is not known. But at any rate they went directly to Dixon, nearly killing their horses by hard driving. At the village of Dixon they represented themselves as Mormon Elders, wanting to see the Prophet. They succeeded in hiring a man with a two-horse team to drive them out to

Wasson's. On the way they passed William Clayton, who had been sent by Joseph to see if he could learn anything of the movements of the officers at Dixon. But as the sheriffs were disguised, Clayton did not recognize them.

The officers arrived at Wasson's and found Joseph walking down the path leading to the barn. They sprang upon him like wild beasts upon their prey, presenting their pistols, and Reynolds exclaimed—"G— d— you, sir, if you stir, I'll shoot!" and this with slight variations he kept repeating. Joseph asked them what was the meaning of all this, for they attempted to serve no process, and to their oft-repeated threats of violence, which they sought to make emphatic with blood-curdling oaths, the Prophet bared his breast and told them to shoot, if they desired to, for he had endured so much oppression that he was weary of life.

By this time Stephen Markham arrived on the scene, and immediately started to the Prophet's assistance, despite the threats of the officers to shoot him if he advanced another step. Nor did the brave man check his advance until Joseph cautioned him not to resist the officers of the law.

Reynolds and Wilson, with much rudeness and many unnecessary imprecations, hustled their prisoner into the wagon they had hired in Dixon, and were for starting off without giving the prisoner a chance to say one word to his friends, bid his wife or children good-by, or even get his hat and coat. But Markham, regardless of the threats of the officers to shoot him, seized the team by the bits and said there was no law requiring an officer to take a man to prison without his clothes, and held on until Emma could bring out Joseph's hat and coat.

All this time they had served no process on their prisoner, and had repeatedly thrust the muzzles of their pistols against his sides until he was badly bruised by the uncalled-for violence.

Joseph shouted to Markham as he was driven away, to go to

Dixon and obtain a writ of *habeas corpus*, but as the horse Markham rode was jaded, and the officers ordered their driver to whip up, they kept up with him, and both parties went into the town together.

The sheriffs thrust their prisoner into a room in a tavern kept by Mr. McKennie, and ordered fresh horses to be ready in five minutes. Joseph told them he wanted to obtain counsel. "G— d— you, you shan't have counsel, one more word and G— d— you, I'll shoot you!" was the brutal answer. Just then, however, a man passed the window and to him Joseph shouted, "I am falsely imprisoned here, and I want a lawyer." Presently Lawyer Southwick, the gentleman who a few days before had rode out to Wasson's to inform the Prophet that a writ was out for him, came to the house, but only to have the door slammed in his face, and be denied admittance. Another lawyer, Shepherd G. Patrick, tried to gain admission to the prisoner but met with the same treatment as the first. But at last, through the influence of a Mr. Sanger and a Mr. Dixon, owner of the hotel building where the Prophet was detained a prisoner, Reynolds was given to understand that his prisoner must have a fair trial, and all the protection the laws afforded him. A writ of *habeas corpus* was sued out before Mr. Chamberlain, the master in chancery, who lived some six miles from Dixon, made returnable before Hon. John D. Caton, judge of the ninth judicial circuit at Ottawa.

Before starting for Ottawa, however, Joseph learned that Cyrus Walker, Esq., was in the vicinity on an electioneering tour, he being the Whig candidate for Congress from that district; and the Prophet attempted to secure his services in his defense, as he was the greatest criminal lawyer in that part of Illinois. Walker, however, refused to engage in his defense unless Joseph would agree to vote for him at the coming election, and the Prophet promised him his vote.

Writs were sued out before the justice of the peace against

Reynolds and Wilson for making threats against the lives of Markham and Joseph; and another writ for a violation of the law in relation to writs of *habeas corpus*; and still another, this time from the circuit court of Lee County, for private injuries, false imprisonment, claiming $10,000 damages. Whether or not the sheriffs were released from the first writ, I cannot learn; but on the last writ they were held in $10,000 bonds, and as they could get no bondsmen this side of Missouri, they were taken in charge by the sheriff of Lee County, and were under the necessity of obtaining a writ of *habeas corpus* themselves. So that while Joseph was the prisoner of Reynolds and Wilson, pending the hearing on the writ of *habeas corpus* he had sued out, they were prisoners under the same circumstances, in charge of the sheriff of Lee County. And in this manner all started for Ottawa for a hearing on the several writs before Judge Caton.

The whole company left Dixon on the twenty-fourth of June, and the same day arrived at Pawpaw Grove, a distance of thirty-two miles. The arrival of the Prophet and party at Pawpaw Grove created no little excitement, and the next morning the people gathered into the largest room in the hotel, and insisted upon hearing the Prophet preach. To this Sheriff Reynolds objected and said to the people, "I wish you to understand this man (pointing to Joseph) is my prisoner, and I want you should disperse." At this an old gentleman by the name of David Town spoke up and said:

You damned infernal Puke,* we'll learn you to come here and interrupt gentlemen! Sit down there, pointing to a very low chair, and sit still. Don't open your head till General Smith gets through talking. If you never learned manners in Missouri, we'll teach you that gentlemen are not to be imposed upon by a nigger-driver. You cannot kidnap men here. There's a committee in this grove that will

---

* A common nick-name for Missourians in those days.

sit on your case; and, sir, it is the highest tribunal in the United States, as *from its decision there is no appeal.*

Old Mr. Town was lame and carried with him a heavy, hickory walking stick with which he emphasized the significant parts of his speech by striking the end of it on the floor. It had the desired effect on Reynolds, who humbly took his seat, while the Prophet without an interruption addressed the company for about an hour and a half on the subject of marriage.

At this point it was learned that Judge Caton was absent in the State of New York, hence the party returned to Dixon, and the officers made returns on the respective writs of *habeas corpus* by endorsing thereon—"Judge absent." New writs, however, were sued out, and at Markham's request, the one in behalf of Joseph was made to read: "Returnable before the nearest tribunal in the Fifth judicial district authorized to hear and determine writs of *habeas corpus*"—and thereby hangs a tale, as the sequel will show.

Arrangements were made with a Mr. Lucien P. Sanger, who was in the stagecoach business, to take the respective prisoners to Quincy, a distance of two hundred and sixty miles, to obtain a hearing on the several writs before Judge Stephen A. Douglass.

En route for Quincy, Joseph convinced his lawyers and Sheriff Campbell, of Lee County, and others, that the municipal court of Nauvoo had the right to try cases under writs of *habeas corpus*, and since the writ that he had sued out and served on Reynolds of Missouri was made "returnable before the nearest tribunal in the Fifth judicial district authorized to hear and determine writs of *habeas corpus*," he insisted on being taken to Nauvoo for a hearing. He prevailed, too, and for that place the now large party directed its course.

CHAPTER XXXII.

MINOR MATTERS IN THE NEW MOVE AGAINST THE PROPHET.

IT now becomes necessary to note a few minor events that occurred. As soon as the sheriffs started for Dixon with Joseph in their power, Emma Smith had her carriage made ready and at once started for Nauvoo with her children, in order to set some scheme or other on foot looking to her husband's deliverance.

Joseph, when arriving at Dixon a prisoner, dispatched William Clayton with a message to his brother Hyrum telling what had befallen him, and requesting that assistance be at once sent to him. Clayton boarded the steamer *Amaranth*, at Rock Island, and arrived in Nauvoo about two o'clock in the afternoon of Sunday, the twenty-fifth of June. Meeting was in progress when Hyrum stepped into the stand and interrupted the proceedings, by announcing that he wanted to meet with the brethren at the Masonic Hall.

The quiet of the Sabbath was immediately changed into excitement, and the brethren rushed to the hall in such numbers that not one-fourth could gain admittance, so the meeting was adjourned to the green, where a hollow square was formed about Hyrum, who related the story Clayton had told him respecting the capture of his brother, and called for volunteers to go to his assistance, and see that he had his rights. Immediately three hundred offered their services and from them a company was selected such as was needed; and before sunset, one hundred and seventy-five men were in the saddle under command of Generals Wilson Law and C. C. Rich, *en route* for Peoria.

Before the company left Nauvoo Elder Wilford Woodruff

opened a barrel of gunpowder and invited every man that was going to the assistance of the Prophet to fill his flask or powder-horn. The company was well armed and well mounted, and presented rather a formidable appearance.

Besides sending out this company to find and protect his brother, Hyrum sent about seventy-five men on the steamer *Maid of Iowa*, a small steamboat purchased by the people of Nauvoo some months before, and placed under the command of Captain Dan Jones.

The company was to go down the Mississippi to the mouth of the Illinois river, thence up that stream as far as Peoria; for it was expected that Joseph was being conveyed to Ottawa, and it was feared by Hyrum that an attempt would be made when the party approached the Illinois river to convey Joseph to one of the crafts plying between Peoria and St. Louis and so take him to Missouri. Hence this company on the *Maid of Iowa* was instructed to take the course mentioned, and to examine the steamboats they met, and if they learned that the Prophet was a prisoner on any one of them, they were to render whatever assistance might be within their power.

The command under Brothers Law and Rich divided and subdivided in going through the country, and on the twenty-seventh a small company under the command of Captain Thomas Grover met Stephen Markham, whom Joseph had dispatched to find the brethren that he suspected had been sent from Nauvoo to his assistance; Markham had instructions to meet the Prophet with any company of brethren he might find at Monmouth.

Near Monmouth, and before the arrival of the main body of Joseph's friends, Reynolds and Wilson planned a scheme of going into that town, raising a mob and taking the Prophet by force into Missouri. The plot failed, however, as it was overheard by P. W. Conover, and Sheriff Campbell took both Wilson and Reynolds into his immediate custody. These men had a strong dislike of going to Nauvoo, as they feared they would never leave the place alive. But the Prophet pledged his word that no harm should befall them. As the friends of Joseph kept dropping in singly, or in squads, the fear of his enemies increased. Reynolds made special inquiries as to whether "Jem Flack" was in the company, and on being answered in the affirmative, he exclaimed, as he turned deathly pale, "I am a dead man!" for he had given Flack a deadly provocation. When Flack rode up, however, the Prophet called him up to him and strictly charged him that whatever insult he had received from Reynolds, not to injure a hair of his head, since he had given his word of honor that he should not be injured; and Flack agreed to let him alone.

Before noon of the thirtieth, Joseph's company, which now numbered about one hundred and forty, approached Nauvoo. Word had previously been sent in as to the probable time of his arrival, and the people prepared to give him a royal reception.

Hyrum Smith and Emma, accompanied by the brass band and a long train of carriages, met the Prophet's company a mile and a half north of the city, and received him. The enthusiasm of the people knew no bounds. The Prophet met his brother and wife with a fond embrace; from the latter, only a few days before, he had been torn away in the most arbitrary and cruel manner, and their reunion was a joy indeed.

Joseph now mounted his favorite horse, "Old Charley," and with Emma riding proudly at his side, and surrounded by his body guard, he led the procession into the city, amid the enthusiastic cheers of the people, the firing of musketry and cannon, and the lively strains of the band. At the gate of the Mansion stood the Prophet's mother, with tears of joy rolling down her aged cheeks, to welcome her son, whom she had seen so many times in the hands of his enemies. Here, too, his children flocked about him and welcomed him with unreserved, childish delight.

The vast crowd that had gathered in front of the Mansion appeared unwilling to leave without some word from their revered leader. When he observed this, he mounted the fence, thanked them and blessed them for their kindness to him, and told them he would address them in the grove, near the temple, at four o'clock.

A company of fifty sat down at the Prophet's table to partake of the feast provided, and Wilson and Reynolds, who had treated him so inhumanly when he was in their power, were placed at the head of the table, and waited upon by Emma with the utmost regard for their comfort, though they had denied her speech with her husband, and were not even willing that she should take to him his hat and coat. Gall to them indeed must have been the kindness of the Prophet and his wife, whom but a few days before they had treated with such harshness.

In the afternoon, several thousand people assembled at the grove, and at four o'clock, the Prophet addressed them in an animated speech of considerable length, in which he related to them his adventures while in the power of his enemies, and contended that the municipal court had the right to hear cases arising under writs of *habeas corpus*. In the course of his speech he allowed himself to be carried away by the fervor of his eloquence beyond the bounds of prudence; a circumstance, however, that will create no astonishment when the excitement and the indignation under which he was laboring, and that arose out of sense of outraged justice and humanity is taken into consideration. Under such circumstances and from such temperaments as that of the Prophet, we shall look in vain at such times for dispassionate discourse, and more than human must that man be, who, under the accumulated wrongs of years of oppression, can always confine his speech, when recounting those wrongs, within the lines that cold, calculating wisdom would draw. The speech, however, was doubtless one of the most characteristic that we have of the Prophet, and for that reason I give it *in extenso*, as reported by Elders Willard Richards and Wilford Woodruff. It should also be remarked that the report was made in long-hand, and doubtless there exist many imperfections in it, and it should only be regarded as a synopsis of his speech:

The congregation is large. I shall require attention. I discovered what the emotions of the people were on my arrival at this city, and I have come here to say, "How do you do?" to all parties; and I do now at this time say to all, "How do you do?" I meet you with a heart full of gratitude to Almighty God, and I presume you all feel the same. I am well—I am hearty. I hardly know how to express my feelings. I feel as strong as a giant. I pulled sticks with the men coming along, and I pulled up with one hand the strongest man that could be found. Then two men tried, but they could not pull me up, and I continued to pull, mentally, until I pulled Missouri to Nauvoo. But I will pass from that subject.

There has been great excitement in the country since Joseph H. Reynolds and Harmon T. Wilson took me; but I have been cool and dispassionate through the whole. Thank God, I am now a prisoner in the hands of the municipal court of Nauvoo, and not in the hands of Missourians.

It is not so much my object to tell of my afflictions, trials, and troubles as to speak of the writ of *habeas corpus*, so that the minds of all may be corrected. It has been asserted by the great and wise men, lawyers, and others, that our municipal powers and legal tribunals are not to be sanctioned by the authorities of the State; and accordingly *they* want to make it lawful to drag away innocent men from their families and friends, and have them put to death by ungodly men for their religion!

Relative to our city charter, courts, right of *habeas corpus*, etc., I wish you to know and publish that we have all power; and if any man from this time forth says anything to the contrary, cast it into his teeth.

There is a secret in this. If there is not power in our charter and courts, then there is not power in the State of Illinois, nor in the Congress or Constitution of the United States; for the United States gave unto Illinois her constitution or charter, and Illinois gave unto Nauvoo her charters, ceding unto us our vested rights, which she has no right or power to take from us. All the power there was in Illinois she gave to Nauvoo; and any man that says to the contrary is a fool.

The municipal court has all the power to issue and determine writs of *habeas corpus* within the limits of this city that the legislature can confer. This city has all the power that the State courts have, and was given by the same authority—the legislature.

I want you to hear and learn, O Israel, this day, what is for the happiness and peace of this city and people. If our enemies are determined to oppress us and deprive us of our constitutional rights and privileges as they have done, and if the authorities that are on the earth will not sustain us in our rights, nor give us that protection which the laws and Constitution of the United States and of this State guarantee unto us, then we will claim them from a higher power—from heaven,—yea, from God Almighty!

I have dragged these men here by my hand, and will do it again; but I swear I will not deal so mildly with them again, for the time has come when *forbearance is no longer a virtue*; and if you or I are again taken unlawfully, you are at liberty to give loose to blood and thunder. But be cool, be deliberate, be wise, act with almighty power; and when you pull, do it effectually—make a *sweepstakes* for once!

My lot has always been cast among the warmest-hearted people. In every time of trouble, friends, even among strangers, have been raised up unto me and assisted me.

The time has come when the vail is torn off from the State of Illinois, and its citizens have delivered me from the State of Missouri. Friends that were raised up unto me would have spilt their life's blood to have torn me from the hands of Reynolds and Wilson, if I had asked them, but I told them no, I would be delivered by the power of God and generalship; and I have brought these men to Nauvoo, and committed them to her from whom I was torn, not as prisoners in chains, but as prisoners of kindness. I have treated them kindly. I have had the privilege of rewarding them good for evil. They took me unlawfully, treated me rigorously, strove to deprive me of my rights, and would have run with me into Missouri to have been murdered, if Providence had not interposed. But now they are in my hands; and I have taken them into my house, set them at the head of my table, and placed before them the best which my house afforded; and they were waited upon by my wife, whom they deprived of seeing me when I was taken.

I have no doubt but I shall be discharged by the municipal court. Were I before any good tribunal, I should be discharged, as the Missouri writs are illegal and good for nothing—they are "without form and void."

But before I will bear this unhallowed persecution any longer—before I will be dragged away again among my enemies for trial, *I will spill the last drop of blood in my veins, and will see all my enemies* IN HELL! To bear it any longer would be a sin, and I will not bear it any longer. Shall we bear it any longer? [One universal "NO!" ran through all that vast assembly, like a loud peal of thunder.]

I wish the lawyer who says we have no powers in Nauvoo may be choked to death with his own words. Don't employ lawyers, or pay them money for their knowledge, for I have learnt that they don't know anything. I know more than they all.

Go ye into all the world and preach the Gospel. He that believeth in our chartered rights may come here and be saved; and he that does not shall remain in ignorance. If any lawyer shall say there is more power in other places and charters with respect to *habeas corpus* than in Nauvoo, believe it not. I have converted this candidate for Congress [pointing to Cyrus Walker, Esq.,] that the right of *habeas corpus* is included in our charter. If he continues converted, I will vote for him.

I have been with these lawyers, and they have treated me well; but I am here in Nauvoo, and the Missourians too. I got here by a lawful writ of *habeas corpus* issued by the master of chancery of Lee County, and made returnable to the nearest tribunal in the fifth judicial district having jurisdiction to try and determine such writs; and here is that tribunal, just as it should be.

However indignant you may feel about the high hand of oppression which has been raised against me by these men, use not the hand of violence against them, for they could not be prevailed upon to come here, till I pledged my honor and my life that a hair of their heads should not be hurt. Will you all support my pledge, and thus preserve my honor? [One universal "YES!" burst from the assembled thousands.] This is another proof of your attachment to me. I know how ready you are to do right. You have done great things, and manifested your love towards me in flying to my assistance on this occasion. I bless you, in the name of the Lord, with all the blessings of heaven and earth you are capable of enjoying.

I have learnt that we have no need to suffer as we have heretofore: we can call others to our aid. I know the Almighty will bless all good men; He will bless you; and the time has come when there will be such a flocking to the standard of liberty as never has been or shall be hereafter. What an era has commenced! Our enemies have prophesied that we would establish our religion by the sword. *Is it true?* No. But if Missouri will not stay her cruel hand in her unhallowed persecutions against us, I restrain you not any longer. I say in the name of Jesus Christ, by the authority of the Holy Priesthood, I this day turn the key that opens the heavens to restrain you no longer from this time forth. I will lead you to the battle; and if you are not afraid to die, and feel disposed to spill your blood in your own defense, you will not offend me. Be not the aggressor: bear until they strike you on one cheek; then offer the other, and they will be sure to strike that; *then defend yourselves,* and God will bear you off, and you shall stand forth clear before His tribunal.

If any citizens of Illinois say that we shall not have our rights, treat them as strangers and not friends, and let them go to hell and be damned! Some say they will mob us. Let them mob and be damned! If we have to give up our chartered rights, privileges, and freedom, which our fathers fought, bled, and died for, and which the Constitution of the United States and of this State guarantee unto us, we will do it only at the point of the sword and bayonet.

Many lawyers contend for those things which are against the rights of men, and *I can only excuse them because of their ignorance.* Go forth and advocate the laws and rights of the people, ye lawyers! If not, don't get into my hands, or under the lash of my tongue.

Lawyers say the powers of the Nauvoo charter are dangerous; but I ask, is the Constitution of the United States or of this State dangerous? No. Neither are the charters granted unto Nauvoo by the legislature of Illinois dangerous, and those who say they are are fools. We have not enjoyed unmolested those rights which the Constitution of the United States of America and our charters grant.

Missouri and all wicked men raise the hue and cry against us, and are not satisfied. Some political aspirants of this State also are raising the hue and cry that the powers in the charters granted unto the city of Nauvoo are dangerous; and although the general assembly have conferred them upon our city, yet the whine is raised—"Repeal them—take them away!" Like the boy who swapped off his jack-knife, and then cried, "Daddy, daddy, I have sold my jack-knife and got sick of my bargain, and I want to get it back again."

But how are they going to help themselves? Raise mobs? And what can mobocrats do in the midst of Kirkpatrickites? No better than a hunter in the claws of a bear. If mobs come upon you any more here, dung your gardens with them. We don't want any excitement; but after we have done all, we will rise up, Washington-like, and break off the hellish yoke that oppresses us, and we will not be mobbed.

The day before I was taken at Inlet Grove, I rode with my wife through Dixon to visit my friends, and I said to her, "Here is a good people." I felt this by the Spirit of God. The next day I was a prisoner in their midst, in the hands of Reynolds, of Missouri, and Wilson, of Carthage. As the latter drove up, he exclaimed, "Ha, ha, ha! By G—, we have got the Prophet now!" He gloried much in it, but he is now our prisoner. When they came to take me, they held two cocked pistols to my head, and saluted me with, "G— d— you, I'll shoot you! I'll shoot you, G— d— you,"—repeating these threats nearly fifty times, from first to last. I asked them what they wanted to shoot me for. They said they would do it, if I made any resistance.

"Oh, very well," I replied, "I have no resistance to make." They then dragged me away, and I asked them by what authority they did these things. They said, "By a writ from the governors of Missouri and Illinois." I then told them I wanted a writ of *habeas corpus*. Their reply was, "G— d— you, *you shan't have it*." I told a man to go to Dixon, and get me a writ of *habeas corpus*. Wilson then repeated, "G— d— you, *you shan't have it:* I'll shoot you."

When we arrived at Dixon, I sent for a lawyer, who came; and Reynolds shut the door in his face, and would not let me speak to him, repeating, "G— d— you, I'll shoot you." I turned to him, opened my bosom, and told him to "shoot away. I have endured so much persecution and oppression that I am sick of life. Why, then, don't you shoot and have done with it, instead of talking so much about it?"

This somewhat checked his insolence. I then told him that I *would* have counsel to consult, and eventually I obtained my wish. The lawyers came to me and I got a writ of *habeas corpus* for myself, and also a writ against Reynolds and Wilson for unlawful proceedings and cruel treatment towards me. Thanks to the good citizens of Dixon, who nobly took their stand against such unwarrantable and unlawful oppression, my persecutors could not get out of the town that night, although, when they first arrived, they swore I should not remain in Dixon five minutes, and I found they had ordered horses accordingly to proceed to Rock Island. I pledged my honor to my counsel that the Nauvoo city charter conferred jurisdiction to investigate the subject; so we came to Nauvoo, where I am now a prisoner in the custody of a higher tribunal than the circuit court.

The charter says that "the city council shall have power and authority to make, ordain, establish and execute such ordinances not repugnant to the Constitution of the United States, or of this State, as they may deem necessary, for the peace, benefit, and safety of the inhabitants of said city." And also that "the municipal court shall have power to grant writs of *habeas corpus* in all cases arising under the ordinances of the city council."

The city council have passed an ordinance "that no citizen of this city shall be taken out of this city by any writ, without the privilege of a writ of *habeas corpus*." There is nothing but what we have power over, except where restricted by the Constitution of the United States. "But," says the mob, "what dangerous powers!" Yes —dangerous, because they will protect the innocent and put down mobocrats. The Constitution of the United States declares that the privilege of the writ of *habeas corpus* shall not be denied. Deny me the writ of *habeas corpus*, and I will fight with gun, sword, cannon, whirlwind, and thunder, until they are used up like the Kilkenny cats. We have more power than most charters confer, because we have power to go behind the writ and try the merits of the case.

If these powers are dangerous, then the Constitution of the United States and of this State are dangerous; but they are not dangerous to good men: they are only so to bad men who are breakers of the laws. So with the laws of the country, and so with the ordinances of Nauvoo: they are dangerous to mobs, but not to good men who wish to keep the laws.

We do not go out of Nauvoo to disturb anybody, or any city, town, or place. Why, then, need they be troubled about us? Let them not meddle with our affair, but let us alone. After we have been deprived of our rights and privileges of citizenship, driven from town to town, place to place, and State to State, with the sacrifice of our homes and lands, our blood has been shed, many having been murdered, and all this because of our religion—because we worship Almighty God according to the dictates of our conscience, shall we longer bear these cruelties which have been heaped upon us for the last ten years in the face of heaven, and in open violation of the Constitution and laws of these United States and of this State? God forbid it. *I will not bear it.* If they take away my rights, I will fight for them manfully and righteously until I am used up. We have done nothing against the rights of others.

You speak of lawyers. I am a lawyer, too; but the Almighty God has taught me the principle of law; and the true meaning and intent of the writ of *habeas corpus* is to defend the innocent and investigate the subject. Go behind the writ, and if the form of one that is issued against an innocent man is right, he should not be dragged to another State, and there be put to death, or be in jeopardy of life and limb, because of prejudice, when he is innocent. The benefits of the Constitution and laws are alike for all; and the great Eloheim has given me the privilege of having the benefits of the Constitution and the writ of *habeas corpus*; and I am bold to ask for this privilege this day; and I ask, in the name of Jesus Christ and all that is sacred, that I may have your lives and all your energies to carry out the freedom which is chartered to us. Will you all help me? If so, make it manifest by raising the right hand. [There was a unanimous response, a perfect sea of hands being elevated.] Here is truly a committee of the whole.

When at Dixon, a lawyer came to me as counsel. Reynolds and Wilson said I should not speak to any man, and they would shoot any man who should dare to speak to me. An old, grey-headed man came up and said I should have counsel, and he was not afraid of their pistols.

The people of Dixon were ready to take me from my persecutors, and I could have killed them, notwithstanding their pistols; but I had no disposition to kill any man, though my worst enemy—not even Boggs. In fact, *he* would have more hell to live in the reflection of his past crimes than to die. After this, I had lawyers enough, and I obtained a writ for Joseph H. Reynolds and Harmon T. Wilson, for damage, assault, and battery, as well as the writ of *habeas corpus*.

We started for Ottoway, and arrived at Pawpaw Grove, thirty-two miles, where we stopped for the night. Esquire Walker sent Mr. Campbell, sheriff of Lee County, to my assistance, and he came and slept by me. In the morning, certain men wished to see me, but I was not allowed to see them. The news of my arrival had hastily circulated about the neighborhood, and very early in the morning the largest room in the hotel was filled with citizens, who were anxious to hear me preach, and requested me to address them.

Sheriff Reynolds entered the room and said, pointing to me, "I wish you to understand this man is my prisoner, and I want you should disperse. You must not gather around in this way." Upon which, an aged gentleman, who was lame and carried a largo, hickory walking-stick, advanced towards Reynolds, bringing his hickory upon the floor, and said, "You damned infernal puke, we'll learn you to come here and interrupt gentlemen! Sit down there, (pointing to a very low chair,) and sit still. Don't open your head till General Smith gets through talking. If you never learned manners in Missouri, we'll teach you that gentlemen are not to be imposed upon by a nigger-driver. You can *not* kidnap men here, if you do in Missouri; and if you attempt it here, there's a committee in this grove that will sit on your case. And, sir, it is the highest tribunal in the United States, *as from its decision there is no appeal.*

Reynolds, no doubt, aware that the person addressing him was at the head of a committee who had prevented the settlers on the public domain from being imposed upon by land speculators, sat down in silence, while I addressed the assembly for an hour and a half on the subject of marriage, my visitors having requested me to give them my views of the law of God respecting marriage.

My freedom commenced from that hour. We came direct from Pawpaw Grove to Nauvoo, having got our writ directed to the nearest court having authority to try the case, which was the municipal court of this city.

It did my soul good to see your feelings and love manifested towards me. I thank God that I have the honor to lead so virtuous and honest a people—to be your leader and lawyer, as was Moses to the children of Israel. Hosannah! *Hosannah!!* HOSANNAH!!! to Almighty God, who has delivered us thus from out of the seven troubles. I commend you to His grace; and may the blessings of heaven rest upon you, in the name of Jesus Christ. Amen.

President Smith then introduced Mr. Cyrus Walker to the assembled multitude, and remarked to him, "these are the greatest dupes, as a body of people, that ever lived, or I am not as big a rogue as I am reported to be. I told Mr. Warren I would not discuss the subject of religion with you. I understand the Gospel and you do not. You understand the quackery of law, and I do not." Mr. Walker then addressed the people to the effect that, from what he had seen in the Nauvoo city charter, it gave the power to try writs of *habeas corpus*, etc. After which, President Smith continued as follows:

"If the legislature have granted Nauvoo the right of determining cases of *habeas corpus*, it is no more than they ought to have done, or more than our fathers fought for. Furthermore if Missouri continues her warfare, and to issue her writs against me and this people unlawfully and unjustly, as she has done, and to take away and trample upon our rights, I swear, in the name of Almighty God, and with uplifted hands to Heaven, I will spill my heart's blood in our defense. They shall not take away our rights; and if they don't stop leading me by the nose, I will lead them by the nose, and if they don't let me alone, I will turn up the world—I will make war. When we shake our own bushes, we want to catch our own fruit. The lawyers themselves acknowledge that we have all power granted us in our charters that we could ask for—that we had more power than any other court in the State; for all other courts were restricted, while ours was not; and I thank God Almighty for it. I will not be rode down to hell by the Missourians any longer; and it is my privilege to speak in my own defense; and I appeal to your integrity and honor that you will stand by and help me according to the covenant you have this day made."

In the meantime, a requisition was made on Sheriff Reynolds, to bring his prisoner before the municipal court of Nauvoo, that the validity of the writ, by virtue of which he held him, might be tested. Reynolds refused to recognize the summons of the court; therefore, his prisoner petitioned the court for a writ of *habeas corpus* to be directed to Sheriff Reynolds, commanding him to bring his prisoner before said court, and there state the cause of his capture and detention, in order that the lawfulness of his arrest might be inquired into. Reynolds complied with the attachment, and the Prophet was delivered into the charge of the city marshal. The next day, the municipal court held a session, William Marks, acting chief justice, D. H. Wells, N. K. Whitney, G. W. Harris, Gustavus Hills and Hiram Kimball, associate justices.

When Joseph was on trial for this same offense before Judge Douglass, on a writ of *habeas corpus* in 1841, as already related in a previous chapter, the court refused to enter into the consideration of the merits of the case, as the judge doubted whether on a writ of *habeas corpus* he had a right to go behind the writ and inquire into the merits of the case. The same point was avoided by Judge Pope in the hearing Joseph had before him on a similar writ, when charged with being accessory before the fact in an assault upon the life of ex-Governor Boggs. But the municipal court had no such scruples, and at once proceeded to try the case *ex parte*, on its merits; and Hyrum Smith, P. P. Pratt, Brigham Young, G. W. Pitkin, Lyman Wight and Sidney Rigdon were examined as witnesses. Their affidavits before that court concerning events that happened to the Saints in Missouri, afford the most circumstantial, reliable, and exhaustive data for the history of The Church while in that State that has ever been published.

After hearing the testimony of these witnesses, and the pleading of counsel, the court ordered that Joseph Smith be released from the arrest and imprisonment of which he complained, for want of substance in the warrant by which he was held, as well as upon the merits of the case.

At the conclusion of the trial the citizens of Nauvoo held a mass meeting and passed resolutions thanking the people of Dixon and vicinity, and of Lee County generally, for the stand they had taken in defense of the innocent, and in favor of law and justice.

A copy of the proceedings of the municipal court of Nauvoo, and of all the papers connected with the case were immediately sent to the governor, as also were affidavits from leading counsel and gentlemen from Dixon, as to the treatment of Wilson and Reynolds, that the governor and the world might know that they had not been injured.

We may conclude the account of this adventure of Joseph's by saying that about a year afterwards, a jury in Lee County awarded forty dollars damages, and costs, against Wilson and Reynolds, for false imprisonment and abuse of the Prophet—a verdict which, while it confirms the unlawful course of those officers, and the fact that their prisoner was abused, insults justice by awarding such an amount for damages.

At the time of this action before the municipal court of Nauvoo, it was a question in Illinois whether said court had the authority to hear and determine writs of *habeas corpus* arising from arrests made by virtue of warrants issued by the courts of the State or of the governor, as in the foregoing case; or whether the clause in the city charter granting the right of issuing such writs was not confined to cases arising from arrests made on account of the violation of some city ordinance. The clause in the charter giving to the municipal court the power to issue writs of *habeas corpus* was as follows:

> The municipal court shall have power to grant writs of *habeas corpus* in all cases arising under the ordinances of the city council.

And in addition there was the general welfare provision, which provided that the

> City council shall have power and authority to make, ordain, establish and execute such ordinances not repugnant to the Constitution of the United States, or of this State, as they may deem necessary for the peace, benefit and safety of the inhabitants of said city.

It was maintained on the part of those who believed that the municipal court had the right to issue writs of *habeas corpus* against process issued from the State courts that all the power there was in Illinois she gave to Nauvoo, and that the municipal court had all the power within the limits of the city that the State courts had, and that power was given by the same authority—the legislature. A number of lawyers of more or less prominence in the State professed to hold the same views; but little reliance can be put in the support they bring to the case, since they were seeking political preferment and would, and did, in their interpretations of the powers granted by the charter, favor that side of the controversy most likely to please the citizens of Nauvoo.

Governor Ford, too, at the time, gave a tacit approval of the course taken by the municipal court in issuing the writ of *habeas corpus*, though he afterwards became very pronounced in his opposition to the exercise of such powers. It occurred in this way: As soon as Joseph was liberated, Sheriff Reynolds applied to Governor Ford for a posse to retake him, representing that the Prophet had been unlawfully taken out of his hands by the municipal court of Nauvoo. The governor refused to grant the petition. Subsequently the governor of Missouri asked Governor Ford to call out the militia to retake Joseph, but this he also refused to do, and gave as a reason that "no process, officer, or authority of the State had been resisted or interfered with," and recited how the prisoner had been released on *habeas corpus* by the municipal court of Nauvoo. The governor acted in this instance with perfect knowledge of what had taken place, for the petition and statement of Reynolds were in his possession as were also complete copies of all the documents, which contained the proceedings before the municipal court of Nauvoo; and in addition to these sources of information, the governor had dispatched a trusted, secret agent, a Mr. Brayman, to Nauvoo who investigated the case and reported the result to him.

On the other hand it was contended that the grant in the charter was intended by the legislature only to give the power to the municipal court to issue writs of *habeas corpus* in cases of arrest for violation of city ordinances, and that giving power to the municipal court to test the warrants or processes issued from the State courts, was never contemplated by the legislature, and that the passage of any ordinance by the city council that would bring about or authorize any such unusual proceeding was an unwarranted assumption of power, utterly wrong in principle and consequently subversive of good government.

But whatever opinion may be entertained on the point under consideration, there can be no question but what upon the broad principles of justice the Prophet Joseph ought to have been set free. The State of Missouri had no just claims upon him. He had been arrested and several times examined on these old charges now revived by the personal malice of John C. Bennett, and after being held a prisoner awaiting indictment and trial for five months, so conscious were the officers of the State that they had no case against him that they themselves connived at his escape. After such proceedings to demand that he be dragged again into Missouri among his old enemies was an outrage against every principle of justice.

CHAPTER XXXIII.

POLITICAL PERPLEXITIES—JOSEPH SMITH A CANDIDATE FOR PRESIDENT OF THE UNITED STATES.

THE events related in the last two chapters occurred on the eve of an election for United States representatives, State and county officers. The Whig and Democratic parties were so divided in Illinois that the citizens of Nauvoo held the balance of power in the congressional district where they were located, and also in the county. Whichever party they voted with, as they voted unitedly, gained the election. This circumstance brought to the people of Nauvoo many concessions, and caused the candidates of both political parties to fawn at their feet. It was a case where "Bell boweth down, and Nebo stoopeth." But we shall see that it also brought with it serious difficulties that contributed in no small degree to hasten the fall of Nauvoo; and yet it was a situation forced upon the Saints rather than a policy deliberately chosen by them. The Prophet himself has given the very best explanation of the enforced necessity of the Saints voting unitedly while in Illinois, and I here quote that explanation:

With regard to elections, some say all the Latter-day Saints vote together and vote as I say. But I never tell any man how to vote, or who to vote for. But I will show you how we have been situated by bringing a comparison. Should there be a Methodist society here and two candidates running for office, one says, "If you will vote for me and put me in governor I will exterminate the Methodists, take away their charters, etc." The other candidate says "If I am governor, I will give all an equal privilege." Which would the Methodists vote for? Of course they would vote *en masse* for the candidate that would give them their rights. Thus it has been with us. Joseph Duncan said, if the people would elect him, he would exterminate the Mormons and take away their charters. As to Mr. Ford he made no such threats, but manifested a spirit in his speeches to give every man his rights; hence The Church universally voted for Mr. Ford, and he was elected governor.*

In the election above referred to a circumstance occurred which greatly intensified the political bitterness. It will be remembered that Cyrus Walker refused to assist Joseph when under arrest at Dixon, unless he would pledge him his vote in the then pending election. This Joseph did and Walker was satisfied that he would go to Congress, as he expected that Joseph's vote would bring to him the entire vote of Nauvoo, which would insure his election; and so expressed himself to Stephen Markham. But the day before election, which was Sunday, Hyrum told Joseph that the Spirit had manifested it to him that it would be to the best interests of the people to vote the Democratic ticket, including Mr. Hoge, the Democratic candidate for Congress. Joseph made that announcement in a public meeting, but in addressing the people he said:

> I am not come to tell you to vote this way, that way, or the other. In relation to national matters I want it to go abroad to the whole world that every man should stand on his own merits. The Lord has not given me a revelation concerning politics. I have not asked Him for one. I am a third party, and stand independent and alone. I desire to see all parties protected in their rights.

Referring to what Hyrum had communicated to him he said:

> I never knew Hyrum to say he ever had a revelation and it failed. Let God speak, and all men hold their peace.

---

* History of Joseph Smith, Mill. Star, vol. xxi, p. 668.

The remarks were made at a public meeting soon after the Prophet's release by the municipal court of Nauvoo from the custody of Reynolds and Wilson.

Joseph kept his pledge personally, and voted for Cyrus Walker; but the Democratic ticket was overwhelmingly successful in Nauvoo.

It ought to be said here in justification of the course of the people of Nauvoo, that very good evidence existed to the effect that the whole difficulty connected with the arrest of Joseph at Dixon on the old Missouri charges of "treason, arson," etc, etc., was a political scheme planned with a view of securing the Mormon vote for the Whig party. The *Illinois State Register* in July published the following on the subject of the arrest of the Prophet at Dixon, to justify the charge it made that the whole affair was but a Whig plot to secure the Mormon vote:

The public is already aware that a demand was lately made upon the governor of this State for the arrest of Joseph Smith, and that a writ was accordingly issued against him. We propose now to state some of the facts, furnishing strong grounds of suspicion that the demand which was made on the governor here was a manœuvre of the Whig party.

1st. A letter was shown to a gentleman of this city, by the agent of Missouri, from the notorious John C. Bennett to a gentleman in one of the western counties of that State, urging the importance of getting up an indictment immediately against Smith, for the five or six years old treason of which he was accused several years ago.

2nd. This charge had been made once before, and afterwards abandoned by Missouri. It is the same charge on which Smith was carried before Judge Douglass and discharged two years ago. After that decision, the indictment against Smith was dismissed, and the charge wholly abandoned.

3rd. But in the letter alluded to, Bennett says to his Missouri agent, Go to the judge, and never leave him until he appoints a special term of court; never suffer the court to adjourn until an indictment is found against Smith for treason. When an indictment shall have been found, get a copy and go immediately to the governor, and never leave him until you get a demand on the governor of Illinois for Smith's arrest; and then dispatch some active and vigilant person to Illinois for a warrant and let him never leave the governor until he gets it; and then never let him come back to Missouri without Smith.

4th. A special term of the circuit court of Daviess County, Missouri, was accordingly called on the 5th day of June last. An indictment was found against Smith for treason five years old. A demand was made and a writ issued, as anticipated, by the 17th of the same month.

5th. Bennett it is well known has for a year past been a mere tool in the hands of the Whig junto at Springfield. He has been under their absolute subjection and control, and has been a regular correspondent of the *Sangamo Journal*, the principal organ of the Whig party. He has been a great pet of both the *Journal* and the junto; and that paper has regularly announced his removals from place to place, until latterly; and within the last year has published more of his writings than of any other person, except the editor.

6th. Cyrus Walker, a short time after his nomination, as the Whig candidate for Congress in the 6th district, made a pilgrimage to Nauvoo, for the purpose of currying favor with the Mormons, and getting their support. But in this he was disappointed and dejected; and it was generally believed that, failing to get the Mormon vote, he would be beaten by his Democratic opponent.

7th. Let it be also borne in mind that the treason of which Smith was accused was five or six years old; that it had been abandoned as a charge by Missouri; that the circuit court of that State sat three times a year; that Smith was permanently settled at Nauvoo, no person dreaming that he would leave there for years to come; that they might have waited in Missouri for a regular term of the court, if the design was simply to revive a charge of treason against Smith, with a perfect assurance that he would always be found at home, and be as subject to arrest at one time as another. But this delay did not suit the conspirators as it would put off an attempt to arrest Smith until after the August election. Let it be borne in mind also that the agent of Missouri, after he had obtained the custody of Smith at Dixon, refused to employ a Democratic lawyer, and insisted upon having a Whig lawyer of inferior abilities, simply upon the ground as he stated, that the Democrats were against him. Let it also be borne in mind that Cyrus Walker, the Whig candidate for Congress, miraculously *happened* to be within six miles of Dixon when Smith was arrested, ready and convenient to be employed by Smith to get him delivered from custody; and that he was actually employed and actually did get Smith enlarged from custody; and withal let it be remembered that John C. Bennett is the pliant tool and pander of the junto at Springfield; and that he was the instigator of an unnecessary special term in Missouri, on the 5th day of June last, for the purpose of getting Smith indicted. We say let all these facts be borne in mind, and they produce a strong suspicion, if not conviction, that the whole affair is a Whig conspiracy to compel a Democratic governor to issue a writ against Smith, pending the congressional elections, so as to incense the Mormons, create a necessity for Walker's and perhaps Browning's professional services in favor of Smith, to get him delivered out of a net of their own weaving, and thereby get the everlasting gratitude of the Mormons and their support for the Whig cause. (*Illinois State Register*, quoted in History of Joseph Smith, Millennial Star, vol. XXI, p. 762.)

Such a plot coming to the knowledge of Joseph and the citizens of Nauvoo would certainly justify them in voting against the perpetrators of such an outrage. Of course it cannot be denied that Cyrus Walker was justified in believing that the vote of Joseph Smith pledged to him at Dixon, and which by him was made a condition precedent to his coming to the assistance of Joseph, was understood as meaning something more than the individual vote of the Prophet, nor do I think the Prophet censurable for using any means at his command under the circumstances to deliver himself from the hands of his enemies. But if afterwards the people of Nauvoo learned—as they evidently did—that a plot had been laid to ensnare them, to secure their vote though it involved the liberty, and perhaps the life of their Prophet-leader, they were justified in casting their votes against the men guilty of such perfidy.

This sudden and unexpected change in the vote of the citizens of Nauvoo, stirred up to the very depths the enmity of the defeated political party; and when, shortly after the election, R. D. Foster, who had been elected school commissioner, and G. W. Thatcher, who had been elected clerk of the commissioner's court for the county, appeared at the courthouse in Carthage to take the oath of office, and file their bonds, an attempt was made to keep them from doing so; and the court was threatened with violence if the Mormons were permitted to qualify.

They qualified, nevertheless; whereupon a call was issued for an anti-Mormon meeting to convene in Carthage on the following Saturday, August the 19th, to protest against the Mormons holding office. The people of Carthage and vicinity assembled at the appointed time, organized with a chairman, Major Reuben Graves; and a secretary, W. D. Abernethy; and a committee of nine to draft resolutions. After listening to speeches by Valentine Wilson, Walter Bagby and others, the meeting adjourned to meet again on the sixth of September.

To enumerate the crimes alleged against the Saints in general and in particular against Joseph Smith, in the preamble to the resolutions adopted at their second meeting, would be drawing up a list of all the crimes that ever threatened the peace, happiness, prosperity and liberty of a nation. They resolved that from recent movements among the Mormons, there were indications that they were unwilling to submit to the ordinary restrictions of law; and therefore concluded that the people of Illinois must assert their rights in some way. That while they deprecated anything like lawless violence, they pledged themselves to resist all wrongs the Mormons should inflict upon them in the future—"peaceably if they could, but forcibly if they must." They called upon all good and honest men to assist in humbling the pride of that "audacious despot," Joseph Smith; pledged themselves to raise a posse and take him if the authorities of Missouri made another demand for him; that it might not be said of them, that they allowed the most outrageous culprits "to go unwhipped of justice." They agreed to support no man of either political party who should truckle to the Mormons for their influence, and finally

> Resolved that when the government ceases to afford protection, the citizens of course fall back upon their original inherent right of self-defense.

One of the principal movers in these meetings was Walter Bagby, the county collector, with whom Joseph had some difficulty in relation to the payment of taxes. In the dispute that arose Bagby told Joseph he lied, and for this insult Joseph struck him, and would doubtless have thrashed him soundly but for the interference of Daniel H. Wells. From that time on, Bagby became the relentless enemy of Joseph and the inspirer of these meetings at Carthage; and afterwards went to Missouri where he conferred with the Prophet's old enemies, and brought about that concerted action between the Missourians and the anti-Mormons of Illinois which resulted finally in his assassination.

Later in the fall, acts of violence began to be perpetrated upon the Mormon people who lived at a distance from Nauvoo; and threats of violence were frequent. In December of the year of which I am now writing—1843—a member of The Church living near Warsaw, by the name of Daniel Avery, and his son Philander, were kidnapped by Levi Williams, of Warsaw, John Elliot and others, and run across the Mississippi to Missouri, where for several weeks Daniel Avery was kept a prisoner in Clark County, while one Joseph McCoy was hunting up witnesses to prove that he had stolen a mare from him. Philander Avery escaped and returned to Illinois; but his father remained a prisoner, and suffered great cruelty at the hands of his captors. Finally, however, he was released by writ of *habeas corpus*, and went to Nauvoo where he made affidavit as to his treatment.

Wild rumors abounded also as to what the Missourians intended to do; and some of the letters from Missouri that fell into Joseph's hands, through friends of his, threatened Illinois with invasion, and for a season it would seem that a border war was inevitable. Joseph was careful to keep Governor Ford informed as to all acts of violence perpetrated upon his people, and especially as to the threats of the Missourians respecting an attack, and went so far as to tender the services of the Legion to repel any attempted invasion of the State should it occur. Governor Ford, however, refused to believe there was any danger in the threats, and therefore would detail no portion of the Legion, or of the other State militia, to be ready for such an assault.

A petition signed by nearly all the citizens of Nauvoo, asking the governor to issue no more warrants at the demand of Missouri for the arrest of Joseph Smith on the old charges, was presented to the executive, but the governor refused to give the people any encouragement that he would favorably entertain their suit.

In the meantime another important event began to take shape. As the time of the presidential election was now approaching the probable candidates for the office began to be discussed.

It was well known that the vote of the citizens of Nauvoo would be important, as it would most likely determine whether Illinois would go Whig or Democratic. The political friends of John C. Calhoun at Quincy, early perceived the importance of securing their favor, and began to work for it. A Colonel Frierson, of Quincy, the political friend of John C. Calhoun, expressed great sympathy for the Saints because of the injustice and persecution they had received at the hands of Missouri, and intimated to Brother Joseph L. Heywood that the Hon. B. Rhett, a representative from South Carolina to the United States Congress, and also a political friend to Mr. Calhoun, had expressed a willingness to present to Congress a memorial for a redress of wrongs suffered by the Saints in Missouri; but was careful to intimate to Brother Heywood, and through him to the citizens of Nauvoo, that he supposed that Mr. Calhoun would be a more acceptable candidate to them than Mr. Van Buren.

Colonel Frierson afterwards went to Nauvoo, met in council with the leading citizens, and drafted a memorial to Congress; a copy of which he took with him to Quincy to obtain signers, but I think it never reached the House of Representatives.

The incident, however, suggested to the Prophet the propriety of addressing letters to each of the candidates for the presidency—five in number, viz.,—John C. Calhoun, Lewis Cass, Richard M. Johnson, Henry Clay and Martin Van Buren—to ascertain what policy they would adopt respecting the Saints and redressing the wrongs done them by Missouri. Only two out of the number, however, gave a reply. They were Calhoun and Clay. The former was of the opinion that the general government possessed such limited and specific powers, that the Missouri troubles did not come within its jurisdiction. As to his treatment of the Latter-day Saints, as the Constitution and the laws of the Union made no distinction between citizens of different religious creeds, he should make none; but so far as the executive was concerned all should have the full benefit of both, and none should be exempted from their operation.*

Clay partially disclaimed being a candidate for the presidency, but said if he ever entered into that high office, he must do so free and unfettered, with no guarantees but such as might be drawn from his whole life, character and conduct. But he was careful to say, that he had watched the progress of the Saints, and sympathized with them in their sufferings under in-

---

* See Appendix I.

justice, which had been inflicted upon them; and thought that they, in common with other religious communities, should enjoy the security and protection of the Constitution and laws.

To these letters the Prophet Joseph wrote scathing replies. The particular portion of Calhoun's answer with which he dealt, was that which claimed that the general government had no jurisdiction in the case of the Saints and Missouri, and handled rather severely the senator's doctrine of the limited powers of the general government.*

In reply to Henry Clay he dealt chiefly with his "no pledge nor guarantee" doctrine, only such as could be drawn from his whole life, character and conduct; and drew such a picture of that statesman's past conduct, that the Kentucky senator could not feel flattered withal, to say the least; and in good round terms he denounced the subterfuges of politicians, and demanded of the nation justice in behalf of his afflicted people. In reading this correspondence one cannot but think that the Prophet is unnecessarily harsh of expression, and some phrases we cannot help but feel are certainly unworthy of him. The faults of these letters, however, are not so much the fault of the individual as the fault of the times. Those were days when moderation in language was certainly not characteristic of the political literature of the times. Personal abuse often seems to have been mistaken for argument, and severity of expression was often thought to out-weigh reason. One other thing should be remembered also, and that is the Prophet Joseph very largely depended upon others for the expression, for the literary form of those ideas which he advanced, and these secondary persons yielded too often to the spirit of the times in what they set down as coming from the Prophet.

When it was ascertained that from none of the candidates in the field, the citizens of Nauvoo could hope for assistance in

---

* See Appendix II.

obtaining justice for the wrongs they suffered in Missouri, Joseph allowed a convention at Nauvoo to put his name in nomination for the office of president; and he published his "Views on the Powers and Policy of the Government of the United States," a document of great strength and one which excited considerable comment from the press of the country, very much of which was favorable.

In this document the Prophet-candidate reviews the growth and development of the American government until it reached the "*Acme* of American glory, liberty, and prosperity" under the administration of General Jackson; and then the beginning of its decline under the "withering touch of Martin Van Buren." He advocated prison reform. Advised the people of the south to petition their respective legislatures to abolish slavery by the year 1850, or now, "and save the abolitionist from reproach and ruin, infamy and shame." He recommended the payment of a reasonable price to the slave-holders of the south for their slaves, to be paid by the surplus revenue, arising from the sale of public lands, and reduction in the wages paid to congressmen. The southern people, said he, are hospitable and noble. They will help to rid so free a country of every vestige of slavery, whenever they are assured of an equivalent for their property. He recommended more economy in the national and state governments, and more equality among the people.

For the accommodation of the people he proposed the establishment of a national bank, with branches in each State, the directors thereof to be elected yearly by the people; and the profits arising from the business to be used as revenue, in defraying the expenses of government, the profits from the branch banks, being used in the respective States where they existed; and those arising from the parent institution by the general government; and reduce taxation to the extent of the net profits of these institutions.

In the light of the experience he and the Latter-day Saints

had passed through in Missouri, he advocated the idea of giving the president full power to send an army to suppress mobs, "and appealed to the States to repeal that relic of folly," which made it necessary for the governor of a State to make a demand of the president for troops in case of invasion or rebellion. "The governor himself," he goes on to say, "may be a mobber; and instead of being punished, as he should be, for murder or treason, he may destroy the very lives, rights and property he should protect."

He favored the annexation of Texas, and the extension of the authority of the United States over contiguous territory on the west, and said:

> When a neighboring realm petitioned to join the Union of the Sons of Liberty, my voice would be, *come*—yea, come Texas, come Mexico, come Canada, and come all the world; let us be brethren, let us be one great family, and let there be a universal peace.*

On the seventeenth of June, 1844, a State convention was held at Nauvoo, which ratified the views of Joseph on the "Powers and Policy of the Government," passed a series of resolutions inviting all men of all parties to assist in the work of reforming the government, and in a formal manner putting in nomination General Joseph Smith for President of the United States, and Sidney Rigdon for vice-president.

James Arlington Bennett, of New York, was asked to take the second place on the ticket first; but, he being of foreign birth, was not eligible. Then the position was offered to Colonel Solomon Copeland, but for some reason he did not accept; so the next choice was Sidney Rigdon, who by that time had removed from Nauvoo to Pennsylvania.

Arrangements were entered into, to hold a national convention in New York on the thirteenth of July following, and

---

*See Appendix III.

preparations were made for an active campaign in favor of the Prophet-nominee; but before the time for the national convention had arrived, the standard bearer of the new party of reform, Jeffersonian Democracy,* free trade and sailors' rights, fell pierced by assassins' bullets—the victim of a cruel mob.

Of course Joseph had no hope that he would be elected to the presidency, but by becoming a candidate, he gave the citizens of Nauvoo an opportunity to act consistently with their views of what ought to be done for the general good of the nation, and at the same time, avoid the wrath of the political parties in the State of Illinois by affiliating with neither of them in the ensuing election; for whenever they voted with one of those parties the other became enraged and *vice versa*. Doubtless the best reasons for, and the best justification of, this movement on the part of the people of Nauvoo is to be found in an editorial article from the *Times and Seasons* for February, 1844—with which I close this chapter:

WHO SHALL BE OUR NEXT PRESIDENT?

This is an inquiry which to us as a people is a matter of the most paramount importance, and requires our most serious, calm, and dispassionate reflection. Executive power, when correctly wielded, is a great blessing to the people of this great commonwealth, and forms one of the firmest pillars of our confederation. It watches the interests of the whole community with a fatherly care; it wisely balances the other legislative powers when overheated by party spirit or sectional feeling; it watches with jealous care our interests and

---

*The fifth resolution adopted at the Nauvoo convention read as follows:

Resolved, that the better to carry out the principles of liberty and equal rights, Jeffersonian Democracy, free trade, and sailors' rights, and the protection of person and property, we will support General Joseph Smith for the President of the United States at the ensuing election.

commerce with foreign nations, and gives tone and efficacy to legislative enactments.

The President stands at the head of these United States, and is the mouth-piece of this vast republic. If he be a man of an enlightened mind and a capacious soul,—if he be a virtuous man, a statesman, a patriot, and a man of unflinching integrity,—if he possess the same spirit that fired the souls of our venerable sires, who founded this great commonwealth, and wishes to promote the universal good of the whole republic, he may indeed be made a blessing to the community.

But if he prostrates his high and honorable calling to base and unworthy purposes,—if he makes use of the power which the people have placed in his hands for their interests to gratify his ambition, for the purpose of self-aggrandizement or pecuniary interest,—if he meanly panders with demagogues, loses sight of the interest of the nation, and sacrifices the Union on the altar of sectional interests or party views, he renders himself unworthy of the dignified trust reposed in him, debases the nation in the eyes of the civilized world, and produces misery and confusion at home. "When the wicked rule the people mourn."

There is perhaps no body of people in the United States who are at the present time more interested about the issue of the presidential contest than are the Latter-day Saints. And our situation in regard to the two great political parties is a most novel one. It is a fact well understood that we have suffered great injustice from the State of Missouri, that we petitioned to the authorities of that State for redress in vain, that we have also memorialized Congress under the late administration, and have obtained the heartless reply that "Congress has no power to redress your grievances."

After having taken all the legal and constitutional steps that we can, we are still groaning under accumulated wrongs. Is there no power anywhere to redress our grievances? Missouri lacks the disposition, and Congress lacks both the disposition and power (?); and thus fifteen thousand inhabitants of these United States can with impunity be dispossessed of their property; have their houses burned, their property confiscated, many of their numbers murdered, and the remainder driven from their homes and left to wander as exiles in this boasted land of freedom and equal rights: and after appealing again and again to the legally constituted authorities of our land for redress, we are coolly told by our highest tribunals, "We can do nothing for you."

We have paid hundreds of thousands of dollars into the coffers of Congress for their lands, and they stand virtually pledged to defend us in our rights, but they have not done it. If a man steals a dollar from his neighbor, or steals a horse or a hog, he can obtain redress; but we have been robbed by wholesale, the most daring murders have been committed, and we are coolly told that we can obtain no redress. If a steamboat is set on fire on our coast by foreigners, even when she is engaged in aiding and abetting the enemies of that power, it becomes a matter of national interference and legislation; or if a foreigner, as in the case of McLeod, is taken on our land and tried for supposed crimes committed by him against our citizens, his nation interferes, and it becomes a matter of negotiation and legislation. But our authorities can calmly look on and see the citizens of a country butchered with impunity: they can see two counties dispossessed of their inhabitants, their houses burned, and their property confiscated; and when the crys of fifteen thousand men, women and children salute their ears, they deliberately tell us that we can obtain no redress!

Hear it, therefore, ye mobbers! Proclaim it to all the scoundrels in the Union! Let a standard be erected around which shall rally all the renegadoes of the land: assemble yourselves and rob at pleasure; murder till you are satisfied with blood; drive men, women and children from their homes: there is no law to protect them, and Congress has no power to redress their grievances; and the great father of the Union (the President) has not got an ear to listen to their complaints.

What shall we do under this state of things? In the event of either of the prominent candidates, Van Buren or Clay, obtaining the presidential chair, we should not be placed in any better situation.

In speaking of Mr. Clay, his politics are diametrically opposed to ours. He inclines strongly to the old school of Federalists, and as a matter of course would not favor our cause; neither could we con scientiously vote for him. And we have yet stronger objections to

Mr. Van Buren on other grounds. He has sung the old song of Congress—"Congress has no power to redress your grievances."

But did the matter rest here, it would not be so bad. He was in the presidential chair at the time of our former difficulties. We appealed to him on that occasion, but we appealed in vain, and his sentiments are yet unchanged.

But all these thing are tolerable in comparison to what we have yet to state. We have been informed from a respectable source that there is an understanding between Mr. Benton, of Missouri, and Mr. Van Buren, and a conditional compact entered into, that if Mr. Benton will use his influence to get Mr. Van Buren elected, Van Buren, when elected, shall use his executive influence to wipe away the stain from Missouri by a further persecution of the Mormons, and wreaking out vengeance on their heads, either by extermination or by some other summary process. We could scarcely credit the statement; and we hope yet for the sake of humanity, that the suggestion is false: but we have too good reason to believe that we are correctly informed.

If, then, this is the case can we conscientiously vote for a man of this description, and put the weapon in his hands to cut our throats with? We cannot. And however much we might wish to sustain the Democratic nomination, we cannot—we will not vote for Van Buren. Our interests, our property, our lives, and the lives of our families are too dear to us to be sacrificed at the shrine of party spirit and to gratify party feelings. We have been sold once in the State of Missouri, and our liberties bartered away by political demagogues, through executive intrigue, and we wish not to be betrayed again by Benton and Van Buren.

Under these circumstances, the question again arises, Whom shall we support? General Joseph Smith—a man of sterling worth and integrity and of enlarged views—a man who has raised himself from the humblest walks in life to stand at the head of a large, intelligent, respectable and increasing society, that has spread not only in this land, but in distant nations,—a man whose talents and genius are of an exalted nature, and whose experience has rendered him in every way adequate to the onerous duty. Honorable, fearless, and energetic, he would administer justice with an impartial hand, and magnify and dignify the office of Chief magistrate of this land; and we feel assured that there is not a man in the United States more competent for the task.

One great reason that we have for pursuing our present course is, that at every election we have been made a political target for the filthy demagogues in the country to shoot their loathsome arrows at. And every story has been put into requisition to blast our fame from the old fabrication of "walk on the water" down to "the murder of ex-Governor Boggs." The journals have teemed with this filthy trash, and even men who ought to have more respect for themselves —men contending for the gubernatorial chair have made use of terms so degrading, so mean, so humiliating, that a Billingsgate fisherwoman would have considered herself disgraced with. We refuse any longer to be thus bedaubed for either party. We tell all such to let their filth flow in its own legitimate channel, for we are sick of the loathsome smell.

Gentlemen, we are not going either to "murder ex-Governor Boggs, nor a Mormon in this State for not giving us his money," nor are we going to "walk on the water," nor "drown a woman," nor "defraud the poor of their property," nor send "destroying angels after General Bennett to kill him," nor "Marry spiritual wives," nor commit any other outrageous act this election to help any party with. You must get some other persons to perform these kind offices for you for the future. We withdraw.

Under existing circumstances, we have no other alternative; and if we can accomplish our object, well: if not, we shall have the satisfaction of knowing that we have acted conscientiously, and have used our best judgment. And if we have to throw away our votes, we had better do so upon a worthy rather than upon an unworthy individual, who might make use of the weapon we put in his hand to destroy us with.

Whatever may be the opinions of men in general in regard to Mr. Smith, we know that he needs only to be known to be admired; and that it is the principles of honor, integrity, patriotism, and philanthropy that have elevated him in the minds of his friends; and the same principles, if seen and known, would beget the esteem and confidence of all the patriotic and virtuous throughout the Union.

Whatever, therefore, be the opinions of other men our course is marked out, and our motto from henceforth will be—GENERAL JOSEPH SMITH.

CHAPTER XXXIV.

THE PROJECTED MOVEMENT TO THE WEST.

AS an evidence that the Prophet entertained no thought of success in his candidacy for the office of Chief Executive, we may mention the fact that, during the time that vigorous preparations were being made for the presidential canvass, he was setting on foot a scheme for taking the body of The Church into the west to settle Oregon. On the twentieth of February, 1844, the Prophet in his journal says:

"I instructed the Twelve Apostles to send out a delegation, and investigate the location of California and Oregon, and hunt out a good location, where we can remove to, after the temple is completed, and where we can build a city in a day, and have a government of our own, get up into the mountains, where the devil cannot dig us out, and live in a healthy climate, where we can live as old as we have a mind too."

In accordance with that instruction, the Twelve called the council on the twenty-first, and Jonathan Dunham, Phinehas H. Young and David Fullmer volunteered to go; and Alphonzo Young, James Emmett, George D. Watt, and Daniel Spencer were called to go.

Subsequently a memorial was drawn up by the Prophet, asking Congress to pass an enactment, authorizing him to raise a company for the purpose of establishing colonies in that vast, unsettled section of the country in the far West, known under the general name of Oregon. At that time there was no particular government existing in the region to which the names Oregon and California were loosely given. Nor was it certain whether that country would fall into the possession of England or the United States, as the northern boundary line question was then unsettled, and England and the United States held the country by a treaty of joint occupancy. As the Prophet preferred having an assurance of protection from the government on his enterprise, he asked Congress to pass the act before alluded to.

Orson Pratt and John E. Page, two of the Twelve, went to Washington in the interest of this scheme, and urged its consideration among the Congressmen. Subsequently, in April, 1844, Orson Hyde was sent to Washington in the interest of the same great project; and through the influence of Mr. Hoge, Representative to Congress from the district in which Nauvoo was included. Mr. Hardin, and Stephen A. Douglass, succeeded in approaching a number of members of Congress on the subject but received small encouragement, as Congressmen then, as now, were extremely cautious in engaging in anything affecting their reputation and prospects for political preferment for the future. But however much these men objected to advocating anything which looked like favoring openly the scheme of the Prophet, they all concurred in affirming that he had the right to lead his people to Oregon to settle, and the government would protect them. Stephen A. Douglass remarked, that if he could command the following that Mr. Smith could, he would resign his seat in Congress, to go to the West. On this subject Orson Hyde made two exhaustive reports to the Prophet in letters from Washington, which I here insert:

WASHINGTON, April 25th, 1844.

HON. SIR,—I take the liberty to transmit through you to the council of our Church the result of my labors thus far. I arrived in this place on the 23rd instant, by way of Pittsburgh, Philadelphia, and New Jersey.

I found Elder Orson Pratt here, Elder Page having been called home to Pittsburgh on account of his wife's ill health. Elder O.

Pratt has been indefatigable in his exertions in prosecuting the business entrusted to his charge. His business has been before the Senate, and referred to the committee on the judiciary; and the report of said committee is not yet rendered, which is the cause of his delay in writing to you.

Yesterday we conversed with Messrs. Hoge, Hardin, Douglass, and Wentworth, and last evening we spent several hours with the Hon. Mr. Semple They all appear deeply interested in the Oregon question, and received us with every demonstration of respect that we could desire. Mr. Hoge thought that the bill would not pass, from the fact that there already exists between England and America a treaty for the joint occupancy of Oregon, and that any act of our Government authorizing an armed force to be raised, and destined for that country, would be regarded by England as an infraction of that treaty, and a cause of her commencing hostilities against us.

But my reply was, These volunteers are not to be considered any part or portion of the army of the United States, neither acting under the direction or authority of the United States; and, said I, for men to go there and settle in the character of emigrants cannot be regarded by our Government as deviating in the least degree from her plighted faith, unless she intends to tamely submit to British monopoly in that country.

Mr. H., said he would present the memorial, if we desired it. I thanked him for his kind offer, but observed that I was not yet prepared for the bill to be submitted, but wished to elicit all the facts relative to the condition of Oregon, and also advise with many other members relative to the matter; and we could better determine then how the bill should be introduced. We do not want it presented and referred to a standing committee, and stuck away with five or ten cords of petitions, and that be the last of it; but we want the memorial read, a move made to suspend the rules of the house, and the bill printed, etc.

Mr. Wentworth said—"I am for Oregon anyhow. You may set me down on your list, and I will go for you if you will go for Oregon."

Judge Douglass has been quite ill, but is just recovered; he will elp all he can; Mr. Hardin likewise. But Major Semple says that he does not believe anything will be done about Texas or Oregon this session, for it might have a very important effect upon the presidential election; and politicians are slow to move when such doubtful and important matters are likely to be affected by it. He says that there are already two bills before the house for establishing a territorial government in Oregon, and to protect the emigrants there; and now he says, Were your bill to be introduced, it might be looked upon that you claimed the sole right of emigrating to and settling that new country to the exclusion of others. He was in favor of the Oregon being settled, and he thought the bills already before the house would extend equal protection to us; and equal protection to every class of citizens was what the government could rightly do; but particular privileges to any one class they could not rightly do.

I observed that the bill asked for no exclusive rights. It asks not for exclusive rights in Oregon, neither do we wish it. Other people might make a move to Oregon, and no prejudices bar their way, and their motives would not be misinterpreted.

But, said I, Missouri knows her guilt; and should we attempt to march to Oregon without the government throwing a protective shield over us, Missouri's crimes would lead her first to misinterpret our intentions, to fan the flame of popular excitement against us, and scatter the firebrands of a misguided zeal among the combustible materials of other places, creating a flame too hot for us to encounter—too desolating for us to indulge the hope of successfully prosecuting the grand and benevolent enterprise we have conceived. We have been compelled to relinquish our rights in Missouri. We have been forcibly driven from our homes, leaving our property and inheritances as spoil to the oppressor; and more or less in Illinois we have been subject to the whims and chimeras of illiberal men, and to threats, to vexatious prosecutions, and lawsuits.

Our government professes to have no power to help us, or to redress the wrongs which we have suffered; and we now ask the government to protect us while raising our volunteers. And when we get into Oregon we will protect ourselves and all others who wish our protection. And after subduing a new country, encountering all its difficulties and hardships, and sustaining the just claims of our nation to its soil, we believe that the generosity of our government towards us will be equal to our enterprise and patriotism, and that they will allow us a grant or territory of land, which will be both honorable in them and satisfactory to us.

This, he says, is all very just and reasonable. But still he thinks that Congress will take no step in relation to Oregon, from the fact that his resolution requesting the President of the United States to give notice to the British government for the abolition of the treaty of joint occupation was voted down; and while that treaty is in force, our government dare do nothing in relation to that country. This resolution was introduced by Mr. Semple to pave the way for the passage of those bills in relation to a territorial government in Oregon.

All our members join in the acknowledgement that you have an undoubted right to go to Oregon with all the emigrants you can raise. They say the existing laws protect you as much as law can protect you; and should Congress pass an additional law, it would not prevent wicked men from shooting you down as they did in Missouri. All the Oregon men in Congress would be glad if we would go to that country and settle it.

I will now give you my opinion in relation to this matter. It is made up from the spirit of the times in a hasty manner, nevertheless I think time will prove it correct:—That Congress will pass no act in relation to Texas or Oregon at present. She is afraid of England, afraid of Mexico, afraid the presidential election will be twisted by it. The members all appear like unskillful players at checkers—afraid to move, for they see not which way to move advantageously. All are figuring and playing round the grand and important questions. In the days of our Lord the people neglected the weightier matters of the law, but tithed mint, rue, anise, and cummin; but I think here in Washington they do little else than tithe the *mint*.

A member of Congress is in no enviable situation: if he will boldly advocate true principles, he loses his influence and becomes unpopular; and whoever is committed and has lost his influence has no power to benefit his constituents, so that all go to figuring and playing round the great points.

Mr. Semple said that Mr. Smith could not constitutionally be constituted a member of the army by law; and this, if nothing else, would prevent its passage. I observed that I would in that case strike out that clause. Perhaps I took an unwarrantable responsibility upon myself; but where I get into a straight place, I can do no better than act according to what appears most correct.

I do not intend the opinion that I have hastily given shall abate my zeal to drive the matter through, but I have given the opinion for your benefit, that your indulgence of the hope that Congress will do something for us may not cause you to delay any important action.

There is already a government established in Oregon to some extent; magistrates have been chosen by the people, &c. This is on the south of the Columbia. North of that river the Hudson Bay Company occupy. There is some good country in Oregon, but a great deal of sandy, barren desert. I have seen a gentleman who has been there, and also in California.

The most of the settlers in Oregon and Texas are our old enemies, the mobocrats of Missouri. If, however, the settlement of Oregon and Texas be determined upon, the sooner the move is made the better; and I would not advise any delay for the action of our government, for there is such a jealousy of our rising power already, that government will do nothing to favor us. If the Saints possess the kingdom, I think they will have to take it; and the sooner it is done the more easily it is accomplished.

Your superior wisdom must determine whether to go to Oregon, to Texas, or to remain within these United States, and send forth the most efficient men to build up churches, and let them remain for the time being; and in the meantime send some *wise* men among the Indians, and teach them civilization and religion, to cultivate the soil, to live in peace with one another and with all men. But whatever you do, don't be deluded with the hope that government will foster us, and thus delay an action which the present is the most proper time that ever will be [in which to accomplish it.—*R.*]

Oregon is becoming a popular question; the fever of emigration begins to rage. If the Mormons become the early majority, others will not come; if the Mormons do not become an early majority, the others will not allow us to come.

Elder Pratt is faithful, useful, and true; he has got the run of matters here very well, and is with me in all my deliberations, visitings, &c.

Major Semple goes with us this evening to introduce us to the President, and to view the White House.

My heart and hand are with you. May heaven bless you and me. As ever, I am

ORSON HYDE.

To the council of The Church of Jesus Christ of Latter-day Saints.

Also the following letter:—

WASHINGTON, April 26, 1844.

DEAR SIR,—Today I trouble you with another communication, which you will please have the goodness to lay before our council.

We were last evening introduced to the President at the White House by the politeness of Major Semple, where we spent an hour very agreeably. The President is a very plain, homespun, familiar, farmer-like man. He spoke of our troubles in Missouri, and regretted that we had met with such treatment. He asked us how we were getting along in Illinois. I told him that we were contending with the difficulties of a new country, and laboring under the disadvantageous consequences of being driven from our property and homes in Missouri.

We have this day had a long conversation with Judge Douglass. He is ripe for Oregon and the California. He said he would resign his seat in Congress if he could command the force that Mr. Smith could, and would be on the march to that country in a month.

I learn that the eyes of many aspiring politicians in this place are now upon that country, and that there is so much jealousy between them that they will probably pass no bill in relation to it. Now all these politicians rely upon the arm of our government to protect them there; and if government were to pass an act establishing a territorial government west of the Rocky Mountains there would be at once a tremendous rush of emigration; but if government pass no act in relation to it, these men have not stamina or sufficient confidence in themselves and their own resources to hazard the enterprise.

The northern Whig members are almost to a man against Texas and Oregon; but should the present administration succceed in annexing Texas, then all the Whigs would turn round in favor of Oregon; for if Texas be admitted, slavery is extended to the south; then free

States must be added to the west to keep up a balance of power between the slave and the free States.

Should Texas be admitted, war with Mexico is looked upon as inevitable. The Senate have been in secret session on the ratification of the treaty of annexation; but what they did we cannot say. General Gaines, who was boarding at the same house with Judge Douglass, was secretly ordered to repair to the Texan frontier four days ago, and left immediately. I asked Judge D. if he did not speak loud for annexation. He says, no. Santa Anna, being a jealous, hot-headed pate, might be suspicious the treaty would be ratified by the Senate, and upon mere suspicion might attempt some hostilities, and Gaines had been ordered there to be on the alert and ready for action if necessary. Probably our navy will in a few days be mostly in the Gulf of Mexico.

There are many powerful checks upon our government, preventing her from moving in any of these important matters; and for aught I know, these checks are permitted, to prevent our government from extending her jurisdiction over that territory which God designs to give to His Saints. Judge Douglass says he would equally as soon go to that country without an act of Congress as with; 'and that in five years a noble State might be formed; and then, if they would not receive us into the Union, we would have a government of our own.' He is decidedly of the opinion that congress will pass no act in favor of any particular man going there; but he says if any man will go, and desires that privilege, and has confidence in his own ability to perform it he already has the right, and the sooner he is off the better for his scheme.

It is the opinion here among politicians that it will be extremely difficult to have any bill pass in relation to the encouragement of emigration to Oregon; but much more difficult to get a bill passed designating any particular man to go. But all concur in the opinion that we are authorized already.

In case of a removal to that country, Nauvoo is the place of general rendezvous. Our course from thence would be westward through Iowa, bearing a little north until we came to the Missouri river, leaving the State of Missouri on the left, thence onward till we come to the Platte, thence up the north fork of the Platte to the mouth of Sweetwater river in longitude 107° 45′ W., and thence up said Sweetwater river to the South Pass of the Rocky Mountains, about eleven hundred miles from Nauvoo; and from said South Pass in latitude 42° 28′ north to the Umpaque and Klamet valleys in Oregon, bordering on California, is about 600 miles, making the distance from Nauvoo to the best portions of Oregon 1,700 miles.

There is no government established there; and it is so near California that when a government shall be established there, it may readily embrace that country likewise. There is much barren country, rocks, and mountains, in Oregon; but the valleys are very fertile. I am persuaded that Congress will pass no act in relation to that country, from the fact that the resolution requesting the President to give notice to the British government for the discontinuance of the treaty of joint occupation of Oregon was voted down with a rush; and this notice must be given before any action can be had, unless Congress violates the treaty; at least so say the politicians here.

Judge Douglass has given me a map of Oregon, and also a report on an exploration of the country lying between the Missouri river and the Rocky Mountains on the line of the Kansas and Great Platte rivers, by Lieutenant J. C. Fremont, of the corps of topographical engineers. On receiving it I expressed a wish that Mr. Smith could see it. Judge D. says it is a public document, and I will frank it to him. I accepted his offer, and the book will be forthcoming to him. The people are so eager for it here that they have even stolen it out of the library. The author is Mr. Benton's son-in-law. Judge D. borrowed it of Mr. B. I was not to tell anyone in this city where I got it. The book is a most valuable document to any one contemplating a journey to Oregon. The directions which I have given may not be exactly correct, but the book will tell correctly. Judge D. says he can direct Mr. Smith to several gentlemen in California who will be able to give him any information on the state of affairs in that country; and when he returns to Illinois, he will visit Mr. Smith.

Brother Pratt and myself drafted a bill this morning, and handed it in to the committee on the judiciary from the Senate, asking an appropriation of two million dollars for the relief of the sufferers among our people in Missouri in 1836-9, to be deposited in the hands of the city council of Nauvoo, and by them dealt out to the sufferers in proportion to their loss. We intend to tease them until we either provoke them or get them to do something for us. I have learned this much—that if we want Congress to do anything for us in drawing up our memorial, we must not ask what is right in the matter, but we must ask what kind of a thing will Congress pass? Will it suit the politics of the majority? Will it be popular or unpopular? For you might as well drive a musket ball through a cotton bag, or the Gospel of Christ through the heart of a priest, case-hardened by sectarianism, bigotry, and superstition, or a camel through the eye of a needle, as to drive anything through Congress that will operate against the popularity of politicians.

I shall probably leave here in a few days, and Brother Pratt will remain. I go to get money to sustain ourselves with.

I shall write again soon, and let you know what restrictions, if any, are laid upon our citizens in relation to passing through the Indian territories. I shall communicate everything I think will benefit. In the meantime if the council have any instructions to us, we shall be happy to receive them here or at Philadelphia.

John Ross is here; we intend to see him. It is uncertain when Congress rises. It will be a long pull in my opinion. As ever, I am,

Yours sincerely,

ORSON HYDE.

Elder Pratt's best respects to the brethren.

An event soon afterwards took place in the House of Representatives before the Prophet's petition was introduced, which put at rest all hopes of Congress doing anything at that time in relation to the Oregon territory. A resolution was introduced giving Great Britain notice that the treaty of joint occupancy of that country was at an end, but it was promptly voted down. That virtually served public notice that the Oregon question was not to be reopened by Congress, at least not until the conclusion of the presidential election.

Sufficient may be gathered from what is set down in the above, to prove that the mind of the Prophet Joseph was bent on establishing his people in the West—somewhere in the Rocky

Mountains—so soon as they could complete the temple. The subject began to take possession of his mind wholly. Some eighteen months before his formal appeal to Congress, for the privilege of settling with his people in the far West, under the protecting ægis of the general government, *viz.*, on the sixth of August, 1842, he prophesied, that his people would continue to suffer much persecution, and at last be driven to the Rocky Mountains. This is the prophecy as it stands in the Prophet's journal:

> Saturday, sixth, [August]. Passed over the river to Montrose, Iowa, in company with General Adams, Colonel Brewer, and others, and witnessed the installation of the officers of the Rising Sun Lodge, of Ancient York Masons, at Montrose, by General James Adams, Deputy Grand Master of Illinois. While the Deputy Grand Master was engaged in giving the requisite instruction to the Master elect, I had a conversation with a number of brethren in the shade of the building on the subject of our persecutions in Missouri, and the constant annoyance which has followed us since we were driven from that State. I prophesied that the Saints would continue to suffer much affliction and would be driven to the Rocky Mountains, many would apostatize, others would be put to death by our persecutors, or lose their lives in consequence of exposure or disease, and some of you will live to go and assist in making settlements and build cities, and see the Saints become a mighty people in the midst of the Rocky Mountains.*—*Millennial Star, Vol. xix, page* 630.

As persecution in Illinois grew more relentless, and mobocrats more bold, until the whole horizon appeared black, and threatening with hatred toward the citizens of Nauvoo, the Prophet told them repeatedly it was "light in the west."

---

* See the author's work, "Succession in the Presidency," where the subject is more exhaustively considered.

CHAPTER XXXV.

THE STANDARD OF PEACE.

MEANTIME the people of Nauvoo, with the Prophet as chief mover in the matter, sought to establish peaceful relations with their neighbors. Armed conflict with surrounding peoples, or with any people, was no part of the policy of Joseph Smith; and no part of the work that he had in hand. It is true that it may be said of the work he introduced, as Jesus said of the work which He began by His personal ministry that it brought not peace but a sword;* in each case, however, "the sword" has been found in the hands, not of those who have accepted the Gospel, but in the hands of those who have rejected it, and opposed it, and made war upon it. Early in the history of the work brought forth by Joseph Smith the Lord commanded His servants to "renounce war and proclaim peace;"† and true to this spirit of the work the Prophet especially sought for peace. In the *Warsaw Signal* of the 14th of February Governor Ford published the following letter to the citizens of Hancock County, in the hope, evidently, of quelling the threatening storm:

SPRINGFIELD, January 29, 1844.

DEAR SIR,—I have received the copy of the proceedings and resolutions of a meeting of the citizens of Hancock County, which you did me the honour to send me.

I have observed with regret that occasions have been presented

---

* Matt. x: 34-40.

† August, 1833, Doc. & Cov. Sec. xcviii.

for disturbing the peace of your county; and if I knew what I could legally do to apply a corrective, I would be very ready to do it. But if you are a lawyer or at all conversant with the law, you will know that, I as a governor, have no right to interfere in your difficulties.

As yet, I believe that there has been nothing like war among you; and I hope that all of you will have the good sense to see the necessity of preserving peace. If there is anything wrong in the Nauvoo charters, or in the mode of administering them, you will see that nothing short of legislative or judiical power is capable of enforcing a remedy.

I myself had the honor of calling the attention of the Legislature to this subject at the last session; but a large majority of both political parties in that body either did not see the evil which you complain of, or, if they did, they repeatedly refused to correct it. And yet a call is made upon me, to do that which all parties refused to do at the last session.

I have also been called upon to take away the arms from the *Mormons*, to raise the militia to arrest a supposed fugitive, and in fact to repeal some of the ordinances of the city of Nauvoo.

Hancock County is justly famed for its intelligence; and I cannot believe that any of its citizens are so ignorant as not to know that I have no power to do these things.

The absurd and preposterous nature of these requests gave some color to the charge that they are made for political effect only. I hope that this charge is untrue: for, in all candor, it would be more creditable to those concerned to have their errors attributed to ignorance than to a disposition to embroil the country in the horrors of war for the advancement of party ends.

But if there should be any truth in the charge, (which God forbid) I affectionately entreat all the good citizens engaged in it to lay aside their designs and yield up their ears to the voice of justice, reason and humanity. All that I can do at present is to admonish both parties to beware of carrying matters to extremity.

Let it come to this—let a state of war ensue, and I will be compelled to interfere with executive power. In that case also, I wish, in a friendly, affectionate, and candid manner, to tell the citizens of

Hancock County, *Mormons* and all, that my interference will be against those who shall be the first transgressors.

I am bound by the laws and Constitution to regard you all as citizens of the State, possessed of equal rights and privileges, and to cherish the rights of one as dearly as the rights of another. I can know no distinction among you except that of assailant and assailed.

I hope, dear sir, you will do me the favor to publish this letter in the papers of your county, for the satisfaction of all persons concerned.

I am, with the highest respect,
Your obedient servant,
THOMAS FORD.

To this letter three days later the Prophet-mayor made the following response in the *Nauvoo Neighbor*, under the caption

PACIFIC INNUENDO.

The very candid, pacific and highly creditable *advice* which Governor Ford has done himself the honor to address to "the citizens of Hancock County, 'Mormons and all,'" and which appears in the *Warsaw Signal* of the 14th instant, is, like the balm of Gilead, well calculated to ease the pain which has troubled the heads and hearts of the Carthagenians, Warsawvians and other over-jealous bodies for *weal and woe*.

It certainly must be admitted, on all hands, that Governor Ford has exalted himself as a mediator, patriot, lawyer, governor, peacemaker, and friend of all, not only to magnify the law and make it honorable, but also in pointing out the *path of peace*.

Such is what the Latter-day Saints have ever sought at the hands of those in authority; and with an approving conscience clear as the crystal spring, and with a laudable intention warm as the summer zephyr, and with a charitable prayer mellow as the morning dew, it is now our highest consolation to hope that all difficulties will cease, and give way to reason, sense, peace and goodwill.

The Saints, if they will be humble and wise, can now *practice* what they *preach*, and soften by good examples, rather than harden by a distinct course of conduct, the hearts of the people.

For general information, it may be well to say that there has never been any cause for alarm as to the Latter-day Saints. The Legislature of Illinois granted a liberal charter for the city of Nauvoo; and let every honest man in the Union who has any knowledge of her say whether she has not flourished beyond the most sanguine anticipations of all. And while they witness her growing glory, let them solemnly testify whether Nauvoo has *wilfully injured* the country, county or a single individual *one cent*.

With the strictest scrutiny publish the facts, whether a particle of law has been evaded or broken: virtue and innocence need no artificial covering. Political views and party distinctions never should disturb the harmony of society; and when the whole truth comes before a virtuous people, we are willing to abide the issue.

We will here refer to the *three late dismissals* upon writs of *habeas corpus*, of Joseph Smith, when arrested under the requisitions of Missouri.

The first, in June, 1841, was tried at Monmouth, before Judge Douglass, of the fifth judicial circuit; and as no exceptions have been taken to that decision by this State or Missouri, but Missouri had previously entered a *nolle prosequi* on all the old indictments against the "Mormons" in the difficulties of 1838, it is taken for granted *that that decision was just.*

The second, in December, 1842, was tried at Springfield before Judge Pope in the United States District Court; and from that honorably discharged, as no exceptions from any source have been made to those proceedings, it follows as a matter of course *that that decision was just!*

And the third, in July, 1843, was tried at the city of Nauvoo, before the municipal court of said city; and as no exceptions to that discharge have been taken, and as the governor says there is "evidence on the other side to show that the sheriff of Lee County *voluntarily* carried Mr. Reynolds (who had Mr. Smith in custody,) to the city of Nauvoo without any coercion on the part of any one" it must be admitted *that that decision was just!*

But is any man still unconvinced of the justness of these strictures relative to the two last cases, let the astounding fact go forth, that *Orin Porter Rockwell*, whom Boggs swore was the principal in his assassination, and accessory to which Mr. Smith was arrested, *has returned home, "clear of that sin."* In fact, there was not a witness to get up an indictment against him.

The Messrs. Averys, who were unlawfully transported out of this State, have returned to their families in peace; and there seems to be no ground for contention, no cause for jealousy, and no excuse for a surmise that any man, woman or child will suffer the least inconvenience from General Smith, the charter of Nauvoo, the city of Nauvoo, or even any of her citizens.

There is nothing for a bone of contention! Even those ordinances which appear to excite the feeling of some people have recently been *repealed*; so that if the "intelligent" inhabitants of Hancock County want peace, want to abide by the governor's advice, want to have a character abroad grow out of their character at home, and really mean to follow the Savior's golden rule, "*To do unto others as they would wish others to do unto them*," they will be still *now*, and let their own works praise them in the gates of justice and in the eyes of the surrounding world. Wise men ought to have understanding enough to conquer men with kindness.

"A soft answer turns away wrath," says the wise man; and it will be greatly to the credit of the Latter-day Saints to show the love of God, by now kindly treating those who may have, in an unconscious moment, done them wrong; for truly said Jesus, "*Pray for thine enemies.*"

Humanity towards all, reason and refinement to enforce virtue, and good for evil are so eminently designed to cure more disorders of society than an appeal to "arms," or even *argument* untempered with *friendship* and the "one thing needful," that no vision for the future, guideboard for the distant, or expositor for the present, need trouble any one with what he ought to do.

His own good, his family's good, his neighbor's good, his country's good, and all good seem to whisper to every person—the governor has told you what to do—*now do it.*

The Constitution expects every man to do his duty; and when he fails the law urges him; or, should he do too much, the same master rebukes him.

Should reason, liberty, law, light and philanthropy now guide the destinies of Hancock County with as much sincerity as has been manifested for her notoriety or welfare, there can be no doubt that peace, prosperity and happiness will prevail, and that future generations as well as the present one will call Governor Ford a peacemaker. The Latter-day Saints will, at all events, and profit by the instruction, and call upon honest men to help them cherish all the love, all the friendship, all the courtesy, all the kindly feelings and all the generosity that ought to characterize *clever people* in a clever neighborhood, and leave candid men to judge which tree exhibits the best fruit—the one with the most clubs and sticks thrown into its boughs and the grass trodden down under it, or the one with no sticks in it, some dead limbs and rank grass growing under it; for by their signs ye can know their fruit, and by the fruit ye know the trees.

Our motto, then, is *Peace with all*! If we have joy in the love of God, let us try to give a reason of that joy, which all the world cannot gainsay or resist. And may be, like as when Paul started with recommendations to Damascus to persecute the Saints, some one who has raised his hand against us with letters to men in high places may see a light at noonday, above the brightness of the sun, and hear the voice of Jesus saying, "*It is hard for thee to kick against the pricks.*"

Intelligence is sometimes the messenger of safety. And, willing to aid the governor in his laubable endeavors to cultivate peace and honor the laws, believing that very few of the citizens of Hancock County will be found in the negative of such a goodly course; and considering his views a kind of manifesto, or olive leaf, which shows that there is rest for the soles of the Saints' feet, we give it a place in the *Neighbor*, wishing it God speed, and saying, *God bless good men and good measures!* And as Nauvoo has been, so it will continue to be, a good city, affording a good market to a good country; and let those who do not mean to try the way of transgressors, say "*Amen.*"

In addition to this in a note to the editor of the *Neighbor*, he advised that he take no further editorial notice of the fulminations of the editor of the *Warsaw Signal* against the people of Nauvoo, but recommended that the advice of Governor

Ford be honored, and that friendship and peace be cultivated with all men.

The Prophet went further than this. He tendered the olive branch of peace even to Missouri. He dictated the following to W. W. Phelps which was published under the title—

A FRIENDLY HINT TO MISSOURI.

One of the most pleasing scenes that can transpire on earth, when a sin has been committed by one person against another, is, *to forgive that sin;* and then, according to the sublime and perfect pattern of the Savior, pray to our Father in heaven *to forgive also.*

Verily, verily, such a friendly rebuke is like the mellow zephyr of summer's eve—it soothes, it cheers and gladdens the heart of the humane and the savage. Well might the wise man exclaim, "A soft answer turneth away wrath;" for men of sense, judgment, and observation, in all the various periods of time, have been witnesses, figuratively speaking, that *water, not wood, checks the rage of fire.*

Jesus said, "Blessed are the peacemakers, for they shall be called the children of God." Wherefore, if the nation, a single state, community, or family ought to be grateful for anything, *it is peace.*

Peace, lovely child of heaven!—peace, like light from the same great parent, gratifies, animates, and happifies the just and the unjust; and is the very essence of happiness below, and bliss above.

He that does not strive with all his powers of body and mind, with all his influence at home and abroad, and to cause others to do so too, to seek peace and maintain it for his own benefit and convenience, and for the honor of his State, nation, and country, has no claim on the clemency of man; nor should he be entitled to the friendship of woman or the protection of government.

He is the canker-worm to gnaw his own vitals, and the vulture to prey upon his own body; and he is, as to his own prospects and prosperity in life, a *felo-de-se* of his own pleasure.

A community of such beings are not far from hell on earth, and should be let alone as unfit for the smiles of the free or the praise of the brave. * * * * * * *

So much to preface this friendly hint to the State of Missouri;

for, notwithstanding some of her private citizens and public officers have committed violence, robbery, and even murder upon the rights and persons of the Church of Jesus Christ of Latter-day Saints, yet compassion, dignity, and a sense of the principles of religion among all classes, and honor and benevolence, mingled with charity by high-minded patriots, lead me to suppose that there are many worthy people in that State who will use their influence and energies to bring about a settlement of all those old difficulties, and use all consistent means to urge the State, for her honor, prosperity, and good name, to restore every person she or her citizens have expelled from her limits, to their rights, and pay them all damage, that the great body of high-minded and well-disposed Southern and Western gentlemen and ladies—the real peacemakers of a western world, will go forth, good Samaritan-like, and pour in the oil and wine, till all that can be healed are made whole; and, after repentance, they shall be forgiven; for verily the Scriptures say, "Joy shall be in heaven over one sinner that repents, more than over ninety-and-nine just persons that need

But the peacemaker, O give ear to him! for the words of his

no repentance." * * * * * *

When you meditate upon the massacre at Haun's mill, forget not that the constitution of your State holds this broad truth to the world, that none shall "be deprived of *life, liberty, or property*, but by the judgment of his peers or the law of the land."

And when you assemble together in towns, counties, or districts, whether to petition your legislature to pay the damage the Saints have sustained in your State, by reason of oppression and misguided zeal, or to restore them to their rights according to Republican principles and benevolent designs, reflect, and make honorable, or annihilate, such statute law as was in force in your State in 1838,—viz., "If twelve or more persons shall combine to levy war against any part of the people of this State, or to remove forcibly out of the State or from their habitations, evidenced by taking arms and assembling to accomplish such purpose, every person so offending shall be punished by imprisonment in the penitentiary for a period not exceeding five years, or by a fine not exceeding five thousand dollars, and imprisonment in the county jail not exceeding six months."

Finally, if honor dignifies an honest people, if virtue exalts a community, if wisdom guides great men, if principle governs intelligent beings, if humanity spreads comfort among the needy, and if religion affords consolation by showing that charity is the first, best, and sweetest token of perfect love, then, O ye good people of Missouri, like the woman in Scripture *who had lost one of her ten pieces of silver*, arise, search diligently till you find the lost piece, and then make a feast, and call in your friends for joy.

With due consideration,

I am the friend of all good men,

JOSEPH SMITH.

Nauvoo, Ill., March 8, 1843.

Surely this was going as far in the interests of peace as men or God could require him to go; but alas! there was to be no peace.

CHAPTER XXXVI.

"IN PERIL AMONG FALSE BRETHREN."

THE winter of 1843-4 was big with events affecting the destinies of Nauvoo. During that winter were set on foot conspiracies which culminated in the destruction of Nauvoo. Men who stood nearest to the Prophet Joseph, and who were bound in honor to defend his life, not bare the knives that were to strike him down, combined together in secret covenant for his overthrow.

Owing to the constant efforts of the Prophet's enemies in Missouri, to capture him and drag him to Missouri where he might be murdered with impunity, the force of police in Nauvoo was increased by the appointment of forty night-guards to patrol the city. These made it less convenient for the conspirators, who worked, as men ever do when engaged in such business—in the darkness. The night guards several times came in contact with men moving about the city in a manner which, to say the least, was suspicious; and soon complaints were made by these same parties that the city government was arbitrary and oppressive; they claimed that these night-watchmen threatened their peace and even started rumors that Joseph had appointed them for the purpose of intimidation.

Among others who complained of the appointment of night-watchmen was William Marks, president of the Nauvoo stake. Joseph, in the course of a speech made at a meeting of the city council at the time of the appointment of the special watchmen, referred to the danger of invasion from Missouri and incidentally remarked: "We have a Judas in our midst." This gave great offense to both William Marks and the Law brothers. The Prophet in his journal, when speaking of the circumstance, says: "What can be the matter with these men? Is it that the wicked flee when no man pursueth, that hit pigeons always flutter, that drowning men clutch at straws, or that Presidents Law and Marks are absolutely traitors to The Church, that my remarks should produce such excitement in their minds? Can it be possible that the traitor whom Porter Rockwell reports to me as being in correspondence with my Missouri enemies is one of my quorum [the First Presidency]? The people in the town were astonished, almost every man saying to his neighbor, 'Is it possible that Brother Law or Marks is a traitor, and would deliver Brother Joseph into the hands of his enemies in Missouri?' If not what can be the meaning of all this? The righteous are bold as a lion."*

In the spring of 1844, the Prophet was apprised by two young men, Denison L. Harris and Robert Scott, the latter living in the family of William Law, of a secret movement then on foot to take his life, and the lives of several other leading men of The Church; among them the Prophet's brother, Hyrum. These young men were invited to the secret meetings by the conspirators, but before going, conferred with the Prophet, who told them to go, but to take no part in the proceedings of these wicked men against himself. They carried out his advice, and at the risk of their lives attended the secret meetings three

---

* Millennial Star, volume xxii: page 631. This Wm. Marks afterwards was prominent among those who induced the Prophet to come back and deliver himself up to his enemies after the Prophet had started west. After the Prophet's death he joined the apostate James J. Strang in his attempt to lead The Church, and still later was a principal factor in bringing into existence the "Josephite" or "Reorganized Church." See the author's work on "Succession in the Presidency of The Church."

times, and brought to Joseph a report of what they had witnessed.*

In addition to the testimonies of these young men was that of M. G. Eaton, who expressed a willingness to make affidavit that there was a plot laid to kill Joseph Smith and others, and would give the names of those who had concocted it. There was also one A. B. Williams who said the same thing. These men went before Daniel H. Wells, at the time a justice of the peace, and made affidavit that such a plot as I have spoken of existed. In their statements they named as leaders of the movement, Chauncey L. Higbee, R. D. Foster, Joseph H. Jackson, and William and Wilson Law. These names correspond with those given by the young men before alluded to, except they also name Austin Cowles, a member of the High Council, at Nauvoo, as one of the active and leading conspirators.

These statements were shortly confirmed by the action of the conspirators themselves, as they soon came out in open as well as secret opposition to the leading Church authorities; and in March a number of them were excommunicated for unchristianlike conduct. Among the number was William Law, a member in the First Presidency, his brother Wilson Law; the Higbee brothers, Chauncey L., and Francis M., and Dr. Robert D. Foster.

An effort was made by these apostates to organize a church after the pattern of the true Church, by the appointment of apostles, prophets, presidents, etc., but it failed miserably, their following was insignificant. These men were desperately wicked; in addition to gross licentiousness they were guilty of theft and of counterfeiting money. They brought much reproach upon the city of Nauvoo, since their crimes were traced to her borders, and that fact went far towards undoing the city's reputa-

---

* A full account of this conspiracy written by Horace Cummings was published in the Contributor, vol. v.

tion abroad. But though these men at one time, and indeed up to the time of their excommunication, held high official positions in The Church and the city, their wickedness was not sustained either by The Church laws or by the members of The Church, or citizens of Nauvoo. It was known that there existed a band of desperate men within the city, and these parties were suspected, but it required some time to obtain proof sufficiently positive to act upon; and where the counterfeiting was done was never learned.

The mask having at last fallen from the faces of this coterie of men, they joined with the avowed enemies of the Saints outside of Nauvoo, and openly advocated the repeal of the city charter, which but a short time before they had assisted to obtain. They violated on several occasions the city ordinances, resisted the city officers, and threatened the life of the mayor. These disturbances led to the arrests and trials before the municipal court, from which the accused generally appealed to the circuit courts; and retaliated by counter arrests of the city authorities for false imprisonment, defamation of character, etc. In all these cases the power of the municipal courts to grant writs of *habeas corpus* was freely exercised, and released the city authorities, as the actions were malicious, and without sufficient cause on which to base the complaints. Thus the affairs of Nauvoo became more and more complicated, and the bitterness constantly increased.

At last the disaffected parties imported a press into the city and proposed publishing a paper to be called the *Nauvoo Expositor*. It avowed its intention in the prospectus it published to agitate for the repeal of the Nauvoo charter, and also announced that since its position in the city of the Saints afforded it opportunities of being familiar with the abuses that prevailed, its publishers intended to give a full, candid and succinct statement of facts as they really existed in the city of Nauvoo, regardless of whose standing in the community might be imperiled.

The proprietors of the paper were the band of conspirators already named, and Sylvester Emmons was employed as editor.

The first, and indeed the only number of the *Expositor* was published on the seventh day of June, 1844, and contained a most scandalous attack upon the most respectable citizens of Nauvoo. It at once filled the entire city with indignation, and the city council immediately took into consideration what would be the best method of dealing with it. The result of the council's meditations was this: Blackstone declared a libelous press a nuisance; the city charter gave to city authorities the power to declare what should be considered a nuisance and to prevent and remove the same; therefore it was

Resolved, by the city council of the city of Nauvoo, that the printing office from whence issues the *Nauvoo Expositor* is a public nuisance, and also all of said *Nauvoo Expositors*, which may be or exist, in said establishment; and the mayor is instructed to cause said printing establishment and papers to be removed without delay, in such manner as he may direct.

On receiving this order the mayor issued instructions to the city marshal to destroy the press without delay, and at the same time gave orders to Jonathan Dunham, acting Major-General of the Nauvoo Legion, to assist the marshal with the Legion if called upon to do so.

The marshal with a small force of men appeared before the *Expositor* printing establishment, informed one or more of the proprietors of the character of his mission, and demanded entrance into the building to carry out his instructions from the mayor. This was denied and the door locked; whereupon the marshal broke in the door, carried out the press, broke it in the street, pied the type and burned all the papers found in the office, and then reported to the mayor, who sent an account of these proceedings to the governor of the State.

This act enraged the conspirators to a higher pitch of desperation. They set fire to their buildings and then fled to Carthage, the county seat of Hancock County, with the lie in their mouths that their lives were in danger in Nauvoo, and that they were driven away from their homes. Fortunately the police discovered the flames started by these incendiaries in time to extinguish them, so that they failed to have the smoking ruins of their own houses to support their story; but their misrepresentations spread like wild-fire and inflamed the public mind, already blinded with prejudice against the people of Nauvoo, to a point which made violence almost certain.

Francis M. Higbee made a complaint before Thomas Morrison, a justice of the peace, against Joseph Smith and all the members of the Nauvoo city council for riot committed in destroying the anti-Mormon press. The warrant issued by the justice was served by Constable Bettisworth upon Joseph Smith at Nauvoo. It required him and the others named in the warrant to go before the justice issuing the warrant, "*or some other justice of the peace.*" Joseph called the attention of the constable to this clause in the writ, and expressed a willingness to go before Esquire Johnson, or any other justice of the peace in Nauvoo. But Bettisworth was determined to take Joseph to Carthage before Justice Morrison, who had issued the writ. Joseph was equally determined not to go, and petitioned the municipal court for a writ of *habeas corpus* which was granted, and under it the prisoner was honorably discharged The other parties mentioned in the writ followed his example and were also discharged.

Meantime indignation meetings were held first at Warsaw, and afterwards in Carthage. The men who had used their uttermost endeavors, for more than two years to incite the people to acts of mob violence against the Saints, had now a popular war cry—"unhallowed hands had been laid upon the liberty of the press." "The law had ceased to be a protection to lives or property in Nauvoo!" "A mob at Nauvoo, under a city ordinance had violated the highest privilege in the government; and to seek redress in the ordinary mode would be utterly ineffectual." Therefore those in attendance upon these meetings adopted resolutions announcing themselves at all times ready to co-operate with their fellow-citizens in Missouri and Iowa to exterminate, *utterly exterminate* the wicked and abominable Mormon leaders, the authors of their troubles.

Committees were appointed to notify all persons in the respective townships suspected of being the "tools of the Prophet to leave immediately, on pain of *instant vengeance.*" And it was further recommended that the adherents of Joseph Smith as a body, be "driven from the surrounding settlements into Nauvoo; that the Prophet and his miscreant adherents should then be demanded at their hands; and, if not surrendered, a war of entire extermination should be waged to the entire destruction, if necessary for the mob's protection, of his adherents; and to carry out these resolutions every citizen was called upon to arm himself."

The mass meeting at Carthage, which had adopted the Warsaw resolutions was in full blast when the news arrived of the failure of Constable Bettisworth, to drag the Prophet into their midst. This increased the excitement, and poured more gall into the cup of bitterness. It was resolved that the "riot" in Nauvoo was still progressing, and of such a serious character as to demand executive interference; and therefore two discreet citizens were appointed to go to Springfield and lay the case before Governor Ford. But this appeal to the executive was not to interfere with the resolutions before passed—active preparations for the extermination of the Mormons were to be continued.

The athorities at Nauvoo also dispatched trusty messengers to Governor Ford with truthful accounts of their proceedings, both as regards the destruction of the press and their action in refusing to accompany Constable Bettisworth to Carthage, that he might not be misled by a false representation of the case, or influenced by the thousand and one falsehoods that had been set on foot by the enemies of the Saints.

Both parties then appealed to the executive of the State: the mob for assistance to carry out their murderous designs, and to give their proceedings a coloring of lawful authority, and the citizens of Nauvoo for protection against the combinations of their avowed enemies bent upon, and publicly pledged to their extermination.

Without waiting the issue of this appeal, however, the mob forces in Carthage, Warsaw and other localities began active operations by sending their committees to the settlements of the Saints outside of Nauvoo, and threatening them with destruction if they did not accept one of three propositions: first, deny that Joseph Smith was a Prophet of God, and take up arms and accompany the mob to arrest him; second, gather up their effects and forthwith remove to the city of Nauvoo; third, give up their arms and remain quiet until the pending difficulties should be settled by the expulsion of their friends. Usually a few days were given the people to consider these propositions, which were utilized by the people in conferring with the Prophet, to know what he advised under the circumstances. The advice given, in its general purport was to yield up none of their rights as American citizens to the demand of mobocrats, but to maintain their rights wherever they were strong enough to resist the mob forces, and when they were not strong enough, retreat to Nauvoo.

Besides the reports which came to Nauvoo from the Saints who were threatened, the air was filled with rumors of mob forces collecting on every hand. Great excitement was reported to exist in upper Missouri, the part of that State from which the Saints had been driven but six years before; and it was reported that the Missourians were going over into Illinois in large numbers to assist the anti-Mormons in and around

Carthage. That arms and ammunition were sent over the Mississippi to the mob, is quite certain; and it is also known that Walter Bagley, the tax-collector for Hancock County, had spent some time in Missouri as an anti-Mormon agent and agitator, seeking to bring about a concerted action between the old enemies of the Saints, and those of like ilk in Illinois.

While these hostile preparations were being made for his destruction, and the extermination of his people, those at all acquainted with the temperament of the Prophet Joseph, might well know that he was not idle. He kept an efficient corps of clerks busy copying reports and affidavits of threatened violence and insurrection, and sent them to the governor, whom he petitioned to come to Nauvoo and in person investigate the causes of the disturbance. Information was also sent to the President of the United States, acquainting him with the prospects of an insurrection, and an invasion of Illinois by Missourians, and asking him for protection.

Nor was Joseph and his associates neglectful of anything that would have a tendency to allay the excitement. Jesse B. Thomas, judge of the circuit in which Hancock County was located, advised him to go before some justice of the peace of the county and have an examination of the charges specified in the writ issued by justice Morrison of Carthage, and that would take away all excuse for a mob, and he would be bound to order them to keep the peace. Some advised the Prophet to go to Carthage, but that he emphatically refused to do. But he and all others named in justice Morrison's warrant went before Squire Wells, a non-Mormon justice of the peace, and after a thorough investigation of the case were acquitted.

In addition to these movements, a mass meeting was held in Nauvoo, at which John Taylor was chairman. Pacific resolutions were adopted, denying the misrepresentations of the apostates, and appointing men to go to the neighboring towns and settlements to present the truth to the people and allay excitement. These men were authorized to say that the members of the city council charged with riot and the violation of law, were willing to go before the circuit court for an investigation of their conduct in respect to the *Nauvoo Expositor*, and refused not to be bound over for such a hearing. But when this announcement was made and it was learned that Judge Thomas had advised this course to allay excitement, the mob threatened that a committee would wait upon the judge and give him a coat of tar and feathers for giving such advice.

These pacific measures appearing to have little or no effect, and active preparations for hostilities continuing on the part of the enemy, Nauvoo was placed under martial law; the Legion was mustered into service, and Joseph in person took command of it. He was in full uniform when he appeared before the Legion, and mounting an unfinished frame building near the Mansion, he took occasion to address the Legion and the people for about an hour and a half; during which time he reviewed the events that had brought upon Nauvoo the issue that confronted them.

To dispel any illusion that any of them might have that he was the only one threatened, he said:

> It is thought by some that our enemies would be satisfied by my destruction, but I tell you as soon as they have shed my blood, they will thirst for the blood of every man in whose heart dwells a single spark of the spirit of the fullness of the Gospel. The opposition of these men is moved by the spirit of the adversary of all righteousness. It is not only to destroy me, but every man and woman who dares believe the doctrines that God hath inspired me to teach to this generation—

Words which subsequent events will prove to have been prophetic. He also said:

> We have forwarded a particular account of all our doings to the governor. We are ready to obey his commands, and we expect that protection at his hands which we know to be our just due.

We may add also, that when a petition was sent to the governor to come to Nauvoo in person to investigate the cause of the disturbance, the service of the Legion was tendered him to keep the peace. But that Joseph had come to a settled determination to maintain the rights of the people at all hazards, and submit no longer to mob violence, may be clearly understood from the spirit of these extracts from the speech made to the Legion on the occasion of his taking command of it.

We are American citizens. We live upon a soil for the liberties of which our fathers periled their lives and spilt their blood upon the battlefield. Those rights so dearly purchased shall not be disgracefully trodden under foot by lawless marauders without at least a noble effort on our part to sustain our liberties. Will you stand by me to the death, and sustain at the peril of our lives, the laws of our country, and the liberties and privileges which our fathers have transmitted unto us, sealed with their sacred blood? (Thousands shouted aye!) It is well. If you had not done it, I would have gone out there, (pointing to the west) and would have raised up a mighty people.

I call upon all men from Maine to the Rocky Mountains, and from Mexico to British America, whose hearts thrill with horror to behold the rights of free men trampled under foot, to come to the deliverance of this people from the cruel hand of oppression, cruelty, anarchy and misrule to which they have long been made subject. * * * I call upon God and angels to witness that I have unsheathed my sword with a firm and unalterable determination that this people shall have their legal rights and shall be protected from mob violence, or my blood shall be spilt upon the ground like water, and my body be consigned to the silent tomb. While I live, I will never tamely submit to the dominion of cursed mobocracy.

There was much more of a like tenor, but this is sufficient to show the determination of the Prophet not to submit to the mobs then rising about him; and the people warmly seconded his resolution.

At this juncture Joseph requested his brother Hyrum to take his family and go with them to Cincinnati. But Hyrum demurred and said, "Joseph, I can't leave you!" Joseph, turning to a number of brethren present, said: "I wish I could get Hyrum out of the way, so that he may live to avenge my blood, and I will stay with you and see it out." But Hyrum Smith was not the kind of man to leave his brother now that the hour of his severest trial had come upon him. His noble nature revolted at the thought, and though the spirit had doubtless whispered Joseph that his life and that of Hyrum's would be sacrificed in the impending crisis, his pathetic words, "Joseph, I can't leave you!" bear testimony to the nobility of the soul that uttered them, and is a witness to the strength of those bonds of love that bound him to his younger brother. Moreover, in consequence of the Prophet's premonitions of his approaching martyrdom, he had ordained his brother Hyrum to succeed him in the presidency of The Church; and hence this consideration as well as his affectionate regard for him as a brother doubtless led him to try to get Hyrum out of harm's way.*

Word was sent to Brigham Young, then on a mission in the eastern States, to return to Nauvoo, and to communicate with the other Apostles and request them also to return to Nauvoo, as likewise all the Elders, and as many more good, faithful men as felt disposed to accompany them, to assist the Saints. Thus every effort was being put forth by the people of Nauvoo to resist oppression and maintain their rights.

---

* "If Hyrum had lived he would not have stood between Joseph and the Twelve, but he would have stood for Joseph. Did Joseph ordain any man to take his place? He did. Who was it? It was Hyrum. But Hyrum fell a martyr before Joseph did."—*Brigham Young*, in a speech at the October conference at Nauvoo, 1844. In *Times and Seasons*, Vol. v. p. 683.

CHAPTER XXXVII.

COMPLIANCE WITH THE DEMANDS OF GOVERNOR FORD.

IN the midst of these preparations, a message was received from Governor Ford, stating that he had arrived in Carthage in the interests of pcace, and hoped to be able to avert the evils of war by his presence; and that he might the better judge of the situation he asked that well-informed and discreet persons be sent to him at Carthage, where he had established for the time his headquarters. This request of the governor's was gladly complied with on the part of the people of Nauvoo; and John Taylor and Dr. J. M. Bernhisel were appointed to represent their version of the situation, and for that purpose were furnished with a copy of the proceedings of the city council, and the affidavits of a number of citizens bearing on the subjects that would likely be discussed.

These representatives of the citizens of Nauvoo, found the governor surrounded by their enemies—the Laws, Fosters, and Higbees, besides others living at Warsaw and Carthage. The only audience given to Messrs. Taylor and Bernhisel was in the presence of these parties, by whom they were frequently interrupted in the most insulting manner, and the parties insulting and abusing them were unchecked by Governor Ford.

After the governor had heard the statements of these gentlemen and read the documents presented by them, he sent a written communication to the mayor, Joseph Smith, in which he said that by destroying the *Expositor* press, the city council of Nauvoo had committed a gross outrage upon the laws and liberties of the people, and had violated the Constitution in several particulars. He also claimed that the municipal court of Nauvoo had exceeded its authority in granting writs of *habeas corpus*. He accepted the statement of the mob at Carthage that Joseph Smith refused to be tried by any other court than the municipal court of Nauvoo, although he had before him the most positive proof that Joseph was willing to go before any justice of the peace in Hancock County, except Justice Morrison of Carthage, where an angry mob had collected, and were threatening his destruction, and since the warrant was made returnable to the magistrate who issued it, or any other justice in the county, the Prophet expressed a willingness to go before any other justice, but very properly refused to go to Carthage. He was even willing to be bound over to appear in the circuit court to answer for the part he took in abating the *Expositor* press as a nuisance. Yet in the face of these facts—in the face of the fact that all the parties charged with riot had appeared before D. H. Wells, a justice of the peace and a non-Mormon, and after investigation were acquitted—yet the governor charged the members of the city council with refusing to appear before any other than the municipal court of Nauvoo for an investigation. He demanded that the mayor and all persons in Nauvoo accused or sued submit in all cases implicitly to the process of the courts and to interpose no obstacles to an arrest, either by writ of *habeas corpus* or otherwise. And in the case of the mayor and a number of the city council charged with riot, he required that they should be arrested by the same constable, by virtue of the same warrant, and tried before the same magistrate, whose authority he insisted had been resisted. "Nothing short of this," he added, "can vindicate the dignity of violated law, and allay the just excitement of the people." Messrs. Taylor and Bernhisel called his attention to the state of excitement in Carthage, and informed him that there were men there bent on killing the Prophet, and that to ensure his safety it would be necessary for him to be accompanied by an armed force which would doubtless provoke a collision. In answer to this the governor advised them to bring no arms, and pledged his faith as governor, and that of the State, to protect those who should go to Carthage for trial. He also made the same pledge in his written communication to Joseph.

The conduct of the governor in thus adopting the reports of the enemies of the citizens of Nauvoo, and menacing the city with destruction, if his arbitrary commands were not complied with, created no small amount of astonishment in Nauvoo. Joseph, however, wrote a courteous reply, corrected the governor's errors, and also represented that the city council of Nauvoo had acted on their best judgment, aided by the best legal advice they could procure; but if a mistake had been made they were willing to make all things right; but asked that the mob might be dispersed, that their lives might not be endangered while on trial. Relative to going to Carthage, however, Joseph pointed out the fact that the governor himself in his written communication had expressed his fears that he could not control the mob; "in which case," he went on to say, "we are left to the mercy of the merciless. Sir, we dare not come for our lives would be in danger, and we are guilty of no crime."

On a hasty consultation with his brother Hyrum, Dr. Richards, and Messrs. Taylor and Bernhisel, after the return of the latter from their conference with Governor Ford it was decided that Joseph should proceed to Washington and lay the case before President Tyler, and he informed Governor Ford of this intention in the letter above referred to. That plan, however, at a subsequent council meeting was abandoned; as Joseph received an inspiration to go to the West, and all would be well. He said to the trusted brethren in that council:

The way is open. It is clear to my mind what to do. All they want is Hyrum and myself; then tell everybody to go about their business, and not collect in groups, but scatter about. There is no danger; they will come here and search for us. Let them search;

they will not harm you in person or in property, and not even a hair of your head. We will cross the river tonight and go away to the West.

This was between nine and ten o'clock on the night of the twenty-second of June, and preparations were at once entered into to carry out this impression of the Spirit. W. W. Phelps was instructed to take the families of the Prophet and his brother to Cincinnati; and that night O. P. Rockwell rowed Joseph, Hyrum and Dr. Richards over the Mississippi to Montrose, and then returned with instructions to procure horses for them and make all necessary preparations to start for "the great basin in the Rocky Mountains."

About ten o'clock the next day the governor's *posse* arrived in Nauvoo to arrest Joseph, but not finding him it returned to Carthage, leaving a man by the name of Yates to watch for the Prophet's appearing. This man said that if the mayor and his brother were not given up, the governor had expressed a determination to send his troops into the city and guard it until they were found, if it took three years.

At this crisis, some of Joseph's friends instead of rendering him all possible assistance to escape from his enemies, complained of his conduct as cowardly and entreated him to return to Nauvoo and not leave them like a false shepherd leaves his flock when the wolves attack them. The parties most forward in making this charge of cowardice were Reynolds Cahoon, L. D. Wasson and Hiram Kimball. Emma Smith, his wife, also sent a letter by the hand of Reynolds Cahoon, entreating him to return and give himself up, trusting to the pledges of the governor for a fair trial. Influenced by these entreaties to return, and stung by the taunts of cowardice from those who should have been his friends, he said: "If my life is of no value to my friends, it is of none to myself." And after a brief consultation with Rockwell and his brother Hyrum, against his better judgment, and with the conviction fixed in his soul that he would be killed, he resolved to return; and crossed over the river that evening to Nauvoo.

His first act after arriving in the beautiful city of which he was the chief founder, was to send word to the governor, by the hand of Theodore Turley and Jedediah M. Grant that he would be ready to go to Carthage as early on the morrow as his (the governor's) *posse* could meet him—provided he could be assured a fair trial, and his witnesses not be abused. That message was delivered to the governor, and he decided at once to send a *posse* to escort Joseph and his party to Carthage; but through the influence which Wilson Law, Joseph H. Jackson and others of like character had over him, he changed his good intention of sending a *posse*, and ordered Joseph's messengers to return that night with orders to him to be in Carthage the next day by ten o'clock without an escort; and he threatened that if Joseph did not give himself up by that time, Nauvoo would be destroyed.

Owing to the jaded condition of their horses the messengers did not reach Nauvoo until daylight of the twenty-fourth. After the orders of the governor were delivered, the faithful brethren who reported them began to warn the Prophet against trusting himself in the hands of his enemies, but he stopped them and would not hear them further—he had decided on his course.

Early on the morning of the twenty-fourth Joseph and the members of the city council, against whom complaints had been made before Justice Morrison, accompanied by a few friends, started for Carthage to give themselves up. As they passed the temple, the party paused, and the Prophet looked with admiration upon the noble edifice and the glorious landscape, which everywhere from that spot greets the eye, and then said: "This is the loveliest place, and the best people under the heavens; little do they know the trials that await them!" On the outskirts of the city they passed the home of Squire D. H.

Wells, who at the time was sick. Joseph dismounted and called to see him. At parting the Prophet said to him cheerfully: "Squire Wells, I wish you to cherish my memory, and not think me the worst man in the world, either."

About ten o'clock the party arrived within four miles of Carthage and there met a company of sixty mounted militiamen under the command of Captain Dunn, on their way to Nauvoo with orders from Governor Ford to demand the State arms in possession of the Nauvoo Legion. It was on the occasion of meeting these troops that Joseph uttered those prophetic words:

"I am going like a lamb to the slaughter; but I am calm as a summer's morning; I have a conscience void of offense towards God, and towards all men. I shall die innocent, and it shall yet be said of me—he was murdered in cold blood."

At the request of Captain Dunn he countersigned the governor's order for the State arms. But the captain prevailed upon him to return to Nauvoo and assist in collecting the arms, promising that afterwards the militia under his command should escort himself and party into Carthage, and he would protect them even at the risk of his own life, to which his men assented by three hearty cheers. It is supposed that Captain Dunn feared the people in Nauvoo might become exasperated and resent the indignity offered them in demanding the surrender of the State arms. Hence his anxiety to have Joseph return. A message was sent to the governor informing him of this new move.

The arms were collected without any difficulty, though the people unwillingly surrendered them, since disarming them and allowing their enemies who had vowed their extermination to keep their arms, smacked of treachery; but the order of the governor and of their Prophet-leader was complied with.

The arms were taken to the Masonic Hall and stacked up, Quartermaster-General Buckmaster receiving them.

This demand for the State arms stirred the fiery indignation of Squire Wells to the very depths of his soul. He arose from his bed of sickness and carried what State arms he had—a pair of horse-pistols—to the appointed place, and threw them at the feet of Officer Buckmaster with the remark, "There's your arms!" Then as he glared at the officer, he said: "I have a pair of epaulets at home, and I have never disgraced them, either," and, too full of righteous wrath for further speech, he walked away.

The arms collected, Captain Dunn thanked the people for their promptness in complying with the demands of the governor, and promised them that while they conducted themselves in such a peaceable manner they should be protected. The company of militia accompanied by Joseph and his party started for Carthage about six o'clock in the evening.

Passing the Masonic Hall where a number of the citizens of Nauvoo still lingered, having been attracted there to witness the surrender of the State arms, the Prophet Joseph raised his hat and said: "Boys, if I don't come back, take care of yourselves. I am going like a lamb to the slaughter." When the company was passing his farm Joseph stopped and looked at it for a long time. Then after he had passed he turned and looked again, and yet again several times. His action occasioned some remarks by several of the company, to which, in reply he said: "If some of you had such a farm, and knew you would not see it any more, you would want to take a good look at it for the last time."

It was midnight when the party entered Carthage, but a militia company encamped on the public square—the Carthage Greys—were aroused and gave vent to profane threats as the company passed, of which the following is a specimen: "Where's the d—n Prophet?" "Stand away, you McDonough boys,* and let us shoot the d—n Mormons!" "G—d d—n you, old Joe,

* Captain Dunn's company was composed chiefly of men from McDonough County, hence the remark.

we've got you now!" Clear the way, and let us have a view of Joe Smith, the Prophet of God. He has seen the last of Nauvoo, we'll use him up now!"

Amid such profanity and abuse, and violent threats, much of which was overheard by Governor Ford, the Prophet's party proceeded to Hamilton's hotel, which it entered and took quarters for the night. Under the same roof were sheltered the wicked apostates of Nauvoo, J. H. Jackson, the Foster brothers, the Higbees and the Laws, besides other desperate men who had sworn to take the life of the Prophet.

The crowd which had followed the Nauvoo party from the public square still hung round the Hamilton House yelling and cursing, and acting like ravenous beasts hungry for their prey. Governor Ford pushed up a window and thus addressed them: "Gentlemen, I know your great anxiety to see Mr. Smith, which is natural enough, but it is quite too late tonight for you to have that opportunity; but I assure you, gentlemen, you shall have that privilege tomorrow morning, as I will cause him to pass before the troops upon the square, and I now wish you, with this assurance, quietly and peaceably to return to your quarters." In answer to this there was a faint "Hurrah, for Tom Ford," and the crowd withdrew. They could afford to wait. God's servants were in the hands of the merciless.

CHAPTER XXXVIII.

THE MARTYRDOM.

EARLY in the morning following their entrance into Carthage, Joseph, his brother Hyrum and the other members of the Nauvoo city council named in the warrant of arrest sworn out by the Higbees, voluntarily surrendered themselves to constable Bettisworth. Shortly afterwards the Prophet was again arrested by the same constable on a charge of treason against the State and people of Illinois, on the oath of Augustine Spencer. Hyrum was arrested on a similar charge, sworn out by Henry O. Norton. And thus the difficulties thickened.

Soon after the second arrest, Governor Ford presented himself at their rooms at the Hamilton house, and requested Joseph to accompany him, as he desired to present him to the troops, to whom he had promised the night before a view of the Prophet. The troops had been drawn up in two lines and Joseph and Hyrum linking arms with Brigadier-General Miner R. Deming passed down them, accompanied by their friends and a company of Carthage Greys. They were introduced as General Joseph and General Hyrum Smith. The Carthage Greys, a few minutes before, at the headquarters of General Deming, had revolted and behaved in an uproarious manner, but were pacified by the governor, and accompanied him, General Deming and the Prophet and his party to where the other troops were drawn up in line. Here they again revolted because the Brothers Smith were introduced to the troops from McDonough County as "Generals" Smith. Some of the officers of the Carthage Greys threw up their hats, drew their swords and said they would introduce themselves to "the d—ned Mormons in a different style." They were again pacified by the governor, who promised them "full" satisfaction. But they continued to act in such an insubordinate manner that General Deming put them under arrest,* but afterwards released them without punishment.

Shortly after this episode with the Carthage Greys, a number of the officers of other militia companies and other gentlemen curious to see the Prophet crowded into the hotel. Joseph took occasion to ask them if there was anything in his appearance to indicate that he was the desperate character his enemies represented him to be. To which they replied, "No, sir, your appearance would indicate the very contrary, General Smith;

---

*The manner of this incident about the revolt of the Carthage Greys is thus related in Gregg's History of Hancock County: "It seems that after the McDonough regiment had been disbanded, and were about to return home, they expressed a desire to see the prisoners, [Joseph and Hyrum] The wish was reasonable, and as the easiest mode of gratifying it, they were drawn up in line, and General Deming with the two prisoners, one on each arm, and the Greys as an escort, passed along the line of troops, Deming introducing them as General Joseph Smith and General Hyrum Smith, of the Nauvoo Legion. The Greys not aware that this was done at the request of the McDonough men, and not satisfied to be made an escort to such a display, exhibited signs of dissatisfaction, and finally gave vent to their feelings by hisses and groans. As a punishment for this offense they were afterward ordered under arrest. In the meantime there was great excitement in the company. As a detachment of the troops was being detailed for the purpose of putting the general's order into execution the officer in command of the Greys addressed them a few words and then said: 'Boys will you submit to an arrest for so trifling an offense?' 'No!' was the unanimous response. 'Then load your pieces with ball,' was the sullen order. In the meantime some explanations had been made, which permitted General Deming to countermand the order of arrest, and the Greys were quietly marched back to their encampment."

This account says nothing of the fact that it was generally known, that the night before, Governor Ford had promised all the troops a but we cannot see what is in your heart, neither can we tell what are your intentions." "Very true, gentlemen," quickly replied the Prophet, "you cannot see what is in my heart, and you are therefore unable to judge me or my intentions; but I can see what is in your hearts, and will tell you what I see. I can see that you thirst for blood, and nothing but my blood will satisfy you. It is not for crime of any description that I and my brethren are thus continually persecuted, and harrassed by our enemies, but there are other motives, and some of them I have expressed, so far as relates to myself; and inasmuch as you and the people thirst for blood, I prophesy in the name of the Lord that you shall witness scenes of blood and sorrow to your entire satisfaction. Your souls shall be perfectly satiated with blood, and many of you who are now present shall have an opportunity to face the cannon's mouth from sources you think not of, and those people that desire this great evil upon me and my brethren shall be filled with sorrow because of the scenes of desolation and distress that await them. They shall seek for peace

---

view of Generals Smith, and the Greys had been in revolt at General Deming's headquarters before the party including Joseph and Hyrum reached the McDonough troops. Moreover, I was informed by Colonel H. G. Ferris, when in Carthage in 1885, investigating these matters, that when word arrived in that place that Joseph Smith would surrender himself to the authorities, if the governor would pledge him protection and a fair trial, the governor made a speech to the mixed multitude of troops and citizens in which he stated the proposition of the Smiths, and wanted to know if they would sustain him in pledging them protection, to which they responded in the affirmative. There was some talk, too, of sending the Greys as a posse to escort the Smiths into Nauvoo. Against this proceeding General Deming protested and told Governor Ford that the pledge of protection made by the crowd and the troops was not to be depended upon, it was insincere, and that the lives of the Smiths were not to be trusted to the Greys. The governor however disregarded the warning of General Deming. Colonel Ferris was present at this meeting.—*B. H. R.*

and shall not be able to find it. Gentlemen, you will find what I have told you will come true." *

The members of the Nauvoo city council under arrest for riot, in destroying the *Expositor* press, were taken before R. F. Smith, justice of the peace and also captain of the Carthage Greys. It will be remembered perhaps that Governor Ford had told Joseph, in a communication referred to in the last chapter, that nothing but his appearing before Justice Morrison, who issued the writ against him would vindicate the majesty of the law, but now the prisoners were at Carthage where Justice Morrison lived, and could have appeared before him, and were willing to do so, they were taken before another justice.

In order to avoid increasing the excitement, the prisoners admitted there was sufficient cause to be bound over to appear at the next term of the circuit court for Hancock County. The bonds amounted to seven thousand five hundred dollars.

Justice Smith dismissed his court without taking any action on the charge of treason under which the Brothers Smith were still held; but about eight o'clock the same evening, Constable Bettisworth appeared at their lodgings at the Hamilton House and insisted on their going to jail. The Prophet demanded to see the copy of the mittimus which was at first denied; but upon his counsel—Messrs Woods & Reid—informing the constable that the accused were entitled to a hearing before a justice, before they could be sent to jail, to the surprise of all present he produced a mittimus, issued by Justice R. F. Smith. It stated that Joseph and Hyrum Smith were under arrest charged with treason; "and have been," so the paper read, "brought before me, a justice of the peace, in and for said county, for trial at the seat of justice hereof, which trial has been necessarily postponed, by reason of the absence of material witnesses." Now, this mittimus, so

---

* In view of the great civil war which a few years later desolated the land it is clear that the above utterance was prophetic.

far as it related to the prisoners appearing before Justice Smith was an infamous falsehood, "unless," as Lawyer Reid says, in the account he published of these proceedings—"unless the prisoners could have appeared before the justice *without being present in person or by counsel!*" The same representation of the case was made to me by Lawyer James W. Woods, who, at the time was associated with Mr. Reid as the Prophet's counsel, whom I met in the summer of 1880, in Iowa, and from whom at that time I received a detailed account of the proceedings.

Joseph and his counsel and his friends protested most vigorously against this unlawful proceeding, but to no avail. R. F. Smith finding his mittimus unlawful, appealed to the governor as to what he should do; to which the governor answered: "You have the Carthage Greys at your command." That hint was sufficient. What the *justice* had illegally begun, the same person as *captain* must with unlawful force consummate! Yet when this same governor was appealed to for protection against this unhallowed as well as unlawful proceeding, he expressed himself as being very sorry the circumstance had occurred, but he really could not interfere with the civic powers!

Elder John Taylor went to the governor and reminded him of his pledges of protection. Elder Taylor expressed his dissatisfaction at the course taken, and told the governor that if they were to be subject to mob rule, and to be dragged contrary to law to prison, at the instance of every scoundrel whose oath could be bought for a dram of whisky, his protection availed very little, and they had miscalculated the executive's promises.

In the meantime a drunken rabble had collected in the street in front of the Hamilton House, and Captain Dunn with some twenty men came to guard the prisoners to the jail. The Prophet's friends stood by him in these trying times and followed him through the excited crowd in the direction of the jail. Stephen Markham walked on one side of the Prophet and his brother Hyrum and Dan Jones on the other, and with their walking sticks kept back the rabble, which several times broke through the guard, while Elder Taylor, Willard Richards and John S. Fullmer walked behind them.

The jail was reached in safety and the prisoners given in charge of Mr. George W. Stigall, who first put them into the criminal's cell, but afterwards gave them the more comfortable quarters known as the "debtors' apartment." When night came] the prisoners and their friends stretched themselves out on the floor of the old jail—and so passed the night of the twenty-fifth.

Governor Ford represents in his "History of Illinois," that these men were placed in prison to protect them from the rabble,* but says not a word about the protests of the prisoners against being thrust into jail, or the illegal means employed in putting them there.

In the forenoon of the twenty-sixth, a lengthy interview took place between Governor Ford and Joseph in which the whole cause of the trouble was reviewed, the causes leading up to the destruction of the *Expositor* press, calling out the Legion on which the charge of treason was based, and all other affairs connected with the difficulties. Governor Ford condemned the action of the city council, but the course pursued by that body was ably defended by Joseph, and showed that even if they had been wrong in following the course they had taken, it was a matter for the courts to decide and not a thing for mobs to settle. In conclusion the Prophet told the Governor that he considered himself unsafe in Carthage, as the town was swarming with men who had openly sworn to take his life. He understood the governor contemplated going to Nauvoo, accompanied by the militia, to investigate certain charges about counterfeit-

---

* Ford's History of Illinois, p. 338.

ing the United States currency, and if possible secure the dies and other implements used in manufacturing it, and Joseph demanded his freedom that he might go with him. The governor promised him that he should go.*

The false mittimus on which Joseph and Hyrum Smith were thrust into prison, ordered the jailor to keep them in custody, "until discharged by due course of law." But on the afternoon of the twenty-sixth, Frank Worrell appeared before the jail in command of the Carthage Greys and demanded that the prisoners be delivered up to the constable to be taken before Justice R. F. Smith for trial. Against this proceeding the jailor protested, as the prisoners were placed in his keeping until "discharged by due course of law," and not at the demand of a constable or military despot. But by threats amounting to intimidation, Worrell compelled the jailor against his conviction of duty to surrender the prisoners to him.

Meantime a mob had gathered at the door of the jail and seeing that things had assumed a threatening aspect, the Prophet stepped into the crowd, locked arms with one of the worst mobocrats, and with his brother Hyrum on the other arm, and followed by his faithful friends, proceeded to the court house. He had been unlawfully thrust into prison, and as illegally dragged out of it and exposed to imminent danger among his worst enemies.

The counsel for the Brothers Smith asked for a continuance until the next day as they were without witnesses, not having been notified when they would come to trial. A continuance was granted until noon the next day. A new mittimus was made out and the prisoners committed again to prison—their old quarters. But after the prisoners were again lodged in jail, and without consulting either them or their counsel,

---

* For this conversation in *extenso* as reported by Elder John Taylor who was present, see Appendix IV.

Justice R. F. Smith changed the time of trial from noon on the twenty-seventh until the twenty-ninth.

This change was made in consequence of a decision reached by Governor Ford and his military council to march all his troops into Nauvoo, except a company of fifty of the Carthage Greys that would be detailed to guard the prisoners. So Mr. R. F. Smith, acting, it will be remembered, in the double capacity of a justice of the peace and captain of the Carthage Greys, as a justice altered the date of the return of the subpœnas and excused the court until the twenty-ninth; that as a captain of a company of militia he might attend the military train entering Nauvoo in triumph!

The evening of the twenty-sixth was spent very pleasantly by the prisoners and their friends—John Taylor, Willard Richards, John S. Fullmer, Stephen Markham and Dan Jones. Hyrum occupied the principal part of the time in reading accounts from the Book of Mormon of the deliverance of God's servants from prison, and in commenting upon them, with a view, doubtless, of cheering his brother Joseph, since the Prophet had expressed himself as having a presentiment of uneasiness as to his safety, that he had never before experienced when in the hands of his enemies.

Late at night all retired to rest except Willard Richards, who by the flickering flame of a tallow candle continued his work of writing out some important documents. Joseph and Hyrum occupied the only bedstead in the room, and their friends lay side by side on the mattresses spread out on the floor. Sometime after midnight a single gun was fired near the prison. Elder Richards started in his chair, and Joseph rose from the bed where he had been lying, and stretched himself out on the floor between Fullmer and Jones.

"Lay your head on my arm for a pillow, Brother John," said the Prophet to Fullmer as he kindly placed his arm under that person's head. Soon all became quiet, except in a low tone

Fullmer and the Prophet continued to talk of presentiments the latter had received of approaching death. "I would like to see my family again," said he, "and I would to God that I could preach to the Saints in Nauvoo once more." Fullmer tried to cheer him by saying he thought he would have that privilege many times.

Again all was silent, and everybody apparently asleep. But Joseph turned to Dan Jones and was heard to say, "Are you afraid to die?" To which the one addressed said: "Has that time come, think you? Engaged in such a cause I do not think death would have many terrors." And then the Prophet said: "You will yet see Wales"—his native land—"and fill the mission appointed you, before you die."* So passed away the night preceding the day which saw enacted that tragedy which robbed earth of two of the noblest men that ever lived upon it.

As the morning light struggled through the windows of Carthage jail, the prisoners and their friends awoke, and the Prophet required Dan Jones to go down stairs and enquire of the guard about the gun that was fired in the night, what the meaning of it was, etc.

Jones went accordingly, and found Frank Worrell in command of the guard and the answer he received to his inquiry was this: "We have had too much trouble to get old Joe here to let him ever escape alive, and unless you want to die with him, you had better leave before sun down; and you are not a d——n bit better than him for taking his part; and you'll see that I can prophesy better than old Joe, for neither he nor his brother, nor anyone who will remain with them, will see the sun set today." This answer Jones related to Joseph, who told him to go to the governor at once and report the words of the guard. On his

---

* This prediction was fulfilled. Elder Dan Jones went on a mission to Wales starting on the 28th of August, 1844, in company with Wilford Woodruff, and performed a most wonderful mission in his native land.

way to the governor's quarters at the Hamilton House, Jones passed a crowd of men who were being addressed by a person unknown to him. He paused long enough to hear these words:

"Our troops will be discharged this morning in obedience to orders, and for a sham we will leave the town; but when the governor and the McDonough troops have left for Nauvoo this forenoon, we will return and kill those men if we have to tear the jail down," (applause.) These words and what the captain of the guard said were faithfully reported to Governor Ford, in reply to which he said: "You are unnecessarily alarmed for the safety of your friends, sir, the people are not that cruel."

Angered at such an answer the following conversation occurred:

Jones. The Messrs. Smith are American citizens, and have surrendered themselves to your excellency upon your pledging your honor for their safety; they are also master Masons, and as such I demand of you the protection of their lives. If you do not this, I have but one more desire, and that is, if you leave their lives in the hands of those men to be sacrificed—

Governor Ford. What is that, sir?

Jones. It is that the Almighty will preserve my life to a proper time and place, that I may testify that you have been timely warned of their danger.

The governor manifested some excitement during this conversation, turning pale at the Masonic warning Jones gave him. The effect, however, was but momentary.

Jones returned to the jail after his conversation with the governor, but was denied admission. He then returned to the governor to secure a pass; and arrived at the square just as that officer was disbanding the militia. It is customary when the militia has been called together to assist in execution of the laws, or to suppress an insurrection, to dismiss the respective companies in charge of their several commanders to be marched home and there be disbanded. But in this instance the governor disbanded all the troops, except the Carthage Greys whom, it appears, he had selected to guard the jail, and the McDonough troops who were to accompany him to Nauvoo.

Governor Ford himself, in his history of Illinois, represents that there were about twelve or thirteen hundred of the militia at Carthage and some five hundred at Warsaw. As the disbanded militia left the square, they acted in a boisterous manner, shouting that they would only go a short distance from town. and then come back and kill old Joe and Hyrum as soon as the governor was far enough out of town. Dan Jones called the attention of the governor to these threats, but he ignored them. I suppose these are the threats of which Governor Ford himself speaks in his history of these unfortunate events, when he says:

> I had heard of some threats being made, but none of an attack upon the prisoners whilst in jail. These threats seemed to be made by individuals not acting in concert. They were no more than the bluster which might have been expected, and furnished no indication of numbers combining for this or any other purpose.

It will be remembered that Governor Ford expressed a determination to march with all his forces into Nauvoo, and Joseph having heard of this, in the interview at the jail before alluded to, expressed a desire to accompany him, and the governor promised him he should go. This promise the governor failed to keep because a council of his officers convinced him that to take the Prophet with him to Nauvoo "would be highly inexpedient and dangerous." Indeed the whole plan of marching all his forces into Nauvoo, was abandoned. The expedition had been formed for the purpose of striking terror into the hearts of the citizens of Nauvoo, by a display of military force in their midst, and to satisfy the wishes of the anti-Mormons.

Speaking of this projected semi-invasion of Nauvoo and the preparations made for the start, Governor Ford says:

> I observed that some of the people became more and more excited and inflammatory the further the preparations were advanced. Occasional threats came to my ears of destroying the city and murdering or expelling the inhabitants.
>
> I had no objection to ease the terrors of the people by such a display of force, and was most anxious also to search for the alleged apparatus for making counterfeit money; and in fact to inquire into all the charges made against that people, if I could have been assured of my command against mutiny and insubordination. But I gradually learned to my entire satisfaction that there was a plan to get the troops into Nauvoo, and there to begin the war, probably by some of our own party, or some of the seceding Mormons, taking advantage of the night to fire on our own force, and then lay it on the Mormons.
>
> I was satisfied that there were those amongst us fully capable of such an act, hoping that in the alarm, bustle and confusion of a militia camp, the truth could not be discovered, and that it might lead to the desired collision.*

Such are the reasons assigned by Governor Ford for abandoning his plan of marching all his forces into Nauvoo. If he could persuade himself to believe that he had those under his command, who would resort to the means he himself alludes to in the foregoing, to bring about a collision with the citizens of Nauvoo; and that he was fearful that his whole command would mutiny when once in the city of the Saints, it is unfortunate for the fame of Governor Ford that his fears could not be aroused for the safety of his prisoners, who were left at the mercy of those same militia forces, of which he himself was distrustful, the only barrier between them and the fury of this mob-militia being a guard made up of their bitterest enemies.

---

* Ford's History of Illinois, page 340.

To satisfy the anti-Mormons the governor told them he would take a small force with him and go in search of counterfeiting apparatus and would make a speech to the citizens of Nauvoo, detailing to them the consequences of any acts of violence on their part. *En route* for Nauvoo, however, some of his officers expressed fears that the Smiths would be killed, and the governor informs us that he reduced his forces, leaving part of his command on the way, and pushed with all speed for Nauvoo; that he might make a speech to the people there and return to Carthage that night. giving up the idea of remaining several days to search for counterfeiting apparatus and making inquiries into the charges against the Mormon people. Leaving him to pursue to his journey to Nauvoo, I return to note the events which took place at the jail.

Cyrus H. Wheelock visited Carthage jail early on the morning of the 27th, and when he departed for Nauvoo to secure witnesses and documents for the impending trial on the charge of treason, he left with the prisoners an old-fashioned, pepperbox revolver. Before leaving Carthage, however, he went to Governor Ford, (he leaving Carthage before the governor started,) and expressed his fears for the safety of the prisoners. He then started for Nauvoo, but with a heavy heart.

Dan Jones was sent to Quincy by the Prophet with a letter to lawyer O. H. Browning, applying for his professional services in the pending trial. The letter was handed to Jones by A. W. Babbitt, the former not being allowed to enter the jail after leaving it in the morning. The mob being informed by the guard of the letter, set up the cry that Joe Smith was sending an order by Jones to the Nauvoo Legion to come and rescue him. A crowd surrounded Jones and demanded the letter but the fearless Welshman refused to give it up; whereupon some were in favor of forcing it from him, but there was a disagreement in the crowd about that, and while they were discussing the point, Jones mounted his horse and rode away.

Stephen Markham being seen on the streets in the afternoon, a number of the Carthage Greys captured him, put him on his horse and forced him out of town at the point of the bayonet, notwithstanding he held a pass from the governor to go in and out of the jail at pleasure. This left but Elders Richards and Taylor with the Prophet and his brother in the prison. They passed the afternoon in pleasant conversation, reading and singing. Elder Taylor sang a hymn entitled "A poor wayfaring man of grief:" a peculiarly plaintive piece of poetry, and admirably suited to their circumstances:

A poor wayfaring man of grief
  Hath often crossed me on the way,
Who sued so humbly for relief
  That I could never answer, Nay.

I had not power to ask His name,
Whereto He went or whence He came,
Yet there was something in His eye
That won my love, I knew not why.

Once when my scanty meal was spread,
  He entered, not a word He spake;
Just perishing for want of bread,
  I gave Him all, He blessed it, brake,

And ate, but gave me part again;
Mine was an angel's portion then,
For while I fed with eager haste,
The crust was manna to my taste.

I spied Him where a fountain burst
  Clear from the rock; His strength was gone,
The heedless water mocked His thirst,
  He heard it, saw it hurrying on.

I ran and raised the suff'rer up;
Thrice from the stream He drained my cup,
Dipped, and returned it running o'er;
I drank and never thirsted more.

'Twas night; the floods were out; it blew
A winter-hurricane aloof;
I heard His voice abroad, and flew
To bid Him welcome to my roof.

I warmed and clothed and cheered my guest,
And laid Him on my couch to rest,
Then made the earth my bed, and seemed
In Eden's garden while I dreamed.

Stript, wounded, beaten nigh to death,
I found Him by the highway side;
I roused His pulse, brought back His breath,
Revived His spirit, and supplied

Wine, oil, refreshment—He was healed;
I had myself a wound concealed,
But from that hour forgot the smart,
And peace bound up my broken heart.

In prison I saw Him next, condemned
To meet a traitor's doom at morn;
The tide of lying tongues I stemmed,
And honored Him 'mid shame and scorn.

My friendship's utmost zeal to try,
He asked if I for Him would die;
The flesh was weak, my blood ran chill,
But the free spirit cried, "I will!"

Then in a moment to my view,
The stranger darted from disguise;
The tokens in His hands I knew,
The Savior stood before mine eyes.

He spake, and my poor name He named,
"Of Me thou hast not been ashamed;
These deeds shall thy memorial be,
Fear not, thou didst them unto Me."

Late in the afternoon Mr. Stigall, the jailor, came in and suggested that they would be safer in the cells. Joseph told him they would go in after supper. Turning to Elder Richards the Prophet said; "If we go to the cell will you go in with us?"

Elder Richards. "Brother Joseph, you did not ask me to cross the river with you [referring to the time when they crossed the Mississippi, *en route* for the Rocky Mountains]—you did not ask me to come to Carthage—you did not ask me to come to jail with you—and do you think I would forsake you now? But I will tell you what I will do; if you are condemned to be hung for treason, I will be hung in your stead, and you shall go free."

Joseph. "But you cannot."

Richards. "I will, though."

This conversation took place a little after five o'clock, and very soon afterwards the attack was made on the jail. It appears that a crowd came from the direction of Warsaw that evidently had an understanding with the Carthage Greys and the members of that company on guard at the jail, since the latter, without question, had but blank cartridges in their guns; and the attack was made under the very eyes of the rest of the company encamped but two or three hundred yards away on the public square, and they made no effort whatever to prevent the assaults on the prison.

The guard at the jail played their part well. They fired blank shots at the advancing mob, or discharged their pieces in the air. They were "overpowered" (?), and the prison was in the hands of an infuriated mob. A rush was made for the room where the prisoners were lodged, and a shower of lead was sent in through the door and the windows from those on the outside.

As no account that I could possibly write would equal that given by an eye-witness of the whole transaction, I here quote entire the account of the tragedy by Elder Willard Richards, as it appeared in the *Times and Seasons* soon after the event, under the caption,

TWO MINUTES IN JAIL.

A shower of musket balls was thrown up the stairway against the door of the prison in the second story, followed by many rapid footsteps.

While Generals Joseph and Hyrum Smith, Mr. Taylor and myself, who were in the front chamber, closed the door of our room against the entry at the head of the stairs, and placed ourselves against it, there being no lock on the door, and no catch that was unsealable.

The door is a common panel, and as soon as we heard the feet at the stair's head, a ball was sent through the door, which passed between us, and showed that our enemies were desperadoes and we must change our position.

General Joseph Smith, Mr. Taylor and myself sprang back to the front part of the room. General Hyrum Smith retreated two-thirds across the chamber directly in front of and facing the door. A ball was sent through the door which hit Hyrum on the side of his nose, when he fell backwards, extending at full length without moving his feet. From the holes in his vest (the day was warm and no one had their coats on but myself) pantaloons, drawers, and shirt, it appeared that a ball must have been thrown from without through the window, which entered the back of his right side, and passing through, lodged against his watch, which was in the right vest pocket, completely pulverizing the crystal and face, tearing off the hands and mashing the whole body of the watch. At the same instant the ball from the door entered his nose.

As he struck the floor he exclaimed emphatically, "*I am a dead man.*" Joseph looked towards him and responded, "*Oh dear! Brother Hyrum,*" and opening the door two or three inches with his left hand, discharged one barrel of a six-shooter (the pistol left him by C. H. Wheelock) at random in the entry, from whence a ball grazed Hyrum's breast, and entering his throat passed into his head, while other muskets were aimed at him as some balls hit him.

Joseph continued snapping his revolver round the casing of the door into the space as before, three barrels of which missed fire, while Mr. Taylor with a walking stick stood by his side and knocked down the bayonets and muskets, which were constantly discharging through the doorway, while I stood by him ready to lend any assistance, with another stick, but could not come within striking distance without going directly in front of the muzzles of the guns.

When the revolver failed, we had no more firearms, and expected an immediate rush of the mob, and the doorway full of muskets half way in the room, and no hope but instant death from within. Mr. Taylor rushed into the window, which is some fifteen or twenty feet from the ground. When his body was nearly on a balance, a ball from the door within entered his leg, and a ball from without struck his watch, a patent lever, in his vest pocket near his left breast, and smashed it into "pie," leaving the hands standing at five o'clock, sixteen minutes, and twenty-six seconds, the force of which ball threw him back on the floor, and he rolled under the bed which stood by his side, where he lay motionless, the mob continuing to fire upon him, cutting away a piece of flesh from his left hip as large as a man's hand, and were hindered only by my knocking down their muzzles with a stick; while they continued to reach their guns into the room, probably left handed, and aimed their discharge so far round as almost to reach us in the corner of the room to where we retreated and dodged, and there I commenced the attack with my stick.

Joseph attempted as a last resort to leap the same window from which Mr. Taylor fell, when two balls pierced him from the door, and one entered his right breast from without, and he fell outward exclaiming, "*O Lord, my God!*" As his feet went out of the window my head went in, the balls whistling all round. He fell on his left side a dead man. At this instant the cry was raised, "*He's leaped the window,*" and the mob on the stairs and in the entry ran out.

I withdrew from the window thinking it no use to leap out on a hundred bayonets, then round Gen. Smith's body. Not satisfied with this, I again reached my head out of the window, and watched some seconds to see if there were any signs of life, regardless of my own, determined to see the end of him I loved. Being fully satisfied that he was dead, with a hundred men near his body and more coming round the corner of the jail, and expecting a return to our room, I rushed toward the prison door at the head of the stairs, and through the entry from whence the firing had proceeded, to learn if the doors into the prison were open. When near the entry Mr. Taylor cried out "*Take me!*" I pressed my way until I found all doors unbarred, returning instantly, caught Mr. Taylor under my arm, and rushed up the stairs into the dungeon, or inner prison, stretched him on the floor and covered him with a bed in such a manner as not likely to be perceived, expecting an immediate return of the mob. I said to Mr. Taylor, "This is a hard case to lay you on the floor, but if your wounds are not fatal, I want you to live to tell the story." I expected to be shot the next moment, and stood before the doors awaiting the onset.

There was, however, no further onset made on the jail.

Three minutes after the attack was commenced, Hyrum Smith lay stretched out on the floor of the prison dead, Elder Taylor lay not far from him savagely wounded, the Prophet was lying by the side of the well curb,* just under the window from

---

* It is said that after Joseph fell by the well curb under the window from which he attempted to leap, he was set up against that curb and Colonel Levi Williams ordered four men to fire at him, which they did. It is then said that a ruffian bareheaded and barefooted, his pantaloons rolled up above his knees and his shirt sleeves above his elbows, approached the dead Prophet bowie-knife in hand with the intention it is supposed of severing the head from the body. He had raised his hand to strike, when a light so sudden and powerful flashed upon the bloody scene that the mob was terror-stricken. The arm of the would-be mutilator of the dead fell powerless at his side, the four muskets of those who fired at him fell to the ground, while their

which he had attempted to leap, the plighted faith of a State was broken, its honor trailed in the dust, and a stain of innocent blood affixed to its escutcheon which shall remain a disgrace forever.

When it was known that the Prophet was killed, consternation seemed to seize the mob and they fled, for the most part, in the direction of Warsaw, in the utmost confusion. Such wild confusion reigned in Carthage that it was nearly midnight before Elder Richards could obtain any help or refreshments for Elder Taylor. At last the wounded man was taken to the Hamilton House and his wounds dressed. The bodies of Joseph and Hyrum were also taken to the same place and laid out.

Meantime Governor Ford had gone to Nauvoo, where he arrived some time in the afternoon. Several thousands assem-

---

owners stood like marble statues unable to move, or join their companions in the hurried and confused retreat they were then making, and Colonel Williams had to call upon some of the retreating mob to carry them away. The history is based upon the statements of Wm. M. Daniels, ——Blackenberry and a Miss Graham, but how far their statements are correct I have no means of judging. When at Carthage I became acquainted with W. R. Hamilton, son of the Mr. Hamilton who kept the Hamilton House, referred to several times in these pages, and who just previous to the murder of the Prophet and his brother had been enrolled as a member of the company of Carthage Greys. At the time of the attack on the jail he was on the public square and at once ran in the direction of the jail and was in full view of it all the time. He saw the Prophet appear at the window and half leap and half fall out of it. After which the mob fled precipitously. According to his statement there was no such an occurrence as setting the body against the well, etc. He claims to have been about the first who went to the body of the murdered man, and afterwards rendered some assistance in removing Elder Taylor and the bodies of the martyrs to his father's house.

It is worthy of note that nothing of all this is recorded by Willard Richards, and it smacks too much of the fanciful. There is too much deliberation in it to believe it to be the action of a mob.—*R.*

bled to hear his speech, that he went there to deliver; and he insulted them, by assuming that all that their worst enemies had said of them was true, and threatened them with most dire calamities. He himself in his history of Illinois, says the people manifested some impatience and anger when he referred to the misconduct alleged against them by their enemies; and well they might, for baser falsehoods were never put in circulation to slander a people.

The governor was invited to stay all night, but he refused and left the city about 6:30 in the evening for Carthage, his escort riding full speed up Main street performing the sword exercise; they passed the temple, and so left the city.

Three miles out the governor and his escort met George D. Grant and David Bettisworth riding toward Nauvoo like madmen with the sad news of the death of Joseph and Hyrum. The governor took them back with him to Grant's house, one and one half miles east of Carthage, that the news might not reach Nauvoo until he had had time to have the county records removed from the court house, and warn the people of Carthage to flee, as he expected an immediate attack from the Nauvoo Legion, and that the whole country would be laid waste.

After being taken back to Carthage, George D. Grant mounted another horse and rode that night with the awful news to Nauvoo.

On the arrival of Governor Ford at Carthage the following note was addressed to Mrs. Emma Smith and Major-General Dunham of the Nauvoo Legion, dated Midnight, Hamilton House, Carthage:

The governor has just arrived; says all things shall be inquired into, and all right measures taken. I say to all citizens of Nauvoo—My brethren, be still, and know that God *reigns*. *Don't rush out of the city*—don't rush to Carthage—stay at home and be prepared for an attack from Missouri mobbers. The governor will render every assistance possible—has sent orders for troops. Joseph and Hyrum are dead, will prepare to move the bodies as soon as possible.

The people of the county are greatly excited, and fear the Mormons will come out and take vengeance. I have pledged my word the Mormons will stay at home as soon as they can be informed, and no violence will be on their part, and say to my brethren in Nauvoo, in the name of the Lord, be still; be patient, only let such friends as choose come here to see the bodies. Mr. Taylor's wounds are dressed, and not serious. I am sound.

WILLARD RICHARDS.

After the note was prepared the governor wrote an order to the people of Nauvoo to defend themselves, and then about one o'clock in the morning went out on the public square and advised all present to disperse, as he expected the Mormons would be so exasperated that they would burn the town. Upon this the people of Carthage fled in all directions, and the governor and his *posse* took flight in the direction of Quincy; but there was no uprising and violence on the part of the Saints.

The next day the bodies of the murdered men were taken to Nauvoo. About one mile east of the temple, on Mullholland street, they were met by the people in solemn procession, under the direction of the city marshal. Neither tongue nor pen can ever describe the scene of sorrow and lamentation which was there beheld. The love of Joseph and Hyrum for the Saints was unbounded, and it had begotten in the people an affection for them that was equally dear and unselfish. They lived in the hearts of the Saints, and thousands would have laid down their lives willingly to have saved theirs. With their beloved and trusted leaders thus brutally snatched from them; under such circumstances of cruelty and official treachery, imagine, if you can, the mingled feelings of sorrow and righteous indignation that struggled in every heart, and sought expression!

Arriving at the Mansion, the bodies were taken into it to be prepared for burial; and Elder Willard Richards and others addressed some eight or ten thousand of the people in the open air. The Saints were advised to keep the peace. Elder Richards stated that he had pledged his honor and his life for their conduct. When the multitude heard that, notwithstanding the sense of outraged justice under which they labored, and this cruel invasion of the rights of liberty and life—in the very midst of their grief and excitement, with the means in their right hands to wreak a terrible vengeance, they voted to a man to trust to the LAW to deal with the assassins, and if that failed them, they would call upon God to avenge them of their wrongs! History records few actions so sublime as this; and it stands to this day a testimony of the devotion of the Latter-day Saints to law and order, the like of which is not paralleled in the history of our country, if in the world.

CHAPTER XXXIX.

CONFUSION—CHOOSING A LEADER.

THE Saints at Nauvoo were now as sheep without a shepherd. They had never contemplated such a crisis as this. That their Prophet would be taken from them had not entered their minds, although in the closing days of his career he had frequently spoken of his fate if again he should fall into the hands of his enemies. On the twenty-second of June, five days preceding his death, at the conclusion of the consultation with several of Nauvoo's leading citizens, and at which time it was decided that the safest thing for himself and Hyrum to do was to go West, he remarks in his journal: "I told Stephen Markham that if I and Hyrum were ever taken again we should be massacred, or I was not a Prophet of God."

When the cowardly appeal made to him by false friends to return to Nauvoo, after he had crossed the Mississippi on his way to the West, was under consideration by himself and a few friends, he said to his brother, Hyrum Smith: "Brother Hyrum, you are the oldest, what shall we do?" Hyrum replied, "Let us go back and give ourselves up, and see the thing out." "If you go back," replied the Prophet, "I shall go with you, but we shall be butchered." Then again, after it was determined to adopt the course suggested by Hyrum, and the party was on the way to the river where they were to take boats for the Nauvoo side, the Prophet lingered behind the rest of the party talking with O. P. Rockwell. Those in advance shouted to them to come on. Joseph replied, "It is no use to hurry, for we are going back to be slaughtered."

On arriving at Nauvoo, Hyrum, too, seemed to have been impressed with a sense of their approaching fate, for on the morning of the twenty-fourth of June, when the first start was made for Carthage, he read the following significant passage in the Book of Mormon, and turned down the leaf upon it:

And it came to pass that I prayed unto the Lord that he would give unto the Gentiles grace, that they might have charity. And it came to pass that the Lord said unto me, if they have not charity it mattereth not unto you, thou hast been faithful; wherefore thy garments are clean. And because thou hast seen thy weakness, thou shalt be made strong, even to the sitting down in the place which I have prepared in the mansions of my father. And now I * * * * bid farewell unto the Gentiles; yea and also unto my brethren whom I love, until we shall meet before the judgment seat of Christ, when all men shall know that my garments are not spotted with your blood.*

I have already quoted the pathetic words of the Prophet on meeting Captain Dunn's company of militia four miles out from Carthage, when he said: "I am going like a lamb to the slaughter; but I am calm as a summer's morning; I have a conscience void of offense towards God and towards all men. I shall die innocent, and it shall yet be said of me—He was murdered in cold blood."

I have also related the circumstance of his lingering to look at his farm as he left Nauvoo for the last time, and clearly intimated that he would never see it again. But notwithstanding these very plain intimations concerning his approaching death, the Saints apparently could not comprehend them. They did not sense them; and when his death so sudden and pitiful did come, it scarcely seemed possible to them that it had taken place. They were unprepared for it, and, as I say, were now like sheep without a shepherd.

---

* Book of Mormon, Ether, Chap. xii.

Sidney Rigdon, the Prophet's first counselor, was in Pittsburg, Pennsylvania. He had removed from Nauvoo to Pittsburg, notwithstanding in a revelation* from God he had been required to make his home in Nauvoo, and stand in his office and calling of counselor and spokesman to the Prophet. The truth is that from the expulsion of the Saints from Missouri in 1838-9, Sidney Rigdon had been of but little service either to the Church or to the Prophet as a counselor. He was a man of admitted ability as an orator, but lacked discretion; a man of fervid imagination, but of inferior judgment; ambitious of place and honor, but without that steadiness of purpose and other qualities of soul which in time secure them. In the early years of The Church he suffered much for the cause of God, but he also complained much; especially was this the case in respect to the hardships endured in Missouri, and subsequently of his poverty and illness at Nauvoo. This habit of complaining doubtless did much to deprive him of the Spirit of the Lord; for at times it bordered upon blasphemy. More than once he was heard to say that Jesus Christ was a fool in suffering as compared with himself! Having lost, in part at least, the Spirit of the Lord, his interest in The Church and its work waned, and after the settlement at Nauvoo he was seldom seen in the councils of the Priesthood. Moreover, it was known that he was in sympathy and even in communication with some of the avowed enemies of Joseph, among others with that arch traitor, John C. Bennett, who was plotting the overthrow of both Joseph and The Church. It was doubtless these considerations which led Joseph to make an effort to get rid of Sidney Rigdon as counselor at the October conference in 1843.

On that occasion the Prophet represented to The Church that such had been the course of Sidney Rigdon that he considered it no longer his duty to sustain him as his counselor.

---

* Doc. & Cov., Sec. cxxiv, 103-106.

Hyrum Smith, however, pleaded the cause of his fellow-counselor, and so strongly urged the Saints to deal mercifully with Sidney Rigdon, that when the question of sustaining him was presented to the conference, the Saints voted in his favor. "I have thrown him off my shoulders, and you have again put him on me," said Joseph. "You may carry him, but I will not." And so confident was he that Sidney Rigdon would continue to fail in the performance of his duty, that he ordained Elder Amasa Lyman to succeed him, both as counselor and spokesman. "Some of the Elders did not understand how Elder Lyman could be ordained to succeed Elder Rigdon, as The Church had voted to try him another year. Elder Joseph Smith was requested to give an explanation. Why, said he, by the same rule that Samuel anointed David to be king over Israel, while Saul was yet crowned. Please read the sixteenth chapter of first Samuel. Elder Smith's explanation, though short, proved a quietus to all their rising conjectures."*

Notwithstanding all his fair promises of amendment, Sidney Rigdon continued neglectful of his high duties, and if for a time his old-time enthusiasm revived—as it seemed to at the April conference following, it was as the flickering flame of a tallow dip only—not the steady rays of the ever-shining sun. He longed to return to the East; and notwithstanding the word of the Lord commanding him to make his home at Nauvoo, he frequently talked with Joseph about going to Pittsburg to live, and finally obtained his consent to go there, and take his family with him, and, as I said before, he was there when the martyrdom occurred.

William Law, who had been the Prophet's second counselor, was in open apostasy and rebellion against him. He had been and was the associate of a corrupt band of men bent on the destruction of the Prophet. Prompted by a spirit of mercy, the

---

*Tract on Sidney Rigdon, by Jedediah M. Grant, pp. 15, 16.

April conference of 1843 had passed without taking action against either William Law, or any of the other apostates; but on the eighteenth of April, at a council of the Priesthood, when six of the Twelve Apostles were present, William Law and several other apostates were excommunicated from The Church; and later William Law undertook the organization of a church after the pattern of the Church of Christ, but it was a miserable failure.

The Twelve Apostles were nearly all absent in the Eastern States on missions; and although messengers were sent to call them to Nauvoo immediately after the Prophet's martyrdom, it would be some time before they could arrive. So that it was a time of general anxiety and depression.

It was in the midst of such circumstances as these that Sidney Rigdon arrived in Nauvoo and demanded that he be appointed "guardian" of The Church. He ignored the members of the quorum of the Twelve who were in the city—Elders Willard Richards, John Taylor and Parley P. Pratt; he conferred with Elder William Marks, president of the stake of Nauvoo, and at once began agitating the question of appointing a "guardian" to The Church. He arrived in Nauvoo on Saturday, the third of August; next day he harangued the Saints, who assembled in the grove near the temple, upon the necessity of appointing a "guardian" to build up The Church to the martyred Prophet, and in the afternoon meeting urged William Marks to make a special appointment for the Saints to assemble on the following Tuesday for that purpose. Elder Marks was in sympathy with Sidney Rigdon, but for some reason he refused to make the appointment for Tuesday, but made it for Thursday, the eighth of August. This was a most fortunate circumstance, since a sufficient number of the Twelve to make a majority of that quorum arrived on the evening of the sixth, and, of course, they were in time to be present at the meeting to be held on the eighth. The day previous to that meeting, however—the seventh of August—the Twelve called a meeting of the high council and high priests, before which they called on Sidney Rigdon to make a statement of his purposes and relate the revelation he claimed to have received at Pittsburg, which prompted his journey to Nauvoo. In substance he replied that the object of his visit was to offer himself to the Saints as a "guardian;" that it had been shown to him in vision at Pittsburg, that The Church must be built up to Joseph the martyr; that all the blessings the Saints could receive would be through their late Prophet; that no man could be a successor to Joseph; that The Church was not disorganized, though the head was gone; that he had been commanded to come to Nauvoo and see that The Church was governed properly, and propose himself to be a "guardian" to the people.*

To this Elder Brigham Young replied:

> I do not care who leads this Church, even though it were Ann Lee; but one thing I must know, and that is, what God says about it. I have the keys and the means of obtaining the mind of God on the subject. * * * Joseph conferred upon our heads all the keys and powers belonging to the Apostleship which he himself held before he was taken away, and no man nor set of men can get between Joseph and the Twelve in this world or in the world to come. How often has Joseph said to the Twelve, I have laid the foundation and you must build thereon, for upon your shoulders the Kingdom rests.†

The next day was the one appointed by Sidney Rigdon for The Church to assemble and choose a "guardian." The attendance was large, as intense interest had been awakened upon the

---

* History of Joseph Smith, Millennial Star, Volume xxv, page 215.

† History of Joseph Smith, Millennial Star, Volume xxv, page 215.

subject to be considered. Sidney Rigdon addressed the assembly, setting forth his claim to the "guardianship" of The Church. He had full opportunity to present his case and for one hour and a half spoke without interruption; but despite his reputation as an orator, he failed to convince the Saints that he was sent of God.

As soon as Sidney Rigdon had closed his speech, Elder Brigham Young arose and made a few remarks. It was on that occasion that he was transfigured before the people, so that through him the Saints heard the voice and felt the presence of their departed leader. George Q. Cannon, who was present on that occasion, says:

> If Joseph had risen from the dead and again spoken in their hearing, the effect could not have been more startling than it was to many present at that meeting, it was the voice of Joseph himself; and not only was it the voice of Joseph which was heard, but it seemed in the eyes of the people as if it were the very person of Joseph which stood before them. A more wonderful and miraculous event than was wrought that day in the presence of that congregation, we never heard of. The Lord gave His people a testimony that left no room for doubt as to who was the man chosen to lead them. They both saw and heard with their natural eyes and ears, and the words which were uttered came, accompanied by the convincing power of God, to their hearts, and they were filled with the Spirit and with great joy. There had been gloom, and in some hearts, probably, doubt and uncertainty, but now it was plain to all that here was the man upon whom the Lord had bestowed the necessary authority to act in their midst in Joseph's stead. On that occasion Brigham Young seemed to be transformed, and a change such as that we read of in the scriptures, as happening to the Prophet Elisha, when Elijah was translated in his presence, seemed to have taken place with him. The mantle of the Prophet Joseph had been left for Brigham. * * * The people said one to another: "The spirit of Joseph rests on Brigham;" they knew that he was the man chosen to lead them and they honored him accordingly. * * * As far as our observation went

(we were only a boy at the time) the people were divided into three classes from the time of the death of Joseph up to this meeting of which we speak. One class felt clearly and understandingly that President Brigham Young was the man whose right it was to preside, he being the president of the Twelve Apostles, and that body being, through the death of Joseph and Hyrum, the presiding quorum of The Church. Another class were not quite clear as to who would be called to preside, but they felt very certain that Sidney Rigdon was not the man. They did not believe that God would choose a coward and traitor to lead His people, to both of which characters they believed Rigdon had a claim. The third class, and we think its members were few, was composed of those who had no clear views one way or the other. They were undecided in their feelings. * * * With very few exceptions, then, the people returned to their homes from that meeting filled with great rejoicing. All uncertainty and anxiety were removed. They had heard the voice of the shepherd and they knew it.

In the journal of Elder William C. Staines, of that date, the following statement is recorded:

Brigham Young said: "I will tell you who your leaders or guardians will be. The Twelve—I at their head!" This was with a voice like the voice of the Prophet Joseph. I thought it was he, and so did thousands who heard it. This was very satisfactory to the people, and a vote was taken to sustain the Twelve in their office, which, with a few dissenting voices, was passed."

President Wilford Woodruff, describing the event, says:

When Brigham Young arose and commenced speaking * * * if I had not seen him with my own eyes, there is no one that could have convinced me that it was not Joseph Smith; and anyone can testify to this who was acquainted with these two men.*

---

* The above remark of President Woodruff's is taken from a testimony of his following a discourse on the subject of Priesthood and the right of succession, delivered by the writer.—*Deseret Evening News*, March 12, 1892.

The remarks of Elder Young, during which he was transfigured before the people, closed the forenoon meeting. When in the afternoon The Church again assembled Elder Young addressed them at some length on the subject of appointing a leader for The Church, representing the claims of the Twelve as the quorum having the right to act in the absence of the late Prophet-President. Following are some quotations from a summary of his speech taken down at the time:

For the first time in my life, for the first time in your lives, for the first time in the Kingdom of God in the nineteenth century, without a prophet at our head, do I step forth to act in my calling in connection with the quorum of the Twelve, as Apostles of Jesus Christ unto this generation—Apostles whom God has called by revelation through the Prophet Joseph, who are ordained and anointed to bear off the keys of the Kingdom of God in all the world.

* * * If any man thinks he has influence among this people, to lead away a party, let him try it, and he will find out that there is a power with the Apostles, which will carry them off victorious through all the world, and build up and defend The Church and Kingdom of God.

* * * If the people want President Rigdon to lead them, they may have him; but I say unto you that the Quorum of the Twelve have the keys of the Kingdom of God in all the world. The Twelve were appointed by the finger of God. Here is Brigham, have his knees ever faltered? Have his lips ever quivered? Here is Heber,* and the rest of the Twelve, an independent body, who have the keys of the Priesthood—the keys of the Kingdom of God—to deliver to all the world; this is true, so help me God. They stand next to Joseph, and are as the First Presidency of The Church.

* * * You must not appoint any man at our head; if you should, the Twelve must ordain him. You cannot appoint a man at our head; but if you do want any other man or men to lead you,

---

* Heber C. Kimball.

take them and we will go our way to build up the Kingdom in all the world.

* * * Brother Joseph, the Prophet, has laid the foundation for a grand work, and we will build upon it; you have never seen the quorums built one upon another. There is an almighty foundation laid, and we can build a kingdom such as there never was in the world; we can build a kingdom faster than the devil can kill the Saints off.

Now if you want Sidney Rigdon or William Law* to lead you, or anybody else, you are welcome to them; but I tell you in the name of the Lord, that no man can put another between the Twelve and the Prophet Joseph. Why? Because Joseph was their file leader, and he has committed into their hands the keys of the Kingdom in this last dispensation, for all the world; don't put a thread between the Priesthood and God.†

Elder Amasa Lyman spoke in support of the Twelve; and then Sidney Rigdon was granted the privilege of speaking; he declined personally, but called on Elder W. W. Phelps to speak in his behalf. Elder Phelps, while evidently having some sympathy with Elder Rigdon, supported the claims of the Twelve. After further discussion Elder Young arose to put the question as to whether The Church would sustain the Twelve or Sidney Rigdon:

I do not ask you to take my counsel or advice alone, but every one of you act for yourselves; but if Brother Rigdon is the person you want to lead you, vote for him, but not unless you intend to follow him and support him as you did Joseph. * * * And I would say the same of the Twelve, don't make a covenant to support them unless you intend to abide by their counsel. * * * I want

---

* William Law had been a counselor to the Prophet Joseph, but was found in transgression and apostasy, had been excommunicated, and was among those who brought about the martyrdom at Carthage.

† Millennial Star, volume xxv: pages 216, 231-32-33.

every man before he enters into a covenant, to know what he is going to do; but we want to know if this people will support the Priesthood in the name of Israel's God. If you say you will, do so.*

Elder Young was then about to put the question to the assembled quorums as to whether they wanted Elder Rigdon for a leader, when, at the request of the latter, the question on supporting the Twelve as the presiding quorum in The Church was first put in the following manner:

Do The Church want, and is it their only desire, to sustain the Twelve as the First Presidency of this people? * * * If The Church want the Twelve to stand as the head of this Kingdom in all the world, stand next to Joseph, walk up into their calling, and hold the keys of this Kingdom—every man, every woman, every quorum is now put in order, and you are now the sole controllers of it—all that are in favor of this in all the congregation of the Saints, manifest it by holding up the right hand. (There was a universal vote.) If there are any of a contrary mind—every man and every woman who does not want the Twelve to preside, lift up your hands in like manner. (No hands up.) This supersedes the other question, and trying it by quorums.†

This disposed of Sidney Rigdon. He had full opportunity to present his case before The Church. The Saints had full opportunity and liberty to vote for him had they wanted him for their leader; but they rejected him and sustained the Twelve.

---

* Millennial Star, volume xxv: page 264.

† That is, whether The Church wanted to have Sidney Rigdon for a "guardian" or leader.

CHAPTER XL.

THE TRIAL OF THE MURDERERS.

MEANTIME there was considerable excitement in Hancock County, since the mob party were determined to elect officers who would screen the murderers of the Prophets. The Saints were equally determined to vote for those whom they believed would sustain law and order; and the following were put forward as candidates for the county and district offices and elected: M. R. Deming, sheriff; D. H. Wells, coroner; George Coulson, commissioner; J. B. Backenstos and A. W. Babbitt, representatives.

The account of the trial of the miscreants charged with the murder of the Prophet I take from Gregg's "History of Hancock County," beginning at page 328:

TRIALS AND ACQUITTALS.

At the October [1844] term of the Hancock Circuit Court—present Jesse B. Thomas, judge; William Elliott, prosecuting attorney; Jacob B. Backenstos, clerk; General Minor R. Deming, sheriff.

The following is the grand jury:

Abram Lincoln, Jas. Reynolds, Th. J. Graham, Wm. M. Owens, Ebenezer Rand, Th. Brawner, Ralph Gorrell, Brant Agnert, Martin Getter, Wm. Smith, Th. Gilmore, Benj. Warrington, Reuben H. Loomis, Samuel Scott, Jas. Ward, Samuel Ramsy, Th. H. Owen, David Thompson, John J. Hickok.

Abraham Golden, E. A. Bedell and Geo. Walker excused for cause. Samuel Marshall refused to serve, and fined $5.00.

The court began its session on Monday the 21st. There had been rumors industriously circulated that the old citizens intended to rally and interpose obstacles in the way of the court and considerable anxiety was felt. The judge in his charge to the grand jury alluded to this rumor and said he was glad to see that no such demonstration was made. He charged them to do their duty in the case likely to come before them and leave the consequences. His charge gave general satisfaction.

There was a rumor that a lot of Mormons and Indians were encamped near the town and this rumor occasioned considerable uneasiness. Orders were issued to investigate. The facts turned out to be that a number of Mormons had come down from Nauvoo to attend court, and had gone into camp to save expense. As to the Indians it was ascertained that a company of them had gone through the county on their way to Iowa, for some purpose unknown; but the two facts had no connection with each other.

On Tuesday the grand jury began their work, and on Saturday about noon they brought into court two bills of indictment against nine individuals—one for the murder of Joseph Smith and the other for the murder of Hyrum Smith. The persons indicted were as follows: Levi Williams, Jacob C. Davis, Mark Aldrich, Thomas C. Sharp, Wm. Voras, John Wills, Wm. N. Grover, ——— Gallaher and ——— Allen.

Murry McConnell, Esq., of Jacksonville by special appointment of the governor was present assisting Mr. Elliot in the prosecution. Messrs. Bushnell and Johnson of Quincy and Calvin A. Warren, and perhaps others appeared for the defendants.

Immediately on announcement of the indictments most of the defendants appeared and asked for an immediate trial. This Mr. McConnell objected to on the grounds of not being ready. His witnesses before the grand jury had departed without being recognized, and besides, Mr. Elliot had gone. It was finally agreed that the causes should be postponed until next term, and that no *capias* should issue from the clerk in the interim if the defendents would pledge themselves to appear at the time. Agreed on—a compact which was afterwards violated by the prosecution.

Subpœnas were asked for by the prosecution for between thirty and forty witnesses, among whom were William M.Daniels and Brackenberry, the two miracle men, and John Taylor, Mrs. Emma Smith and Governor Ford.

On May 19, 1845, court again met in special term at Carthage. Present, Richard M. Young, judge; James H. Ralston, prosecuting attorney; David E. Head, clerk; and R. H. Deming, sheriff. The cause of the people *vs.* Williams *et al* coming up, Messrs. Williams, Davis, Aldrich, Sharp and Grover appeared and were admitted to bail on personal recognizance in the sums of $5,000.00 jointly and severally. Josiah Lamborn of Jacksonville as assistant prosecuting attorney and William A. Richardson, O. H. Browning, Calvin A. Warren, Archibald Williams, O. C. Skinner and Tho. Morrison for defendants. Motion of defendants to quash the array of jurors for first week, on account of supposed prejudice of county commissioners who selected them and of the sheriff and deputies was sustained. Also motion for the appointment of elisors for the same cause, and absence of coroner from county. The array was set aside, and Tho. H. Owen and Wm. D. Arbenethy appointed elisors for the case. These gentlemen had a thankless and arduous duty to perform. Usually it is not difficult to find men willing to sit on juries; in this case few were willing to try the experiment of going into court, with the almost certainty of being rejected by one or the other party, and the position was not an enviable one, if taken. Ninety-six men were brought into court before the requisite panel of 12 was full. The following are names of the jurors chosen:

Jesse Griffiths, Joseph Jones, Wm. Robertson, William Smith, Joseph Massey, Silas Griffiths, Jonathan Foy, Solomon J. Hill, James Gittings, F. M. Walton, Jabez A. Beebe, Gilmore Callison.

The trial lasted till the 30th when the jury was instructed by the court and after a deliberation of several hours returned a verdict of *not guilty*.

Instructions to the jury had been asked by both parties, the following among a list of nine asked by defendants' counsel, were given, and probably had most influence on the verdict.

"That where the evidence is circumstantial admitting all to be proven that the evidence tends to prove, if then the jury can make any supposition consistent with the facts, by which the murder might have been committed without the agency of the defendants, it will be their duty to make that supposition, and find defendants not guilty.

"That in making up their verdict, they will exclude from their consideration all that was said by Daniels, Brackenberry and Miss Graham. [Witnesses, see note, p. 319.]

"That whenever the probability is of a definite and limited nature whether in proportion of 100 to 1 or 1,000 to 1 or any rate is immaterial, it cannot be made the ground of conviction, for to act upon it in any case would be to decide that for the sake of convicting many criminals, the life of one innocent man might be sacrificed [Starkie 508.]"

Same defendants, for murder of Hyrum Smith were requested to enter into recognizance of $5,000 each (with fourteen sureties) to the June term, 1845. At said term case was called, and Elliot and Lamborn not answering, the cause was dismissed for want of prosecution and defendants discharged.

Colonel John Hay, in the *Atlantic Monthly* for December, 1869, published an article on this subject. Although but a mere boy at the time of this trial he had within his reach sources of correct information. (He was a member of the State department subsequently.) He says: "The case was closed. There was not a man on the jury, in the court, in the county, that did not know the defendants had done the murder. But it was not proven, and the verdict of not guilty was right in law. * * * The elisors presented 99 men before 12 were found ignorant enough and indifferent enough to act as jurors."

The fact is, the trial amounted to nothing more than a farce. The law had been outraged, the honor of the State betrayed, her plighted faith was shamefully broken, and there was not virtue enough in the people to demand its vindication. Nor is this at all an exaggerated statement of the matter. The governor of Illinois himself—Thomas Ford—admits all that is here said. Of the atrocious deed itself and his determination to bring the murderers to justice he says:

I had determined from the first that some of the ringleaders in the foul murder of the Smiths should be brought to trial. If these men had been the incarnation of Satan himself, as was believed by many, their murder was a foul and treacherous action, *alike disgraceful to those who perpetrated the crime, to the State, and to the governor, whose word had been pledged for the protection of the prisoners in jail, and which had been so shamefully violated; and required that the most vigorous means should be used to bring the assassins to punishment.**

Speaking of the trial, Governor Ford says:

Accordingly, I employed able lawyers to hunt up the testimony, procure indictments, and prosecute the offenders. A trial was had before Judge Young in the summer of 1845. The sheriff and panel of jurors, selected by the Mormon court, were set aside for prejudice, and elisors were appointed to select a new jury. One friend of the Mormons and one anti-Mormon were appointed for this purpose; but as more than a thousand men had assembled under arms at the court, to keep away the Mormons and their friends, the jury was made up of these military followers of the court, who all swore that they had never formed or expressed any opinion as to the guilt or innocence of the accused. The Mormons had one principal* witness who was with the troops at Warsaw, had marched with them until they disbanded heard their consultations, went before them to Carthage, and saw them murder the Smiths. But before the trial came on, they induced him to become a Mormon; and being much more anxious for the glorification of the Prophet than to avenge his death, the Mormons made him publish a pamphlet giving an account of the murder; in which he professed to have seen a bright and shining light descend upon the head of Joe Smith to strike some of the conspirators with blindness; and that he heard supernatural voices in the air confirming his mission as a Prophet! Having published this in a book, he was compelled to swear to it in court, which of course destroyed the credit of his evidence. This witness was afterwards expelled by the Mormons, but no doubt they will cling to his evidence in favor of the divine mission of the Prophet.† Many other wit-

---

*Ford's History of Illinois, page 367.

† This the "Mormons," however, have not done; and no well informed "Mormon," regards the story as being vouched for in any

nesses were examined who knew the facts, but under the influence of the demoralization of faction, denied all knowledge of them. It has been said, that faction may find men honest, but it scarcely ever leaves them so. This was verified to the letter in the history of the Mormon quarrel. The accused were all acquitted.

During the progress of these trials, the judge was compelled to permit the courthouse to be filled and surrounded by armed bands who attended court to browbeat and overawe the administration of justice. The judge himself was in a duress, and informed me that he did not consider his life secure any part of the time. The consequence was that the crowd had everything their own way; the lawyers for the defense defended their clients by a long and elaborate attack upon the governor; the armed mob stamped with their feet and yelled their approbation at every sarcastic and smart thing that was said, and the judge was not only forced to hear it, but to lend it a kind of approval.*

And now in conclusion, as promised in the footnote on this page, I quote the statement of the martyrdom as vouched for by The Church, and published in the book of Doctrine and Covenants:

To seal the testimony of this book and the Book of Mormon, we announce the martyrdom of Joseph Smith the Prophet, and Hyrum Smith the Patriarch. They were shot in Carthage jail, on the 27th of June, 1844, about five o'clock p. m., by an armed mob, painted black—of from 150 to 200 persons. Hyrum was shot first and fell calmly, exclaiming, "I am a dead man!" Joseph leaped from the window, and was shot dead in the attempt, exclaiming, "O Lord, my God!" They were both shot after they were dead in a brutal manner and both received four balls.

---

authoritative way by The Church. The only authoritative account of the sad martyrdom of the Prophets for which The Church stands responsible is that published in the Doctrine and Covenants, section CXXXV (and which is published at the close of this chapter); and in that account the element of the miraculous enters not at all.

*Ford's History of Illinois, pages 367, 368.

John Taylor and Willard Richards, two of the Twelve, were the only persons in the room at the time; the former was wounded in a savage manner with four balls, but has since recovered; the latter, through the providence of God, escaped, "without even a hole in his robe."

Joseph Smith, the Prophet and Seer of the Lord, has done more (save Jesus only,) for the salvation of men in this world, than any other man that ever lived in it. In the short space of twenty years, he has brought forth the Book of Mormon, which he translated by the gift and power of God, and has been the means of publishing it on two continents; has sent the fullness of the everlasting gospel which it contained to the four quarters of the earth; has brought forth the revelations and commandments which compose this Book of Doctrine and Covenants, and many other wise documents and instructions for the benefit of the children of men; gathered many thousands of the Latter-day Saints, founded a great city; and left a fame and name that cannot be slain. He lived great, and he died great in the eyes of God and his people, and like most of the Lord's anointed in ancient times, has sealed his mission and his works with his own blood—and so has his brother Hyrum. In life they were not divided, and in death they were not separated!

When Joseph went to Carthage to deliver himself up to the pretended requirements of the law, two or three days previous to his assassination, he said, "I am going like a lamb to the slaughter; but I am calm as a summer's morning; I have a conscience void of offense towards God, and towards all men. I SHALL DIE INNOCENT, AND IT SHALL YET BE SAID OF ME—HE WAS MURDERED IN COLD BLOOD." The same morning, after Hyrum had made ready to go—shall it be said to the slaughter? Yes, for so it was,—he read the following paragraph, near the close of the fifth chapter of Ether, in the Book of Mormon, and turned down the leaf upon it:—

"And it came to pass that I prayed unto the Lord that he would give unto the Gentiles grace, that they might have charity. And it came to pass that the Lord said unto me, if they have not charity, it mattereth not unto you, thou hast been faithful; wherefore thy garments are clean. And because thou hast seen thy weakness, thou shalt be made strong, even unto the sitting down in the place which

I have prepared in the mansions of my Father. And now I * * bid farewell unto the Gentiles; yea and also unto my brethren whom I love, until we shall meet before the judgment-seat of Christ, where all men shall know that my garments are not spotted with your blood." The testators are now dead, and their testament is in force.

Hyrum Smith was 44 years old, February, 1844, and Joseph Smith was 38 in December, 1843; and henceforward their names will be classed among the martyrs of religion; and the reader in every nation will be reminded that the "Book of Mormon," and this book of Doctrine and Covenants of the Church, cost the best blood of the nineteenth century to bring them forth for the salvation of a ruined world: and that if the fire can scathe a *green tree* for the glory of God, how easy it will burn up the "dry trees" to purify the vineyard of corruption. They lived for glory; they died for glory; and glory is their eternal reward. From age to age shall their names go down to posterity as gems for the sanctified.

They were innocent of any crime, as they had often been proved before, and were only confined in jail by the conspiracy of traitors and wicked men; and their *innocent blood* on the floor of Carthage jail, is a broad seal affixed to "Mormonism" that cannot be rejected by any court on earth; and their *innocent blood* on the escutcheon of the State of Illinois, with the broken faith of the State as pledged by the governor, is a witness to the truth of the everlasting Gospel, that all the world cannot impeach; and their *innocent blood* on the banner of liberty, and on the *magna charta* of the United States, is an ambassador for the religion of Jesus Christ, that will touch the hearts of honest men among all nations; and their *innocent blood*, with the innocent blood of all the martyrs under the altar that John saw, will cry unto the Lord of hosts, till He avenges that blood on the earth. Amen.

CHAPTER XLI.

THE EXODUS—THE FALL OF NAUVOO.

IT is thought by some that our enemies would be satisfied with my destruction; but I tell you that as soon as they have shed my blood, they will thirst for the blood of every man in whose heart dwells a single spark of the spirit of the fullness of the Gospel. The opposition of these men is moved by the spirit of the adversary of all righteousness. It is not only to destroy me, but every man and woman who dares believe the doctrines that God hath inspired me to teach in this generation.

Such were the words of the Prophet Joseph Smith to the Nauvoo Legion on the eighteenth of June, 1844. And the action of the old citizens of Hancock and the surrounding counties subsequent to the murder of the Prophet, prove how truly inspired were the words we have quoted. For no sooner did they discover that the work which Joseph had begun refused to die with him, than they renewed hostilities, and sought by every means their wicked hearts could devise to harass and destroy those who devoted their energies to the consummation of the work which had been started.

The mockery of a trial given those who had murdered the Prophets, emboldened the enemies of the Saints, for they saw justice powerless to vindicate outraged law, and that with impunity they could prey upon the citizens of Nauvoo, whom, it would seem, their hatred had selected for a sacrifice. Thieves and blacklegs generally, saw the opportunity of having their crimes charged upon an innocent people, and established themselves in the vicinity of Nauvoo, though principally on the Iowa side of the river, and all the thefts and acts of violence committed by those renegades were charged up to the account of the citizens of Nauvoo, and too gladly believed by the people in the surrounding counties.

Not only were the charges of theft and robbery made against the Sainst, but they were also accused of hiding from justice any and all criminals who came into their midst—that Nauvoo, in short, was a rendezvous for outlaws, counterfeiters and desperate men generally. These charges led the city council on the thirteenth of January, 1845, to investigate the allegations and a series of resolutions were adopted stating that the charges of theft for the most part were fabrications of their enemies bent on ruining the reputation of the city, and defied those who made the charges to sustain with proof a single case where the citizens of Nauvoo had screened criminals from justice.

The council also extended an invitation to all who had reasons to believe that their stolen property was concealed in Nauvoo to come and make diligent search for it, and pledged them the assistance of the council. To hunt out crime and put away everything that could give rise to even a suspicion of concealing criminals, the mayor was authorized to increase the force of police if necessary to five hundred; and the people were called upon to redouble their diligence in preventing criminals from coming among them, and all such persons as soon as discovered were to be given up to the officers of the law.

The next day the action of the city council was submitted to the citizens of Nauvoo, and they approved of it. Fifty delegates were chosen and sent into the surrounding counties to disabuse the public mind relative to the false accusations made against the Saints, and to ask their co-operation in ridding the country of the counterfeiters and thieves which infested it. But all these efforts were fruitless. The falsehoods of their enemies outweighed the truths of the Saints, and prejudice more cruel than hell itself hardened the hearts of the people of Illinois against the appeals of the citizens of Nauvoo, and made them deaf to all entreaties for justice.

Twice during the summer of 1845, Governor Ford himself went to Nauvoo to investigate these charges against her people; and when he came to deal with the "Mormon troubles," in his message to the legislature that fall, after speaking of the charges made, he said:

> Justice, however, requires me to say that I have investigated the charge of promiscuous stealing, and find it to be greatly exaggerated. I could not ascertain that there were a greater proportion of thieves in that community than in any other of the same number of inhabitants, and perhaps if the city of Nauvoo were compared with St. Louis, or any other western city, the proportion would not be so great.

The prejudice, not to say bitterness, of Governor Ford against the Saints would rob his statement of any suspected exaggeration favorable to them.

Nor is Governor Ford's voice the only one which vindicates the character of the citizens of Nauvoo. The deputy sheriff of Hancock County exonerated the Mormon people from any participation in the thefts perpetrated in the surrounding country. He testified that stolen property was brought through the country *via* Nauvoo, passed over the river to the Iowa side and taken into the interior, where it was concealed. He also stated that there were some five or six persons in Nauvoo who were assisting in this nefarious business, but said he, "they are not Mormons nor are they fellowshiped by them."

Notwithstanding all this, misrepresentation so far succeeded in poisoning the minds of the public and the leading men in the State, that in January, 1845, the city charter of Nauvoo and the charter of the Legion were both repealed, and thus the protecting ægis of the city government was snatched away from her citizens, when most they needed it, and left them exposed to the fury of their enemies.

Of this act of punic faith on the part of the State legislature, the State attorney, Josiah Lamborn, in a letter to Brigham Young, said:

> I have always considered that your enemies have been prompted by political and religious prejudices, and by a desire for plunder and blood, more than for the common good. By the repeal of your charter, and by refusing all amendments and modifications, our legislature has given a kind of sanction to the barbarous manner in which you have been treated. Your two representatives exerted themselves to the extent of their ability in your behalf, but the tide of popular passion and frenzy was too strong to be resisted. It is truly a melancholy spectacle to witness the law-makers of a sovereign State condescending to pander to the vices, ignorance and malevolence of a class of people who are at all times ready for riot, murder and rebellion.

Senator Jacob C. Davis was one among those who had been indicted for the murder of Joseph and Hyrum, and of him the attorney-general said:

> Your senator, Jacob C. Davis, has done much to poison the minds of members against anything in your favor. He walks at large in defiance of law an indicted murderer. If a Mormon was in his position, the senate would afford no protection, but he would be dragged forth to jail or the gallows, or be shot down by a cowardly and brutal mob.

In the meantime the Twelve Apostles, sustained by the Saints, put forth every exertion to carry out the designs of their martyred Prophet respecting Nauvoo. The Nauvoo House was hurried on, and the walls were growing rapidly under the constant labor of the masons. Work, too, was vigorously prosecuted at the temple. At the time of Joseph's death that edifice was but one story high, yet on the twenty-fourth of May, 1845, about six o'clock in the morning the cap-stone was laid amid the general rejoicing and shouts of "Hosanna" from the assembled thousands of the Saints. As President Brigham Young finished laying the cap-stone he stood upon it and said:

> The last stone is laid upon the temple, and I pray the Almighty in the name of Jesus to defend us in this place, and sustain us until the temple is finished and we have all got our endowments.
>
> The whole congregation then following the motion of President Young shouted as loud as possible: Hosanna! Hosanna! Hosanna! to God and the Lamb! Amen! Amen! and Amen!*
>
> "So let it be, thou Almighty God," solemnly concluded President Young.

Thus the world began to understand that Mormonism was not born to die with its earthly leaders. And it began to be whispered that the Prophet Joseph dead was even more potent than when living. His testimony had been sealed with his blood, and it gave to his life and his labors an additional sanctity in the eyes of his followers, as well as making it more binding upon the world.

Seeing then the continued prosperity of Nauvoo and her citizens, the people in the vicinity of that city and in the surrounding counties again commenced hostilities, if, indeed, it may be said that they had ever ceased. The enormity of the murder at Carthage jail had checked them temporarily; for an instant the torch and assassin's knife had dropped from their nerveless hands and they stood aghast, at that deed of blood. But seeing the work the murdered Prophet had started surviving his fall, they took up again the weapons of fell destruction and rushed once more upon their victims.

Early in September, 1845, mobbing the scattered families of the Saints began in earnest. A meeting was held by anti-

---

* Wm. Clayton's journal, under date of May 24, 1845.

Mormons near what was called the "Morley settlement," to devise means of getting rid of the Mormons. During the meeting guns were fired at the house where it was held, and the assault charged upon the Saints, though most likely it was done by some of their own party—that they might have an excuse for their meditated acts of violence upon the people of Nauvoo. Such was the general belief at the time; and Governor Ford in his "History of Illinois," speaking of this circumstance, says:

> In the fall of 1845, the anti-Mormons of Lima and Green Plains, held a meeting to devise means for the expulsion of the Mormons from their neighborhood. They appointed some persons of their own number to fire a few shots at the house where they were assembled; but to do it in such a way as to hurt none who attended the meeting. The meeting was held, the house was fired at, but so as to hurt no one; and the anti-Mormons suddenly breaking up their meeting, rode all over the country spreading the dire alarm, that the Mormons had commenced the work of massacre and death.*

The attack was made upon the Morley settlement, and on the eleventh of the month twenty-nine houses were burned down, while their occupants were driven into the bushes where men, women and children laid drenched with rain, anxiously awaiting the breaking of day.

Speaking of this outrage, the editor of the Quincy *Whig*, Mr. Bartlett, said:

> Seriously, these outrages should be put a stop to at once; if the Mormons have been guilty of crime why punish them, but do not visit their sins upon defenseless women and children. This is as bad as the savages. * * * It is feared that this rising against the Mormons is not confined to the Morley settlement, but that there is an understanding among the anties in the northern part of this [Adams] and Hancock counties to make a general sweep, burning and destroying the property of the Mormons wherever it can be found. If this

---

* Ford's History of Illinois, p. 406.

is the case, there will be employment of the executive of the State, and that soon. * * * Still later news from above [referring to Hancock County] was received late on Monday night. The outrages were still continued. The flouring mill, carding machine, etc., of Norman Buel, a Mormon, one mile and a half west of Lima is now a heap of ashes. Colonel Levi Williams, of Green Plains has ordered out his brigade, it is said to aid the anti-Mormons. The anti-Mormons from Shuyler [county] and the adjoining counties, are flocking in and great distress of life and property may be expected. Heaven only knows where these proceedings will end. It is time the strong arm of power was extended to quell them.*

In the midst of the exciting scenes which followed, the sheriff of Hancock County, Mr. J. B. Backenstos proved himself a friend to law and order. He did all in his power to arrest the spread of violence and called upon all law-abiding citizens to act as a *posse comitatus*, but announced it as his opinion that the citizens of Nauvoo had better take no part in suppressing the mob-violence, since that might lead to a civil war. At the same time he told the people of Hancock, that "the Mormon community had acted with more than ordinary forbearance, remaining perfectly quiet, and offering no resistance when their dwellings, their buildings, stacks of grain, etc., were set on fire in their presence. They had forborne until forbearance was no longer a virtue." His vigorous efforts were making headway against the violators of the law; but in consequence of some parties who had sought his life, while acting in his official capacity, being killed, he was arrested† by General John J. Hardin and placed on trial for murder; after which mob-violence went unchecked of justice.

In the midst of these tumultuous scenes a mass meeting of the citizens was convened at Quincy on the twenty-second of

---

* The Hancock Mob., p. 4, by J. B. Conyers, M. D.

† He was acquitted at his trial which took place at Peoria.

September. It was generally known that the Prophet Joseph had contemplated going west with the main body of The Church, and it was one of the objects of this meeting to appoint a committee to confer with The Church authorities and learn what their present intentions were as to leaving the State. It was expressed as the opinion of that meeting that the only basis upon which the Mormon troubles could be settled would be the removal of that people from Illinois. "It is a settled thing," said Mr. Bartlett, editor of the Quincy *Whig*, in his issue following the meeting of the above date—

> It is a settled thing that the public sentiment of the State is against the Mormons, and it will be in vain for them to contend against it; and to prevent bloodshed, and the sacrifice of many lives on both sides, it is their duty to obey the public will, and leave the State as speedily as possible. That they will do this we have a confident hope—and that too, before the last extreme is resorted to—that of force.

We are sorry to say that many of the leading men of Quincy, principally prominent members of the bar, who before had been kindly disposed towards the citizens of Nauvoo, now turned against them, and became the advocates of violence, and lent the weight and influence of their characters to the support and spread of mob-law. Among such we are sorry to publish Major Warren and O. H. Browning, the latter having defended the Prophet Joseph on more than one occasion when unjustly charged with crime before the courts of the country. His burning words of eloquence, in reciting the wrongs of the Saints, when cruelly expelled from Missouri, would, one would think, have enlisted the sympathy of adamantine hearts; and now to see him leagued with those bent upon bringing about a repetition of these sorrows, is an event to be truly deplored.

In answer to the Quincy committee to state what their present intentions were relative to leaving the State, the Twelve handed them the following communication:

NAUVOO, September 24, 1845.

Whereas, a council of the authorities of the Church of Jesus Christ of Latter-day Saints, at Nauvoo have this day received a communication from Messrs. Henry Asbury, John P. Robins, Albert G. Pearson, P. A. Goodwin, J. N. Ralston, M. Rogers and E. Congers, committee of the citizens of Quincy, requesting us to communicate in writing our disposition and intention at this time, particularly with regard to removing to some place where the peculiar organization of our Church will not be likely to engender so much strife and contention as unhappily exists at this time in Hancock and some of the adjoining counties;

And, whereas, said committee have reported to us the doings of a public meeting of the citizens of Quincy on the twenty-second inst., by which it appears there are some feelings concerning us as a people, and in relation to which sundry resolutions were passed, purporting to be for the purpose of maintaining or restoring peace to the country;

And, whereas, it is our desire and ever has been, to live in peace with all men, so far as we can, without sacrificing the right to worship God according to the dictates of our own consciences which privilege is granted by the Constitution of these United States; and, whereas, we have time and again, been driven from our peaceful homes, and our women and children have been obliged to live on the prairies, in the forests, on the roads and in tents, in the dead of winter, suffering all manner of hardships—even to death itself—as the people of Quincy well know; the remembrance of whose hospitality, in former days, still causes our hearts to burn with joy, and raise the prayer to heaven for blessing on their heads; and, whereas, it is now so late in the season that it is impossible for us, as a people, to remove this fall without causing a repetition of like sufferings; and, whereas, it has been represented to us from other sources than those named, and even in some communications from the executive of the State, that many of the citizens of the State were unfriendly to our views and principles; and, whereas, many scores of our homes in this country have been burned to ashes without any justifiable cause or provocation, and we have made no resistance, till compelled by the authorities of the county so to do, and that authority not connected with our Church; and, whereas, said resistance to mobocracy, from legally constituted authority, appears to be misunderstood by some, and misconstrued by others, so as to produce an undue excitement in the public mind; and, whereas, we desire peace above all earthly blessings;

Therefore, we would say to the committee above mentioned, and to the governor, and all the authorities and people of Illinois, and the surrounding States and Territories that we propose to leave this county next spring, for some point so remote, that there will not need be any difficulty with the people and ourselves, provided certain propositions necessary for the accomplishment of our removal shall be observed, as follows, to-wit:

That the citizens of this and surrounding counties, and all men, will use their influence and exertion to help us to sell or rent our properties, so as to get means enough that we can help the widow, the fatherless and the destitute to remove with us.

That all men will let us alone with their vexatious law-suits so that we may have time, for we have broken no laws; and help us to cash, dry goods, groceries, etc., to good oxen, beef cattle, sheep, wagons, mules horses, harness, etc., in exchange for our property, at a fair price, and deeds given on payment, that we may have means to accomplish a removal without the suffering of the destitute to an extent beyond the endurance of human nature.

That all exchange of property shall be conducted by a committee, or by committees of both parties; so that all the business may be transacted honorably and speedily.

That we will use all lawful means, in connection with others to preserve the public peace while we tarry; and shall expect, decidedly, that we be no more molested with house-burning, or any other depredations, to waste our property and time, and hinder our business.

That it is a mistaken idea, that we have proposed to leave in six months, for that would be so early in the spring that grass may not grow nor water run; both of which would be necessary for our removal But we propose to use our influence, to have no more seed time and harvest among our people in this county after gathering our present crops; and that all communications be made to us in writing.

By order of the council,

BRIGHAM YOUNG,
President.

W. RICHARDS,
Clerk.

The Quincy committee reported to the citizens of that city, the propositions of The Church authorities, which were regarded as satisfactory in part, but thought they were not so full or decisive as was necessary. The mass meeting to which they reported, however, accepted the propositions and decided to recommend the people in the surrounding counties to do the same. "But," said one of the resolutions:

We accept it [the proposition of The Church authorities] as an unconditional proposition to remove. We do not intend to bring ourselves under any obligation to purchase their property or furnish purchasers for the same, but we will in no way hinder or obstruct them in their efforts to sell; and will expect them to dispose of their property, and remove at the time appointed.

Resolved, that it is now too late to attempt the settlement of the difficulties in Hancock County upon any other basis than that of the removal of the Mormons from the State.

Resolved, that whilst we shall endeavor, by all the means in our power, to prevent the occurrence of anything which might operate against their removal, and afford the people of Nauvoo any grounds of complaint, we shall equally expect good faith upon their part; and if they shall not comply with their own proposition, the consequence must rest upon those who violate faith. And we now solennly pledge ourselves to be ready at the appointed time to act, as the occasion may require, and that we will immediately adopt a preliminary military organization, for prompt future action, if occasion should demand it.

Resolved, that in our opinion, the peace of Hancock County cannot so far be restored as to allow the desired progress to be made, in preparing the way for the removal of the Mormons, while J. B.

Backenstos remains sheriff of said county: and that he ought to resign said office.

Of the first of these resolutions Josiah B. Conyers, the author of "A Brief History of the Hancock Mob," says with just indignation and sarcasm:

> The first one, in our opinion, is unique. They accepted and recommended to the people of the surrounding counties to accept an unconditional proposition to remove. But understand, Mr. Mormon, though we accept it and recommend the surrounding counties to do so, likewise, (reprobate you, unconditionally) we do not intend to bring ourselves under any obligation to purchase your property, or to furnish purchasers; but we will be very kind and obliging, and will in no way, hinder or obstruct you in your efforts to sell, provided, nevertheless, this shall not be so construed as to prevent us from running off the purchaser. But we expect this small favor of you, viz., that you must dispose of your property, and leave at the appointed time.*

This mass meeting closed its business by arranging a plan for adopting a preliminary military organization for prompt future action, if occasion should demand.

On the first and second of October an anti-Mormon convention assembled at Carthage, in which nine counties, those immediately surrounding Hancock, were represented. A committee on evidence, was appointed, on which Archibald Williams, one of the Saints' bitterest enemies, was chairman. It was its business to collect evidence in relation to the depredations of the Mormons. The chairman made a report to which were appended a number of affidavits, charging various crimes on the people of Nauvoo. It is needless to say that the whole thing was an *ex patre* affair, and sustained by the men who had assisted in the murder of Joseph and Hyrum Smith; and it was upon their evidence the convention acted.

---

* Hancock Mob, Conyers, pp. 13, 14.

The convention adopted the course followed by the mass meeting at Quincy—that is, it agreed to accept the propositions of The Church authorities, to remove, in the same spirit they were received at Quincy, and proceeded to prepare a preliminary military organization to act with promptitude, provided the Saints did not remove. The convention also,

Resolved, that it is expected as an indispensable condition to the pacification of the county, that the old citizens be permitted to return to their homes unmolested by the present sheriff (Backenstos,) and the Mormons, for anything alleged against them; any attempt on their part to arrest or prosecute such persons for pretended offenses, will inevitably lead to a renewal of the late disorder.

O. H. Browning moved the following:

Resolved, that the Hon. W. N. Purple, judge of this judicial circuit court be requested not to hold a court in Hancock County this fall; as, in the opinion of this convention, such court could not be holden without producing a collision between the Mormons and anti-Mormons, and renewing the excitement and disturbances which have recently affected said county.

And thus those guilty of mob violence and house burning were to be protected by the Carthage convention from prosecution before the courts; and those who might have the temerity to prosecute them and vindicate the law, were threatened by a renewal of that same lawless violence! Where, then, proud State of Illinois, was your majesty! Your honor! Can you answer? If you, out of very shame, cannot look up and reply, history answers for you, and tells you it was trailed in the dust, under the very feet of as vile a set of traitors as ever brought shame to their country! And where was your virtuous populace, the true watch and guard of a State's honor? Alas, they were blinded by the falsehoods prompted by malice and envy, and started on foot to shield the guilty murderers of innocence, or quelled by the bold front of a traitorous but successful mob.

In the meantime every exertion was made by the citizens of Nauvoo, to be ready for the great exodus in the spring. The temple had been so far completed that a conference was held in it on the sixth of October, and committees appointed to negotiate the sale of property and attend to other branches of business.

Nauvoo presented a busy scene in those days. Men were hurrying to and fro collecting wagons and putting them in repair; the roar of the smith's forge was well nigh perpetual, and even the stillness of night was broken by the steady beating of the sledge and the merry ringing of the anvil. Committees were seeking purchasers of real estate and converting both that and personal property into anything that would be of service to those just about to plunge into an unknown and boundless wilderness.

But while these efforts were being put forth on the part of the people of Nauvoo, to fulfill their agreement with the mob forces, the conditions of removal on the part of the old settlers were frequently violated; and instances of mob violence were almost every day occurrences. The people, who were making preparations to leave the farms, gardens and homes they had redeemed from the wilderness, were constantly threatened with destruction by the hostile demonstrations of their heartless neighbors.

To give an earnest of the intentions of the Mormons to leave the State where they had suffered so much, and to thereby remove all occasion for the implacable wrath of their enemies, that was so impatient that it could not wait for the springtime to come, for the sacrifice of its victims, the Twelve and the High Council, with about four hundred families, crossed the Mississippi on the ice, on the eleventh of February, 1846, and were soon lost to view in the wilderness of Iowa. Others continued to follow as fast as they could make ready, until by the latter part of April, the great body of The Church at Nauvoo had gone.

But now, purchasers for their property failed those who remained. The people surrounding Nauvoo saw no need of purchasing that which inevitably must become theirs. The result was that it became impossible for this remnant, consisting for the most part, of the destitute, the aged, infirm and sick, to remove. And surely a people who had still any faith left in humanity, would be justified in the belief that these could remain until an asylum was found for them by their friends, who had already gone in search of new homes. But in this, be it said, to the shame of Illinois, they were deceived. In the hardened hearts of their enemies, however, there was no mercy, even for the helpless; no pity for the sick or destitute. In their enemies' veins the milk of human kindness had dried up.

During the preparations for the exodus, Major Warren had been stationed with a small military force in Hancock, to keep the peace; but about the middle of April he received orders to disband his force on the first of May, as that was adjudged by "the public expectation," to use a phrase of Major Warren's, when the last of the Mormons should have left the State. So soon as it was understood that there were still left in Nauvoo a number of Mormons who would likely remain through the summer to continue their efforts to dispose of property, an uproar was raised in the surrounding counties, meetings were held and resolutions adopted, demanding that they leave at once, under threats of extermination. When the governor saw this new furore breaking out, he countermanded the order for Major Warren to disband his forces, and commanded him to hold his position and to preserve the peace until he received further orders.

The new impetus given to mob violence, however, was not to spend its force without perpetrating some outrage, and a number of cowardly attacks were made upon Mormons. On the eleventh of May, Major Warren found it necessary to issue a circular from which I quote the following:

> The undersigned again deems it his duty to appear before you in a circular. It may not be known to all of you, that the day after my detachment was disbanded at Carthage, I received orders from the executive to muster them into service again, and remain in the county until further orders.
>
> I have now been in Nauvoo with my detachment a week and can say to you with perfect assurance that the demonstrations made by the Mormon population, are unequivocal. They are leaving the State, and preparing to leave, with every means that God and nature has placed in their hands. * * * The anti-Mormons desire the removal of the Mormons; this is being effected peaceably and with all possible dispatch. All aggressive movements, therefore, against them at this time, must be actuated by a wanton desire to shed blood, or to plunder. * * *
>
> A man of near sixty years of age, living about seven miles from this place, was taken from his house a few nights since, stripped of his clothing, and his back cut to pieces with a whip, for no other reason than because he was a Mormon, and too old to make successful resistance. Conduct of this kind would disgrace a horde of savages. * * * To the Mormons I would say, go on with your preparations and leave as fast as you can. Leave the fighting to be done by my detachment. If we are overpowered, then recross the river, and defend yourselves and property.

To those busy trying to raise mob forces, principally Squire M'Calla and Colonel Levi Williams, Major Warren gave warning that a previous order to the effect that not more than four armed men, other than State troops, should assemble together, would be enforced; and that any mob which assembled would be dispersed; his force or the mob would leave the field in double quick time. This had the effect of quieting matters down for a season, but only until Major Warren's detachment was disbanded.

A meeting was held at Carthage on the sixth of June, to

make preparations for celebrating the fourth of July, the nation's natal day. It was suggested at that meeting that, as all the Mormons had not left the State, the people of Hancock County could not be considered free; and under those circumstances, they ought not to celebrate the fourth with the usual rejoicings. The meeting was therefore adjourned to meet on the twelfth, for the purpose of taking into consideration why it was that all Mormons had not left the city of Nauvoo. That happened to be the day fixed by the governor on which to raise volunteers for the Mexican war, which, in the meantime, had broken out; so that there was considerable excitement among the militia of Hancock County, and the mob leaders doubtless thought the time propitious for making a demonstration against the few Saints still remaining in Nauvoo.

A large body of men were found willing to march into Nauvoo, but it was learned that the new citizens who had purchased much of the property of the now exiled people, were unwilling to allow the mob forces to enter the city, and meeting with this unexpected opposition, the mob forces marched to Golden's point, distant from Nauvoo some five or six miles down the river. At this juncture, Stephen Markham returned to Nauvoo from the camp of the Apostles for some Church property; but it was rumored that he had returned with a large body of men, and as Markham's name was a terror among the enemies of the Saints, the mob took to flight, though no one was in pursuit. It was a case of the wicked fleeing when no man pursued.

The committee at Quincy having control of the mob forces, either chagrined by the cowardice of those who had collected at Golden's point, or appalled at the prospect of innocent blood being found upon their skirts, retired from the position which had been assigned them. This disorganized the mob and they dispersed to their homes, but agreed to assemble again at the call of their leaders; and laid an injunction upon the Mormons in Nauvoo not to go outside of the city limits, except in making their way westward.

This order of the mob was disregarded by a party of new citizens and a few Saints who went into the country several miles, to harvest a field of grain. While engaged in their work, they were surrounded by a mob and captured. They were robbed of their arms, stripped of their clothing, and cruelly beaten with hickory goads. This outrage created intense excitement in Nauvoo, and the new citizens and Saints made common cause in bringing the perpetrators of it to justice. But while the parties accused of the crime were under arrest in the hands of the officers, a second party, consisting of P. H. Young and his son, Richard Ballantyne, James Standing and Mr. Herring were kidnapped, and held by their tormentors fourteen days, during which time they were constantly threatened with death. They finally escaped, however, and returned to Nauvoo.

The parties accused of making the assault on those in the harvest field, took a change of venue to Quincy, but whether they were ever brought to trial or not, I cannot learn, but think they were not.

Among those arrested for attacking the party of harvesters was Major M'Calla; and in his possession was found a gun taken from the party. The gun was recognized by several persons, among whom was Wm. Pickett, and taken from him. The mobbers then and there made out a charge of stealing, and got out warrants for the arrest of Pickett, Furness and Clifford. Pickett, it would seem, had incurred the hatred of the mob, and they desired to get him into their power. Word was brought to him by a friend that the warrant was merely a subterfuge to get him into the hands of his enemies; consequently, when one John Carlin, a special constable from Carthage, undertook to arrest him, he asked if he would guarantee his safety; being answered in the negative, he resisted the officer and would not be taken. Though it is claimed that afterwards, in company with several friends he went before the magistrate of Green Plains, who, it was said, issued the warrant for his arrest. But as he had no record of the warrant he refused to put him under arrest. The other parties accused were acquitted on examination.

The mob now, however, saw an opportunity to accomplish their full purpose of destroying the city of Nauvoo. An officer had been resisted by a citizen, and his fellow citizens approved his course! "Nauvoo was in rebellion against the laws!" Carlin issued a proclamation calling upon the citizens to come as a *posse comitatus*, to assist him in executing the law. And to his clarion call,

There was mounting in hot haste.

The old mob forces were soon assembled at Carthage, and the command given to Captain Singleton.

The citizens of Nauvoo petitioned the governor for protection, and he sent to them Major J. R. Parker, with a force of ten men from Fulton County, and also authorized him to take command of such forces as might volunteer to defend the city against any attacks that might be threatened. He was also empowered "to pursue, and in aid of any peace officer with a proper warrant, arrest the rioters who may threaten or attempt such an attack, and bring them to trial;" and to assist with an armed posse any peace officer in making an arrest, and with a like force to guard the prisoners, during the trial, and as long as he believed them in danger of mob violence. The commission bears date August 24, 1846.

Thus equipped, Major Parker went to Nauvoo and issued a proclamation calling upon the mobs then collecting, "*in the name of the people of Illinois, and by virtue of the authority vested in him by the governor of the State to disperse.*" The issue, then, was no longer between the mob forces and the Mormons; it was between the recognized authority of the State and this lawless banditti. Major Parker also announced that he was authorized and prepared to assist the proper officers in serving any writs in their hands.

In answer to this proclamation Carlin issued a counter one to the effect that if he met with resistance from Parker, he would consider his detachment as a mob, and proceed accordingly. To which Parker replied, if the forces under Carlin undertook to enter Nauvoo, he would treat them as a mob. Parker also wrote to Singleton, and expressed a desire to bring about a settlement of the difficulty without shedding blood. To this communication Singleton replied that in Parker's proposition he saw nothing looking to the expulsion of the remnant of the Mormon people left in Nauvoo, and "that is," said he "a *sine qua non* with us." It will be remembered that Carlin's professed object in calling for a posse was to arrest William Pickett; but now something more is demanded—the immediate removal of the Mormons, the surrender of Nauvoo, etc. Singleton concluded his terms to Parker, the representative of the governor of the State, in these words:

> When I say to you, the Mormons must go, I speak the mind of the camp and the country. They can leave without force or injury to themselves or their property, but I say to you, sir, with all candor, *they shall go*—they may fix the time within sixty days, or I will fix it for them.

At this juncture a committee of one hundred, which had been appointed by the citizens of Quincy, arrived on the scene, to act—ostensibly—as mediators, to bring about a peaceful solution of the trouble, but one cannot help thinking their true mission was to insiduously carry out the project of the mob. But I leave the reader to draw his own inference respecting that; when he hears the terms proposed by that committee, and which all classes of citizens in Nauvoo, seeing no alternative, accepted:

The terms offered were that the Mormons move out of the city, or disperse within sixty days. A force of twenty-five to remain in the city during that time, half the expense of maintaining them was to be paid by the people of Nauvoo; for which amount they were to give bond; that the Mormons surrender their arms, which should be returned to them after they left the State; that as soon as those arms were surrendered, the forces under Singleton were to disperse; that all hostilities cease between the respective parties as soon as the agreement was accepted.

The singularity about this agreement is that not one word is said about giving up Pickett, to arrest whom the forces under Singleton were ostensibly called out. Does it not reveal the fact that the Pickett episode was merely a ruse—a pretext for gathering a mob to sack Nauvoo and drive away the Mormons?

This proposed settlement, however, was rejected by the mob forces. It did not sufficiently gratify their implacable hatred. They did, in very deed, as the Prophet Joseph foretold his people they would, thirst for the blood of every man in whose heart dwelt a single spark of the spirit of the fullness of the Gospel. But when the mob rejected these terms, Singleton and other leaders left them; saying the Mormons had done all that could be required of them.

On the retirement of Singleton and others, the command of the mob was given to Thomas S. Brockman, a Campbellite preacher, known familiarly as "Old Tom," among his followers. He at once went into active preparations for bombarding the city; and with a force of more than one thousand men, and six pieces of cannon, took up a position about one mile east of the city, in a cornfield just at the head of Mulholland street; and not far from the house of Squire D. H. Wells.

From this position Brockman issued the terms upon which he would grant peace. The terms he offered were much more outrageous than those proposed by the Quincy committee, and therefore were rejected by the people of Nauvoo, both by Mormon and non-Mormon. Brockman addressed his insolent terms of peace to "the commanding officer of Nauvoo, and the trustees of the Mormon Church." The "commanding officer" was Major Clifford, who had succeeded Major Parker in that position. He was vested with the governor's commission as Parker had been, and it was to this representative of Illinois' executive that the demand of Brockman to surrender the city, and stack his arms, was addressed; so that he and his mob forces were pitted against the laws and lawful authority of the State, and we shall see, as we proceed, how mobs were more powerful than the State authorities; or rather, how the lawful authorities of the State were so lost to all sense of shame, so recreant to the trust reposed in them, so neglectful of the honor and dignity of the State, that they permitted their own representatives to be driven in disgrace from the field by the mob led by Brockman: and furthermore, those same authorities were so lost to every principle of humanity, that they permitted the helpless and unoffending people to be driven from their homes out into the wilderness to perish from exposure.

The citizens of Nauvoo were not willing to allow Brockman's mob to enter the city without making some effort to prevent him; and although their forces numbered not more than three or four hundred, they presented a determined front to the mob. They converted some steam-boat shafts into cannon—five pieces in all—and threw up some fortifications on the north of Mulholland street, facing the mob's camp. These works were under command of Captain Lamareux. On the south of of Mulholland street, the companies of Gates and Cutler were stationed.

On September 10th, 11th, and 12th, there was some desultory firing on both sides, without much advantage being gained. On the thirteenth, however, the mob-forces advanced in solid column, making a desperate effort to reach Mulholland street, the principal street leading into Nauvoo from the east. If the onset was desperate, the resistance was equally determined. The main shock of the conflict was sustained for a time by Gates' and Cutler's companies, and they must inevitably have been overpowered by the superior numbers of the mob, had not Squire Wells come up with Lamareux's company to reinforce them. The doughty squire had ridden across an open field exposed to the fire of the enemy, to where Lamareux's company lay behind their fortifications. He called upon them to advance at once to check the approach of the mob. There was one brave spirit who needed no second call to perform his duty. That was William Anderson, captain of what was known as the "Spartan Band." He leaped from behind the trenches and calling on his men to follow, started for the front. The rest of Lamareux's company did not so readily respond, and manifested a disposition to retreat rather than advance. Squire Wells, observing this, and seeing Anderson and his few brave followers rushing headlong into the conflict, raised in his stirrups, and swinging his hat, shouted: "Hurrah for Anderson! Who wouldn't follow the brave Anderson!" This rallied their spirits, and they followed the squire to the front, where they were soon firing at the enemy as steadily as their comrades.

The mob forces by this time had nearly reached Mulholland street, but now they recoiled from the rapid firing of the reinforcements and beat a retreat to the house of a Mr. Carmichael, but a short distance from Squire Wells' house. Here they waited until wagons came from their camp, and putting their dead and wounded into them, returned to where they were encamped in the morning. The number of killed and wounded of the mob has never been ascertained, as the facts were kept concealed. The intrepid Anderson and his equally brave son, a lad not more than fifteen years of age, fell in the engagement; and one Morris was killed while crossing a field by a cannon ball.

Negotiations were now renewed, and the citizens of Nauvoo, seeing that the State authorities rendered them no assistance, but permitted even their own authority to be braved by a lawless mob, and knowing that they would eventually be overpowered, accepted the following terms of settlement, in order to stop the further effusion of blood:—

1. The city of Nauvoo will surrender. The force of Colonel Brockman to enter and take possession of the city tomorrow, the seventeenth of September, at three o'clock p. m.

2. The arms to be delivered to the Quincy committee, to be returned on the crossing of the river.

3. The Quincy committee pledge themselves to use their influence for the protection of persons and property from all violence, and the officers of the camp and the men pledge themselves to protect all persons and property from violence.

4. The sick and helpless to be protected and treated with humanity.

5. The Mormon population of the city to leave the State or disperse as soon as they can cross the river.

6. Five men, including the Trustees of The Church, and five clerks, with their families (Wm. Pickett not one of the number) to be permitted to remain in the city, for the disposition of property, free from all molestation and personal violence.

7. Hostilities to cease immediately, and ten men of the Quincy committee to enter the city, in the execution of their duty as soon as they think proper.

These terms of capitulation were signed on the part of the citizens of Nauvoo, by Almon W. Babbitt, Joseph L. Heywood and John S. Fullmer; and on the part of the mob by Thomas S. Brockman and John Carlin; and by Andrew Johnson on behalf of the Quincy committee.

The rest of my story is soon told. There was a hasty flight of the "Mormon" population and a number of the new citizens who had assisted in the defense of Nauvoo. They left their homes without being able to carry with them anything for their comfort. The sick, aged and infirm, together with the youth, without regard to sex or condition, shared the same fate; they had to lie out on the Mississippi bottoms where many perished through exposure, and beyond all doubt, all would have famished from hunger, had not their camp been filled with innumerable flocks of quail, so tame that women and children caught hundreds of them in their hands, and thus was the cry of hunger relieved, by what would generally be regarded as a miraculous occurrence.*

Brockman and his forces entered the city, and once in, he insolently violated every condition of the treaty of surrender. But lest I should be charged with inaccuracy—for such events as I am recording seem almost too much to believe—I quote from the report made by Mr. Brayman to Governor Ford. Mr. Brayman had acted as the Governor's agent, for some time, in a secret capacity from the commencement of the difficulties at Nauvoo, and the following abstract is from an elaborate report he gives of the final struggle for the defense of the city. Moreover, the fact that I have never seen this matter reproduced in any of our books encourages me to insert it here:

The force of General Brockman marched into the city at three o'clock. From fifteen hundred to two thousand men marched in procession, through the city, and encamped on the south side, near the river. The march was conducted without the least disorder or trespass upon persons or property. The streets were deserted—the obnoxious persons had left the city, leaving but little to provoke the resentment of the victors. But a few Mormons remained in the city, and these were hastening their preparations for crossing the river as soon as possible. On my return from Carthage to the city, about noon, I learned that the Quincy committee had closed its labors at sunrise and had left for home, leaving a sub-committee to complete

* The condition of the exiled Saints at this period is graphically described by General Thomas L. Kane, see appendix—

the reception and delivery of the arms of those Mormons who had not yet departed.

I also learned that in addition to the duty General Brockman had assumed, under the treaty, of superintending the removal of the Mormons from the State, he had issued an order for the expulsion from the State, of all who had borne arms in defense of the city against his force, and all who were in any manner identified with the Mormons.

It could scarcely be believed that such an order in such palpable and gross violation of the unanimous pledge which had been signed by the officers, agreed to by the whole force, and endorsed by the Quincy committee, had been given. But on applying to General Brockman, I learned that such an order had been given, and would be executed. This order was rigorously enforced throughout the day, with many circumstances of the utmost cruelty and injustice. Bands of armed men traversed the city, entering the houses of citizens, robbing them of arms, throwing their household goods out of doors, insulting them, and threatening their lives. Many were seized and marched to the camp, and after military examination, set across the river, for the crime of sympathizing with the Mormons, or the still more heinous offense of *fighting in the defense of the city, under command of officers commissioned by* YOU, [Governor Ford], and instructed to make that defense. It is, indeed, painfully true, that many citizens of this State, have been driven from it by an armed force, because impelled by our encouragement, and a sense of duty, they have bravely defended their homes and homes of their neighbors from the assaults of a force assembled for unlawful purposes.

In the face of the pledge given to protect persons and property from all violence, (excepting of course Mormon persons and property), it may be estimated that nearly one half of the new citizens of Nauvoo have been forced from their homes and dare not return. Thus far, these citizens have appealed in vain for protection and redress.

It remains yet to be seen whether there is efficacy in the law, power in the executive arm, or potency in public opinion sufficient to right their grievous wrongs. It is disgraceful to the character of the State, and a humiliation not to be borne, to permit a military leader, acting without a shadow of lawful authority, but in violation of law and right, not only to thwart the will of the executive, but to impose upon citizens the penalty of banishment, for acting under it.*

Was this arch traitor, Brockman, hung for his treason against the State? No; nor even tried or questioned, neither he nor his followers. Perhaps it was thought that an investigation might reveal the fact to the world that many high officials, and chief among them the governor of the State, had been engaged in an unlawful conspiracy to drive from Illinois an innocent community, whose rights they had not the moral courage to defend against the fierce attacks of lawless mobs, whose hands were crimson in the blood of innocence; and who repeatedly trampled the honor and dignity of the State under their feet.

After a time the most of the new citizens returned to the homes they had purchased for little or nothing from the now exiled founders of the beautiful city. But Nauvoo never prospered under its new masters. Out of sympathy for those who had redeemed it from a wilderness, and some portions of it from a swamp, its fields and gardens refused to yield in their strength to the industry of other hands. Its decline was as rapid and disastrous as its rise had been sudden and glorious.

A French communistic society had purchased considerable property in the deserted city, and into their hands passed the splendid temple the Saints at such sacrifice had erected. Externally, the building had been completed in the spring of 1846, even to the gilding of the angel and the trumpet at the top of the spire. During the winter of 1845-6 various rooms of the temple were dedicated for ordinance work, and there hundreds of the faithful Saints received their endowments—the sacred

---

*The Hancock Mob, by J. B. Conyers, M. D., pages 73, 74.

mysteries of the faith. The main court of worship was also prepared; and on the evening of April 30th, 1846, the building was privately dedicated, Joseph Young, the senior president of the First Council of Seventy, offering the dedicatory prayer. On the first of May, 1846, under the direction of Apostles Orson Hyde and Wilford Woodruff, the edifice was publicly dedicated, according to the order of the Holy Priesthood, revealed through the Prophet Joseph Smith.

The temple was always a source of envy to the enemies of the Saints, and it was feared that if it continued to stand it would be a bond between its exiled builders and the city from which they had been cruelly driven, and an inducement for them to return. On the tenth of November, 1848, an incendiary, therefore, set it on fire, and the tower was destroyed, and the whole building so shattered, that on the twenty-seventh of May, 1850, a tornado blew down the north wall. I was informed by M. M. Morrill, who at the time of my visit was mayor of Nauvoo, and, by the way, one who had assisted in its defense when attacked by the mob, that one Joseph Agnew, confessed to being the incendiary. Finally all the walls were pulled down and the stone hauled away for building purposes, until now, not one stone stands upon another. Even the very foundation has been cleared away, and the excavation for the basement filled up and the site covered with inferior buildings.

At the time of my visit, in the summer of 1885, the population of Nauvoo numbered about seventeen hundred, nine-tenths of whom were Germans. The principal occupation is grape-growing, vineyards covering some portions of the city plat, which was once the principal business center. The whole place has a half-deserted, half-dilapidated appearance, and seems to be withering under a blight, from which it refuses to recover.

Such is the fate of Nauvoo, which once promised to be the first city of Illinois, and beyond all question would have been so had there existed sufficient virtue and honor in that State to have protected its founders in their rights.

* * * * * * *

Still stands the forest primeval; but under the
Shade of its branches
Dwells another race, with other customs
And languages.

The quotation connects me with my introduction, and reminds me that I have completed the task proposed in these pages. But in the fate which overtook the survivors of the Acadian peasant-exiles from Nova Scotia, and the Mormon exiles from Illinois, the former fails altogether to suggest the faintest hint of a parallel.

Only along the shores of the mournful and
mystic Atlantic
Linger a few Acadian peasants, whose fathers
from exile
Wandered back to their native land to die
in its bosom,

Finishes the story of the Acadian exiles. Not so the story of the exiles from Illinois. They did not perish in exile, nor did merely a handful of them, broken in spirits as in fortunes return to live silent and sad on the site of their former homes. The Mormon exiles were not broken and scattered—they remained a people; beyond their exile they were destined to have a glorious history. Their faith in their religion was not shattered. Their church was not disrupted. Their hearts were not turned against their prophets. Their spirits were not blighted nor their hearts bowed down beyond the power of recovery; nor their fortunes so blasted that they could not hope for prosperity—for God was with them.

The institution—The Church—brought into existence, and its doctrines developed amid so much of spiritual tempest and pursued so relentlessly by mob violence, and which may be said to have had a second birth at Nauvoo, and to have received sanctification from the martyrdom of her earthly founder—The Church which these exiles bore with them into the western wilderness was not born to die. Whatever might be the fate of The Church and the Saints in other dispensations of the Gospel, God had now introduced the Dispensation of the Fullness of Times, in which He has decreed that all things in Christ shall be gathered together in one—even in Him.* A dispensation in which the salvation of man and the redemption of the earth itself shall be consummated. And the earth and men made ready for the all glorious reign of truth and righteousness so long promised by God and His prophets. Hence The Church was not destroyed; and the people who fled with her to the wilderness did not perish. The blinding storms of sleet and rain which enveloped their principal companies as in melancholy trains they penetrated the wilderness of the then territory of Iowa, might easily have been taken for God's curtain rung down upon the most melancholy scene in America's history—the scene of a people in free America—the boasted asylum for the oppressed, where religious freedom is guaranteed by express constitutional provision—fleeing from the worst forms of oppression—the oppression of mob violence invoked in Illinois to crush their religious faith. But the curtain so rung down was not upon the final act. The hand of God again rolled it up; and when He did, it was to reveal to the world the exiles as the redeemers of desert wastes; the planters of cities; the builders of temples, the founders of States; and for themselves and for their religious faith so entrenched, so strengthened, so enlarged that the world shall never, while the earth itself remains, or sun or stars en-

* Eph. 1: 9, 10.

dure be rid of that faith founded—under God—by JOSEPH SMITH, THE PROPHET-MARTYR OF NAUVOO.

APPENDICES.

APPENDIX I.

CORRESPONDENCE BETWEEN JOSEPH SMITH AND JOHN C. CALHOUN.

HON. JOHN C. CALHOUN.

DEAR SIR,—As we understand you are a candidate for the Presidency at the next election; and as the Latter-day Saints (sometimes called Mormons, who now constitute a numerous class in the school politic of this vast republic,) have been robbed of an immense amount of property, and endured nameless sufferings by the State of Missouri, and from her borders have been driven by force of arms, contrary to our national covenants; and as in vain we have sought redress by all constitutional, legal, and honorable means, in her courts, her executive councils and her legislative halls; and as we have petitioned Congress to take cognizance of our sufferings without effect, we have judged it wisdom to address you this communication, and solicit an immediate, specific and candid reply to "*What will be your rule of action relative to us as a people*," should fortune favor your ascension to the chief magistracy?

Most respectfully, sir, your friend,
and the friend of peace, good order,
and constitutional rights,
JOSEPH SMITH.
In behalf of the Church of Jesus Christ of Latter-day Saints.

FORT HILL, 2ND DECEMBER, 1843.

SIR,—You ask me what would be my rule of action relative to the Mormons or Latter-day Saints, should I be elected President; to which I answer, that if I should be elected, I would strive to administer the government according to the Constitution and the laws of the Union; and that as they make no distinction between citizens of different religious creeds, I should make rone. As far as it depends on the executive department, all should have the full benefit of both, and none should be exempt from their operation.

But as you refer to the case of Missouri, candor compels me to repeat what I said to you at Washington, that, according to my views, the case does not come within the jurisdiction of the federal government, which is one of limited and specific powers.

With respect, I am, &c., &c.,

J. C. CALHOUN.

Mr. Joseph Smith.

NAUVOO, ILLINOIS, JANUARY 2, 1844.

SIR,—Your reply to my letter of last November, concerning your rule of action towards the Latter-day Saints, if elected president, is at hand; and that you and your friends of the same opinion relative to the matter in question may not be disappointed as to me or my mind upon so grave a subject, permit me, as a law-abiding man, as a well-wisher to the perpetuity of constitutional rights and liberty, and as a friend to the free worship of Almighty God by all, according to the dictates of every person's own conscience, to say *I am surprised* that a man or men in the highest stations of public life should have made up such a fragile "view" of a case, than which there is not one on the face of the globe fraught with so much consequence to the happiness of men in this world or the world to come.

To be sure, the first paragraph of your letter appears very complacent and fair on a white sheet of paper. And who, that is ambitious for greatness and power, would not have said the same thing? Your oath would bind you to support the Constitution and laws; and as all creeds and religions are alike tolerated, they must, of course, all be justified or condemned according to merit or demerit. But why—tell me why are all the principal men held up for public stations *so cautiously careful* not to publish to the world that they *will judge a righteous judgment*, law or no law? for laws and opinions, like the vanes of steeples, change with the wind.

One Congress passes a law, another repeals it; and one statesman says that the Constitution means this, and another that; and who does not know that all may be wrong? The opinion and pledge, therefore, in the first paragraph of your reply to my question, like the forced steam from the engine of a steam-boat, makes the show of a bright cloud at first; but when it comes in contact with a purer atmosphere, dissolves to common air again.

Your second paragraph leaves you naked before yourself, like a likeness in a mirror, when you say that, "according to your view, the federal government is one of limited and specific powers," and has no jurisdiction in the case of the Mormons. So then a State can at any time expel any portion of her citizens with impunity, and, in the language of Mr. Van Buren, frosted over with your gracious "*views of the case,*" though the cause is ever so just, Government can do nothing for them, because it has no power.

Go on, then, Missouri, after another set of inhabitants (as the Latter-day Saints did,) have entered some two or three hundred thousand dollars' worth of land; and made extensive improvements thereon. Go on, then, I say; banish the occupants or owners, or kill them, as the mobbers did many of the Latter-day Saints, and take their land and property as spoil; and let the legislature, as in the case of the Mormons, appropriate a couple of hundred thousand dollars to pay the mob for doing that job; for the renowned senator from South Carolina, Mr. J. C. Calhoun, says the powers of the federal government are so *specific and limited that it has no jurisdiction of the case!* O ye people who groan under the oppression of tyrants!—ye exiled Poles, who have felt the iron hand of Russian grasp!—ye poor and unfortunate among all nations! come to the asylum of the oppressed; buy ye lands of the general government; pay in your money to the treasury to strengthen the army and the navy; worship God according to the dictates of your own consciences; pay in your taxes to support the great heads of a glorious nation: but remember a "*sovereign State*" is so much more powerful than the United States, the parent government, that it can exile you at pleasure, mob you with impunity, confiscate your lands and property, have the legislature sanction it,—yea, even murder you as an edict of an emperor, *and it does no wrong;* for the noble senator of South

Carolina says the power of the federal government is *so limited and specific that it has no jurisdiction of the case!* What think ye of *imperium in imperio?*

Ye spirits of the blessed of all ages, hark! Ye shades of departed statesmen listen! Abraham, Moses, Homer, Socrates, Solon, Solomon, and all that ever thought of right and wrong, look down from your exaltations, if you have any; for it is said, "In the midst of counsellors there *is safety;*" and when you have learned that fifteen thousand innocent citizens, after having purchased their lands of the United States and paid for them, were expelled from a "sovereign State," by order of the governor, at the point of the bayonet, their arms taken from them by the same authority, and their right of migration into said State denied, under pain of imprisonment, whipping, robbing, mobbing, and even death, and no justice or recompense allowed; and, from the legislature with the governor at the head, down to the justice of the peace, with a bottle of whisky in one hand and a bowie-knife in the other, hear them all declare that there is no justice for a Mormon in that State; and judge ye a righteous judgment, and tell me when the virtue of the States was stolen, where the honor of the general government lies hid, and what clothes a senator with wisdom. O nullifying Carolina! O little tempestuous Rhode Island! Would it not be well for the great men of the nation to read the fable of the *partial judge;* and when part of the free citizens of a State had been expelled contrary to the Constitution, mobbed, robbed, plundered, and many murdered, instead of searching into the course taken with Joanna Southcott, Ann Lee, the French Prophets, the Quakers of New England, and rebellious niggers in the slave states, to hear both sides and then judge, rather than have the mortification to say, "Oh, it is *my* bull that has killed *your* ox! That alters the case! I must inquire into it; *and if, and if*——

If the general government has no power to reinstate expelled citizens to their rights, there is a monstrous hypocrite fed and fostered from the hard earnings of the people! A real "bull beggar" upheld by sycophants. And although you may wink to the priests to stigmatize, wheedle the drunkards to swear, and raise the hue-and-cry of—"Impostor! false prophet! G— d— old Joe Smith!" yet remember, if the Latter-day Saints are not restored to all their rights and paid for all their losses, according to the known rules of justice and judgment, reciprocation and common honesty among men, that God will come out of His hiding place, and vex this nation with a sore vexation: yea, the consuming wrath of an offended God shall smoke through the nation with as much distress and woe as independance has blazed through with pleasure and delight. Where is the strength of government? Where is the patriotism of a Washington, a Warren, and Adams? And where is a spark from the watch-fire of '76, by which one candle might be lit that would glimmer upon the confines of Democracy? Well may it be said that one man is not a state, nor one state the nation.

In the days of General Jackson, when France refused the first installment for spoliations, there was power, force, and honor enough to resent injustice and insult, and the money came; and shall Missouri, filled with negro-drivers and white men stealers, go "unwhipped of justice" for tenfold greater sins than France? No! verily, no! While I have power of body and mind—while water runs and grass grows—while virtue is lovely and vice hateful, and while a stone points out a sacred spot where a fragment of American liberty once was, I or my posterity will plead the cause of injured innocence, until Missouri makes atonement for all her sins, or sinks disgraced, degraded, and damned to hell, "where the worm dieth not, and the fire is not quenched."

Why, sir, the power not delegated to the United States and the States belong to the people, and Congress sent to do the people's business have all power; and shall fifteen thousand citizens groan in exile? O vain men! will ye not, if ye do not restore them to their rights and two million dollars' worth of property, relinquish to them (the Latter-day Saints,) as a body, their portion of power that belongs to them according to the Constitution? Power has its convenience as well as inconvenience. "The world was not made for Cæsar alone, but for Titus too.

I will give you a parable. A certain lord had a vineyard in a goodly land, which men labored in at their pleasure. A few meek men also went and purchased with money from some of these chief men that labored at pleasure a portion of land in the vineyard, at a very remote part of it, and began to improve it, and to eat and drink the fruit thereof,—when some vile persons, who regarded not man, neither feared the lord of the vineyard, rose up suddenly and robbed these meek men, and drove them from their possessions, killing many.

This barbarous act made no small stir among the men in the vineyard; and all that portion who were attached to that part of the vineyard where the men were robbed rose up in grand council, with their chief man, who had firstly ordered the deed to be done, and made a covenant not to pay for the cruel deed, but to keep the spoil, and never let those meek men set their feet on that soil again, neither recompense them for it.

Now, these meek men, in their distress, wisely sought redress of those wicked men in every possible manner, and got none. They then supplicated the chief men, who held the vineyard at pleasure, and who had the power to sell and defend it, for redress and redemption; and those men, loving the fame and favor of the multitude more than the glory of the lord of the vineyard, answered—"Your cause is just, but we can do nothing for you, because we have no power."

Now, when the lord of the vineyard saw that virtue innocence was not regarded, and his vineyard occupied by wicked men, he sent men and took the possession of it to himself, and destroyed these unfaithful servants, and appointed them their portion among hypocrites.

And let me say that all men who say that Congress has no power to restore and defend the rights of her citizens have not the love of the truth abiding in them. Congress has power to protect the nation against foreign invasion and internal broil; and whenever that body passes an act to maintain right with any power, or to restore right to any portion of her citizens, it is the SUPREME LAW OF THE LAND; and should a State refuse submission, that State is guilty of *insurrection or rebellion,* and the President has as much power to repel it as Washington had to march against the "whisky boys at Pittsburg," or General Jackson had to send an armed force to suppress the rebellion of South Carolina.

To close, I would admonish you, before you let your "*candor compel*" you again to write upon a subject great as the salvation of man, consequential as the life of the Savior, broad as the principles of eternal truth, and valuable as the jewels of eternity, to read in the eighth section and first article of the Constitution of the United States, the *first, fourteenth,* and *seventeenth* "specific" and not very "limited powers" of the federal government, what can be done to protect the lives, property, and rights of a virtuous people, when the administrators of the law and law-makers are unbought by bribes, uncorrupted by patronage, untempted by gold, unawed by fear, and uncontaminated tangling alliances—even like Cæser's wife, not only *unspotted, but unsuspected!* And God, who cooled the heat of a Nebuchadnezzar's furnace or shut the mouths of lions for the honor of a Daniel, will raise your mind above the narrow notion that the general government has no power, to the sublime idea that Congress, with the President as executor, is as almighty in its sphere as Jehovah is in His.

With great respect, I have the honor to be

Your obedient servant,

JOSEPH SMITH.

Hon. ("Mr.") J. C. Calhoun,
Fort Hill, S. C.

APPENDIX II.

CLAY'S LETTER TO JOSEPH SMITH AND THE LATTER'S REPLY.

ASHLAND, November 15, 1843.

DEAR SIR:—I have received your letter in behalf of the Church of Jesus Christ of Latter-day Saints, stating that you understand that I am a condidate for the presidency, and inquiring what will be my rule of action relative to you as a people, should I be elected.

I am profoundly grateful for the numerous and strong expressions of the people in my behalf as a candidate for President of the United States; but I do not so consider myself. That must depend upon future events and upon my sense of duty.

Should I be a condidate, I can enter into no engagements, make no promises, give no pledges to any particular portion of the people of the United States. If I ever enter into that high office, I must go into it free and unfettered, with no guarantees but such as are to be drawn from my whole life, character and conduct.

It is not inconsistent with this declaration to say that I have viewed with a lively interest the progress of the Latter-day Saints; that I have sympathized in their sufferings under injustice, as it appeared to me, which has been inflicted upon them; and I think, in common with other religious communities, they ought to enjoy the security and protection of the Constitution and the laws.

I am, with great respect, your friend and obedient servant,

H. CLAY.

To Joseph Smith, Esq.

NAUVOO, ILL., May 13, 1844.

SIR:—Your answer to my inquiry, "What would be your rule of action towards the Latter-day Saints, should you be elected President of the United States?" has been under consideration since last November, in the fond expectation that you would give (for every honest citizen has a right to demand it,) to the country a manifesto of your views of the best method and means which would secure to the people, *the whole people*, the most freedom, the most happiness, the most union, the most wealth, the most fame, the most glory at home, and the most honor abroad, at the least expense. But I have waited in vain. So far as you have made public declarations, they have been made, like your answer to the above, soft to flatter, rather than solid to feed the people. You seem to abandon all former policy which may have actuated you in the discharge of a statesman's duty, when the vigor of intellect and the force of virtue should have sought out an everlasting habitation for liberty; when, as a wise man, a true patriot, and a friend to mankind, you should have resolved to ameliorate the lawful condition of our *bleeding* country by a mighty plan of wisdom, righteousness, justice, goodness and mercy, that would have brought back the golden days of our nation's youth, vigor and vivacity, when prosperity crowned the efforts of a youthful republic, when the gentle aspirations of the sons of liberty were, "We are one!"

In your answer to my questions last fall, that peculiar tact of modern politicians declaring, "*If you ever enter into that high office, you must go into it free and unfettered, with no guarantees but such as are to be drawn from your whole life, character and conduct,*" so much resembles a lottery-vendor's sign, with the goddess of good luck sitting on the car of fortune, a-straddle of the horns of plenty, and driving the merry steeds of beatitude, without reins or bridle, that I cannot help exclaiming—O frail man, what have you done that will exalt you? Can anything be drawn from your *life, character or conduct* that is worthy of being held up to the gaze of this nation as a model of *virtue*, charity and wisdom? Are you not a lottery picture, with more than two blanks to a prize? Leaving many things prior to your Ghent treaty, let the world look at that, and see where is the wisdom, honor and patriotism which ought to have characterized the plenipotentiary of the only free nation upon the earth? A quarter of a century's negotiation to obtain our rights on the north-eastern boundary, and the motley manner in which Oregon tries to shine as American territory, coupled with your presidential race and some-by-chance secretaryship in 1825, all go to convince the friends of freedom, the golden patriots of Jeffersonian democracy, free trade and sailors' rights, and the protectors of person and property, that an honorable war is better than a dishonorable peace.

But had you really wanted to have exhibited the wisdom, clemency, benevolence and dignity of a great man in this boasted republic, when fifteen thousand free citizens were exiled from their own homes, lands and property, in the wonderful patriotic State of Missouri, and you then upon your oath and honor occupying the exalted station of a Senator of Congress from the noble-hearted State of Kentucky, why did you not show the world your loyalty to law and order, by using all honorable means to restore the innocent to their rights and property? Why, sir, the more we search into your character and conduct, the more we must exclaim from Holy Writ, "The tree is known by its fruit."

Again: this is not all. Rather than show yourself an honest man, by guaranteeing to the people what you will do in case you should be elected president, "you can enter into no engagement, make no promises, and give no pledges as to what you will do. Well, it may be that some hot-headed partisan would take such nothingarianism upon trust; but sensible men and even *ladies* would think themselves insulted by such an evasion of coming events! If a tempest is expected, why not prepare to meet it, and, in the language of the poet, exclaim—

> Then let the trial come; and witness thou
> If terror be upon me,—If I shrink
> Or falter in my strength to meet the storm
> When hardest it besets me.

True greatness never wavers; but when the Missouri compromise was entered into by you for the benefit of *slavery*, there was a mighty shrinkage of *western honor*; and from that day, sir, the sterling Yankee, the struggling Abolitionist, and the staunch Democrat, with a large number of the liberal-minded Whigs, have marked you as a *black-leg* in politics, begging for a chance to *shuffle* yourself into the Presidential chair, where you might deal out the destinies of our beloved country for a *game of brag* that would end in—"*Hark from the tombs a doleful sound.*" Start not at this picture: for your "whole life, character and conduct" have been spotted with deeds that cause a blush upon the face of a virtuous patriot. So you must be contented in your lot, while crime, cowardice, cupidity or low cunning have handed you down from the high tower of a statesman to the black-hole of a gambler. A man that accepts a challenge or fights a duel is nothing more nor less than a murderer; for Holy Writ declares that, "*Whoso sheds man's blood, by man shall his blood be shed:*" and when in the renowned city of Washington the notorious *Henry Clay* dropped from the summit of a Senator to the sink of a scoundrel to shoot at that chalk-line of a Randolph, he not only disgraced his own fame, family and friends, but he polluted the *sanctum sanctorum* of American glory; and the kingly blackguards throughout the whole world are pointing the finger of scorn at the boasted "asylum of the oppressed," and hissing at American statesmen as *gentlemen vagabonds and murderers*, holding the olive branch of peace in one hand and a pistol for death in the other! Well might the Savior rebuke the heads of this nation with "*Wo unto you scribes, Pharisees, hyyocrites!*" for the United States Government and Congress, with a few honorable exceptions, have gone the way of Cain, and must perish in their gainsayings, like Korah and his wicked host. And honest men of every clime, and the innocent, poor and oppressed, as well as heathens, pagans and Indians, everywhere, who could but hope that the tree of liberty would yield some precious fruit for the hungry human race, and shed some balmy leaves for the healing of nations, have long since given up all hopes of equal rights, of justice and judgment, and of truth and virtue, when such polluted, vain, heaven-daring, bogus patriots are forced or flung into the front rank of Government to guide the destinies of millions. Crape the heavens with weeds of wo, gird the earth with sack-cloth, and let hell mutter one melody in commemoration of fallen splendor! for the glory of America has departed, and God will set a flaming sword to guard the tree of liberty, while such mint-tithing Herods as Van Buren, Boggs, Benton, Calhoun and Clay are thrust out of the realms of virtue as fit subjects for the kingdom of fallen greatness. *Vox reprobi, vox Diaboli!*

In your late addresses to the people of South Carolina, where rebellion budded, but could not blossom, you "renounced ultraism," "high tariff," and almost banished your "banking system" for the more certain standard of "public opinion." This is all very well, and marks the intention of a politician, the calculations of a demagogue, and the allowance for leeings of a shrewd manager, just as truly as the weathercock does the wind when it turns upon the spire. Hustings for the South, barbacues for the West, confidential letters for the North and "American System" for the East.

Lull-a-by baby upon the tree top,
And when the wind blows the cradle will rock.

Suppose you should also, taking your "whole life, character and conduct" into consideration, and, as many hands make light work, stir up the old "Clay party," the "National Republican party," the "High Protective Tariff party," and the late coon-skin party, with all their paraphernalia, *ultraism, ne plus ultraism, sine qua non,* which have grown with your growth, strengthened with your strength, and shrunk with your shrinkage, and ask the people of this enlightened republic what they think of your powers and policy as a statesman; for verily it would seem, from all past remains of parties, politics, projects and pictures, that you are the *Clay*; and the people the *potter*; and as some vessels are marred in the hands of the potter, the natural conclusion is that *you are a vessel of dishonor.*

You may complain that a close examination of your "whole life, character and conduct" places you, as a Kentuckian would pleasantly term it, "in a bad fix." But, sir, when the nation has sunk deeper and deeper into the mud at every turn of the great wheels of the Union, while you have acted as one of the principal drivers, it becomes the bounden duty of the whole community, as one man, to whisper you on every point of government, to uncover every act of your life, and inquire what mighty acts you have done to benefit the nation, how much you have tithed the mint to gratify your lust, and why the fragments of your raiment hang upon the thorns by the path as signals to *beware.*

But your *shrinkage* is truly wonderful! Not only your banking system and high tariff project have vanished from your mind "like the baseless fabric of a vision," but the "annexation of Texas" has touched your pathetic sensibilities of national pride so acutly, that the poor Texans, your own *brethren,* may fall back into the ferocity of Mexico, or be sold at auction to British stock-jobbers, and all is well. For "I," the old Senator from Kentucky, and fearful it would militate against my interest in the north to enlarge the borders of the Union in the south. Truly "a poor wise child is better than an old foolish king who will be no longer admonished." Who ever heard of a nation that had too much territory? Was it ever bad policy to make friends? Has any people ever become too good to do good? No, never. But the ambition and vanity of some men have flown away with their wisdom and judgment, and left a croaking *skeleton* to occupy the place of a noble *soul!*

Why, sir, the condition of the whole earth is lamentable. Texas dreads the teeth and the nails of Mexico. Oregon has the rheumatism, brought on by a horrid exposure to the heat and cold of British and American trappers. Canada has caught a bad cold from extreme fatigue in the patriot war. South America has the headache cause by bumps against the beams of Catholicity and Spanish Sovereignty. Spain has the gripes from age and inquisition. France trembles and wastes under the effects of contagious diseases. England groans with the gout, and wiggles with wine. Italy and the German States are pale with the consumption. Prussia, Poland, and the little contiguous dynasties, duchies and domains, have the mumps so severely, that "the whole head is sick, and the whole heart is faint." Russia has the cramp by lineage. Turkey has the numb palsy. Africa, from the curse of God, has lost the use of her limbs China is ruined by the queen's evil, and the rest of Asia fearfuly exposed to the small-pox, the natural way, from British peddlers. The islands of the sea are almost dead with the scurvy. The Indians are blind and lame; and the United States, which ought to be the good physician with "balm from Gilead" and an "*asylum for the oppressed,*" has boosted and is boosting up into the council chamber of the Government a clique of political gamblers, to play for the old clothes and old shoes of a sick world, and "*no pledge, no promise to any particular portion of the people*" that the rightful heirs will ever receive a cent of their Father's legacy. Away with such self-important, self-aggrandizing and self-willed demagogues! Their friendship is colder than polar ice, and their profession meaner than the damnation of hell.

O man! when such a great dilemma of the globe, such a tremendous convulsion of kingdoms shakes the earth from centre to circumference; when castles, prison-houses, and cells raise a cry to God against the cruelty of man; when the mourning of the fatherless and the widow causes anguish in heaven; when the poor among all nations cry day and night for bread, and a shelter from the heat and storm; and wher the degraded black slave holds up his manacled hands to the great statesmen of the United States, and sings—

"O liberty, where are thy charms,
That sages have told me are sweet?"

And when fifteen thousand free citizens of the high-blooded republic of North America are robbed and driven from one State to another without redress or redemption, it is not only time for a candidate for the presidency to pledge himself to execute judgment and justice in righteousness, law or no law; but it is his bounden duty as a man, for the honor of a disgraced country, and for the salvation of a once virtuous people, to call for a union of all honest men, and appease the wrath of God by acts of wisdom, holiness, and virtue! "The fervent prayer of a righteous man availeth much."

Perhaps you may think I go too far with my strictures and innuendos, because in your concluding paragraph you say "it is not inconsistent with your declarations to say that you have viewed with a lively interest the progress of the Latter-day Saints, that you have sympathized in ther sufferings under injustice; as it appeared to you, which has been inflicted upon them, and that you *think*, in common with all other religious communities, they ought to enjoy the security and protection of the Constitution and the laws." If words were not wind, and imagination not a vapor, such "views" "*with a lively interest*" might coax out a few Mormon votes; such "sympathy" for their suffering under injustice might heal some of the sick yet lingering amongst them, raise some of the dead, and recover some of their property from Missouri; and finally, if thought was not a phantom, we might, in common with other religious communities, "*you think, enjoy the security* and *protection of the Constitution and laws*." But during ten years, while the Latter-day Saints have bled, been robbed, driven from their own lands, paid oceans of money into the treasury to pay your renowned self and others for legislating and *dealing* out equal rights and privileges to those *in common with all other religious communities*, they have waited and expected in vain! If you have possessed any patriotism, it has been veiled by your *popularity*, for fear the Saints would fall in love with its charms. Blind charity and dumb justice never do much towards alleviating the wants of the needy; but straws show which way the wind blows. It is currently rumored that your *dernier resort* for the Latter-day Saints is to migrate to Oregon or California. Such cruel humanity, such noble injustice, such honorable cowardice, such foolish wisdom, and such vicious virtue could only emanate from Clay. After the Saints have been plundered of three or four millions of land and property by the people and powers of the *sovereign* State of Missouri—after they have sought for redress and redemption, from the county court to Congress, and been denied through religious prejudice and sacerdotal dignity— after they have builded a city and two temples at an immense expense of labor and treasure—after they have increased from hundreds to hundreds of thousands, and after they have sent missionaries to the various nations of the earth to gather Israel, according to the predictions of all the holy prophets since the world began, that great plenipotentiary, the renowned secretary of state, the ignoble duelist, the gambling senator, and Whig candidate for the presidency, *Henry Clay*, the wise Kentucky lawyer, advises the Latter-day Saints to go to Oregon to obtain justice and set up a government of their own.

O ye crowned heads among all nations, is not Mr. Clay a wise man, and very patriotic? Why, great God! to transport 200,000 people through a vast prairie, over the Rocky Mountains, to Oregon, a distance of nearly two thousand miles, would cost more than *four millions!* or should they go by Cape Horn in ships to California, the cost would be more than *twenty millions!* and all this to save the United States from inheriting the disgrace of Missouri for murdering and robbing the Saints with impunity! Benton and Van Buren, who make no secret to say that if they get into power they will carry out Boggs' exterminating plan to rid the country of the Latter-day Saints, are

"Little nipperkins of milk,"

compared to "Clay's" great aquafortis jars. Why, he is a real giant in humanity! "Send the Mormons to Oregon, and free Missouri from debt and disgrace!" Ah! sir, let this doctrine go to-and-fro throughout the whole earth—that we, as Van Buren said, know your cause is just, but the United States government can do nothing for you, because it has no power. "*You must go to Oregon, and get justice from the Indians!*"

I mourn for the depravity of the world; I despise the hypocrisy of Christendom; I hate the imbecility of American statesmen; I detest the shrinkage of candidates for office from pledges and responsibility; I long for a day of righteousness, when "He whose right it is to reign shall judge the poor, and reprove with equity for the meek of the earth;" and I pray God, who hath given our fathers a promise of a perfect government in the last days, to purify the hearts of the people and hasten the welcome day.

With the highest consideration for virtue and unadulterated freedom,

I have the honor to be,

Your obedient servant,

JOSEPH SMITH.

Hon. Henry Clay, Ashland, Ky.

APPENDIX III.

JOSEPH SMITH'S VIEWS OF THE POWERS AND POLICY OF THE GOVERNMENT OF THE UNITED STATES.

BORN in a land of liberty, and breathing an air uncorrupted with the sirocco of barbarous climes, I ever feel a double anxiety for the happiness of all men, both in time and in eternity.

My cogitations, like Daniel's have for a long time troubled me, when I viewed the condition of men throughout the world, and more especially in this boasted realm, where the Declaration of Independence "holds these truths to be self-evident, that all men are created equal; that they are endowed by their Creator with certain unalienable rights; that among these are life, liberty, and the pursuit of happiness;" but at the same time some two or three millions of people are held as slaves for life, because the spirit of them is covered with a darker skin than ours; and hundreds of our own kindred for an infraction, or supposed infraction, of some over-wise statute, have to be incarcerated in dungeon glooms, or suffer the more moral penitentiary gravitation of mercy in a nutshell, while the duelist, the debauchee, and the defaulter for millions, and other criminals, take the uppermost rooms at feasts, or, like the bird of passage, find a more congenial clime by flight.

The wisdom which ought to characterize the freest, wisest, and most noble nation of the nineteenth century, should, like the sun in his meridian splendor, warm every object beneath its rays; and the main efforts of her officers, who are nothing more or less than the servants of the people, ought to be directed to ameliorate the condition of all, black or white, bond or free; for the best of books says, "God hath made of one blood all nations of men for to dwell on all the face of the earth."

Our common country presents to all men the same advantages,

the same facilities, the same prospects, the same honors, and the same rewards; and without hypocrisy, the Constitution, when it says, "We, the people of the United States, in order to form a more perfect union, establish justice, ensure domestic tranquility, provide for the common defense, promote the general welfare, and secure the blessings of liberty to ourselves and our posterity, do ordain and establish this Constitution for the United States of America," meant just what it said without reference to color or condition, *ad infinitum.*

The aspirations and expectations of a virtuous people, environed with so wise, so liberal, so deep, so broad, and so high a charter of *equal rights* as appear in said Constitution, ought to be treated by those to whom the administration of the laws is entrusted with as much sanctity as the prayers of the Saints are treated in heaven, that love, confidence, and union, like the sun, moon, and stars, should bear witness,

(For ever singing as they shine,)
" *The hand that made us is divine.*"

Unity is power; and when I reflect on the importance of it to the stability of all governments, I am astounded at the silly moves of persons and parties to foment discord in order to ride into power on the current of popular excitement; nor am I less surprised at the stretches of power or restrictions of right which too often appear as acts of legislators to pave the way to some favorite political scheme as destitute of intrinsic merit as a wolf's heart is of the milk of human kindness. A Frenchman would say, "*Presque tout aimer richesses et pouvoir.*" (Almost all men like wealth and power.)

I must dwell on this subject longer than others; for nearly one hundred years ago that golden patriot, Benjamin Franklin, drew up a plan of union for the then colonies of Great Britain, that *now* are such an independent nation, which, among many wise provisions for obedient children under their father's more rugged hand, had this:—"They have power to make laws, and lay and levy such general duties, imports, or taxes as to them shall appear most equal and just, (considering the ability and other circumstances of the inhabitants in the several colonies,) and such as may be collected with the least inconvenience to the people, rather discouraging luxury than loading industry with unnecessary burdens." Great Britain surely lacked the laudable humanity and fostering clemency to grant such a just plan of union; but the sentiment remains, like the land that honored its birth, as a pattern for wise men *to study the convenience of the people more than the comfort of the cabinet.*

And one of the most noble fathers of our freedom and country's glory, great in war, great in peace, great in the estimation of the world, and great in the hearts of his countrymen, (the illustrious Washington,) said in his first inaugural address to Congress—"I behold the surest pledges that as, on one side, no local prejudices or attachments, no separate views or party animosities will misdirect the comprehensive and equal eye which ought to watch over this great assemblage of communities and interests, so, on another, that the foundations of our national policy will be laid in the pure and immutable principles of private morality, and the pre-eminence of free government be exemplified by all the attributes which can win the affections of its citizens and command the respect of the world."

Verily, here shine the virtue and wisdom of a statesman in such lucid rays, that had every succeeding Congress followed the rich instruction, in all their deliberations and enactments, for the benefit and convenience of the whole community and the communities of which it is composed, no sound of rebellion in South Carolina, no rupture in Rhode Island, no mob in Missouri expelling her citizens by executive authority, corruption in the ballot boxes, a border warfare between Ohio and Michigan, hard times and distress, outbreak upon outbreak in the principal cities, murder, robbery, and defalcation, scarcity of money, and a thousand other difficulties, would have torn asunder the bonds of the Union, destroyed the confidence of man with man, and left the great body of the people to mourn over misfortunes in poverty brought on by corrupt legislation in an hour of proud vanity for self-aggrandizement.

The great Washington, soon after the foregoing faithful admonition for the common welfare of his nation, further advised Congress that "among the many interesting objects which will engage your attention, that of providing for the common defense will merit particular regard. To be prepared for war is one of the most effectual means of preserving peace." As the Italian would say—"*Buono aviso.*" (Good advice.)

The elder Adams, in his inaugural address, gives national pride such a grand turn of justification, that every honest citizen must look back upon the infancy of the United States with an approving smile, and rejoice that patriotism in their rulers, virtue in the people, and prosperity in the Union once crowned the expectations of hope, unveiled the sophistry of the hypocrite, and silenced the folly of foes. Mr. Adams said, "If national pride is ever justifiable or excusable, it is when it springs not from *power* or riches, grandeur or glory, but from conviction of national innocence, information and benevolence."

There is no doubt that such was actually the case with our young realm at the close of the last century. Peace, prosperity, and union filled the country with religious toleration, temporal enjoyment, and virtuous enterprise; and grandly, too, when the deadly winter of the "Stamp Act," "Tea Act," and other *close communion* acts of royalty had chocked the growth of freedom of speech, liberty of the press, and liberty of conscience, did light, liberty, and loyalty flourish like cedars of God.

The respected and venerable Thomas Jefferson, in his inaugural address, made more than forty years ago, shows what a beautiful prospect an innocent, virtuous nation presents to the sage's eye where there is space for enterprise, hands for industry, heads for heroes, and hearts for moral greatness. He said, "A rising nation spread over a wide and fruitful land, traversing all the seas with the rich productions of their industry, engaged in commerce with nations who feel power and forget right, advancing rapidly to destinies beyond the reach of mortal eye,—when I contemplate these transcedent objects, and see the honor, the happiness of this beloved country committed to the issue and auspices of this day, I shrink from the contemplation, and humble myself before the magnitude of the undertaking."

Such a prospect was truly soul-stirring to a good man. But "since the fathers have fallen asleep," wicked and designing men have unrobed the government of its glory; and the people if not in dust and ashes, or in sackcloth have to lament in poverty her departed greatness while demagogues build fires in the north and the south, east and west to keep up their spirits *till it is better times*. But year after year has left the people to *hope* till the very name of *Congress* or *State Legis-*

lature is as horrible to the sensitive friend of his country as the house of "Bluebeard" is to his children, or "Crockford's Hell of London" to meek men.

When the people are secure and their rights properly respected, then the four main pillars of prosperity—viz., agriculture, manufactures, navigation, and commerce, need the fostering care of government; and in so goodly a country as ours, where the soil, the climate, the rivers, the lakes, and the sea coast, the productions, the timber, the minerals, and the inhabitants are so diversified, that a pleasing variety accomodates all tastes, trades, and calculations, it certainly is the highest point of supervision to protect the whole northern and southern, eastern and western, center and circumference of the realm, by a judicious tariff. It is an old saying and a true one, "If you wish to be *respected,* respect yourselves."

I will adopt in part the language of Mr. Madison's inaugural address—"To cherish peace and friendly intercourse with all nations, having corresponding dispositions; to maintain sincere neutrality towards beligerant nations; to prefer in all cases amicable discussion and reasonable accommodation of differences to a decision of them by an appeal to arms; to exclude foreign intrigues and foreign partialities, so degrading to all countries, and so baneful to free ones; to foster a spirit of independence too just to invade the rights of others, too proud to surrender our own, too liberal to indulge unworthy prejudices ourselves, and too elevated not to look down upon them in others; to hold the union of the States as the basis of their peace and happiness; to support the Constitution, which is the cement of the Union, as well in its limitations as in its authorities; to respect the rights and authorities reserved to the States and to the people as equally incorporated with and essential to the success of the general system; to avoid the slightest interference with the rights of conscience or the functions of religion, so wisely exempted from civil jurisdiction; to preserve in their full energy the other salutary provisions in behalf of private and personal rights, and of the freedom of the press,"—so far as intention aids in the fulfillment of duty, are consummations too big with benefits not to captivate the energies of all honest men to achieve them, when they can be brought to pass by reciprocation, friendly alliances, wise legislation, and honorable treaties.

The government has once flourished under the guidance of trusty servants; and the Hon. Monroe, in his day, while speaking of the Constitution, says, "Our commerce has been wisely regulated with foreign nations and between the States. New States have been admitted into our Union. Our territory has been enlarged by fair and honorable treaty, and with great advantage to the original States; the States respectively protected by the national government, under a mild paternal system against foreign dangers, and enjoying within their separate spheres, by a wise partition of power, a just proportion of the sovereignty, have improved their police, extended their settlements, and attained a strength and maturity which are the best proofs of wholesome laws well administered. And if we look to the condition of individuals, what a proud spectacle does it exhibit! On whom has oppression fallen in any quarter of the Union? Who has been deprived of any right of person or property?—who restrained from offering his vows in the mode which he prefers to the divine Author of his being? It is well known that all these blessings have been enjoyed in their fullest extent; and I add, with peculiar satisfaction, that there has been no example of a capital punishment being inflicted on any one for the crime of high treason." What a delightful picture of power, policy, and prosperity! Truly the wise man's proverb is just—"*Sedaukauh teromain goy, veh-ka-sade le-u-meem khahmaut.*" (Righteousness exalteth a nation, but sin is a reproach to any people.)

But this is not all. The same honorable statesman, after having had about forty years' experience in the government, under the full tide of successful experiment, gives the following commendatory assurance of the efficacy of the *Magna Charta* to answer its great end and aim—*to protect the people in their rights.* "Such, then, is the happy government under which we live; a government adequate to every purpose for which the social compact is formed; a government elective in all its branches, under which every citizen may by his merit obtain the highest trust recognized by the Constitution, which contains within it no cause of discord, none to put at variance one portion of the community with another; a government which protects every citizen in the full enjoyment of his rights, and is able to protect the nation against injustice from foreign powers."

Again, the younger Adams, in the silver age of our country's advancement to fame, in his inaugural address (1825), thus candidly declares the majesty of the youthful republic in its increasing greatness:—"The year of jubilee, since the first formation of our union, has just elapsed: that of the Declaration of Independence is at hand. The consummation of both was effected by this Constitution. Since that period, a population of four millions has multiplied to twelve. A territory, bounded by the Mississippi, has been extended from sea to sea. New States have been admitted to the Union, in numbers nearly equal to those of the first confederation. Treaties of peace, amity, and commerce have been concluded with the principal dominions of the earth. The people of other nations, the inhabitants of regions acquired, not by conquest, but by compact, have been united with us in the participation of our rights and duties, of our burdens and blessings. The forest has fallen by the ax of our woodsman. The soil has been made to teem by the tillage of our farmers. Our commerce has whitened every ocean. The dominion of man over physical nature has been extended by the invention of our artists. Liberty and law have marched hand in hand. All the purposes of human association have been accomplished as effectively as under any other government on the globe, and at a cost little exceeding, in a whole generation, the expenditures of other nations in a single year."

In continuation of such noble sentiments, General Jackson, upon his ascension to the great chair of the chief magistracy, said, "As long as our government is administered for the good of the people, and is regulated by their will, as long as it secures to us the rights of person and property, liberty of conscience, and of the press, it will be worth defending; and so long as it is worth defending, a patriotic militia will cover it with an impenetrable *ægis*."

General Jackson's administration may be denominated the *acme* of American glory, liberty, and prosperity; for the national debt, which in 1815, on account of the late war, was $125,000,000, and being lessened gradually, was paid up in his golden day, and preparations were made to distribute the surplus revenue among the several States; and that august patriot, to use his own words in his farewell address, retired, leaving "a great people prosperous and happy, in the full enjoyment of liberty and peace, honored and respected by every nation of the world."

At the age, then, of sixty years, our blooming republic began to decline under the withering touch of Martin Van Buren! Disappointed ambition, thirst for power, pride, corruption, party spirit, faction, patronage, perqisites, fame, tangling alliances, priestcraft, and spiritual wickedness in *high places,* struck hands and revelled in midnight splendor.

Trouble, vexation, perplexity, and contention, mingled with hope, fear, and murmuring, rumbled through the Union and agitated the whole nation, as would an earthquake at the center of the earth, the world heaving the sea beyond its bounds and shaking the everlasting hills; so, in hopes of better times, while jealousy, hypocritical pretensions, and pompous ambition were luxuriating on the ill-gotten spoils of the people, they rose in their majesty like a tornado, and swept through the land, till General Harrison appeared as a star among the storm-clouds for better weather.

The calm came, and the language of that venerable patriot, in his inaugural address, while descanting upon the merits of the Constituiton and its framers, thus expressed himself:—"There were in it features which appeared not to be in harmony with their ideas of a simple representative democracy or republic. And knowing the tendency of power to increase itself, particularly when executed by a single individual, predictions were made that, at no very remote period, the government would terminate in virtual monarchy.

"It would not become me to say that the fears of these patriots have been already realized. But as I sincerely believe that the tendency of measures and of men's thanions for some years past has been in that direction, it is, I conceive, strictly proper that I should take this occasion to repeat the assurances I have heretofore given of my determination to arrest the progress of that tendency, if it really exists, and restore the government to its pristine health and vigor."

This good man died before he had the opportunity of applying one balm to ease the pain of our groaning country, and I am willing the nation should be the judge, whether General Harrison, in his exalted station, upon the eve of his entrance into the world of spirits, *told the truth, or not*, with acting President Tyler's three years of perplexity, and pseudo-Whig-Democrat reign to heal the breaches or show the wounds, *secundum artem* (according to art).

Subsequent events, all things considered, Van Buren's downfall, Harrison's exit, and Tyler's self-sufficient turn to the whole, go to show, as a Chaldean might exclaim—"*Beram etai elaugh beshmayauh gauhah rauzeen.*" (Certainly there is a God in heaven to reveal secrets.)

No honest man can doubt for a moment but the glory of American liberty is on the wane, and that calamity and confusion will sooner or later destroy the peace of the people. Speculators will urge a national bank as a savior of credit and comfort. A hireling psuedo-priesthood will plausibly push abolition doctrines and doings and "human rights" into Congress, and into every other place where conquest smells of fame, or opposition swells to popularity. Democracy, Whiggery, and cliquery will attract their elements and foment divisions among the people, to accomplish fancied schemes and accumulate power, while poverty, driven to despair, like hunger forcing its way through a wall, will break through the statutes of men to save life, and mend the breach in prison glooms.

A still higher grade of what the "nobility of nations" call "great men" will dally with all rights, in order to smuggle a fortune at "one fell swoop," mortgage Texas, possess Oregon, and claim all the unsettled regions of the world for hunting and trapping; and should an humble, honest man, red, black, or white, exhibit a better title, these gentry have only to clothe the judge with richer ermine, and spangle the lawyer's finger with finer rings, to have the judgment of his peers and the honor of his lords as a pattern of honesty, virtue, and humanity, while the motto hangs on his nation's escutcheon—"*Every man has his price!*"

Now, O people! people! turn unto the Lord and live, and reform this nation. Frustrate the designs of wicked men. Reduce Congress at least two-thirds. Two senators from a State and two members to a million of population will do more business than the army that now occupy the halls of the national legislature. Pay them two dollars and their board per diem (except Sundays). That is more than the farmer gets, and he lives honestly. Curtail the officers of government in pay, number, and power; for the Philistine lords have shorn our nation of its goodly locks in the lap of Delilah.

Petition your State legislatures to pardon every convict in their several penitentiaries, blessing them as they go, and saying to them, in the name of the Lord, *Go thy way, and sin no more.*

Advise your legislators, when they make laws for larceny, burglary, or any felony, to make the penalty applicable to work upon roads, public works, or any place where the culprit can be taught more wisdom and more virtue, and become more enlightened. Rigor and seclusion will never do as much to reform the propensities of men as reason and friendship. Murder only can claim confinement or death. Let the penitentiaries be turned into seminaries of learning, where intelligence, like the angels of heaven, would banish such fragments of barbarism. Imprisonment for debt is a meaner practice than the savage tolerates, with all his ferocity. "*Amor vincit omnia.*" (Love conquers all.)

Petition, also, ye goodly inhabitants of the slave States, your legislators to abolish slavery by the year 1850, or now, and save the abolitionist from reproach and ruin, infamy and shame.

Pray Congress to pay every man a reasonable price for his slaves out of the surplus revenue arising from the sale of public lands and from the deduction of pay from the members of Congress.

Break off the shackles from the poor black man, and hire him to labor like other human beings; for "an hour of virtuous liberty on earth is worth a whole eternity of bondage." Abolish the practice in the army and navy of trying men by court-martial for desertion. If a soldier or marine runs away, send him his wages, with this instruction, that *his country will never trust him again; he has forfeited his honor.*

Make HONOR the standard with all men. Be sure that good is rendered for evil in all cases; and the whole nation, like a kingdom of kings and priests, will rise up in righteousness, and be respected as wise and worthy on earth, and as just and holy for heaven, by Jehovah, the Author of perfection.

More economy in the national and state governments would make less taxes among the people; more equality through the cities, towns, and country, would make less distinction among the people; and more honesty and familiarity in societies would make less hypocrisy and flattery in all branches of the community; and open, frank, candid decorum to all men, in this boasted land of liberty, would beget esteem, confidence, union, and love; and the neighbor from any State or from any country, of whatever color, clime, or tongue, could rejoice when he put his foot on the sacred soil of freedom, and exclaim, The very name of "*American*" is fraught with *friendship!* Oh, then, create confidence, restore freedom, break down slavery, banish imprisonment for debt, and be in love, fellowship, and peace with all the world! Remember that honesty is not subject to law. The law was made for transgressors. Wherefore a Dutchman might exclaim—"*Ein eherlicher name ist besser als Reichthum.*" (A good name is better than riches.)

For the accommodation of the people in every State and Territory let Congress show their wisdom by granting a national bank, with branches in each State and Territory, where the capital stock shall be held by the nation for the mother bank, and by the States and Territories for the branches; and whose officers and directors shall be elected yearly by the people, with wages at the rate of two dollars per day for services; which several banks shall never issue any more bills than the amount of capital stock in her vaults and the interest.

The net gain of the mother bank shall be applied to the national revenue, and that of the branches to the States' and Territories' revenues. And the bills shall be par throughout the nation, which will mercifully cure that fatal disorder known in cities as *brokerage*, and leave the people's money in their own pockets.

Give every man his constitutional freedom, and the President full power to send an army to suppress mobs, and the States authority to repeal and impugn that relic of folly which makes it necessary for the governor of a State to make the demand of the President for troops, in case of invasion or rebellion.

The governor himself may be a mobber; and instead of being punished, as he should be, for murder or treason, he may destroy the very lives, rights, and property he should protect. Like the good Samaritan, send every lawyer, as soon as he repents and obeys the ordinances of heaven, to preach the Gospel to the destitute, without purse or scrip, pouring in the oil and the wine. A learned priesthood is certainly more honorable than "*an hireling clergy.*"

As to the contiguous territories to the United States, wisdom would direct no tangling alliance. Oregon belongs to this government honoraby; and when we have the red man's consent, let the Union spread from the east to the west sea; and if Texas petitions Congress to be adopted among the sons of liberty, give her the right hand of fellowship, and refuse not the same friendly grip to Canada and Mexico. And when the right arm of freemen is stretched out in the character of a navy for the protection, of rights, commerce and honor, let the iron eyes of power watch from Maine to Mexico, and from California to Columbia. Thus may union be strengthened, and foreign speculation prevented from opposing broadside to broadside.

Seventy years have done much for this goodly land. They have burst the chains of oppression and monarchy, and multiplied its inhabitants from two to twenty millions, with a proportionate share of knowledge keen enough to circumnavigate the globe, draw the lightning from the clouds, and cope with all the crowned heads of the world.

Then why—oh, why will a once floushing people not arise, phœnix-like, over the cinders of Martin Van Buren's power, and over the sinking fragments and smoking ruins of other catamount politicians, and over the windfalls of Benton, Calhoun, Clay, Wright and a caravan of other equally unfortunate law doctors, and cheerfully help to spread a plaster and bind up the *burnt, bleeding wounds* of a sore but blessed country.

The Southern people are hospitable and noble. They will help to rid so free a country of every vestige of slavery, whenever they are assured of an equivalent for their property. The country will be full of money and confidence when a national bank of twenty millions,and a State bank in every State, with a million or more, gives a tone to monetary matters, and make a circulating medium as valuable in the purses of a whole community, as in the coffers of a speculating banker or broker.

The people may have faults, but they should never be trifled with. I think Mr. Pitt's quotation in the British parliament of Mr.

Prior's couplet for the husband and wife, to apply to the course which the king and ministry of England should pursue to the then colonies of the *now* United States, might be a genuine rule of action for some of the *breath-made* men in high places to use towards the posterity of this noble, daring people:—

Be to her faults a little blind;
Be to her virtues very kind.

We have had Democratic Presidents, Whig Presidents, a pseudo-Democratic-Whig President, and now it is time to have *a President of the United States;* and let the people of the whole Union, like the inflexible Romans, whenever they find a *promise* made by a candidate that is not *practiced* as an officer, hurl the miserable sycophant from his exaltation, as God did Nebuchadnezzar, to crop the grass of the field with a beast's heart among the cattle.

Mr. Van Buren said, in his inaugural address, that he went "into the Presidential chair the inflexible and uncompromising opponent of every attempt, on the part of Congress, to abolish slavery in the district of Columbia, against the wishes of the slave holding States, and also with a determination equally decided to resist the slightest interference with it in the States where it exists.

Poor little Matty made this rhapsodical sweep with the fact before his eyes, that the State of New York, his native State, had abolished slavery without a struggle or a groan. Great God, how independent! From henceforth slavery is tolerated where it exists, constitution or no constitution, people or no people, right or wrong: *Vox Matti—Vox Diaboli* ("the voice of Matti"—"the voice of the Devil.") And, peradventure, his great "sub-treasury" scheme was a piece of the same mind. But the man and his measures have such a striking resemblance to the anecdote of the Welshman and his cart-tongue, that when the Constitution was so long that it allowed slavery at the capitol of a free people, it could not be cut off; but when it was so short that it needed a *sub-treasury* to save the funds of the nation, *it could be spliced!* Oh, granny, granny, what a long tail our puss has got! (As a Greek might say, *Hysteron proteron,* (the cart before the horse). But his mighty whisk through the great national fire, for the presidential chestnuts, *burnt the locks of his glory with the blaze of his folly!*

In the United States the people are the government, and their united voice is the only sovereign that should rule, the only power that should be obeyed, and the only gentlemen that should be honored at home and abroad, on the land and on the sea. Wherefore, were I the President of the United States, by the voice of a virtuous people, I would honor the old paths of the venerated fathers of freedom; I would walk in the tracks of the illustrious patriots who carried the ark of the government upon their shoulders with an eye single to the glory of the people; and when that people petitioned to abolish slavery in the slave States, I would use all honorable means to have their prayers granted, and give liberty to the captive by paying the Southern gentlemen a reasonable equivalent for his property; that the whole nation might be free indeed!

When the people petitioned for a national bank, I would use my best endeavors to have their prayers answered, and establish one on national principles to save taxes, and make them the controllers of its ways and means. And when the people petitioned to possess the Territory of Oregon, or any other contiguous territory, I would lend the influence of a chief magistrate to grant so reasonable a request, that they might extend the mighty efforts and enterprise of a free people from the east to the west sea, and make the wilderness blossom as the rose. And when a neighboring realm petitioned to join the union of the sons of liberty, my voice would be *come*—yea, come, Texas; come, Mexico; come, Canada; and come, all the world: let us be brethren, let us be one great family, and let there be a universal peace. Abolish the cruel custom of prisons (except certain cases), penitentiaries, courts-martial for desertion; and let reason and friendship reign over the ruins of ignorance and barbarity; yea, I would, as the universal friend of man, open the prisons, open the eyes, open the ears, and open the hearts of all people, to behold and enjoy freedom—unadulterated freedom; and God, who once cleansed the violence of the earth with a flood, whose Son laid down His life for the salvation of all His Father gave Him out of the world, and who has promised that He will come and purify the world again with fire in the last days, should be supplicated by me for the good of all people. With the highest esteem, I am a friend of virtue and of the people.

JOSEPH SMITH.

Nauvoo, Illinois, Feb. 7, 1844.

APPENDIX IV.

AN ACCOUNT OF THE MARTYRDOM OF JOSEPH SMITH, BY PRESIDENT JOHN TAYLOR.

BEING requested by Elders George A. Smith and Wilford Woodruff, Church historians, to write an account of events that transpired before, and took place at, the time of the martyrdom of Joseph Smith, in Carthage jail, in Hancock County, State of Illinois, I write the following, principally from memory, not having access at this time to any public documents relative thereto farther than a few desultory items contained in Ford's "History of Illinois." I must also acknowledge myself considerably indebted to George A. Smith, who was with me when I wrote it, and who, although not there at the time of the bloody transaction, yet, from conversing with several persons who were in the capacity of Church historians, and aided by an excellent memory, has rendered me considerale service.

These and the few items contained in the note at the end of this account are all the aid I have had. I would further add that the items contained in the letter, in relation to dates especially, may be considered strictly correct.

After having written the whole, I read it over to the Hon. J. M. Bernhisel, who with one or two slight alterations, pronounced it strictly correct. Brother Bernhisel was present most of the time. I am afraid that, from the length of time that has transpired since the occurrence, and having to rely almost exclusively upon my memory, there may be some slight inaccuracies, but I believe that in the general it is strictly correct. As I figured in those transaction from the commencement to the end, they left no slight impression on my mind.

In the year 1844, a very great excitement prevailed in some

parts of Hancock, Brown and other neighboring counties of Illinois, in relation to the Mormons, and a spirit of vindictive hatred and persecution was exhibited among the people, which was manifested in the most bitter and acrimonious language, as well as by acts of hostility and violence, frequently threatening the destruction of the citizens of Nauvoo and vicinity, and utter annihilation of the Mormons and Mormonism, and in some instances breaking out in the most violent acts of ruffianly barbarity. Persons were kidnapped, whipped, persecuted and falsely accused of various crimes; their cattle and houses injured, destroyed, or stolen; vexatious prosecutions were instituted to harass and annoy. In some remote neighborhoods they were expelled from their homes without redress, and in others violence was threatened to their persons and property, while in others every kind of insult and indignity were heaped upon them, to induce them to abandon their homes, the County or the State.

These annoyances, prosecutions and persecutions were instigated through different agencies and by various classes of men, actuated by different motives, but all uniting in the one object—prosecution, persecution and extermination of the Saints.

There were a number of wicked and corrupt men living in Nauvoo and its vicinity, who had belonged to the Church, but whose conduct was incompatible with the Gospel; they were accordingly dealt with by the Church and severed from its communion. Some of these had been prominent members, and held official stations either in the city or Church. Among these were John C. Bennett, formerly mayor; William Law, counselor to Joseph Smith; Wilson Law, his natural brother, and general in the Nauvoo Legion; Dr. R. D. Foster, a man of some property, but with a very bad reputation; Francis and Chauncey Higbee, the latter a young lawyer, and both sons of a respectable and honored man in the Church, known as Judge Elias Higbee, who died about twelve months before.

Besides these, there were a great many apostates, both in the city and county, of less notoriety, who for their delinquencies, had been expelled from the Church. John C. Bennett and Francis and Chauncey Higbee were cut off from the Church; the former was also cashiered from his generalship for the most flagrant acts of seduction and adultery; and the developments in the cases were so scandal ous that the High Council, before which they were tried, had to sit with closed doors.

William Law, although counselor to Joseph, was found to be his most bitter foe and maligner, and to hold intercourse, contrary to all law, in his own house, with a young lady resident with him; and it was afterwards proven that he had conspired with some Missourians to take Joseph Smith's life, and was only saved by Josiah Arnold and Daniel Garn, who, being on guard at his house, prevented the assassins from seeing him. Yet, although having murder in his heart, his manners were generally courteous and mild, and he was well calculated to deceive.

General Wilson Law was cut off from the Church for seduction, felsehood, and defamation; both the above were also court-martialed by the Nauvoo Legion, and expelled. Foster was also cut off I believe, for dishonesty, fraud and falsehood. I know he was eminently guilty of the whole, but whether these were the specific charges or not, I don't know, but I do know that he was a notoriously wicked and corrupt man.

Besides the above characters and Mormonic apostates, there were other three parties. The first of these may be called religionists, the second politicians, and the third counterfeiters, black-legs, horse-thieves and cut-throats.

The religious party were chagrined and maddened because Mormonism came in contact with their religion, and they could not oppose it from the scriptures. Thus like the ancient Jews, when enraged at the exhibition of their follies and hypocrisies by Jesus and His apostles, so these were infuriated against the Mormons because of their discomfiture by them; and instead of owning the truth and rejoicing in it, they were ready to gnash upon them with their teeth, and to persecute the believers in principles which they could not disprove.

The political party were those who were of opposite politics to us. There were always two parties, the Whigs and Democrats, and we could not vote for one without offending the other; and it not unfrequently happened that candidates for office would place the issue of their election upon opposition to the Mormons, in order to gain political influence from the religious prejudice, in which case the Mormons were compelled, in self-defense, to vote against them, which resulted almost invariably against our opponents. This made them angry; and although it was of their own making, and the Mormons could not be expected to do otherwise, yet they raged on account of their discomfiture, and sought to wreak their fury on the Mormons. As an instance of the above, when Joseph Duncan was candidate for the office of governor of Illinois, he pledged himself to his party that, if he could be elected, he would exterminate or drive the Mormons from the State.* The consequence was that Governor Ford was elected. The Whigs, seeing that they had been out-generaled by the Democrats in securing the Mormon vote, became seriously alarmed, and sought to repair their disaster by raising a crusade against the people. The Whig newspapers teemed with accounts of the wonders and enormities of Nauvoo, and of the awful wickedness of a party which could consent to receive the support of such miscreants. Governor Duncan, who was really a brave, honest man, and who had nothing to do with getting the Mormon charters passed through the Legislature, took the stump on this subject in good earnest, and expected to be elected governor almost on this question alone.

The third party, composed of counterfeiters, black-legs, horse-thieves and cut-throats, were a pack of scoundrels that infested the whole of the western country at that time. In some districts their influence was so great as to control important State and County offices. On this subject Governor Ford has the following:

"Then, again, the northern part of the State was not destitute of its organized bands of rogues, engaged in murders, robberies, horse-stealing and in making and passing counterfeit money. These rogues were scattered all over the north, but the most of them were located in the counties of Ogle, Winnebago, Lee and De Kalb.

"In the County of Ogle they were so numerous, strong, and well organized that they could not be convicted for their crimes. By getting some of their numbers on the juries, by producing a host of witnesses to sustain their defense, by perjured evidence, and by changing the venue of one County to another, by continuances from term

---

* See his remarks as contained in his History of Illinois, page 269.

to term, and by the inability of witnesses to attend from time to time at distant and foreign Counties, they most generally managed to be acquitted."*

There was a combination of horse-thieves extending from Galena to Alton. There were counterfeiters engaged in merchandising, trading, and store-keeping in most of the cities and villages, and in some districts, I have been credibly informed by men to whom they have disclosed their secrets, the judges, sheriffs, constables, and jailors, as well, as professional men, were more or less associated with them. These had in their employ the most reckless, abandoned wretches, who stood ready to carry into effect the most desperate enterprises, and were careless alike of human life and property. Their object in persecuting the Mormons was in part to cover their own rascality, and in part to prevent them from exposing and prosecuting them; but the principal reason was plunder, believing that if they could be removed or driven they would be made fat on Mormon spoils, besides having in the deserted city a good asylum for the prosecution of their diabolical pursuits.

This conglomeration of apostate Mormons, religious bigots, political fanatics and black-legs, all united their forces against the Mormons, and organized themselves into a party, denominated anti-Mormons. Some of them, we have reason to believe, joined The Church in order to cover their infamous practices, and when they were expelled for their unrighteousness only raged with greater violence. They circulated every kind of falsehood that they could collect or manufacture against the Mormons. They also had a paper to assist them in their nefarious designs, called the *Warsaw Signal*, edited by a Mr. Thomas Sharp, a violent and unprincipled man, who shrunk not from any enormity. The anti Mormons had public meetings, which were very numerously attended, where they passed resolutions of the most violent and inflammatory kind, threatening to drive, expel and exterminate the Mormons from the State, at the same time accusing them of every evil in the vocabulary of crime.

They appointed their meetings in various parts of Hancock,

---

* Ford's History of Illinois, page 246.

M'Donough, and other counties, which soon resulted in the organization of armed mobs, under the direction of officers who reported to their headquarters, and the reports of which were published in the anti-Mormon paper, and circulated through the adjoining counties. We also published in the *Times and Seasons* and the *Nauvoo Neighbor* (two papers published and edited by me at that time) an account, not only of their proceedings, but our own. But such was the hostile feeling, so well arranged their plans, and so desperate and lawless their measures, that it was with the greatest difficulty that we could get our papers circulated; they were destroyed by postmasters and others, and scarcely ever arrived at the place of their destination, so that a great many of the people, who would have been otherwise peaceable, were excited by their misrepresentations, and instigated to join their hostile or predatory bands.

Emboldened by the acts of those outside, the apostate Mormons, associated with others, commenced the publication of a libelous paper in Nauvoo, called the *Nauvoo Expositor*. This paper not only reprinted from the others, but put in circulation the most libelous, false, and infamous reports concereing the citizens of Nauvoo, and especially the ladies. It was, however, no sooner put in circulation than the indignation of the whole community was aroused; so much so, that they threatered its annihilation; and I do not believe that in any other city of the United States, if the same charges had been made against the citizens, it would have been permitted to remain one day. As it was among us, under these circumstances, it was thought best to convene the city council to take into consideration the adoption of some measures for its removal, as it was deemed better that this should be done legally than illegally. Joseph Smith, therefore, who was mayor, convened the city council for that purpose; the paper was introduced and read, and the subject examined. All, or nearly all present, expressed their indignation at the course taken by the *Expositor*, which was owned by some of the aforesaid apostates, associated with one or two others. Wilson Law, Dr. Foster, Charles Ivins and the Higbees before referred to, some lawyers, storekeepers, and others in Nauvoo who were not Mormons, together with the anti-Mormons outside of the city, sustained it. The calculation was, by false statements, to unsettle the minds of many in the city, and to form combinations there similar to the anti-Mormon associations outside of the city. Various attempts had heretofore been made by the party to annoy and irritate the citizens of Nauvoo; false accusations had been made, vexatious lawsuits instituted, threats made, and various devices resorted to, to influence the public mind, and, if possible, to provoke us to the commission of some overt act that might make us amenable to the law. With a perfect knowledge, therefore, of the designs of these infernal scoundrels who were in our midst, as well as those who surrounded us, the city council entered upon an investigation of the matter. They felt that they were in a critical position, and that any move made for the abating of that press would be looked upon, or at least represented, as a direct attack upon the liberty of speech, and that, so far from displeasing our enemies, it would be looked upon by them as one of the best circumstances that could transpire to assist them in their nefarious and bloody designs. Being a member of the city council, I well remember the feeling of responsibility that seemed to rest upon all present; nor shall I soon forget the bold, manly, independent expressions of Joseph Smith on that occasion in relation to this matter. He exhibited in glowing colors the meanness, corruption, and ultimate designs of the anti-Mormons; their despicable characters and ungodly influences, especially of those who were in our midst. He told of the responsibility that rested upon us, as guardians of the public interest, to stand up in the defense of the injured and oppressed, to stem the current of corruption, and, as men and Saints, to put a stop to this flagrant outrage upon this people's rights.

He stated that no man was a stronger advocate for the liberty of speech and of the press than himself: yet, when this noble gift is utterly prostituted and abused, as in the present instance, it loses all claim to our respect, and becomes as great an agent for evil as it can possibly be for good; and notwithstanding the apparent advantage we should give our enemies by this act, yet it behooved us, as men, to act independent of all secondary influences, to perform the part of men of enlarged minds, and boldly and fearlessly to discharge the duties devolving upon us by declaring as a nuisance, and removing this filthy, libelous, and seditious sheet from our midst.

The subject was discussed in various forms, and after the remarks made by the mayor, every one seemed to be waiting for some one else to speak.

After a considerable pause, I arose and expressed my feelings frankly, as Joseph had done, and numbers of others followed in the same strain; and I think, but am not certain, that I made a motion for the removal of that press as a nuisance. This motion was finally put, and carried by all but one; and he conceded that the measure was just, but abstained through fear.

Several members of the city council were not in The Church. The following is the bill referred to:

Bill for Removing of the Press of the "Nauvoo Expositor." *

Resolved by the city council of the city of Nauvoo, that the printing-office from whence issues the *Nauvoo Expositor* is a public nuisance; and also of said *Nauvoo Expositors* which may be or exist in said establishment; and the mayor is instructed to cause said establishment and papers to be removed without delay, in such manner as he shall direct.

Passed June 10th, 1844. GEO. W. HARRIS, President *pro tem.*

W. RICHARDS, Recorder.

After the passage of the bill, the marshal, John P. Greene, was ordered to abate or remove, which he forthwith proceeded to do by summoning a posse of men for that purpose. The press was removed or broken, I don't remember which, by the marshal, and the types scattered in the street.

This seemed to be one of those extreme cases that require extreme measures, as the press was still proceeding in its inflammatory course. It was feared that, as it was almost universally execrated, should it continue longer, an indignant people might commit some overt act which might lead to serious consequences, and that it was better to use legal than illegal means.

This, as was foreseen, was the very course our enemies wished us to pursue, as it afforded them an opportunity of circulating a very

---

* *Deseret News*, No. 29, Sept. 23, 1857, p. 226.

plausible story about the Mormons being opposed to the liberty of the press and of free speech, which they were not slow to avail themselves of. Stories were fabricated, and facts perverted; false statements were made, and this act brought in as an example to sustain the whole of their fabrications; and, as if inspired by Satan, they labored with an energy and zeal worthy of a better cause. They had runners to circulate their reports, not only through Hancock County, but in all the surrounding counties. These reports were communicated to their anti-Mormon societies, and these societies circulated them in their several districts. The anti-Mormon paper, the *Warsaw Signal*, was filled with inflammatory articles and misrepresentations in relation to us, and especially to this act of destroying the press. We were represented as a horde of lawless ruffians and brigands, anti-American and anti-republican, steeped in crime and iniquity, opposed to freedom of speech and of the press, and all the rights and immunities of a free and enlightened people; that neither person nor property were secure: that we had designs upon the citizens of Illinois and of the United States, and the people were called upon to rise *en masse*, and put us down, drive us away, or exterminate us as a pest to society, and alike dangerous to our neighbors, the State, and commonwealth.

These statements were extensively copied and circulated throughout the United States. A true statement of the facts in question was published by us both in the *Times and Seasons* and the *Nauvoo Neighbor;* but it was found impossible to circulate them in the immediate counties, as they were destroyed in the post-offices or otherwise by the agents of the anti-Mormons, and in order to get the mail to go abroad, I had to send the papers a distance of thirty or forty miles from Nauvoo, and sometimes to St. Louis (upward of two hundred miles), to insure their proceeding on their route, and then one-half or two-thirds of the papers never reached the place of destination, being intercepted or destroyed by our enemies.

These false reports stirred up the community around, of whom many, on account of religious prejudice, were easily instigated to join the anti-Mormons and embark in any crusade that might be undertaken against us: hence their ranks swelled in numbers, and new organizations were formed, meetings were held, resolutions passed, and men and means volunteered for the extirpation of the Mormons.

On these points Governor Ford writes: "These also were the active men in blowing up the fury of the people, in hopes that a popular movement might be set on foot, which would result in the expulsion or extermination of the Mormon voters. For this purpose public meetings had been called, inflammatory speeches had been made, exaggerated reports had been extensively circulated, committees had been appointed, who rode night and day to spread the reports and solicit the aid of neighboring counties, and at a public meeting at Warsaw resolutions were passed to expel or exterminate the Mormon population. This was not, however, a movement which was unanimously concurred in. The county contained a goodly number of inhabitants in favor of peace, or who at least desired to be neutral in such a contest. These were stigmatized by the name of Jack-Mormons, and there were not a few of the more furious exciters of the people who openly expressed their intention to involve them in the common expulsion or extermination.

"A system of excitement and agitation was artfully planned and executed with tact. It consisted in spreading reports and rumors of the most fearful character. As examples: On the morning before my arrival at Carthage, I was awakened at an early hour by the frightful report, which was asserted with confidence and apparent consternation, that the Mormons had already commenced the work of burning, destruction, and murder, and that every man capable of bearing arms was instantly wanted at Carthage for the protection of the county.

"We lost no time in starting; but when we arrived at Carthage we could hear no more concerning this story. Again, during the few days that the militia were encamped at Carthage, frequent applications were made to me to send a force here, and a force there, and a force all about the country, to prevent murders, robberies, and larcenies which, it was said, were threatened by the Mormons. No such forces were sent, nor were any such offenses committed at that time, except the stealing of some provisions, and there was never the least proof that this was done by a Mormon. Again, on my late visit to Hancock County, I was informed by some of their violent enemies that the larcenies of the Mormons had become unusually numerous and insufferable.

"They admitted that but little had been done in this way in their immediate vicinity, but they insisted that sixteen horses had been stolen by the Mormons in one night near Lima, and, upon inquiry, was told that no horses had been stolen in that neighborhood, but that sixteen horses had been stolen in one night in Hancock County. This last informant being told of the Hancock story, again changed the venue to another distant settlement in the northern edge of Adams."*

In the meantime legal proceedings were instituted against the members of the city council of Nauvoo. A writ, here subjoined, was issued upon the affidavit of the Laws, Fosters, Higbees, and Ivins, by Mr. Morrison, a justice of the peace in Carthage, the county seat of Hancock, and put into the hands of one David Bettesworth, a constable of the same place.

Writ issued upon affidavit by Thomas Morrison, J. P., State of Illinois, Hancock County, ss.

"The people of the State of Illinois, to all constables, sheriffs, and coroners of said State, greeting:

"Whereas complaint hath been made before me, one of the justices of the peace in and for the county of Hancock aforesaid, upon the oath of Francis M. Higbee, of the said county, that Joseph Smith, Samuel Bennett, John Taylor, William W. Phelps, Hyrum Smith, John P. Greene, Stephen Perry, Dimick B. Huntington, Jonathan Dunham, Stephen Markham, William Edwards, Jonathan Holmes, Jesse P. Harmon, John Lytle, Joseph W. Coolidge, Harvey D. Redfield, Porter Rockwell, and Levi Richards, of said county, did, on the tenth day of June instant, commit a riot at and within the county aforesaid, wherein they with force and violence broke into the printing office of the *Nauvoo Expositor*, and unlawfully and with force burned and destroyed the printing press, type and fixtures of the same, being the property of William Law, Wilson Law, Charles Ivins, Francis M. Higbee, Chauncey L. Higbee, Robert D. Foster and Charles A. Foster.

---

* Ford's History of Illinois, page 330, 331.

"These are therefore to command you forthwith to apprehend the said Joseph Smith, Samuel Bennett, John Taylor, William W. Phelps, Hyrum Smith, John P. Greene, Stephen Perry, Dimick B. Huntington, Jonathan Dunham, Stephen Markham, William Edwards, Jonathan Holmes, Jesse P. Harmon, John Lytle, Joseph W. Coolidge, Harvey D. Redfield, Porter Rockwell, and Levi Richards, and bring them before me, or some other justice of the peace, to answer the premises, and farther to be dealt with according to law.

"Given under my hand and seal at Carthage, in the county aforesaid, this 11th day of June, A. D. 1844.

"THOMAS MORRISON, J. P." (Seal.)*

The council did not refuse to attend to the legal proceedings in the case, but as the law of Illinois made it the privilege of the persons accused to go "or appear before the issuer of the writ, or any other justice of the peace," they requested to be taken before another magistrate, either in the city of Nauvoo or at any reasonable distance out of it.

This the constable, who was a mobocrat, refused to do; and as this was our legal privilege we refused to be dragged, contrary to law, a distance of eighteen miles, when at the same time we had reason to believe that an organized band of mobocrats were assembled for the purpose of extermination or murder, and among whom it would not be safe to go without a superior force of armed men. A writ of *habeas corpus* was called for, and issued by the municipal court of Nauvoo, taking us out of the hands of Bettesworth, and placing us in the charge of the city marshal. We went before the municipal court and were dismissed. Our refusal to obey this illegal proceeding was by them construed into a refusal to submit to law, and circulated as such, and the people either did believe, or professed to believe, that we were in open rebellion against the laws and the authorities of the State. Hence mobs began to assemble, among which all through the country inflammatory speeches were made, exciting them to mobocracy and violence. Soon they commenced their

---

**Deseret News*, No. 30, September 30, 1857, page 233.

depredations in our outside settlements, kidnapping some, and whipping and otherwise abusing others.

The persons thus abused fled to Nauvoo as soon as practicable, and related their injuries to Joseph Smith, then mayor of the city, and lieutenant general of the Nauvoo Legion. They also went before magistrates, and made affidavits of what they had suffered, seen and heard. These affidavits, in connection with a copy of all our proceedings were forwarded by Joseph Smith to Mr. Ford, then governor of Illinois, with an expression of our desire to abide law, and a request that the governor would instruct him how to proceed in the case of arrival of an armed mob against the city. The governor sent back instructions to Joseph Smith that, as he was lieutenant general of the Nauvoo Legion, it was his duty to protect the city and surrounding country, and issued orders to that effect. Upon the reception of these orders Joseph Smith assembled the people of the city, and laid before them the governor's instructions; he also convened the officers of the Nauvoo Legion for the purpose of conferring in relation to the best mode of defense. He also issued orders to the men to hold themselves in readiness in case of being called upon. On the following day General Joseph Smith, with his staff, the leading officers of the Legion, and some prominent strangers who were in our midst, made a survey of the outside boundaries of the city, which was very extensive, being about five miles up and down the river, and about two and a half back in the center, for the purpose of ascertaining the position of the ground, and the feasibility of defense, and to make all necessary arrangements in case of an attack.

It may be well here to remark that numbers of gentlemen, strangers to us, either came on purpose or were passing through Nauvoo, and upon learning the position of things, expressed their indignation against our enemies, and avowed their readiness to assist us by their counsel or otherwise. It was some of these who assisted us in reconnoitering the city, and finding out its adaptability for defense, and how to protect it best against an armed force. The Legion was called together and drilled, and every means made use of for defense. At the call of the officers, old and young men came forward, both from the city and the country, and mustered to the number of about five thousand.

In the meantime our enemies were not idle in mustering their forces and committing depredations, nor had they been; it was, in fact, their gathering that called ours into existence; their forces continued to accumulate; they assumed a threatening attitude, and assembled in large bodies, armed and equipped for war, and threatened the destruction and extermination of the Mormons.

An account of their outrages and assemblages was forwarded to Governor Ford almost daily; accompanied by affidavits furnished by eye-witnesses of their proceedings. Persons were also sent out to the counties around with pacific intentions, to give them an account of the true state of affairs, and to notify them of the feelings and dispositions of the people of Nauvoo, and thus, if possible, quell the excitement. In some of the more distant counties these men were very successful, and produced the salutary influence upon the minds of many intelligent and well-disposed men. In neigboring counties, however, where anti-Mormon influence prevailed, they produced little effect. At the same time guards were stationed around Nauvoo, and picket-guards in the distance. At length opposing forces gathered so near that more active measures were taken; reconnoitering parties were sent out, and the city proclaimed under martial law. Things now assumed a belligerent attitude, and persons passing through the city were questioned as to what they knew of the enemy, while passes were in some instances given to avoid difficulty with the guards. Joseph Smith continued to send on messengers to the governor, (Philip B. Lewis and other messengers were sent.) Samuel James, then residing at La Harpe, carried a message and dispatches to him, and in a day or two after Bishop Edward Hunter and others went again with fresh dispatches, representations, affidavits, and instructions; but as the weather was excessively wet, the rivers swolen, and the bridges washed away in many places, it was with great difficulty that they proceeded on their journeys. As the mobocracy had at last attracted the governor's attention, he started in company with some others from Springfield to the scene of trouble, and missed, I believe, both Brothers James and Hunter on the road, and, of course, did not see their documents. He came to Carthage, and made that place, which was a regular mobocratic den, his headquarters; as it was the county seat, however, of Hancock County, that circumstance might, in a measure, justify his staying there.

To avoid the appearance of all hostility on our part, and to fulfill the law in every particular, at the suggestion of Judge Thomas, judge of that judicial district, who had come to Nauvoo at the time, and who stated that we had fulfilled the law, but, in order to satisfy all he would council us to go before Esquire Wells, who was not in our Church, and have a hearing, we did so, and after a full hearing we were again dismissed.

The governor on the road collected forces, some of whom were respectable, but on his arrival in the neighborhood of the difficulties he received as militia all the companies of the mob forces who united with him. After his arrival at Carthage he sent two gentlemen from there to Nauvoo as a committee to wait upon General Joseph Smith, informing him of the arrival of his excellency, with a request that General Smith would send out a committee to wait upon the governor and represent to him the state of affairs in relation to the difficulties that then existed in the county. We met this committee while we were reconnoitering the city, to find out the best mode of defense as aforesaid. Dr. J. M. Bernhisel and myself were appointed as a committee by General Smith to wait upon the governor. Previous to going, however, we were furnished with affidavits and documents in relation both to our proceedings and those of the mob; in addition to the general history of the transaction, we took with us a duplicate of those documents which had been forwarded by Bishop Hunter, Brother James, and others. We started from Nauvoo in company with the aforesaid gentlemen at about 7 o'clock on the evening of the 21st of June, and arrived at Carthage about 11 p. m.

We put up at the same hotel with the governor, kept by a Mr. Hamilton. On our arrival we found the governor in bed, but not so with the other inhabitants. The town was filled with a perfect set of rabble and rowdies, who, under the influence of Bacchus, seemed to be holding a grand saturnalia, whooping, yelling and vociferating as if Bedlam had broken loose.

On our arrival at the hotel, and while supper was preparing, a man came to me, dressed as a soldier, and told me that a man named Daniel Garn had just been taken prisoner, and was about to be committed to jail, and wanted me to go bail for him. Believing this to be a ruse to get me out alone, and that some violence was intended, after consulting with Dr. Bernhisel, I told the man that I was well acquainted with Mr. Garn, that I knew him to be a gentleman, and did not believe that he had transgressed law, and, moreover, that I considered it a very singular time to be holding courts and calling for security, particularly as the town was full of rowdyism.

I informed him that Dr. Bernhisel and myself would, if necessary go bail for him in the morning, but that we did not feel ourselves safe among such a set at that late hour of the night.

After supper, on retiring to our room, we had to pass through another, which was separated from ours only by a board partition, the beds in each room being placed side by side, with the exception of this fragile partition. On the bed that was in the room which we passed through I discovered a man by the name of Jackson, a desperate character, and a reputed, notorious cut-throat and murderer. I hinted to the doctor that things looked rather suspicious, and looked to see that my arms were in order. The doctor and I occupied one bed. We had scarcely laid down when a knock at the door, accompanied by a voice announced the approach of Chauncey Higbee, the young lawyer and apostate before referred to.

He addressed himself to the doctor, and stated that the object of his visit was to obtain the release of Daniel Garn; that Garn he believed to be an honest man; that if he had done anything wrong, it was through improper counsel, and that it was a pity that he should be incarcerated, particularly when he could be so easily released; he urged the doctor, as a friend, not to leave so good a man in such an unpleasant situation; he finally prevailed upon the doctor to go and give bail, assuring him that on his giving bail Garn would be immediately dismissed.

During this conversation I did not say a word.

Higbee left the doctor to dress, with the intention of returning and taking him to the court. As soon as Higbee had left, I told the doctor that he had better not go; that I believed this affair was all a ruse to get us separated; that they knew we had documents with us from General Smith to show to the governor; that I believed their object was to get possession of those papers, and, perhaps, when they had separated us, to murder one or both. The doctor, who was actuated by the best of motives in yielding to the assumed solicitude of Higbee, coincided with my views; he then went to Higbee, and told him that he had concluded not to go that night, but that he and I would both wait upon the justice and Mr. Garn in the morning.

That night I lay awake with my pistols under my pillow, waiting for any emergency. Nothing more occurred during the night. In the morning we arose early, and after breakfast sought an interview with the governor, and were told that we could have an audience, I think, at ten o'clock. In the meantime we called upon Mr. Smith, a justice of the peace, who had Mr. Garn in charge. We represented that we had been called upon the night before by two different parties to go bail for a Mr. Daniel Garn, whom we were informed he had in custody, and that, believing Mr. Garn to be an honest man, we had now come for that purpose, and were prepared to enter into recognizances for his appearance, whereupon Mr. Smith, the magistrate, remarked that, under the present excited state of affairs, he did not think he would be justified in receiving bail from Nauvoo, as it was a matter of doubt whether property would not be rendered valueless there in a few days.

Knowing the party we had to deal with, we were not much surprised at this singular proceeding; we then remarked that both of us possessed property in farms out of Nauvoo in the country, and referred him to the county records. He then stated that such was the nature of the charge against Mr. Garn that he believed he would not be justified in receiving any bail. We were thus confirmed in our opinion that the night's proceedings before, in relation to their desire to have us give bail, was a mere ruse to separate us. We were not permitted to speak with Garn, the real charge against whom was that he was traveling in Carthage or its neighborhood: what the fictitious one was, if I knew, I have since forgotten, as things of this kind were of daily occurrence.

After waiting the governor's pleasure for some time we had an audience; but such an audience!

He was surrounded by some of the vilest and most unprincipled men in creation; some of them had an appearance of respectability, and many of them lacked even that. Wilson, and, I believe, William

Law, were there, Foster, Frank and Chauncey Higbee, Mr. Mar, a lawyer from Nauvoo, a mobocratic merchant from Warsaw, the aforesaid Jackson, a number of his associates, among whom was the governor's secretary, in all, some fifteen or twenty persons, most of whom were recreant to virtue, honor, integrity, and everything that is considered honorable among men. I can well remember the feelings of disgust that I had in seeing the governor surrounded by such an infamous group, and on being introduced to men of so questionable a character; and had I been on private business, I should have turned to depart, and told the governor that if he thought proper to associate with such questionable characters, I should beg leave to be excused; but coming as we did on public business, we could not, of course, consult our private feelings.

We then stated to the governor that, in accordance with his request, General Smith had, in response to his call, sent us to him as a committee of conference; that we were acquainted with most of the circumstances that had transpired in and about Nauvoo lately, and were prepared to give him all information; that, moreover, we had in our possession testimony and affidavits confirmatory of what we should say, which had been forwarded to him by General Joseph Smith; that communications had been forwarded to his excellency by Messrs. Hunter, James, and others, some of which had not reached their destination, but of which we had duplicates with us. We then, in brief, related an outline of the difficulties, and the course we had pursued from the commencement of the trouble up to the present, and handing him the documents, respectfully submitted the whole.

During our conversation and explanations with the governor we were frequently, rudely and impudently contradicted by the fellows he had around him, and of whom he seemed to take no notice.

He opened and read a number of the documents himself, and as he proceeded he was frequently interrupted by, "that's a lie!" "that's a God damned lie!" that's an infernal falsehood!" "that's a blasted lie!" etc.

These men evidently winced at the exposure of their acts, and thus vulgarly, impudently, and falsely repudiated them. One of their number, Mr. Mar, addressed himself several times to me while in conversation with the governor. I did not notice him until after a frequent repetition of his insolence, when I informed him that "my business at that time was with Governor Ford," whereupon I continued my conversation with his excellency. During the conversation, the governor expressed a desire that Joseph Smith, and all parties concerned in passing or executing the city law in relation to the press, had better come to Carthage; that, however repugnant it might be to our feelings, he thought it would have a tendency to allay public excitement, and prove to the people what we professed, that we wished to be governed by law. We represented to him the course we had taken in relation to this matter, and our willingness to go before another magistrate other than the municipal court; the illegal refusal of our request by the constable; our dismissal by the municipal court, a legally constituted tribunal; our subsequent trial before 'Squire Wells at the instance of Judge Thomas, the circuit judge, and our dismissal by him; that we had fulfilled the law in every particular; that it was our enemies who were breaking the law, and, having murderous designs, were only making use of this as a pretext to get us into their power. The governor stated that the people viewed it differently, and that, notwithstanding our opinions, he would recommend that the people should be satisfied. We then remarked to him that, should Joseph Smith comply with his request, it would be extremely unsafe, in the present excited state of the country, to come without an armed force; that we had a sufficiency of men, and were competent to defend ourselves, but there might be danger of collision should our forces and those of our enemies be brought into such close proximity. He strenuously advised us not to bring our arms, and *pledged his faith as governor, and the faith of the State, that we should be protected, and that he would guarantee our perfect safety.*

We had at that time about five thousand men under arms, one thousand of whom would have been amply sufficient for our protection.

At the termination of our interview, and previous to our withdrawal, after a long conversation and the perusal of the documents which we had brought, the governor informed us that he would prepare a written communication for General Joseph Smith, which he desired us to wait for. We were kept waiting for this instrument some five or six hours.

About five o'clock in the afternoon we took our departure with not the most pleasant feelings. The associations of the governor, the spirit he manifested to compromise with these scoundrels, the length of time that he had kept us waiting, and his general deportment, together with the infernal spirit that we saw exhibited by those whom he had admitted to his counsels, made the prospect anything but promising.

We returned on horseback, and arrived at Nauvoo, I think, at about eight or nine o'clock at night, accompanied by Captain Yates in command of a company of mounted men, who came for the purpose of escorting Joseph Smith and the accused in case of their complying with the governor's request, and going to Carthage. We went directly to Brother Joseph's, when Captain Yates delivered to him the governor's communication. A council was called, consisting of Joseph's brother, Hyrum, Dr. Richards, Dr. Bernhisel, myself, and one or two others.

We then gave a detail of our interview with the governor. Brother Joseph was very much dissatisfied with the governor's letter and with his general deportment, and so were the council, and it became a serious question as to the course we should pursue. Various projects were discussed, but nothing definitely decided upon for some time.

In the interim two gentlemen arrived; one of them, if not both, sons of John C. Calhoun. They had come to Nauvoo, and were very anxious for an interview with Brother Joseph.

These gentlemen detained him for some time; and, as our council was held in Dr. Bernhisel's room in the Mansion House, the doctor lay down; and as it was now between 2 and 3 o'clock in the morning, and I had had no rest on the previous night, I was fatigued, and thinking that Brother Joseph might not return, I left for home and rest.

Being very much fatigued, I slept soundly, and was somewhat surprised in the morning by Mrs. Thompson entering my room about 7 o'clock, and exclaiming in surprise, "What, you here! the brethren have crossed the rive some time since."

"What brethren?" I asked.

"Brother Joseph, and Hyrum, and Brother Richards," she answered.

I immediately arose upon learning that they had crossed the river, and did not intend to go to Carthage. I called together a number of persons in whom I had confidence, and had the type, stereotype plates, and most of the valuable things removed from the printing office, believing that, should the governor and his force come to Nauvoo, the first thing they would do would be to burn the printing office, for I knew they would be exasperated if Brother Joseph went away. We had talked over these matters the night before, but nothing was decided upon. It was Brother Joseph's opinion that, should we leave for a time, public excitement, which was then so intense, would be allayed; that it would throw on the governor the responsibility of keeping the peace; that in the event of an outrage, the onus would rest upon the governor, who was amply prepared with troops, and could command all the forces of the State to preserve order; and that the act of his own men would be an overwhelming proof of their seditious designs, not only to the governor, but to the world. He moreover thought that, in the east, where he intended to go, public opinion would be set right in relation to these matters, and its expression would partially influence the west, and that, after the first ebullition, things would assume a shape that would justify his return.

I made arrangements for crossing the river, and Brother Elias Smith and Joseph Cain, who were both employed in the printing office with me, assisted all that lay in their power together with Brother Brower and several hands in the printingoffice. As we could not find out the exact whereabouts of Joseph and the brethren, I crossed the river in a boat furnished by Brother Cyrus H. Wheelock and Alfred Bell; and after the removal of the things out of the printing office, Joseph Cain brought the account books to me, that we might make arrangements for their adjustment; and Brother Elias Smith, cousin to Brother Joseph, went to obtain money for the journey, and also to find out and report to me the location of the brethren.

As Cyrus H. Wheelock was an active, enterprising man, and in the event of not finding Brother Joseph I calculated to go to Upper Canada for the time being, and should need a companion, I said to Brother Cyrus H. Wheelock, "Can you go with me ten or fifteen hundred miles?"

He answered, "Yes."

"Can you start in half an hour?"

"Yes."

However, I told him that he had better see his family, who lived over the river, and prepare a couple of horses and the necessary equippage for the journey, and that, if we did not find Brother Joseph before, we would start at nightfall.

A laughable incident occurred on the eve of my departure. After making all the preparations I could, previous to leaving Nauvoo, and having bid adieu to my family, I went to a house adjoining the river, owned by Brother Eddy. There I disguised myself so as not to be known, and so effectually was the transformation that those who had come after me with a boat did not know me. I went down to the boat and sat in it. Brother Bell, thinking it was a stranger, watched my moves for some time very impatiently, and then said to Brother Wheelock, "I wish that old gentleman would go away; he has been pottering around the boat for some time, and I am afraid Elder Taylor will be coming." When he discovered his mistake, he was not a little amused.

I was conducted by Brother Bell to a house that was surrounded by timber on the opposite side of the river. There I spent several hours in a chamber with Brother Joseph Cain, adjusting my accounts; and I made arrangements for the stereotype plates of the Book of Mormon and Doctrine and Covenants, to be forwarded east, thinking to supply the company with subsistence money through the sale of these books in the east.

My horses were reported ready by Brother Wheelock, and funds on hand by Brother Elias Smith. In about half an hour I should have started, when Brother Elias Smith came to me with word that he had found the brethren; that they had concluded to go to Carthage, and wished me to return to Nauvoo and accompany them. I must confess that I felt a good deal disappointed at this news, but I immediately made preparations to go. Escorted by Brother Elias Smith, I and my party went to the neighborhood of Montrose, where we met Brother Joseph, Hyrum, Brother Richards and others. Dr. Bernhisel thinks that W. W. Phelps was not with Joseph and Hyrum in the morning, but that he met him, myself, Joseph and Hyrum, W. Richards and Brother Cahoon, in the afternoon, near Montrose, returning to Nauvoo.

On meeting the brethren I learned that it was not Brother Joseph's desire to return, but that he came back by request of some of the brethren, and that it coincided more with Brother Hyrum's feelings than those of Brother Joseph. In fact, after his return, Brother Hyrum expressed himself as perfectly satisfied with the course taken, and said he felt much more at ease in his mind than he did before. On our return the calculation was to throw ourselves under the immediate protection of the governor, and to trust to his word and faith for our preservation.

A message was, I believe, sent to the governor that night, stating that we should come to Carthage in the morning, the party that came along with us to escort us back, in case we returned to Carthage, having returned.

It would seem from the following remarks of General Ford that there was a design on foot, which was, that if we refused to go to Carthage at the governor's request, there should be an increased force called for by the governor, and that we should be destroyed by them. In accordance with this project, Captain Yates returned with his *posse*, accompanied by the constable who held the writ.

The following is the governor's remark in relation to this affair:

"The constable and his escort returned. The constable made no effort to arrest any of them, nor would he or the guard delay their departure one minute beyond the time, to see whether an arrest could be made. Upon their return they reported that they had been informed that the accused had fled, and could not be found. I immediately proposed to a council of officers to march into Nauvoo with the small force then under my command, but the officers were of the opinion that it was too small, and many of them insisted upon a further call of the militia. Upon reflection I was of the opinion that the officers were right in the estimate of our force, and the project for immediate action was abandoned.

"I was soon informed, however, of the conduct of the constable and guard, and then I was perfectly satisfied that a most base fraud had been attempted, that, in fact, it was feared that the Mormons would submit, and thereby entitle themselve to the protection of the law. It was very apparent that many of the bustling, active spirits were afraid that there would be no occasion for calling out an overwhelming militia force, for marching into Nauvoo, for probable mutiny when there, and for the extermination of the Mormon race. It appeared that the constable and the escort were fully in the secret, and acted well their part to promote the conspiracy." *

In the morning Brother Joseph had an interview with the officers of the Legion, with the leading members of the city council, and with the principal men of the city. The officers were instructed to dismiss their men, but to have them in a state of readiness to be called upon in any emergency that might occur.

About half past six o'clock the members of the city council, the marshal, Brothers Joseph and Hyrum, and a number of others, started for Carthage, on horseback. We were instructed by Brother Joseph Smith not to take any arms, and we consequently left them behind. We called at the house of Brother Fellows on our way out. Brother Fellows lived about four miles from Carthage.

While at Brother Fellow's house, Captain Dunn, accompanied by Mr. Coolie, one of the governor's aides-de-camp, came up from Carthage *en route* for Nauvoo with a requisition from the governor for the State arms. We all returned to Nauvoo with them; the governor's request was complied with, and after taking some refreshments, we all returned to proceed to Carthage. We arrived there late in the night. A great deal of excitement prevailed on and after our arrival. The governor had received into his company all of the companies that had been in the mob; these fellows were riotous and disorderly, hallooing, yelling, and whooping about the streets like Indians, many of them intoxicated; the whole presented a scene of rowdyism and low-bred ruffianism only found among mobocrats and desperadoes, and entirely revolting to the best feelings of humanity. The governor made a speech to them to the effect that he would show Joseph and Hyrum Smith to them in the morning.

About here the companies with the governor were drawn up in line, and General Demming, I think, took Joseph by the arm and Hyrum(Arnold says that Joseph took the governor's arm), and as he passed through between the ranks, the governor leading in front,

---

* Ford's History of Illinois, page 333.

very politely introduced them as General Joseph Smith and General Hyrum Smith.*

---

*The *Deseret News* gives the following account of Joseph and Hyrum Smith's passing through the troops in Carthage:

"CARTHAGE, June 25, 1844.

"Quarter past nine. The governor came and invited Joseph to walk with him through the troops. Joseph solicited a few moments' private conversation with him, which the governor refused.

"While refusing, the governor looked down at his shoes, as though he was ashamed. They then walked through the crowd, with Brigadier General Miner R. Demming, and Dr. Richards, to General Demming's quarters. The people appeared quiet until a company of Carthage Grays flocked round the doors of General Demming in an uproarious manner, of which notice was sent to the governor. In the meantime the governor had ordered the McDonough troops to be drawn up in line, for Joseph and Hyrum to pass in front of them, they having requested that they might have a clear view of the General Smiths. *Joseph had a conversation with the governor for about ten minutes, when he again pledged the faith of the State that he and his friends should be protected from violence.*

"Robinson, the postmaster, said, on report of martial law being proclaimed in Nauvoo, he had stopped the mail, and notified the postmaster general of the state of things in Hancock County.

"From the general's quarters Joseph and Hyrum went in front of the lines, in a hollow square of a company of Carthage Grays. At seven minutes before ten they arrived in front of the lines, and passed before the whole, Joseph being on the right of General Demming and Hyrum on his left, Elders Richards, Taylor and Phelps following. Joseph and Hyrum were introduced by Governor Ford about twenty times along the line as General Joseph Smith and General Hyrum Smith, the governor walking in front on the left. The Carthage Grays refused to receive them by that introduction, and some of the officers threw up their hats, drew their swords, and said they would introduce themselves to the damned Mormons in a different style. The governor mildly entreated them not to act so rudely, but their excitement increased; the governor, however, succeeded in pacifying them by making a speech, and promising them that they should have 'full satisfaction.' General Smith and party returned to their lodgings at five minutes past ten."—*Deseret News, No. 35, Nov. 4, 1857, page 274.*

All were orderly and courteous except one company of mobocrats —the Carthage Grays—who seemed to find fault on account of too much honor being paid to the Mormons. There was afterwards a row between the companies, and they came pretty near having a fight; the more orderly not feeling disposed to endorse or submit to the rowdyism of the mobocrats. The result was that General Demming, who was very much of a gentleman, ordered the Carthage Grays, a company under the command of Captain Smith, a magistrate in Carthage, and a most violent mobocrat, under arrest. This matter, however, was shortly afterward adjusted, and the difficulty settled between them.

The mayor, aldermen, councilors, as well as the marshal of the city of Nauvoo, together with some persons who had assisted the marshal in removing the press in Nauvoo, appeared before Justice Smith, the aforesaid captain and mobocrat, to again answer the charge of destroying the press; but as there was so much excitement, and as the man was an unprincipled villain before whom we were to have our hearing, we thought it most prudent to give bail, and consequently became security for each other in $500 bonds each, to appear before the County Court at its next session. We had engaged as counsel a lawyer by the name of Wood, of Burlington, Iowa; and Reed, I think, of Madison, Iowa After some little discussion the bonds were signed, and we were all dismissed.

Almost immediately after our dismissal, two men—Augustine Spencer and Norton—two worthless fellows, whose words would not have been taken for five cents, and the first of whom had a short time previously been before the mayor in Nauvoo for maltreating a lame brother, made affidavits that Joseph and Hyrum Smith were guilty of treason, and a writ was accordingly issued for their arrest, and the constable Bettesworth, a rough, unprincipled man, wished immediately to hurry them away to prison without any hearing. His rude, uncouth manner in the administration of what he considered the duties of his office made him exceedingly repulsive to us all. But, independent of these acts, the proceedings in this case were altogether illegal. Providing the court was sincere, which it was not, and providing these men's oaths were true, and that Joseph and Hyrum were guilty of treason, still the whole course was illegal.

The magistrate made out a mittimus, and committed them to prison without a hearing, which he had no right legally to do. The statute of Illinois expressly provides that "all men shall have a hearing before a magistrate before they shall be committed to prison;" and Mr. Robert H. Smith, the magistrate, had made out a mittimus committing them to prison contrary to law without such hearing. As I was informed of this illegal proceeding, I went immediately to the governor and informed him of it. Whether he was apprised of it before or not, I do not know; but my opinion is that he was.

I represented to him the characters of the parties who had made oath, the outrageous nature of the charge, the indignity offered to men in the position which they occupied, and declared to him that he knew very well it was a vexatious proceeding, and that the accused were not guilty of any such crime. The governor replied, he was very sorry that the thing had occurred; that he did not believe the charges, but that he thought the best thing to be done was to let the law take its course. I then reminded him that we had come out there at his instance, not to satisfy the law, which we had done before, but the prejudices of the people, in relation to the affairs of the press; that at his instance we had given bonds, which we could not by law be required to do to satisfy the people, and that it was asking too much to require gentlemen in their position in life to suffer the degredation of being immured in a jail at the instance of such worthless scoundrels as those who had made this affidavit. The governor replied that it was an unpleasant affair, and looked hard; but that it was a matter over which he had no control, as it belonged to the judiciary; that he, as the executive, could not interfere with their proceedings, and that he had no doubt but that they would immediately be dismissed. I told him that we had looked to him for protection from such insults, and that I thought we had a right to do so from the solemn promises which he had made to me and to Dr. Bernhisel in relation to our coming without guard or arms; that we had relied upon his faith, and had a right to expect him to fulfill his engagements after we had placed ourselves implicity under his care, and complied with all his requests, although extrajudicial.

He replied that he would detail a guard, if we required it, and see us protected, but that he could not interfere with the judiciary.

I expressed my dissatisfaction at the course taken, and told him, that, if we were to be subject to mob rule, and to be dragged, contrary to law, into prison at the instance of every infernal scoundrel whose oaths could be bought for a dram of whiskey, his protection availed very little, and we had miscalculated his promises.

Seeing there was no prospect of redress from the governor, I returned to the room, and found the constable Bettesworth very urgent to hurry Brothers Joseph and Hyrum to prison, while the brethren were remonstrating with him. At the same time a great rabble was gathered in the streets and around the door, and from the rowdyism manifested I was afraid there was a design to murder the prisoners on the way to jail.

Without conferring with any person, my next feelings were to procure a guard, and seeing a man habited as a soldier in the room, I went to him and said, "I am afraid there is a design against the lives of the Messrs. Smith; will you go immediately and bring your captain; and, if not convenient, any other captain of a company, and I will pay you well for your trouble?" He said he would, and departed forthwith, and soon returned with his captain, whose name I have forgotten, and introduced him to me. I told him of my fears, and requested him immediately to fetch his company.

He departed forthwith, and arrived at the door with them just at the time when the constable was hurrying the brethren down stairs. A number of the brethren went along, together with one or two strangers; and all of us, safely lodged in prison, ramained there during the night.

At the request of Joseph Smith for an interview with the governor, he came the next morning, Thursday, June 26th, at half past 9 o'clock, accompanied by Colonel Geddes, when a lengthy conversation was entered into in relation to the existing difficulties; and after some preliminary remarks, at the governor's request, Brother Joseph gave him a general outline of the state of affairs in relation to our difficulties, the excited state of the country, the tumultuous mobocratic movements of our enemies, the precautionary measures used by himself (Joseph Smith), the acts of the city council, the destruction of the press, and the moves of the mob and ourselves up to that time.

The following report is, I believe, substantially correct:

Governor—"General Smith, I believe you have given me a general outline of the difficulties that have existed in the country in the documents forwarded to me by Dr. Bernhisel and Mr. Taylor; but, unfortunately, there seems to be a great discrepancy between your statements and those of your enemies. It is true that you are substantiated by evidence and affidavit, but for such an extraordinary excitement as that which is now in the country there must be some cause, and I attribute the last outbreak to the destruction of the *Expositor*, and to your refusal to comply with the writ issued by Esquire Morrison. The press in the United States is looked upon as the great bulwark of American freedom, and its destruction in Nauvoo was represented and looked upon as a high-handed measure, and manifests to the people a disposition on your part to suppress the liberty of speech and of the press. This, with your refusal to comply with the requisition of a writ, I conceive to be the principal cause of this difficulty; and you are moreover represented to me as turbulent, and defiant of the laws and institutions of your country."

General Smith—"Governor Ford, you, sir, as governor of this State, are aware of the persecutions that I have endured. You know well that our course has been peaceable and law-abiding for I have furnished this State ever since our settlement here with sufficient evidence of my pacific intentions, and those of the people with whom I am associated, by the endurence of every conceivable indignity and lawless outrage perpetrated upon me and upon this people since our settlement here; and you know yourself that I have kept you well posted in relation to all matters associated with the late difficulties. If you have not got some of my communications, it has not been my fault.

"Agreeably to your orders, I assembled the Nauvoo Legion for the protection of Nauvoo and the surrounding country against an armed band of marauders; and ever since they have been mustered I have almost daily communicated with you in regard to all the leading events that have transpired; and whether in the capacity of mayor of the city, or lieutenant general of the Nauvoo Legion, I have striven, according to the best of my judgment, to preserve the peace and to administer even-handed justice; but my motives are impugned, my acts are misconstrued, and I am grossly and wickedly misrepresented. I suppose I am indebted for my incarceration to the oath of a worthless man, who was arraigned before me and fined for. abusing and maltreating his lame, helpless brother. That I should be charged by you, sir, who know better, of acting contrary to law, is to me a matter of surprise. Was it the Mormons or our enemies who first commenced these difficulties? You know well it was not us; and when this turbulent, outrageous people commenced their insurrectionary movements I made you acquainted with them officially, and asked your advice, and have followed strictly your counsel in every particular. Who ordered out the Nauvoo Legion? I did, under your direction. For what purpose? To suppress the insurrectionary movements. It was at your instance, sir, that I issued a proclamation calling upon the Nauvoo Legion to be in readiness at a moment's warning to guard against the incursions of mobs, and gave an order to Jonathan Dunham, acting major-general, to that effect.

"Am I, then, to be charged with the acts of others? and because lawlessness and mobocracy abound, am I, when carrying out your instructions, to be charged with not abiding law? Why is it that I must be made accountable for other men's acts? If there is trouble in the country, neither I nor my people made it; and all that we have ever done, after much endurance on our part, is to maintain and uphold the Constitution and institutions of our country, and to protect an injured, innocent, and persecuted people against misrule and mob violence.

"Concerning the destruction of the press to which you refer, men may differ somewhat in their opinions about it; but can it be supposed that after all the indignities to which they have been subjected outside, that people could suffer a set of worthless vagabonds to come into their city, and, right under their own eyes and protection, vilify and calumniate not only themselves, but the character of their wives and daughters, as was impudently and unblushingly done in that infamous and filthy sheet?

"There is not a city in the United States that would have suffered such an indignity for twenty-four hours. Our whole people were indignant, and loudly called upon our city authorities for a redress of their grievances, which, if not attended to, they themselves would have taken into their own hands, and have summarily punished the audacious wretches as they deserved. The principle of equal rights that has been instilled into our bosoms from our cradles as American citizens forbids us submitting to every foul indignity, and succumbing and pandering to wretches so infamous as these. But, independent of this, the course that we pursued we consider to be strictly legal; for, notwithstanding the result, we were anxious to be governed strictly by law, and therefore we convened the city council; and being desirous in our deliberations to abide by law, we summoned legal counsel to be present on the occasion. Upon investigating the matter, we found that our city charter gave us power to remove all nuisances. Furthermore, after consulting Blackstone upon what might be considered a nuisance, it appeared that that distinguished lawyer, who is considered authority, I believe, in all our courts, states among other things that 'a libelous and filthy press may be considered a nuisance, and abated as such.' Here, then, one of the most eminent English barristers, whose works are considered standard with us, declares that a libelous and filthy press may be considered a nuisance; and our own charter, given us by the Legislature of this State, gives us power to remove nuisances; and by ordering that press to be abated as a nuisance, we conceived that we were acting stricly in accordance with law. We made that order in our corporate capacity, and the city marshal carried it out. It is possible there may have been some better way, but I must confess that I could not see it.

"In relation to the writ served upon us, we are willing to abide the consequences of our own acts, but are unwilling, in answering a writ of that kind, to submit to illegal exactions, sought to be imposed upon us under the pretense of law, when we knew they were in open violation of it. When that document was presented to me by Mr. Bettesworth, I offered, in the presence of more than twenty persons, to go to any other magistrate, either in our city, in Appanoose, or any other place where we should be safe, but we all refused to put ourselves into the power of a mob. What right had that constable to refuse our request? He had none according to law; for you know, Governor Ford, that the statute law in Illinois is, that the parties served with the writ 'shall go before him who issued it, or some other justice of the peace.' Why, then, should we be dragged to Carthage, where the law does not compel us to go? Does not this look like many others of our persecutions with which you are acquainted? and have we not a right to expect foul play? This very act was a breach of law on his part, an assumption of power that did not belong to him, and an attempt, at least, to deprive us of our legal and constitutional rights and privileges. What could we do, under the circumstances, different from what we did do? We sued for, and obtained a writ of *habeas corpus* from the municipal court, by which we were delivered from the hands of Constable Bettesworth, and brought before and acquitted by the municipal court. After our acquittal, in a conversation with Judge Thomas, although he considered the acts of the party illegal, he advised that, to satisfy the people, we had better go before another magistrate who was not in our Church. In accordance with his advice, we went before Esquire Wells, with whom you are well acquainted; both parties were present, witnesses were called on both sides, the case was fully investigated, and we were again dismissed. And what is this pretended desire to enforce law, and wherefore are these lying, base rumors put into circulation but to seek, through mob influence, under pretense of law, to make us submit to requisitons which are contrary to law and subversive of every principle of justice? And when you, sir, required us to come out here, we came, not because it was legal, but because you required it of us, and we were desirous of showing to you, and to all men, that we shrunk not from the most rigid investigation of our acts. We certainly did expect other treatment than to be immured in a jail at the instance of these men, and I think, from your plighted faith, we had a right so to expect, after disbanding our own forces, and putting ourselves entirely in your hands. And now, after having fulfilled my part, sir, as a man and an American citizen, I call upon you, Governor Ford, to deliver us from this place, and rescue us from this outrage that is sought to be practiced upon us by a set of infamous scoundrels."

Governor Ford.—"But you have placed men under arrest, detained men as prisoners, and given passes to others, some of which I have seen,"

John P. Greene, City Marshal.—"Perhaps I can explain. Since these difficulties have commenced, you are aware that we have been placed under very peculiar circumstances; our city has been placed under a very rigid police guard; in addition to this, frequent guards have been placed outside the city to prevent any sudden surprise, and those guards have questioned suspected or suspicious persons as to their business. To strangers, in some instances, passes have been given to prevent difficulty in passing those guards; it is some of these passes that you have seen. No person, sir, has been imprisoned without a legal cause in our city."

Governor.—"Why did you not give a more speedy answer to the posse that I sent out?"

General Smith.—We had matters of importance to consult upon; your letter showed anything but an amiable spirit. We have suffered immensely in Missouri from mobs, in loss of property, imprisonment, and otherwise. It took some time for us to weigh duly these matters; we could not decide upon matters of such importance immediately, and your posse were too hasty in returning; we were consulting for a large people, and vast interests were at stake. We had been outrageously imposed upon, and knew not how far we could trust any one; besides, a question necessarily arose, How shall we come? Your request was that we should come unarmed. It became a matter of serious importance to decide how far promises could be trusted, and how far we were safe from mob violence."

Colonel Geddes.—"It certainly did look, from all I have heard, from the general spirit of violence and mobocracy that here prevails, that it was not safe for you to come unprotected."

Governor Ford.—"I think that sufficient time was not allowed by the posse for you to consult and get ready. They were too hasty; but I suppose they found themselves bound by their orders. I think, too, there is a great deal of truth in what you say, and your reasoning is plausible, but I must beg leave to differ from you in relation to the acts of the City Council. That Council, in my opinion, had no right to act in a legislative capacity, and in that of the judiciary. They should have passed a law in relation to the matter, and then the Municipal Court, upon complaint, could have removed it; but for the City Council to take upon themselves the law-making and the execution of the law, is, in my opinion, wrong; besides, these men ought to have had a hearing before their property was destroyed; to destroy it without was an infringement on their rights; besides, it is so contrary to the feelings of American people to interfere with the press. And, furthermore, I cannot but think that it would have been more judicious for you to have gone with Mr. Bettesworth to Carthage, notwithstanding the law did not require it. Concerning your being in jail, I am sorry for that; I wish it had been otherwise. I hope you will soon be released, but I can not interfere."

Joseph Smith.—"Governor Ford, allow me, sir, to bring one thing to your mind that you seem to have overlooked. You state that you think it would have been better for us to have submitted to the requisition of Constable Bettesworth, and to have gone to Carthage. Do you not know, sir, that that writ was served at the instance of an anti-Mormon mob, who had passed resolutions, and published them, to the effect that they would exterminate the Mormon leaders? And are you not informed that Captain Anderson was not only threatened but had a gun fired at his boat by this said mob in Warsaw when coming up to Nauvoo, and that this very thing was made use of as a means to get us into their hands; and we could not, without taking an armed force with us, go there without, according to their published declarations, going into the jaws of death? To have taken a force with us would only have fanned the excitement, and they would have stated that we wanted to use intimidation; therefore, we thought it the most judicious to avail ourselves of the protection of the law."

Governor Ford.—"I see, I see."

Joseph Smith.—"Furthermore, in relation to the press, you say that you differ from me in opinion. Be it so; the thing, after all, is only a legal difficulty, and the courts, I should judge, are competent to decide on that matter. If our act was illegal, we are willing to meet it; and although I cannot see the distinction that you draw about the acts of the City Council, and what difference it could have made in point of fact, law, or justice between the City Council's acting together or separate) or how much more legal it would have been for the Municipal Court, who were a part of the City Council, to act separately instead of with the councilors, yet, if it is deemed that we did a wrong in destroying that press, we refuse not to pay for it; we are desirous to fulfill the law in every particular, and are responsible for our acts. You say that the parties ought to have a hearing. Had it been a civil suit, this of course, would have been proper; but there was a flagrant violation of every principle of right—a nuisance; and it was abated on the same principle that any nuisance, stench, or putrefied carcass would have been removed. Our first step, therefore, was to stop the foul, noisome, filthy sheet, and then the next in our opinion would have been to have prosecuted the man for a breach of public decency. And, furthermore, again let me say, Governor Ford, I shall look to you for our protection. I believe you are talking of going to Nauvoo; if you go, sir, I wish to go along. I refuse not to answer any law, but I do not consider myself safe here."

Governor.—"I am in hopes that you will be acquitted, and if I go I will certainly take you along. I do not, however, apprehend danger. I think you are perfectly safe either here or anywhere else. I can not, however, interfere with the law. I am placed in peculiar circumstances and seem to be blamed by all parties."

Joseph Smith.—"Governor Ford, I ask nothing but what is legal; I have a right to expect protection, at least from you; for, independent of law, you have pledged your faith and that of the State for my protection, and I wish to go to Nauvoo."

Governor.—"And you shall have protection, General Smith. I did not make this promise without consulting my officers, who all pledged their honor to its fulfillment. I do not know that I shall go tomorrow to Nauvoo, but if I do I will take you along."

At a quarter past ten o'clock the governor left.

At about half past twelve o'clock, Mr. Reed, one of Joseph's counsel, came in, apparently much elated; he stated that, upon an examination of the law, he found that the magistrate had transcended his jurisdiction, and that having committed them without an examination, his jurisdiction ended, that he had him upon a pinhook; that he ought to have examined them before he committed them, and that, having violated the law in this particular, he had no further power over them; for, once committeed, they were out of his jurisdiction, as the power of the magistrate extended no farther than their committal, and that now they could not be brought out except at the regular session of the Circuit Court, or by a writ of *habeas corpus;* but that if

Justice Smith would consent to go to Nauvoo for trial, he would compromise matters with him, and overlook this matter.

Mr. Reed further stated that the anti-Mormons, or mob, had concocted a scheme to get out a writ from Missouri, with a demand upon Governor Ford for the arrest of Joseph Smith, and his conveyance to Missouri, and that a man by the name of Wilson had returned from Missouri the night before the burning of the press for this purpose.

At half past two o'clock Constable Bettesworth came to the jail with a man named Simpson, professing to have some order, but he would not send up his name, and the guard would not let him pass. Dr. Bernhisel and Brother Wasson went to inform the governor and council of this. At about twenty minutes to three Dr. Bernhisel returned, and stated that he thought the governor was doing all he could. At about ten minutes to three Hyrum Kimball appeared with news from Nauvoo.

Soon after Constable Bettesworth came with an order from Esquire Smith to convey the prisoners to the court-house for trial. He was informed that the process was illegal, that they had been placed there contrary to law, and that they refused to come unless by legal process. I was informed that Justice Smith (who was also captain of the Carthage Grays) went to the governor and informed him of the matter, and that the governor replied, "You have your forces, and of course can use them." The constable certainly did return, accompanied by a guard of armed men, and by force, and under protest, hurried the prisoners to the court.

About four o'clock the case was called by Captain Robert F. Smith, J. P. The counsel for the prisoners called for subpœnas to bring witnesses. At twenty-five minutes past four he took a copy of the order to bring the prisoners from jail to trial, and afterwards he took names of witnesses.

Counsel present for the State; Higbee, Skinner, Sharp, Emmons, and Morrison. Twenty-five minutes to five the writ was returned as served, June 25th.

Many remarks were made at the court that I paid but little attention to, as I considered the whole thing illegal and a complete burlesque. Wood objected to the proceedings in toto, in consequence of its illegality, showing that the prisoners were not only illegally committed, but that, being once committed, the magistrate had no further power over them; but as it was the same magistrate before whom he was pleading who imprisoned them contrary to law, and the same who, as captain, forced them from jail, his arguments availed but little. He then urged that the prisoners be remanded until witnesses could be had, and applied for a continuance for that purpose. Skinner suggested until twelve o'clock next day. Wood again demanded until witnesses could be obtained; that the court meet at a specified time, and that, if witnesses were not present, again adjourn, without calling the prisoners. After various remarks from Reed, Skinner, and others, the court stated that the writ was served yesterday, and that it will give until tomorrow at twelve m. to get witnesses.

We then returned to jail. Immediately after our return Dr. Bernhisel went to the governor, and obtained from him an order for us to occupy a large open room containing a bedstead. I rather think that the same room had been appropriated to the use of debtors; at any rate, there was free access to the jailer's house, and no bars or locks except such as might be on the outside door of the jail. The jailer, Mr. George W. Steghall, and his wife, manifested a disposition to make us as comfortable as they could; we ate at their table, which was well provided, and, of course, paid for it.

I do not remember the names of all who were with us that night and the next morning in jail, for several went and came; among those that we considered stationery were Stephen Markham, John S. Fullmer, Captain Dan Jones, Dr. Willard Richards, and myself. Dr. Bernhisel says that he was there from Wednesday in the afternoon until eleven o'clock next day. We were, however, visited by numerous friends, among whom were Uncle John Smith, Hyrum Kimball, Cyrus H. Wheelock, besides lawyers, as counsel. There was also a great variety of conversation, which was rather desultory than otherwise, and referred to circumstances that had transpired, our former and present grievances, the spirit of the troops around us, and the disposition of the governor; the devising for legal and other plans for deliverance, the nature of testimony required; the gathering of proper witnesses, and a variety of other topics, including our religious hopes, etc.

During one of these conversations Dr. Richards remarked: "Brother Joseph, if it is necessary that you die in this matter, and if they will take me in your stead, I will suffer for you." At another time, when conversing about deliverance, I said, "Brother Joseph, if you will permit it, and say the word, I will have you out of this prison in five hours, if the jail has to come down to do it." My idea was to go to Nauvoo, and collect a force sufficient, as I considered the whole affair a legal farce, and a flagrant outrage upon our liberty and rights. Brother Joseph refused.

Elder Cyrus H. Wheelock came in to see us, and when he was about leaving drew a small pistol, a six-shooter, from his pocket, remarking at the same time, "Would any of you like to have this?" Brother Joseph immediately replied, "Yes, give it to me;" whereupon he took the pistol, and put it in his pantaloons pocket. The pistol was a six-shooting revolver, of Allen's patent; it belonged to me, and was one that I furnished to Brother Wheelock when he talked of going with me to the east, previous to our coming to Carthage. I have it now in my possession. Brother Wheelock went out on some errand, and was not suffered to return. The report of the governor having gone to Nauvoo without taking the prisoners along with him caused very unpleasant feelings, as we were apprised that we were left to the tender mercies of the Carthage Grays, a company strictly mobocratic, and whom we knew to be our most deadly enemies; and their captain, Esquire Smith, was a most unprincipled villain. Besides this, all the mob forces, comprising the governor's troops, were dismissed, with the exception of one or two companies, which the governor took with him to Nauvoo. The great part of the mob was liberated, the remainder was our guard.

We looked upon it not only as a breach of faith on the part of the governor, but also as an indication of a desire to insult us, if nothing more, by leaving us in the proximity of such men. The prevention of Wheelock's return was among the first of their hostile movements.

Colonel Markham then went out, and he was also prevented from returning. He was very angry at this, but the mob paid no attention to him; they drove him out of town at the point of the bayonet, and threatened to shoot him if he returned. He went, I am informed, to Nauvoo for the purpose of raising a company of men for our protection. Brother Fullmer went to Nauvoo after witnesses; it is my opinion that Brother Wheelock did also.

Some time after dinner we sent for some wine. It has been reported by some that this was taken as a sacrament. It was no such thing; our spirits were generally dull and heavy, and it was sent for to revive us. I think it was Captain Jones who went after it, but they would not suffer him to return. I believe we all drank of the wine, and gave some to one or two of the prison guards. We all of us felt unusually dull and languid, with a remarkable depression of spirits. In consonance with those feelings I sang a song, that had lately been introduced into Nauvoo, entitled, "A poor, wayfaring man of grief," etc.

The song is pathetic, and the tune quite plaintive, and was very much in accordance with our feelings at the time, for our spirits were all depressed, dull and gloomy, and surcharged with indefinite ominous forebodings. After a lapse of some time, Brother Hyrum requested me again to sing that song. I replied, "Brother Hyrum, I do not feel like singing;" when he remarked, "Oh, never mind; commence singing, and you will get the spirit of it." At his request I did so. Soon afterwards I was sitting at one of the front windows of the jail, when I saw a number of men, with painted faces, coming around the corner of the jail, and aiming towards the stairs. The other brethern had seen the same, for, as I went to the door, I found Brother Hyrum Smith and Dr. Richards already leaning against it. They both pressed against the door with their shoulders to prevent its being opened, as the lock and latch were comparatively useless. While in this position, the mob, who had come up stairs, and tried to open the door, probably thought it was locked, and fired a ball through the keyhole; at this Dr. Richards and Brother Hyrum leaped back from the door, with their faces towards it; almost instantly another ball passed through the panel of the door, and struck Brother Hyrum on the left side of the nose, entering his face and head. At the same instant, another ball from the outside entered his back, passing through his body and striking his watch. The ball came from the back, through the jail window, opposite the door, and must, from its range, have been fired from the Carthage Grays, who were placed there ostensibly for our protection, as the balls from the fire-arms, shot close by the jail, would have entered the ceiling, we being in the second story, and there never was a time after that when Hyrum could have received the latter wound. Immediately, when the balls struck him, he fell flat on his back, crying as he fell, "I am a dead man." He never moved afterwards.

I shall never forget the deep feeling of sympathy and regard manifested in the countenance of Brother Joseph as he drew nigh to Hyrum, and, leaning over him, exclaimed, "Oh! my poor, dear brother Hyrum!" He, however, instantly arose, and with a firm, quick step, and a determined expression of countenance, approached the door, and pulling the six-shooter left by Brother Wheelock from his pocket, opened the door slightly, and snapped the pistol six successive times; only three of the barrels, however, were discharged. I afterwards understood that two or three were wounded by these discharges, two of whom, I am informed, died. I had in my hands a large, strong hickory stick, brought there by Brother Markham, and left by him, which I had seized as soon as I saw the mob approach; and while Brother Joseph was firing the pistol, I stood close behind him. As soon as he had discharged it he stepped back, and I immediately took his place next to the door, while he occupied the one I had done while he was shooting. Brother Richards, at this time, had a knotty walking-stick in his hands belonging to me, and stood next to Brother Joseph, a little farther from the door, in an oblique direction, apparently to avoid the rake of the fire from the door. The firing of Bother Joseph made our assailants pause for a moment; very soon after, however, they pushed the door some distance open, and protruded and discharged their guns into the room, when I parried them off with my stick, giving another direction to the balls.

It certainly was a terrible scene: streams of fire as thick as my arm passed by me as these men fired, and, unarmed as we were, it looked like certain death. I remember feeling as though my time had come, but I do not know when, in any critical position, I was more calm, unruffled, energetic, and acted with more promptness and decision. It certainly was far from pleasant to be so near the muzzles of those fire-arms as they belched forth their liquid flames and deadly balls. While I was engaged in parrying the guns, Brother

Joseph said, "That's right, Brother Taylor, parry them off as well as you can." These were the last words I ever heard him speak on earth.

Every moment the crowd at the door became more dense, as they were unquestionably pressed on by those in the rear ascending the stairs, until the whole entrance at the door was literally crowded with muskets and rifles, which, with the swearing, shouting and demoniacal expressions of those outside the door and on the stairs, and the firing of the guns, mingled with their horrid oaths and execrations, made it look like Pandemonium let loose, and was, indeed, a fit representation of the horrid deed in which they were engaged.

After parrying the guns for some time, which now protruded thicker and farther into the room, and seeing no hope of escape or protection there, as we were now unarmed, it occurred to me that we might have some friends outside, and that there might be some chance of escape in that direction, but here there seemed to be none. As I expected them every moment to rush into the room—nothing but extreme cowardice having thus far kept them out—as the tumult and pressure increased, without any other hope, I made a spring for the window which was right in front of the jail door, where the mob was standing, and also exposed to the fire of the Carthage Grays, who were stationed some ten or twelve rods off. The weather was hot, we all of us had our coats off, and the window was raised to admit air. As I reached the window, and was on the point of leaping out, I was struck by a ball from the door about midway of my thigh, which struck the bone, and flattened out almost to the size of a quarter of a dollar, and then passed on throug the fleshy part to within about half an inch of the outside. I think some prominent nerve must have been severed or injurd, for, as soon as the ball struck me, I fell like a bird when shot, or an ox when struck by a butcher, and lost entirely and instantaneously all power of action or locomotion. I fell upon the window-sill, and cried out, "I am shot!" Not possessing any power to move, I felt myself falling outside of the window, but immediately I fell inside, from some, at that time, unknown cause. When I struck the floor my animation seemed restored, as I have seen it sometimes in squirrels and birds after being shot. As soon as I felt the power of motion I crawled under the bed which was in a corner of the room, not far from the window where I received my wound. While on my way and under the bed I was wounded in three other places; one ball entered a little below the left knee, and never was extracted; another entered the forepart of my left arm, a little above the wrist, and, passing down by the joint, lodged in the fleshy part of my hand, about midway, a little above the upper joint of my little finger; another struck me on the fleshy part of my left hip, and tore away the flesh as large as my hand, dashing the mangled fragments of flesh and blood against the wall.

My wounds were painful, and the sensation produced was as though a ball had passed through and down the whole length of my leg. I very well remember my reflections at the time. I had a very painful idea of becoming lame and decrepid, and being an object of pity, and I felt as though I would rather die than be placed in such circumstances.

It would seem that immediately after my attempt to leap out of the window, Joseph also did the same thing, of which circumstance I have no knowledge only from information. The first thing that I noticed was a cry that he had leaped out of the window. A cessation of firing followed, the mob rushed down stairs, and Dr. Richards went to the window. Immediately afterwards I saw the doctor going towards the jail door, and as there was an iron door at the head of the stairs adjoining our door which led into the cells for criminals, it struck me that the doctor was going in there, and I said to him, "Stop, doctor, and take me along." He proceeded to the door and opened it, and then returnod and dragged me along to a small cell prepared for criminals.

Brother Richards was very much troubled, and exclaimed, "Oh! Brother Taylor, is it possible that they have killed both Brother Hyrum and Joseph? it cannot surely be, and yet I saw them shoot them;" and, elevating his hands two or three times, he exclaimed, "Oh Lord, my God, spare thy servants!" He then said, "Brother Taylor, this is a terrible event;" and he dragged me farther into the cell, saying, "I am sorry I can do no better for you;" and, taking an old, filthy mattress, he covered me with it, and said, "That may hide you, and you may yet live to tell the tale, but I expect they will kill me in a few moments." While lying in this position I suffered the most excruciating pain.

Soon afterwards Dr. Richards came to me, informed me that the mob had precipitately fled, and at the same time confirmed my worst fears that Joseph was assuredly dead. I felt a dull, lonely, sickening sensation at the news. When I reflected that our noble chieftain, the prophet of the living God, had fallen, and that I had seen his brother in the cold embrace of death, it seemed as though there was a void or vacuum in the great field of human existence to me, and a drak, gloomy chasm in the kingdom, and that we were left alone. Oh how lonely was that feeling! How cold, barren and desolate! In the midst of difficulties he was always the first in motion; in critical positions his counsel was always sought. As our prophet he approached our God, and obtained for us his will; but now our prophet, our counselor, our general, our leader was gone, and amid the fiery ordeal that we then had to pass through, we were left alone without his aid, and as our future guide for things spiritual or temporal, and for all things pertaining to this world or the next, he had spoken for the last time on earth!

These reflections and a thousand others flashed upon my mind. I thought, Why must the good perish, and the virtuous be destroyed? Why must God's nobility, the salt of the earth, the most exalted of the human family, and the most perfect types of all excellence, fall victims to the cruel, fiendish hate of incarnate devils?

The poignancy of my grief, I presume, however, was somewhat allayed by the extreme suffering that I endured from my wounds.

Soon afterwards I was taken to the head of the stairs and laid there, where I had a full view of our beloved and now murdered Brother Hyrum. There he lay as I had left him; he had not moved a limb; he lay placid and calm, a monument of greatness even in death; but his noble spirit had left its tenement, and was gone to dwell in regions more congenial to its exalted nature. Poor Hyrum! he was a great and good man, and my soul was cemented to his. If ever there was an exemplary, honest, and virtuous man, an embodiment of all that is noble in the human form, Hyrum Smith was its representative.

While I lay there a number of persons came around, among whom was a physician. The doctor, on seeing a ball lodged in my left hand, took a penknife from his pocket and made an incision in it for the purpose of extracting the ball therefrom, and having obtained a pair of carpenter's compasses, made use of them to draw or pry out the ball, alternately using the penknife and compasses. After sawing for some time with a dull penknife, and prying and pulling with the compasses, he ultimately succeded in extracting the ball, which weighed about half an ounce. Some time afterwards he remarked to a friend of mine that I had "nerves like the devil," to stand what I did in its extraction. I really thought I had need of nerves to stand such surgical butchery, and that, whatever my nerves may be, his practice was devilish.

This company wished to remove me to Mr. Hamilton's hotel, the place where we had staid previous to our incarceration in jail. I told them, however, that I did not wish to go; I did not consider it safe. They protested that it was, and that I was safe with them; that it was a perfect outrage for men to be used as we had been; that they were my friends; that it was for my good they were counseling me, and that I could be better taken care of there than here.

I replied, "I don't know you. Who am I among? I am surrounded by assassins and murderers; witness your deeds! Don't talk to me of kindness or comfort; look at your murdered victims. Look at me! I want none of your counsel nor comfort. There may be some safety here; I can be assured of none anywhere," etc.

They G—— d—— their souls to hell, made the most solemn asservations, and swore by God and the devil, and everything else that they could think of, that they would stand by me to death and protect me. In half an hour every one of them had fled from the town.

Soon after a coroner's jury were assembled in the room over the body of Hyrum. Among the jurors was Captain Smith, of the Carthage Grays, who had assisted in the murder, and the same justice before whom we had been tried. I learned of Francis Higbee as being in the neighborhood. On hearing his name mentioned, I immediately arose and said, "Captain Smith, you are a justice of the peace; I have heard his name mentioned; I want to swear my life against him." I was informed that word was immediately sent to him to leave the place, which he did.

Brother Richards was busy during this time attending to the coroner's inquest, and to the removal of the bodies, and making arrangements for their removal from Carthage to Nauvoo.

When he had a little leisure, he again came to me, and at his suggestion I was removed to Hamilton's tavern. I felt that he was the only friend, the only person, that I could rely upon in that town. It was with difficulty that sufficient persons could be found to carry me to the tavern; for immediately after the murder a great fear fell upon all the people, and men, women, and children fled with great precipitation, leaving nothing nor anybody in the town but two or three women and children and one or two sick persons.

It was with great difficulty that Brother Richards prevailed upon Mr. Hamilton, hotel-keeper, and his family, to stay; they would not until Brother Richards had given a solemn promise that he would see them protected, and hence I was looked upon as a hostage. Under these circumstances, notwithstanding, I believe they were hostile to the Mormons, and were glad that the murder had taken place, though they did not actually participate in it; and, feeling that I should be a protection to them, they staid.

The whole community knew that a dreadful outrage had been perpetrated by those villains, and fearing lest the citizens of Nauvoo, as they possessed the power, might have a disposition to visit them with a terrible vengeance, they fled in the wildest confusion. And, indeed, it was with very great difficulty that the citizens of Nauvoo could be restrained. A horrid, barbarous murder had been committed, the most solemn pledge violated, and that, too, while the victims were, contrary to the requirements of the law, putting themselves into the hands of the governor to pacify a popular excitement. This outrage was enhanced by the reflection that our people were able to protect themselves against not only all the mob, but against three times their number and that of the governor's troops put together. They were also exasperated by the speech of the governor in town.

The whole events were so faithless, so dastardly, so mean, cowardly, and contemptible, without one extenuating circumstance, that it would not have been surprising if the citizens of Nauvoo had arisen *en masse*, and blotted the wretches out of existence. The citizens of Carthage knew they would have done so under such circumstances, and, judging us by themselves, they were all panic-stricken, and fled. Colonel Markham, too, after his expulsion from Carthage, had gone home, related the circumstances of his ejectment, and was using his influence to get a company to go out. Fearing that when the people heard that their prophet and patriarch had been murdered under the above circumstances they might act rashly, and knowing that if they once got roused, like a mighty avalanche they would lay the country waste before them and take a terrible vengeance—as none of the Twelve were in Nauvoo, and no one, perhaps, with sufficient influence to control the people, Dr. Richards, after consulting me, wrote the following note, fearing that my family might be seriously affected by the news. I told him to insert that I was slightly wounded.

*Willard Richards' Note from Carthage Jail to Nauvoo.**

"Carthage jail, 8 o'clock 5 min. p. m., June 27th, 1844.

"Joseph and Hyrum are dead. Taylor wounded, not very badly. I am well. Our guard was forced, as we believe, by a band of Missourians from 100 to 200. The job was done in an instant, and the party fled towards Nauvoo instantly. This is as I believe it. The citizens here are afraid of the 'Mormons' attacking them; I promise them no.

W. RICHARDS.

"N. B.—The citizens promise us protection; alarm guns have been fired.

"JOHN TAYLOR."

I remember signing my name as quickly as possible, lest the tremor of my hand should be noticed, and the fears of my family excited.

A messenger was dispatched immediately with the note, but he was intercepted by the governor, who, on hearing a cannon fired at Carthage, which was to be the signal for the murder, immediately fled with his company, and fearing that the citizens of Nauvoo, when apprised of the horrible outrage, would immediately rise and pursue, he turned back the messenger, who was George D. Grant. A second

---

* *Deseret News*, No. 38, Nov. 25, 1857, p. 297.

one was sent, who was treated similarly; and not until a third attempt could news be got to Nauvoo.

Samuel H. Smith, brother to Joseph and Hyrum, was the first brother I saw after the outrage; I am not sure whether he took the news or not; he lived at the time in Plymouth, Hancock County, and was on his way to Carthage to see his brothers, when he was met by some of the troops, or rather mob, that had been dismissed by the governor, and who were on their way home. On learning that he was Joseph Smith's brother they sought to kill him, but he escaped, and fled into the woods, where he was chased for a length of time by them; but, after severe fatigue, and much danger and excitement, he succeeded in escaping, and came to Carthage. He was on horseback when he arrived, and was not only very much tired with the fatigue and excitement of the chase, but was also very much distressed in feelings on account of the death of his brothers. These things produced a fever, which laid the foundation for his death, which took place on the 30th of July. Thus another of the brothers fell a victim although not directly, but indirectly to this infernal mob.

I lay from about five o'clock until two next morning without having my wounds dressed, as there was scarcely any help of any kind in Carthage, and Brother Richards was busy with the dead bodies, preparing them for removal. My wife Leonora started early the next day, having had some little trouble in getting a company or a physician to come with her; after considerable difficulty she succeeded in getting an escort, and Dr. Samuel Bennet came along with her. Soon after my father and mother arrived from Oquakie, near which place they had a farm at that time, and hearing of the trouble hastened along.

General Demming, Brigadier General of the Hancock County Militia, was very much of a gentleman, and showed me every courtesy, and Colonel Jones also was very solicitous about my welfare.

I was called upon by several gentlemen of Quincy and other places, among whom was Judge Ralston, as well as by our own people, and a medical man extracted a ball from my left thigh that was giving me much pain; it lay about half an inch deep, and my thigh was considerably swollen. The doctor asked me if I would be tied during the operation; I told him no; that I could endure the cutting associated with the operation as well without, and I did so; indeed, so great was the pain I endured that the cutting was rather a relief than otherwise.

A very laughable incident occurred at the time; my wife Leonora went into an adjoining room to pray for me, that I might be sustained during the operation. While on her knees at prayer, a Mrs. Bedell, an old lady of the Methodist association, entered, and, patting Mrs. Taylor on her back with her hand, said, "There's a good lady, pray for God to forgive your sins, pray that you may be converted, and the Lord may have mercy on your soul."

The scene was so ludicrous that Mrs. Tayloy knew not whether to laugh or be angry. Mrs. Taylor informed me that Mr. Hamilton, the father of the Hamilton who kept the house, rejoiced at the murder, and said in company that "it was done up in the best possible style, and showed good generalship;" and she further believed that the other branches of the family sanctioned it. These were the associates of the old lady referred to, and yet she could talk of conversion and saving souls in the midst of blood and murder: such is man and such consistency.

The ball being extracted was the one that first struck me, which I before referred to: it entered on the outside of my left thigh, about five inches from my knee, and, passing rather obliquely towards my body, had, it would seem, struck the bone, for it was flatted out nearly as thin and large as a quarter of a dollar.

The governor passed on, staying at Carthage only a few minutes, and he did not stop until he got fifty miles from Nauvoo. There had been various opinions about the complicity of the governor in the murder, some supposing that he knew all about it, and assisted or winked at its execution. It is somewhat difficult to form a correct opinion; from the facts presented it is very certain that things looked more than suspicious against him.

In the first place, he positively knew that we had broken no law.

Secondly. He knew that the mob had not only passed inflammatory resolutions, threatening extermination to the Mormons, but that they had actually assembled armed mobs and commenced hostilities against us.

Thirdly. He took those very mobs that had been arrayed against us, and enrolled them as his troops, thus legalizing their acts.

Fourthly. He disbanded the Nauvoo Legion, which had never violated law, and disarmed them, and had about his person in the shape of militia known mobocrats and violaters of the law.

Fifthly. He requested us to come to Carthage without arms, promising protection, and then refused to interfere in delivering us from prison, although Joseph and Hyrum were put there contrary to law.

Sixthly. Although he refused to interfere in our behalf, yet, when Captain Smith went to him and informed him that the persons refused to come out, he told him that he had a command and knew what to do, thus sanctioning the use of force in the violation of law when opposed to us, whereas he would not for us interpose his executive authority to free us from being incarcerated contrary to law, although he was fully informed of all the facts of the case, as we kept him posted in the affairs all the time.

Seventhly. He left the prisoners in Carthage jail contrary to his plighted faith.

Eightly. Before he went he dismissed all the troops that could be relied upon, as well as many of the mob, and left us in charge of the "Carthage Grays," a company that he knew were mobocratic, our most bitter enemies, and who had passed resolutions to exterminate us, and who had been placed under guard by General Demming only the day before.

Ninthly. He was informed of the intended murder, both before he left and while on the road, by several different parties.

Tenthly. When the cannon was fired in Carthage, signifying that the deed was done, he immediately took up his line of march and fled. How did he know that this signal portrayed their death if he was not in the secret? It may be said some of the party told him. How could he believe what the party said about the gun signal if he could not believe the testimony of several individuals who told him in positive terms about the contemplated murder?

He has, I believe, stated that he left the "Carthage Grays" there because he considered that, as their town was contiguous to ours, and as the responsibility of our safety rested solely upon them, they would not dare suffer any indignity to befall us. This very admission shows that he did really expect danger; and then he knew that these people had published to the world that they would exterminate us, and his leaving us in their hands and taking of their responsibilities was like leaving a lamb in charge of a wolf, and trusting to its humanity and honor for its safe-keeping.

It is said, again that he would not have gone to Nauvoo, and thus placed himself in the hands of the Mormons, if he had anticipated any such event, as he would be exposed to their wrath. To this it may be answered that the Mormons did not know their signals, while he did; and they were also known in Warsaw, as well as in other places; and as soon as the gun was fired, a merchant of Warsaw jumped upon his horse and rode directly to Quincy, and reported "Joseph and Hyrum killed, and those who were with them in jail." He reported further that "they were attempting to break jail, and were all killed by the guard." This was their story; it was anticipated to kill all, and the gun was to be the signal that the deed was accomplished. This was known in Warsaw. The governor also knew it and fled; and he could really be in no danger in Nauvoo, for the Mormons did not know it, and he had plenty of time to escape, which he did.

It is said that he made all his officers promise solemnly that they would help him to protect the Smiths; this may or may not be. At any rate, some of these same officers helped to murder them.

The strongest argument in the governor's favor, and one that would bear more weight with us than all the rest put together, would be that he could not believe them capable of such atrocity; and, thinking that their talk and threatenings were a mere ebullition of feeling, a kind of braggadocio, and that there was enough of good moral feeling to control the more violent passions, he trusted to their faith. There is, indeed, a degree of plausibility about this, but when we put it in juxtaposition to the amount of evidence that he was in possession of, it weighs very little. He had nothing to inspire confidence in them, and everything to make him mistrust them. Besides, why his broken faith? why his disregard of what was told him by several parties? Again, if he knew not the plan, how did he understand the signal? Why so oblivious to everything pertaining to the Mormon interest, and so alive and interested about the mobocrats? At any rate, be this as it may, he stands responsible for their blood, and it is dripping on his garments. If it had not been for his promises of protection, they would have protected themselves; it was plighted faith that led them to the slaughter; and to make the best of it, it was a breach of that faith and a non-fulfillment of that promise, after repeated warning, that led to their death.

Having said so much, I must leave the governor with my readers and with his God. Justice, I conceive, demanded this much, and truth could not be told with less; as I have said before, my opinion is that the governor would not have planned this murder, but he had not sufficient energy to resist popular opinion, even if that opinion led to blood and death.

It was rumored that a strong political party, numbering in its ranks many of the prominent men of the nation, were engaged in a plot for the overthrow of Joseph Smith, and that the governor was of this party, and Sharp, Williams, Captain Smith, and others were his accomplices, but whether this was the case or not I do not know. It is very certain that a strong political feeling existed against Joseph Smith, and I have reason to believe that his letters to Henry Clay, were made use of by political parties opposed to Mr. Clay, and were the means of that statesman's defeat. Yet, if such a combination as the one referred to existed, I am not apprised of it.

While I lay at Carthage, previous to Mrs. Taylor's arrival, a pretty good sort of a man, who was lame of a leg, waited upon me, and sat up at night with me; afterwards Mrs. Taylor, mother and others waited upon me.

Many friends called upon me, among whom were Richard Ballantyne, Elizabeth Taylor, several of the Perkins family, and a number of the brethren from Macedonia and La Harpe. Besides these, many strangers from Quincy, some of whom expressed indignant feelings against the mob and sympathy for myself. Brother Alexander Williams called upon me, who suspected that they had some designs in keeping me there, and stated that he had, at a given point in some woods, fifty men, and if I would say the word he would raise other fifty, and fetch me out of there. I thanked him, but told him I thought there was no need. However, it would seem that I was in some danger; for Colonel Jones, before referred to, when absent from me, left two loaded pistols on the table in case of an attack, and some time afterward, when I had recovered and was publishing the affair, a lawyer, Mr. Backman, stated that he had prevented a man by the name of Jackson, before referred to, from ascending the stairs, who was coming with a design to murder me, and that now he was sorry he had not let him do the deed.

There were others also, of whom I heard, that said I ought to be killed, and they would do it, but that it was too damned cowardly to shoot a wounded man; and thus, by the chivalry of murderers, I was prevented from being a second time mutilated or killed. Many of the mob, came around and treated me with apparent respect, and the officers and people generally looked upon me as a hostage, and feared that my removal would be the signal for the rising of the Mormons.

I do not remember the time that I staid at Carthage, but I think three or four days after the murder, when Brother Marks with a carriage, Brother James Allred with a wagon, Dr. Ells, and a number of others on horseback, came for the purpose of taking me to Nauvoo. I was very weak at the time, occasioned by the loss of blood and the great discharge of my wounds, so when my wife asked me if I could talk I could barely whisper, no. Quite a discussion arose as to the propriety of my removal, the physician and people of Carthage protesting that it would be my death, while my friends were anxious for my removal if possible.

I suppose the former were actuated by the above-named desire to keep me. Colonel Jones was, I believe, sincere; he had acted as a friend all the time, and he told Mrs. Taylor she ought to persuade me not to go, for he did not believe I had strength enough to reach Nauvoo. It was finally agreed, however, that I should go; but it was thought that I could not stand riding in a wagon or carriage, they prepared a litter for me; I was carried down stairs and put upon it. A number of men assisted to carry me, some of whom had been engaged in the mob. As soon as I got down stairs, I felt much better and strengthened, so that I could talk; I suppose the effect of the fresh air.

When we got near the outside of the town I remembered some

woods that we had to go through, and telling a person near to call for Dr. Ells, who was riding a very good horse, I said, "Doctor, I perceive that the people are getting fatigued with carrying me; a number of Mormons live about two or three miles from here, near our route, will you ride to their settlement as quick as possible, and have them come and meet us?" He started off on a gallop immediately. My object in this was to obtain protection in case of an attack, rather than to obtain help to carry me.

Very soon after the men from Carthage made one excuse after another until they had all left, and I felt glad to get rid of them. I found that the tramping of those carrying me produced violent pain, and a sleigh was produced and attached to the hind end of Brother James Allred's wagon, a bed placed upon it, and I propped up on the bed. Mrs. Taylor rode with me, applying ice and ice-water to my wounds. As the sleigh was dragged over the grass on the prairie, which was quite tall, it moved very easy and gave me very little pain.

When I got within five or six miles of Nauvoo the brethren commenced to meet me from the city, and they increased in number as we drew nearer, until there was a very large company of people of all ages and both sexes, principally, however, men.

For some time there had been almost incessant rain, so that in many low places on the prairie it was from one to three feet deep in water, and at such places the brethren whom we met took hold of the sleigh, lifted it, and carried it over the water; and when we arrived in the neighborhood of the city, where the roads were excessively muddy and bad, the brethren tore down the fences, and we passsed through the fields.

Never shall I forget the difference of feeling that I experienced between the place that I had left and the one that I had now arrived at. I had left a lot of reckless, bloodthirsty murderers, and had come to the City of the Saints, the people of the living God; friends of truth and righteousness, thousands of whom stood there with warm, true hearts to offer their friendship and services, and to welcome my return. It is true it was a painful scene, and brought sorrowful remembrance to mind, but to me it caused a thrill of joy to find myself once more in the bosom of my friends, and to meet with the cordial welcome of true, honest hearts. What was very remarkable, I found myself very much better after my arrival at Nauvoo than I was when I started on my journey, although I had traveled eighteen miles.

The next day as some change was wanting, I told Mrs. Taylor that if she could send to Dr. Richards, he had my purse and watch, and they would find money in my purse.

Previous to the doctor leaving Carthage, I told him that he had better take my purse and watch, for I was afraid the people would steal them. The doctor had taken my pantaloons' pocket, and put the watch in it with the purse, cut off the pocket, and tied a string around the top; it was in this position when brought home. My family, however, were not a little startled to find that my watch had been struck with a ball. I sent for my vest, and, upon examination, it was found that there was a cut as if with a knife, in the vest pocket which had contained my watch. In the pocket the fragments of the glass were found literally ground to powder. It then occurred to me that a ball had struck me at the time I felt myself falling out of the window, and that it was this force that threw me inside. I had often remarked to Mrs. Taylor the singular fact of finding myself inside the room, when I felt a moment before after being shot, that I was falling out, and I never could account for it until then; but here the thing was fully elucidated, and was rendered plain to my mind. I was indeed falling out, when some villain aimed at my heart. The ball struck my watch, and forced me back; If I had fallen out I should assuredly have been killed, if not by the fall, by those around, and this ball intended to dispatch me, was turned by an overruling Providence into a messenger of mercy, and saved my life. I shall never forget the feelings of gratitude that I then experienced towards my Heavenly Father; the whole scene was vividly portrayed before me, and my heart melted before the Lord. I felt that the Lord had preserved me by a special act of mercy; that my time had not yet come, and that I had still a work to perform upon the earth.

(Signed),

JOHN TAYLOR.